THE 60-YEAR CURRICULUM

The 60-Year Curriculum explores models and strategies for lifelong learning in an era of profound economic disruption and reinvention. Over the next half-century, globalization, regional threats to sustainability, climate change, and technologies such as artificial intelligence and data mining will transform our education and workforce sectors. In turn, higher education must shift to offer every student life-wide opportunities for the continuous upskilling they will need to achieve decades of worthwhile employability. This cutting-edge book describes the evolution of new models—covering computer science, inclusive design, critical thinking, civics, and more—by which universities can increase learners' trajectories across multiple careers from mid-adolescence to retirement. Stakeholders in workforce development, curriculum and instructional design, lifelong learning, and higher and continuing education will find a unique synthesis offering valuable insights and actionable next steps.

Christopher J. Dede is Timothy E. Wirth Professor in Learning Technologies at Harvard Graduate School of Education, USA, where he served as Chair of the Learning and Teaching Department.

John Richards is Lecturer at Harvard Graduate School of Education, USA, and President of Consulting Services for Education, Inc. (CS4Ed). He has served as President of the JASON Foundation for Education and Senior Vice President and General Manager of Turner Learning, Inc.

The 60-Year Curriculum

New Models for Lifelong Learning in the Digital Economy

Edited by Christopher J. Dede and John Richards

Routledge
Taylor & Francis Group

NEW YORK AND LONDON

First published 2020
by Routledge
52 Vanderbilt Avenue, New York, NY 10017

and by Routledge
2 Park Square, Milton Park, Abingdon, Oxon, OX14 4RN

Routledge is an imprint of the Taylor & Francis Group, an informa business

Library of Congress Cataloging-in-Publication Data
A catalog record for this title has been requested

ISBN: 978-0-367-42319-3 (hbk)
ISBN: 978-0-367-82127-2 (pbk)
ISBN: 978-1-003-01361-7 (ebk)

Typeset in Minion
by codeMantra

Contents

Foreword

A letter from my future self:

It is 2030. I'm turning 70 and thinking back to some key moments in my academic life. No, I am not talking about the day in my freshman year that I met my wife of 49 years. I am thinking about the year 2007 when, without knowing the journey I was beginning, I started pursuing the 60-Year Curriculum (*60YC*) idea. I had been working at Colorado State University (CSU) for six years. This was my second career. After helping build data communications and wireless companies around the world for 20 years, I came to teach at CSU in the classroom and the distance MBA program. Then, I built an entrepreneurship center, helped re-engineer tech transfer in order to use my students to write plans for commercializing technology from our labs, and assisted in launching 14 successful companies from researchers' inventions.

Because of this success, l was asked to create a new Office of Economic Development at the university. To be clear, I was as much of an outsider as is possible in a research university. Research universities are optimized to invent (spending money and time to create and disseminate knowledge). I had spent my life as an innovator (spending knowledge and time to make money). Invention and innovation are operational opposites and very hard to do in the same organization at the same time. I was invited to try because the state of Colorado had its major financial disruption starting in 2001 when the technology sector crashed, not in the Great Recession in 2008. The financial challenges of 2001–2007 were close to existential for the university because the state could not fund public higher education under the Taxpayer Bill of Rights (TABOR) constitutional restrictions. The state legislature had essentially no other discretionary spending to manage deficits not allowed by TABOR. It was a difficult time. But, in retrospect, this meant CSU was prepared for later economic challenges in ways many other universities were not.

The dilemma I faced in 2007 was to keep proving CSU's worth as a part of the state economy while it survived financially in order to serve our public mission as a land-grant university. As the new AVP of Economic Development, I had the job of helping to solve this riddle. Being new to the very mature practice of "economic development" as a profession, I had to reduce all the political, strategic, geographic, and other concerns to something simple that I could manage. I made it simple by saying, "If more money comes into an area than goes out, then economic development will occur." My role was thus to make more money come into Colorado, and Colorado State University in particular, than went out. That, I was prepared to do—based on my industry experience combined with my deep respect for the academic institution, its faculty, and its land-grant mission.

I started my study of how research universities contribute to their communities. At the time, most universities and colleges talked about the local impact of high-wage employment of faculty and staff as well as student spending in the local economy. The research universities added to that the impact of federal grants and the local impact of the research enterprise. A few universities were starting to talk about the impact of technology commercialization and new jobs created. However, very few universities talked about the total public good of their graduates beyond citing general income statistics.

As a data-driven person from MIT, I decided to quantify each of these paths to help me focus on the best one for CSU to follow. Here is what I learned and concluded. I have left out the detailed numbers because they do not matter to our *60YC* discussion.

- The public contribution of faculty, staff, and student spending carries little-to-no new political influence because legislators know that the school is not going anywhere, so the economic development benefit is already captured. This is not a path to new economic development unless the school is growing.
- The impact of increased research funding is highly desirable, and the legislature and statewide economic development offices support these efforts. But for the university itself, research is at best break-even. Most schools lose money overall on research because indirect cost recovery levels are not high enough to cover the true, fully-allocated indirect costs of the research enterprise. Moreover, while the short-term impact on local economic development can be high, its long-term impact is constrained by the overall federal funding levels and approved federal and state indirect cost recovery rules. Only the very few schools with rapidly growing, sponsored research can follow this path to sustained economic development. Since Colorado State was already one of the largest Carnegie 1 Research Universities without a medical school, its potential for increased economic development by this means was limited.
- The impact of technology transfer licensing and commercialization has the potential for very large new economic development, but it is almost completely unpredictable for any given university. Venture capitalists, the best risk investors in the world, are proud if they make two out of ten successful investments. Most have one winner, two to three break-even outcomes, and the rest of the investments lose. Venture capitalists invest at the stage where a great deal is known. The market is proven, the product or service exists, the value proposition and needs are well articulated, and the risks quantifiable. Go one level upstream in funding and look at angel investors. They are usually successful at a much lower rate because so much less is known at the time they invest. Now, go the rest of the way upstream to a university

lab where technology emerges from faculty passion. The need in the market is unknown, manufacturing feasibility is unknown, distribution channels are uncertain, and intellectual property protection is unclear and expensive. You cannot convince me that the ability to predict winners is better than one in a thousand. In other words, the risk is so high that one cannot bet on sustained new economic development from technology commercialization unless one can afford to spin off more than 100 new companies or licenses per year for a decade in the hope that one of them is successful enough to pay for 999 disappointments. Discovering that success here would be luck, not skill, was a great disappointment to me because following this path had been my hypothesis for success in my new job, and I had already spent several years helping CSU to do this better.

- Then, I did the math on the contribution of our graduates to the public good of the state of Colorado as compared to their peers who did not go to college. The simple measure I used was tax receipts on the income difference, plus higher real estate taxes paid, plus higher sales and excise taxes paid, based on the well-known wage difference. I ignored the benefits of better health and lower social costs. The number was huge. It dwarfed all the others combined. I had found the answer. Many already knew this, but it was a great discovery for me. And answering this question had started me on my path to online and distance education and ultimately the 60 Year-Curriculum.

If the answer to sustained, new economic development from a university was to graduate more learners, then we needed to figure out how. Our intense financial constraints allowed no new investment money; no new money for faculty, buildings, dorms, or classrooms; no extra space on our campuses; and no new money to launch new programs. As I studied the economic impact of education in Colorado, one statistic kept showing up. There were 750,000 Colorado residents who had started but never finished college. The impact of helping them complete would be enormous.

This was when I discovered the age 25–55 hole in the *60YC*. Almost no one except for-profit universities served this market segment. Their business models were suspect because of very low completion rates and high federal loan defaults. Many of the potential students were strong learners, but they all worked full time and needed to control time and place to be able to learn. I had spent 20 years building high-speed data systems that sit behind the global Internet. I already had taught online with video lectures and LMS-hosted courses. I knew what the private for-profits were doing in terms of pedagogy and course delivery, and much of that work was much better than their business results.

So, the obvious answer was to put all this knowledge together to create a new, public, online university that was much better, and lower cost, than the for-profit providers. In this way, Colorado's land-grant-based system might again extend its 1860s mission of educating the "rest of the people" as proposed by Senator Morrill and signed into law by President Lincoln. From these ideas, I became part of a team that founded and launched Colorado State University Global Campus.

We studied the needs of this narrow market segment and designed a master-teacher course university for degree completion and professionally oriented master's degrees. We set tuition as low as possible ($250 per credit hour for undergraduates and $350 per credit hour for graduates), and we locked tuition for students until they graduated. Eleven months from first funding, CSU Global launched with seven different degree programs. The rest is history. Nine months to 1,000 students, 30 months to break even, 40 months to full repayment of the startup funds, and 10 years later over 25,000 admitted adult learners and over 15,000 graduates. The math of 15,000 additional graduates worked out to a huge economic impact in Colorado and around the region. In addition, think of the personal pride of all those learners. And it all was done and continues to be done with no state funds. In fact, CSU Global sends a significant surplus back to the system to support the other campuses.

Now extrapolate that idea to include others with the same plan like Arizona State University Online; Southern New Hampshire University; Georgia Institute of Technology; University of California, Berkeley; University of California, Irvine; Oregon State University; the University of Washington; and the other innovators. You can see how plugging just one hole in the *60YC* creates massive economic, individual, and social value.

While filling the role of CEO of Global Campus, I also was asked to lead the campus-based Division of Continuing Education. This forced me to answer the corollary question of how to extend a research faculty to distant learners who could not quit their jobs to come to campus. We solved that with video lecture capture and a new LMS that allowed us to extend existing programs to new learners at very low cost, again entirely self-funded. As an internal "Outsource Program Manager," we were able to operate, fund growth, and reserve money on less than 25% of revenue, allowing the rest of the funds to flow to the campus to help it overcome state budget cuts. We reached 34 degree programs and 15,000 students by the time I left Colorado to lead Harvard's Division of Continuing Education.

Harvard's Extension School had been offering night classes to adult learners since 1910 and had an amazing brand, a solid technology platform, early online courses, and a great team to build from. Arriving at Harvard's DCE and learning the details of our Extension School, Summer School, Professional Development Programs, and Institute for Learning in Retirement, I quickly recognized the average student age of 34 was similar to Global Campus and CSU Online, but I also quickly realized Harvard DCE's student's age range was much wider, from 12 to 92. Taking the tails off the curve, we have significant enrollment from age 15 to 75 with a mean age of 34. Early in my tenure, I was talking with Gary Matkin from UC Irvine Extension, and he outlined his concept of comprehensive, lifelong educational services that he called the "60-Year Curriculum." I was immediately hooked on the name and idea. My *60YC* journey had become formal.

By the time I retired from Harvard at the end of 2019, DCE had grown to over 30,000 learners annually, up from about 18,000 in 2013. In the Extension school, there were 1,400 courses year-round with 900 available online to serve

4,000 students in stackable, graduate-certificate programs; 4,000 students who were admitted to degree programs; 4,000 more who were earning their way into admission; and about 4,000 taking course without explicit program intentions. We had grown degree graduates from 637 to 1,207 in six years by packaging for and serving the needs of the *60YC* learner. In the Summer School, we had developed 550 courses, with 250 online, serving 3,500 high school learners, 3,500 college students from other universities, and 3,000 Extension students. In addition, we had built a Professional Development Program of short, non-credit courses taken by about 4,000 learners, and our Harvard Institute for Learning in Retirement had 550 members. We also hosted 92 high school students a year in our Crimson Summer Academy.

All of the programs were growing, especially the stackable, graduate-certificate program. When I retired in 2019, Harvard had all the ingredients for quality teaching and learning as well as the architecture of flexible, CRM-centered information systems to support access globally to *60YC* learners. All of us at DCE, including me, owe our university leadership thanks for their insight to allow Harvard to be both the most exclusive and the most inclusive university on earth.

The easy part implementing the *60YC* was providing courses with technology-enhanced pedagogy in hybrid environments. Universities already knew how to do this well. But what was going to be the higher education strategic information system of the future? There was lots of work already going on with Salesforce, Robots and Pencils, and dozens of others. Yet no one had pulled it all together to formulate the learner-centered, cloud-based service suite of the future.

Here are a few examples of *60YC* efforts during that challenging and creative time that I am very proud to have watched, studied, and supported.

- Two global workshops on the *60YC* hosted at Harvard in partnership between DCE and the Harvard Graduate School of Education in 2018 and 2019 started the broad recognition of the *60YC* as important to the higher-education sector. Professor Dede's work has been an inspiration for decades, and his effort and leadership led to this book. The ongoing workshops, conferences, publications, and Harvard-demonstrated leadership in its DCE have enabled hundreds of universities to be confident as they find their role in serving the lifelong learning needs of their communities. This includes Harvard DCE with its adoption of the *60YC* as one of its three, big, long-term strategies along with Learning Engineering (Dede, Richards, & Saxberg, 2019) and CRM-centered information systems. This third component provides the services and products needed from higher education as they serve the broad program and service needs of the *60YC* learner (perhaps the next book).
- Georgia Tech was the first to offer graduate degrees at scale. Their early $6,000 Master's in Computer Science created a new type of access. They and dozens of others followed with sub-$10,000 degrees. The data shows that tens of thousands of learners earned master's degrees this way with essentially identical learning outcomes to the equivalent campus programs; almost all

were learners who could not have gone back to school otherwise. Further, the dominant share of graduates is Americans, in contrast to then-current on-campus programs, whose growth is mostly international students. This was how America stayed competitive in the knowledge economy. Bravo to all the large-scale providers for one of the greatest economic, personal, and social impacts of the next 20 years.

• The University of California, Irvine, was the first to integrate the Office of Career Services into its Extension School. Gary Matkin, as the coiner of the "60-Year Curriculum," recognized that serving a learner over a very long period of time required a service-based relationship not a product-based relationship. By integrating career services, UCI was the first to be able to engage learners over the long term and to predict future product needs based on job trends and career paths. With this knowledge, UCI Extension and the rest of the university expanded their already diverse offerings, creating ever more higher education onramps and offramps for learners, and became one of California's most valued public entities.

• The University of Washington's Continuum College was the first to purposefully integrate up and down the employment lifecycle. By investing in a trust network of blockchain-based credentials, Continuum achieved the amazing goal of democratizing credentials. In the trust-based network, all credentials earned anywhere, both credit and noncredit, had learning outcome and competencies embedded in their meta-data, along with electronic pointers to actual work products so the learner could control how their knowledge and skills were represented to employers. With credentials validated by the university on blockchain, control moved to the learner with true portability outcomes to higher education for the first time.

In 2030, we live in the future these innovators created. Learning is always on, and personal capability is a recorded and integrated lifetime of courses and experiences. That was the promise of a successful *60YC*. That is how the *60YC* led to economic development, personal freedom, and long-term social value, as well as economic sustainability for the universities and colleges that engaged. Thank you for reading this book.

Hunt Lambert
Cambridge, MA
November, 2030

Reference

Dede, C., Richards, J., & Saxberg, B. (Eds.). (2019). *Learning engineering for online education: Theoretical contexts and design-based examples*. New York, NY: Routledge.

Acknowledgments

The editors wish to acknowledge the contributions of those whose dedicated work made the success of the 60-Year Curriculum Workshop and its culmination in this book possible.

The Harvard Division of Continuing Education and the Harvard Graduate School of Education—for co-hosting this and previous pioneering workshops focused on life-long engagement between learners and institutions.

Mark Wittcoff—for his generous support of the 60-Year Curriculum movement, given in honor of his late father, Raymond Wittcoff.

The participants in the *60YC* Workshop—for their energetic and informed discussion of the topics raised during the workshop.

Amie Evans—for her deft coordination of the organizers, authors, participants, and supporting staff, and for her patient attention to the logistical details of conducting the *60YC* Workshop.

Katie Sievers—for her copious notes and insightful summaries of the first day's proceedings.

Kurt Moellering—for his empathetic respect for substance and his fastidious attention to detail in copy-editing manuscripts for this volume.

Michelle Murray and Sarah Ledoux—for providing emergency technical support on very short notice.

The staff of the Harvard Division of Continuing Education—for the essential technical and administrative support they provided during the organization and conduct of the *60YC* Workshop.

1

Introduction
Reconceptualizing Higher Education and Lifelong Learning in the Era of the Synergistic Digital Economy

CHRISTOPHER J. DEDE

Defining the "60-Year Curriculum"

Teenagers' serious thinking about a career begins by middle adolescence, gradually moving beyond visions of being a rock star or a professional athlete to develop realistic conceptions about their first occupational role (Porfeli & Lee, 2012). Looking ahead, the average lifespan of children born in 2020 is projected to be 90–100 years (Gratton & Scott, 2016), so many current students will need to work until their mid-70s to have enough savings for retirement or some other form of post-work life. In progressing through about 60 years of employment, they will face not only evolving jobs requiring expanding skillsets but also multiple careers as some occupations disappear and new roles appear in workplaces shaped by globalization, environmental crises, and artificial intelligence (AI) (Dede, 2018). As a result of these developments, society must prepare today's young people for six decades of career growth (e.g., moving from student teacher to lead teacher) and career change (e.g., moving from automobile welding supervisor to high school science teacher) followed by retirement. To fulfill their responsibilities, educators at every level are faced with the increasing challenge of developing young people's capacity for unceasing reinvention to face an uncertain and changing workplace and for taking on occupations that do not yet exist.

Dr. Gary Matlin at UC-Irvine coined the term the "60-Year Curriculum" (*60YC*) to refer to continuing education centered on lifelong learning about occupational changes and transitions (Branon, 2018). This book describes a *60YC* initiative sponsored by Harvard's Division of Continuing Education (DCE) and focuses on a transformational evolution of higher education toward novel strategies to enable adults to add skills—via formal instruction, employment, and daily life—as their occupational and personal context evolves and shifts. On-the-job learning is familiar to most people; many of us learn to take on tasks that fall outside of our initial academic training. For example, as a professor in learning technologies I have had to reinvent my teaching and research every few years because of advances in digital technologies and globalization. Young adults today face challenges in finding stable jobs that provide benefits and upward mobility for their occupational role. Now, nations face challenges with continuing employability greater than at any prior time in history. I tell my students to prepare simultaneously for their first two careers, determining which is a better foundation as an initial job while building skills that enable shifting to new work-roles in a future neither they nor I can imagine.

> The *60YC* is often described in occupational terms, but our initiative is based on a broader educational mission. As argued by Sizer and Sizer:
>
> High schools have long had three core tasks: to prepare young people for the world of work; to prepare them to use their minds well, to think deeply and in an informed way; and to prepare them to be thoughtful citizens and decent human beings.
>
> (1999, p. 10)

In the 21st century, work, civic participation, and family life rely heavily on the ability to collaborate, mentor, and network. Doing these activities well requires moral and ethical capacities that foster mutual benefits. In particular, low-cost videoconferencing and social media have expanded the toolset and skillset required for sharing, co-creating, and negotiating with others, including people of different linguistic and cultural backgrounds whom one may never meet face-to-face (Fadel, Trilling, & Bialik, 2015). Thus, all three core tasks posited by Sizer and Sizer are important aspects of what educators must inculcate and evolve via the *60YC*.

Achieving the goals of the *60YC* requires rethinking the objectives of education. The importance of this shift was highlighted in a 2012 report by the US National Research Council (NRC), *Education for Life and Work: Developing Transferable Knowledge and Skills in the 21st Century*, which posits that flexibility, creativity, initiative, innovation, intellectual openness, collaboration, leadership, and conflict resolution are essential for each person (2012). The report argued that cognitive, intrapersonal, and interpersonal dimensions of knowledge and skills are best developed in combination. Table 1.1 categorizes a broad range of knowledge and skills vital in the 21st century, grouped by these dimensions.

TABLE 1.1 Dimensions of Knowledge and Skills

Cognitive Outcomes	*Intra-personal Outcomes*	*Inter-personal Outcomes*
Cognitive processes & strategies	Intellectual openness	Teamwork & collaboration
Knowledge	Work ethic & conscientiousness	Leadership
Creativity	Positive core self-evaluation	Communication
Critical thinking	Metacognition	Responsibility
Information literacy	Flexibility	Conflict resolution
Reasoning	Initiative	
Innovation	Appreciation of diversity	

Some of these skills are seldom included in current educational objectives; others are under-emphasized; and still others have changed due to advances in digital technologies (e.g., filtering information has become more important than finding information). Moreover, and in contrast to industrial-style multiple choice and short-answer testing, achieving and assessing mastery now requires the ability to apply knowledge and skills in real-world contexts, demonstrating proficiency via effective, authentic performances. Accenture (2017) summarized and synthesized a variety of frameworks for 21st-century skills.

A report from the UK-based innovation foundation Nesta predicted the nature of work in developed countries in 2030 when the pupils currently starting elementary school begin their careers (Bakhshi, Downing, Osborne, & Schneider, 2017). Its forecast spans only the initial stage of these students' employment, yet the report describes a future—a little more than a decade away—quite different from the present. Political, environmental, and economic instability are driving rapid, chaotic shifts in work and society. Given this rate of change, education's role must be long-term capacity building—enhancing students' interpersonal and intrapersonal skills for a lifetime of flexible adaptation and creative innovation—as well as providing short-term preparation so that they are college-or-career ready. The Nesta report stressed that current educational objectives overemphasize the acquisition of knowledge and underemphasize the mastery of generalizable skills for lifelong employability. Similar to the 2012 NRC report, the skills Nesta highlighted include fluency of ideas, social perceptiveness, systems evaluation, originality, judgment, and decision-making. Nesta emphasized educators must raise aspirations for sophisticated educational outcomes and prepare all students—not only an elite few—to reach ambitious, individual proficiencies in these skills.

A recent Organization for Economic Co-operation and Development (OECD) report (2018) complemented the NRC and Nesta studies by emphasizing personal well-being, which goes beyond income, wealth, jobs, and earnings to stress equitable access to health, civic engagement, social connections, education, security, life satisfaction, and the environment. This OECD report described knowledge and skills people need for lifelong employability but adds an emphasis on attitudes and values, such as creating new value, reconciling tensions and dilemmas, and taking responsibility through personal agency. This formulation of what students need has less emphasis on cognitive factors and more on intrapersonal (including moral and ethical dimensions) and interpersonal capabilities. These align with Sizer and Sizer's goals for educational outcomes that produce thoughtful citizens and decent human beings.

Moving beyond Preparation for One's First Job

Society must help workers who have exhausted their resources for formal education and are faced with ongoing occupational change (Rodrik, 2017). However, the above reports are focused primarily on preparing students at the start of their working lives, getting them ready for their first career, and building transferable skills for future career growth and career change. For that reason, the *60YC* initiative centers on the least understood aspect of the lifelong learning and employability challenge: What are the organizational and societal mechanisms by which people can upskill later in their lives when they do not have the time or resources for a full-time academic experience that results in a degree or certificate? Creating these mechanisms requires developing novel services for adults who are learning while working—the focus of this book—and then applying insights from the new organizations delivering those services to the related tasks of improving preparation for initial jobs and of having a satisfying life after retirement.

Because the digitalization of the economy is unprecedented historically, an uncertainty not addressed in these reports is the extent to which advances in technology will create as many jobs as they eliminate (Frey & Osborne, 2013). If not, then new challenges will arise in ensuring that people who are structurally unemployed have adequate incomes and meaningful opportunities outside of paid work.

Adult learners need educational opportunities and stackable credentials not limited to formal degrees and certifications. Thus far, attempts to address learning post-matriculation have centered on what individual institutions might do. For example, in 2015 Stanford developed an aspirational vision called "Open Loop University" (Stanford2025, n.d.), and Georgia Tech has released its report *Deliberate Innovation, Lifetime Education* (Georgia Tech Commission on Creating the Next in Education, 2018). The hallmarks of these and similar models center on providing a lifelong commitment to alumni that includes periodic opportunities to upskill through services offered by the institution: micro-credentials, minimester classes, and credit for accomplishments in life; personalized advising and coaching as new challenges and opportunities emerge; and blended-learning experiences with distributed worldwide availability. Some of these services will require partnerships and collaborations with organizations outside of academia that have complementary strengths and missions (e.g., mentoring the transition to a new job or occupation).

Further, the educational emphasis in college shifts to acquisition of competencies (skills, knowledge, and abilities) rather than disciplinary topics and knowledge communication—the student's goal is to develop a suite of skills and strategic attitudes to make a difference in the world rather than just attaining formal academic certification to meet the immediate requirements of a particular occupational role. Beyond these models of how universities might help, partnerships with employers are important in recognizing the value and complementarity of situated workplace learning and acculturation.

Models like these are a useful step forward but are not sufficient because they focus on a single institution's ability to serve its alumni rather than on meeting the more general need to equip and help all adults from any background at any stage of their lives. For this reason, DCE's *60YC* is exploring models in which a coalition of extension schools might accomplish this broader task by working together to extend their mission, moving beyond episodic "continuing education" to iterative, cyclical, continuous adult learning. Another organizational model could be regional higher education coalitions parallel to Western Governors

University in their cross-institutional cooperation. Useful insights about institutional partnerships and coalitions can come from fields like medicine that provide approaches for continuous recertification, as well as from sectors like the military that have well-developed approaches for employee career growth and career change. That said, expanding the mission of current institutions designed for different educational purposes is unlikely to provide the full range of services necessary for continuous lifelong learning. This book sketches strategies and models that could provide a novel comprehensive solution, including models from non-profits and workforce development boards.

Frameworks for Adult Learning and Education

Thompson (2009) provided a brief history of research and theory on adult learning and cognition. Relevant to occupational learning, Knowles (1970) identified andragogy (instructional strategies for aiding the learning of adults, as opposed to children) as including five basic assumptions:

1. Adults are more independent and self-directed than children.
2. As adults mature, their life experience grows as a resource on which to base new learning.
3. Adults' motivation for learning is largely focused on life tasks, issues, and challenges.
4. For adults, learning just-in-time is valued more than learning just-in-case.
5. For adults, learning is problem-centered rather than content-centered.

Cross (1981) applied these principles to the design of adult learning experiences. Brookfield (1986) and Mezirow (1991) emphasized the self-directed nature of adult learning and the importance of critical awareness.

Bryson defined adult education as "all activities with an educational purpose that are carried on by people in the ordinary business of life" (1936, pp. 3–4). In contrast to informal learning from life, Cremin (1970) defined education as an intentional and organized activity to transmit or acquire knowledge, skills, and attitudes. Recent work in the learning sciences has emphasized the importance of context and culture (National Academies of Science, Engineering, and Medicine, 2018), which shape learning from life as well as through education. Marsick and Watkins defined informal and incidental learning as "learning outside of formally structured, institutionally sponsored, classroom-based activities" (1990, pp. 6–7) and asserted that responding to non-routine circumstances outside of standard procedures exposes erroneous tacit assumptions and leads to learning through reflection on what was expected versus what actually happened. In this process, they differentiated between informal workplace learning, which may be planned and intentional, versus incidental workplace learning, which is "a byproduct of some other activity, such as task accomplishment, interpersonal interaction, sensing the organizational culture, or trial-and-error experimentation" (pp. 6–7).

Informal and incidental learning draws on various frameworks: Dewey's (1938) reflective thought, Lewin's (1947) action research, Polanyi's (1967) tacit knowledge, and Argyris and Schon's (1978) action science, a systematic process for learning from experimentation in groups and organizations. Marsick and Watkins (1990) identified conditions that might delimit or enhance informal and incidental learning. Delimiters include the ways that understanding is framed and reframed (Polanyi, 1967) and the capacity to engage in goal-directed behavior in everyday work (Inkster, 1987). Consistent with the 21st-century skills described earlier, enhancers include creativity, proactivity, and critical reflectivity. Situated cognition and learning by doing in workplace settings are also important forms of informal learning (National Academy of Sciences, Engineering, and Medicine, 2018), as are deliberate and focused actions by adult learners.

As adult education has evolved over time, its use of these learning principles has become more pervasive. Fostering career growth and career change via the *60YC* will require research to deepen our understanding of adult learning, as well as applications of personalized learning to this distinct set of students. The process of *learning engineering* will support the development of new models and refined approaches for adults (Dede, 2019).

The History of Institutions Fostering Adult Learning in America

Understanding the approaches organizations have historically used to promote adult learning and education in the United States is important as a context for developing future-oriented strategies. This section briefly summarizes this evolution and the many types of institutions and media involved, and it then draws implications for the *60YC*.

In the Colonial Period, adults primarily drew on sources of informal learning, such as coffeehouses and taverns. Public lectures were 'another source of information, but the required fees limited access to the leisured, business, and professional classes (Stubblefield & Keane, 1994). In contrast, public libraries provided more open means of learning. In 1727, Benjamin Franklin founded a learned society, a mutual-improvement club whose members aided each other's learning; some of these groups incorporated multiple disciplines and fields, such as the American Philosophical Society. Evening schools offered basic courses in reading, writing, and arithmetic, as well as more advanced offerings in classic and modern languages or in business and technical subjects (Seybolt, 1925). Apprenticeships were the basis of most workplace learning; the mutual obligations of mentor and apprentice were specified in contracts of indenture, typically for seven years (Towner, 1966).

By the early 1800s, social reformers saw adult education as a means of providing access to learning for everyone, including marginalized populations like women, ethnic groups, and the poor (Wecter, 1937). Agricultural societies worked to modernize the practices of farming (Rossiter, 1975), and evening schools helped to educate immigrants who worked all day in factories and shops. Knowledge that served a useful economic purpose was promoted by industrialists; this included a particular emphasis on science, engineering, and technology communicated through mechanics' institutes (Bates, 1965). Newspapers flourished and complemented the rapid expansion of libraries as published sources of information (Bode, 1960).

During this period, lyceums emerged as a popular form of adult education. Their emphasis was on the sciences and useful knowledge, the development of libraries and museums, and the encouragement of temperance and morality; politics and religions were excluded as topics (Noffsinger, 1926). A competitor to lyceums as an organized movement was the rise of professional lecturing, which developed national educational associations in fields such as geology, dentistry, and civil engineering (Scott, 1980).

Between the Civil War and World War I, adult education flourished (Knowles, 1977). The Morrill Act of 1862 created Land Grant colleges (Andrews, 1918). As a complement to lyceums and lectures, chautauquas emerged: weeks-long summer institutes devoted to learning (Morrison, 1974). These events organized into circuits on which a traveling chautauqua might visit about 30 towns over the course of a summer. Perhaps in response to these non-academic methods of adult education, universities developed *extension* activities that focused on subjects such as mechanics, farming, and teaching (Van Hise, 1915). Magazines joined books and newspapers as media for informal learning (Tebbel, 1974). World's Fairs provided a complement to museums.

The development and implementation of the first correspondence courses were credited to Sir Isaac Pitman of England, the inventor of shorthand. In 1840, he used the postal service in England to reach learners at a distance. A more formal version of the early-American correspondence course was created by Anna Ticknor of Boston in 1873. In order to increase educational opportunities for women, she originated the Society to Encourage Studies at Home. The society provided courses of study for women of all social classes and served over 10,000 women over its 24-year lifespan (Nasseh, 1997; Stevens-Long & Crowell, 2002).

Advances in industrialization and a move away from agricultural labor led to an increasing focus on preparation for work, both for career growth and for career change (Gutman, 1976). Technics and the useful arts linked science and economic development (Daniels, 1971). Businesses pushed for vocational education, trade schools, and in-plant apprenticeships. Taylor's "scientific management" promoted training for workers to act like machines (Neumann, 1979), while corporate "industrial welfare" programs taught safety and sanitation. Workers sometimes pushed back against this top-down training, creating their own educational systems like the Grange, the Farmers' Alliance, and the Knights of Labor (McLaurin, 1978). On America's entry into World War I, the military developed methods of mass training and classification by aptitude, including the origination of intelligence testing (Gould, 1981).

In the period between the two world wars, the Carnegie Corporation of New York professionalized adult education through forming the American Association for Adult Education (AAAE). Annual conferences and the *Journal of Adult Education* brought rigor and research to the field. That said, the AAAE focused on the professionalization of adults more than on providing access to career growth and change to marginalized populations (Lagemann, 1987). In parallel and with a similarly elitist perspective, the National University Extension Association helped to professionalize those offerings (Rohfeld, 1990). Government programs associated with the New Deal reached more of a general adult audience (Maskin, 1973).

Commissioned by the American Association of Museums, the research of Edward S. Robinson aided with the design of exhibits to maximize learning (Alexander, 1979). *Life* magazine invented the picture essay, and movie theatre audiences enjoyed newsreels (Marquis, 1986). Radio broadened the range of educative media and reached national audiences, supplanting the newspaper as the preferred source of news (Perrett, 1985). Despite the rapid rise of radio technology, distance education courses were rarely if ever offered for credit in higher education. The education community, along with society as a whole, regarded legitimate education as only possible in conventional locales such as classrooms (Funk, 1998).

Corporations blended emerging media into their training, establishing formal schools such as the Westinghouse Technical Night School and the General Motors Institute of Technology (Stubblefield & Keane, 1994). The US entry into World War II brought coordinated efforts to train not only military personnel but also civilian workers (Grace, 1948). Post-war, the GI bill brought many former military personnel into higher education.

The past seven decades have brought expansion for many of the adult educational mechanisms and organizations described above. Community colleges provided educational and certification options that were less time consuming and expensive than four year colleges. Workplace education programs sponsored by large corporations for their employees became the norm (Eurich, 1985), and unions responded with educational initiatives of their own (Aronowitz, 1990). IBM (2005) established a model for blending formal and informal learning with its On Demand learning system. Professional associations, such as the American Bar Association and the American Medical Association, became core licensing bodies for people who wanted to practice those professions.

In the decades after World War II, television became a powerful vehicle for adult education (Chafe, 1991). Tele-courses (Verduin & Clark, 1991), which developed in the 1970s, showed promise for minimizing some of these problems. The development of videotape allowed educators to customize the same content for different learning environments. This medium also allowed increased flexibility; course content could be stored, delivered, and repeated at will. However, despite their advantages, the cost and complexity of producing tele-courses made them impractical for teaching large numbers of students.

The British Open University began in 1969 through video broadcasting its weekly courses on the BBC. Over time and with the advent of new technologies, the British Open University's model of distance learning evolved into a student-centered delivery system and administrative structure separate from a campus setting. More economically practical than tele-courses, this system envisioned each student as "a node in the network" (Granger, 1990, p. 189) that provided individualized instruction in a virtual classroom. The students had access to a virtual library—customizable based on their particular learning style—and to collaborative tools that encouraged discourse and critical thinking (Prewitt, 1998). By encouraging a community of learners without admission requirements, this model enabled outreach to adults facing career growth and career change.

During the 1990s, government policy and investment led to workforce innovation boards, public funding for workforce development, and public employability offices. Also, widespread usage of the Internet transformed the nature of distance education. In particular, with the development of the World Wide Web (WWW) as a means of representing and accessing information, Internet use expanded exponentially. By 2000, the number of webpages rose to at least one billion (Maddux, 2001). With its capability to facilitate communication between people in various geographic locations and to disseminate information quickly and relatively inexpensively, the Internet appeared well-matched for distance education of adults. However, change has been very slow in both face-to-face and distance-based educational practice (Cuban, 2013), with a perennial emphasis on presentational instruction and content coverage despite research-based findings emphasizing active learning and skill development (Clark & Mayer, 2016; National Academies of Science, Engineering, and Medicine, 2018). In informal learning, however, social media (such as YouTube videos) have transformed how adults gain and interpret information (Dede, 2016).

In online learning, although massively open online courses (MOOCs) were hailed as a breakthrough, their instructional practices have remained entrenched in outdated models of teaching (Dede, 2013). In particular, methods for personalization such as individualizing a student's path to content mastery—through adaptive learning or competency-based education—have typically not been utilized (Dede, Ho, & Mitros, 2016). Similarly, more efficient and effective learning as a result of faster and more in-depth diagnosis of student needs or course trouble-spots has languished, including assessment of skills such as systems thinking, collaboration, and problem solving in the context of deep, authentic, subject-area knowledge assessments.

In summary, over the past few centuries, beyond participants' desire for self-improvement, adult education has been influenced by those who sought to shape individuals and society as well as by the sequential emergence of various media that could support learning (Stubblefield & Keane, 1994). Almost every conceivable combination of the dimensions of adult education have been tried— formal, informal, and incidental; community-based and classroom-based; top-down from employers and government and bottom-up from workers and individuals; isolated, collaborative/peer-based, and massive numbers of participants—all with an ever-evolving array of media. While the future may bring new capabilities such as immersion in designed experiences that simulate career growth and career change (Dede, Grotzer, Kamarainen, & Metcalf, 2017), the rich knowledge from the past about participants, instructional designs, and organizational structures should inform emerging models for the *60YC*. These models must address lifetime (as opposed to life-stage) learning and lifetime (versus career-stage) employability, incorporating strategic, long-term investments as well as tactical preparation. As discussed earlier, the *60YC* also must extend beyond people's work to include their personal wellbeing and social contribution.

The Challenges of Maintaining Workforce Value and Lifetime Employability

This section draws on studies and current reports from many organizations, so that a variety of viewpoints is represented. All these analyses present a consistent message about the core issues and ways that stakeholders should act in response. No term acceptable to all stakeholders has emerged from these studies; this chapter uses the phrase "synergistic digital economy" to reflect the interweaving and mutual empowerment of physical and biological technologies by advances in digital technologies.

Recently, the chair of the World Economic Forum posited that civilization is entering a historically unprecedented, transformational economic change. As Schwab explains in *The Fourth Industrial Revolution: What it Means, How to Respond*:

> [The Fourth Industrial Revolution] is characterized by a fusion of technologies that is blurring the lines between the physical, digital, and biological spheres. . . . When compared with previous industrial revolutions, the Fourth is evolving at an exponential rather than a linear pace. Moreover, it is disrupting almost every industry in every country. And the breadth and depth of these changes herald the transformation of entire systems of production, management, and governance. . . . The possibilities of billions of people connected by mobile devices, with unprecedented processing power, storage capacity, and access to knowledge, are unlimited. And these possibilities will be multiplied by emerging technology breakthroughs in fields such as artificial intelligence, robotics, the Internet of Things, autonomous vehicles, 3-D printing, nanotechnology, biotechnology, materials science, energy storage, and quantum computing.
>
> (2016, p. 1)

Schwab indicates that, in this new economic system, human talent will become the most important factor in production, outweighing historically central factors such as financial capital and technological infrastructure. He sees inequality as the greatest concern of the coming decades, with jobs segregated into low-skill/low-wage and high-skill/high-wage occupations, losing many jobs in the middle class.

In its 2019 report *Leading through the Fourth Industrial Revolution: Putting People at the Centre*, the World Economic Forum uses manufacturing as an illustration of the importance of talent and the challenge of inequality. Manufacturing is currently 16% of the world's economy and employs nearly one quarter of the world's workers (2019c, p. 6). The report describes how an emerging economic transformation is disrupting long-established business models, creating shifts in production-value chains, digitizing almost every manufacturing process, and fostering demand for customized products. Trends in the concentration of product demand and labor supply across geographies, as well as the localization and consolidation of production supply chains, are accelerating shifts in the nature of work and occupations. All this is driving a rise in protectionism and populism, as many see their financial security threatened or lost. For better or for worse, these pervasive economic factors are driving an inevitable, world-wide, long-term rise in career growth and career change.

Autor (2019) contrasts the work of the past and the work of the future from an economics perspective. The International Labour Organization's Global Commission on the Future of Work (2019) calls for a human-centered agenda for the future of work, with increasing investments in people's capabilities, in the institutions of work (universal labor guarantees, time sovereignty, collective representation of workers and employers, harnessing of technology for meaningful work), and in decent and sustainable work. Without investments in increasing human capabilities, the gulf between the affluent and the poor will persist and perhaps widen.

In its 2019 report *Dialogue Series on New Economic and Social Frontiers: Shaping the New Economy in the Fourth Industrial Revolution*, the World Economic Forum describes how other sectors of the world economy beyond manufacturing are also contributing to occupational instability, insecurity, and inequality:

> Although many advanced economies have reaped enormous benefits from technological advances, they have also experienced a hollowing out of the middle class; growing market concentration within many sectors; a "great decoupling" between productivity growth and the evolution of wages; and concerns about algorithm bias solidifying patterns of exclusion. Largely because of increasing polarization and reduced social mobility, perceptions within these economies around the opportunities and risks are diverging.... Part of this insecurity comes from the very real experience of shifts in labour markets already underway; and it is compounded by growing uncertainty about what the future will look like, with the only area of consensus being that the biggest part of the transformation is still ahead of us.
>
> (2019a, p. 1)

These concerns are echoed in the World Economic Forum's *Global Risks Report 2019*, which warns about the psychological stresses people are facing worldwide due to lack of control in the face of uncertainty given complex social, technological, and work-related transformations. The report notes that declining psychological and social well-being is not only a risk in itself but also adds to other risks related to social cohesion and politics (2019b, p. 7).

The World Economic Forum's *Leading Through the Fourth Industrial Revolution: Putting People at the Centre* report described earlier identifies the primary societal and leadership challenge as enabling workers; although technology is an important differentiator for organizations, people are seen as the most important source of competitive strength (2019c). In their book, *Human+Machine: Reimagining Work in the Age of AI*, Daugherty and Wilson (2018) indicate that organizations are quickly realizing that humans are necessary to leverage the full potential of intelligence technologies. Accenture (2018) estimates that, if workforce enablement does not catch up with the rate of technological progress, G20 economies could lose up to $11.5 trillion in cumulative GDP growth over the next ten years. This is equivalent to more than an entire percentage point from the average growth rate every year during this period.

The World Economic Forum's report *Strategies for the New Economy: Skills as the Currency of the Labour Market* describes the types of leadership actions needed to meet these challenges, centering on three types of initiatives: skills-building strategies in the learning ecosystem; labor market strategies to identify necessary skills and provide mechanisms for certifying these as warrants of employability; and enabling strategies, such as encouraging lifelong learning and aligning skills taxonomies (2019d, p. 8). Summarizing these strategies is beyond the scope of this chapter, but the cases offer models valuable in actualizing the *60YC*. The research of Deming and Kahn (2018) addresses several of these strategies, examining skill requirements across firms and labor markets, and Deming (2017) highlights the growing importance of social skills in the labor market. Resolving difficulties in measuring social skills and understanding effective ways to help people learn these are central to achieving the leadership actions recommended by the World Economic Forum.

Like learning ecosystem strategies and labor market strategies, educational technologies are another avenue to address the challenges raised by the synergistic digital economy. An inquiry into the "skills gap" at the 2018 Stanford Shaping the Workforce of the Future design series highlighted that there was a significant opportunity for workforce educational technologies to help close a translation gap between workers and how their skills apply to the future of work. As a follow-up from the series, the organizers developed a web-based application that leverages principles from the learning sciences to prompt the process of analogical reasoning so that users might transfer their skills to new and different types of work. This tool ingests existing data about a user from their LinkedIn profile, resume, and other text-based sources and visualizes them as the competencies needed for the future of work. Early studies in partnership with the Los Angeles Chamber of Commerce revealed participants exposed to their skill-visualization map were three times more likely to be recommended by the chamber for an internship with one of their partner organizations such as Snap, LinkedIn, Google, and Microsoft and self-reported having 356% more skills (Forshaw, Rosas, & Maples, 2019).

Shifts in Workforce Skills

The World Economic Forum's The *Future of Jobs Report 2018* report describes a new human-machine frontier within existing tasks:

> Companies expect a significant shift on the frontier between humans and machines when it comes to existing work tasks between 2018 and 2022. In 2018, an average of 71% of total task hours across the 12 industries covered in the report are performed by humans, compared to 29% by machines. By 2022 this average is expected to have shifted to 58% task hours performed by humans and 42% by machines. In 2018, in terms of total working hours, no work task was yet estimated to be predominantly performed by a machine or an algorithm. By 2022, this picture is projected to have somewhat changed, with machines and algorithms on average increasing their contribution to specific tasks by 57%. For example, by 2022, 62% of organization's information and data processing and information search and transmission tasks will be performed by machines compared to 46% today. Even those work tasks that have thus far remained overwhelmingly human—communicating and interacting (23%); coordinating, developing, managing and advising (20%); as well as reasoning and decision making (18%)—will begin to be automated (30%, 29%, and 27% respectively). Relative to their starting point today, the expansion of machines' share of work task performance is particularly marked in the reasoning and decision-making, administering, and looking for and receiving job-related information tasks.
>
> (2018, p. viii)

Similar conclusions about the challenge of technology-driven career growth and career change are reached in reports from the Organization for Economic Cooperation and Development (2019)—*Trends Shaping Education, 2019*—and the Southern Regional Education Board (2019)—*Unprepared and Unaware: Upskilling the Workforce for a Decade of Uncertainty*.

The Brookings report *Automation and Artificial Intelligence: How Machines are Affecting People and Places* indicates that almost no occupations will be unaffected by AI, and about one quarter of US jobs will face high exposure to automation in the coming decades (Muro, Maxim, & Whiton, 2019). In response, the authors recommend five major public policy agendas; the two closely related to this chapter are to promote a constant learning mindset and to create a universal adjustment benefit to support all displaced workers. The latter could be actualized through federal initiatives such as employability insurance, which could serve as a potential funding source for the *60YC*. Acemoglu and Restrepo (2018) note that AI focused on automation reduces employment, but AI focused on new tasks where labor can be productively employed may increase jobs and develop new types of meaningful work. Further, all types of occupations must be fully available to the diverse groups who are marginalized in our current economy.

The Brookings report also notes that a cultural shift must take place in business practices for hiring:

> As the market for accelerated learning continues to expand, companies will need to be able to effectively evaluate which skills workers have mastered. Therefore, state and local governments, in partnership with industry associations, business services groups, and other employer intermediaries, should develop and push wide acceptance of skill-based hiring. This would stand in contrast to current standard hiring practices, which designate a high school diploma or university degree as the primary, and often sole, credential. Skill-based hiring efforts could in turn be leveraged to facilitate "stackable credentials" by laying out which skills and certifications can be combined into the equivalent of a degree.
>
> (Muro et al., 2019, p. 53)

On the demand side, skill-based learning will be a difficult shift to accomplish, just as it is on the supply side where educators have long-standing, entrenched practices related to what degrees represent and how they are acquired.

New types of credentials and novel mechanisms for obtaining them are essential for most adults facing career change because they do not have the resources to complete the extensive formal education associated with degrees and certifications. Goldin and Katz present a historical analysis of the co-evolution of educational attainment and the wage structure in the United States through the 20th century in their book *The Race between Education and Technology* (2010). Recent publications that discuss this challenge of meaningful work and fair wages and present promising approaches to credentialing include the American Enterprise Institute report, *Non-Degree Credentials, Work-based Learning, and the American Working Class* (Columbus, 2019); the International Council for Open and Distance Education report, *The Present and Future of Alternative Digital Credentials* (ICDE Working Group, 2019); and Northeastern University's analysis, *Educational Credentials Come of Age*, a survey on the use and value of educational credentials in hiring (Gallagher, 2018). A crucial issue in this is applying AI to create a division of labor in which mid-range and lower-range jobs are worthwhile and respected as opposed to making people the eyes and hands of machines that govern their behavior (Acemoglu & Restrepo, 2018; International Labor Organization, 2019).

The World Bank (2019, p. 9) makes similar recommendations on what governments can do to ameliorate problems caused by the changing nature of work. Its *World Development Report* argues for investing in human capital, particularly early childhood education, to develop higher order cognitive and sociobehavioral skills in addition to the standard foundational skills taught through current curricula. Also, a solid, guaranteed social-minimum-income and strengthened social-insurance are seen as key in helping the labor market meet the challenges of increasing work in the informal economy, which often offers no protections. Further, the World Bank recommends creating the necessary public funding for these measures through property taxes in large cities, excise taxes on goods such as sugar or tobacco, and carbon taxes.

The World Economic Forum report *Towards a Reskilling Revolution: Industry-Led Action for the Future of Work* argues that business and government have strong economic reasons for making these shifts in labor market and business practices:

> Drawing from average reskilling costs, we find that the 1.37 million workers who are projected to be displaced fully out of their roles in the next decade according to the US Bureau of Labor Statistics, may be reskilled to new viable (similar skillset) and desirable (higher wages) growing roles at a cost of US$34 billion. On average this would entail US$24,800 per displaced worker. . . . In the US alone, with an overall investment of US$4.7 billion, the private sector could reskill 25% of all workers in disrupted jobs with a positive cost-benefit balance . . . if industry-led collaboration could reduce reskilling costs and times by 30%, nearly half of the disrupted workforce could be reskilled by employers with a positive cost-benefit balance. . . . With the set of assumptions applied and with an investment of US$19.9 billion, the US government could reskill 77% of workers expected to be displaced by technology into growing jobs while generating a positive return in the form of taxes and lower welfare payments.
>
> (2019e, p. vii)

This shows a strong economic case can be made for funding the *60YC*.

How big a skill shift will be necessary in career growth and career change? Some of what will occur is shifts in the division of labor between person and machine; the Brookings report discussed above details what those changes may be. Also, people may change to new careers that do not now exist. Beyond supply-side analyses of which current jobs will be eliminated or de-skilled and which new roles employers will need, the demand-side creation of new occupations by entrepreneurial young people is important to consider. The 2017 report from Accenture, *New Skills Now: Inclusion in the Digital Economy*, analyzes the core skills important for workplace success in the coming decades and presents six personas that illustrate what skills are needed to enter particular careers, such as functional-test engineer or aged-care worker. Two reports from Cognizant (2017, 2018), *21 Jobs of the Future* and *21 More Jobs of the Future*, sketch some interesting hypothetical possibilities for new occupations. These include personal memory curator, man-machine teaming manager, genomic portfolio director, augmented reality journey builder, and tidewater architect. An interesting exercise for the reader is to imagine how much the content, process, and personnel of current higher education and adult learning organizations would need to shift to enable helping students master these new roles.

Overall, this book discusses the roles that higher education can play in the organizational and societal mechanisms by which people can upskill later in their lives when they do not have the time or resources for a full-time academic experience that results in a degree or certificate. Creating this transformational evolution of higher education requires developing novel services for adults learning while working—through formal instruction—or informally in daily life, and then applying insights from the new organizations delivering those services—within and outside of higher education—to the related tasks of improving preparation for initial jobs and of having a satisfying life after retirement.

Overview of the Chapters in This Volume

The book begins with a foreword by Huntington Lambert, Dean of Harvard's Division of Continuing Education. Next is this introductory chapter introducing terms and conceptual frameworks as well as providing a brief summary of the contents of each chapter, grouped into two types of discussions. *Challenges and Opportunities for Stakeholders* are delineated in chapters by Scott, Servoz, and Brewer. *Current Models and Strategies* are provided by Harmon and Baker, Mishra and Smith, Wingard and Farrugia, Honan, and Lambert and Leitner. The book concludes with a chapter by Richards summarizing cross-cutting themes from the chapters and delineating important next steps in research and practice for the evolution of *60YC*.

Challenges and Opportunities for Stakeholders

Scott's chapter, "Education, Age, and the Machine," describes how the combined influences of technological change and longevity are likely to transform the educational system. What we learn, when and how we learn it, and who we learn it from all will change. The good news for the educational system is that the continued growth it has benefited from over the last 100 years looks set to continue, as these forces should raise the return on education. The more challenging news is that this expansion will manifest itself as a shift into new areas that are currently poorly served: adult education, intergenerationally mixed courses, skills- and employment-based learning, and shorter cumulative programs.

Servoz's chapter, "Are We Ready for the Jobs that the Digital Economy Will Offer to Us?" indicates that previous historical waves of automation have been overwhelmingly positive for the economy and society. However, AI, as the latest manifestation of the digitalization transformation, is in a different league, with the potential to amplify major socio-economic changes and be much more disruptive. What do recent developments in digitalization, AI, and robotization foreshadow for the economy, businesses, and jobs? Should we be worried or excited? Where will jobs be destroyed or new ones created? How do education systems, businesses, governments, and social partners need to adapt to successfully manage the forthcoming transitions?

Brewer's chapter, "Employing the 60-Year Curriculum as a Strategic Approach," discusses how, until recently, employers controlled the career paths of individuals. Today, career paths are in the hands of the individual. People are faced with sponsoring their own learning and all that this entails—time, distance, costs, and outcomes. Steering a pathway through this uncertain and high-investment terrain is nigh impossible without some guidance. It is critical for educational institutions to understand how strategic- and student-centric foci can support their efforts to achieve educational objectives and learning outcomes for students and educators alike. There is no doubt that a transdisciplinary approach will be one of the factors that will be necessary to bring the dynamism of the 60YC to fulfill its value proposition. Student transition into a 60YC context is an important aspect in terms of curriculum design by linking content, delivery, and assessment with each prospective student's previous learning. Designing a curriculum *with* rather than *for* adults necessitates a democratic, active, and stratified environment that facilitates learning. Engaging external stakeholders to participate in curriculum design allows educational institutions to harvest and harness information from the most suitable sources and will lead to developing new ideas that return value to students and, subsequently, to the institution.

Current Models and Strategies

Harmon and Baker's chapter, "Creating the Next in Higher Education at Georgia Tech," delineates that trying to envision the best possible future is always challenging, but putting in place a process and set of actions that might enable that future is even more challenging. This chapter provides a description of and context for Georgia Tech's efforts to envision and create its educational future. It identifies factors we think are driving change in higher education and how this institution is responding to them. It identifies activities already in process at Georgia Tech and describes actions yet to be determined and/or defined to help reach that future. This work is based upon the efforts of a group of faculty, staff, and students who engaged in a multi-year effort, called the Commission on Creating the Next in Education, resulting in the publication of a guiding report titled "Deliberate Innovation, Lifetime Education." With this report, Georgia Tech is striving to provide options that will enable the university to succeed in the future and not suggesting that these are the only steps one should take. We firmly believe that higher education in the future must be different than it is now in several meaningful dimensions in order to fulfill our social contract.

Mishra and Smith's chapter, "Known for Whom We Include: Designing Models for Lifelong Education at Arizona State University," indicates that the development and implementation of a 60YC requires a broad conceptualization of university design grounded in a deep understanding of the learners we are trying to reach. Mishra and Smith argue that we need to expand our view from those we have traditionally served to others who may have significantly different lived experiences and educational needs. In particular, we need to focus on the variable, fluid, and evolving nature of learner narrative-identities over a student's lifespan and meet all students where they are in terms of their current and aspirational identity development. In this chapter, Mishra and Smith provide examples of (and initial learnings from) some key initiatives currently underway at Arizona State University (ASU) that align with the 60YC. An important aspect of ASU's work has been developing new pathways to learners in addition to the standard direct-to-learner model. These include the education-to-business model, in which ASU delivers a learning experience in partnership with an employer. The authors argue that, in response to the upskilling needs of adult learners, universities will re-imagine how they engage learners at scale (such as partnerships with community-based organizations).

Wingard and Farrugia's chapter, "Market-Driven Education: The Imperative for Responsive Design and Application," describes how the higher education sector faces the imminent challenge of how to prepare students with the applicable skills and abilities necessary to secure a job after graduation and to adapt continuously to ever-changing workplace demands throughout their careers. Currently, higher education falls short of expectations in producing market-ready, employable graduates; inadequate employer engagement is the principle culprit for this failure. This chapter describes the existing gap between higher education and employers and discusses the relative implications of this disconnect for workers and employers alike. The chapter delineates a framework of higher education-employer engagement, and its connection to employability, and applies this framework to the case of the Columbia University School of Professional Studies—focusing on how the school approaches employer engagement throughout its academic and co-curricular activities in service of maximizing the employability of its graduates.

Honan's chapter, "The Role and Potential of University-Based Executive Education and Professional Development Programs in the 60-Year Curriculum: A Case Example of an Intensive Residential Program for Higher Education Leaders," examines an example of a long-standing, university-based program designed for senior-level leaders of colleges and universities. Through a detailed description of key design features of this program, the chapter attempts to illustrate some of the key challenges and opportunities associated with effectively meeting the learning needs of individuals who are in the latter stages of the *60YC* continuum. The chapter concludes with a discussion of the roles that university-based executive education programs could play for this audience in the coming years. Among the challenges discussed is the need for empirical evidence to document the efficacy of these types of programs; that might support continued investments in this type of learning experience.

Lambert and Leitner's chapter, "Implementing *60YC* Learning at the Harvard Division of Continuing Education," explains that the mission of Harvard's Division of Continuing Education (HDCE) is to provide open access to high-quality affordable courses, certificates, and degrees for adult learners. Implementing the *60YC* at HDCE has been, and will continue to be, a work in progress with both successful innovations and missteps. Thus far, it has involved successive strategic planning exercises to guide an evolution from a lecture-oriented pedagogical model with administration-centric services to supporting multiple online and hybrid pedagogical models with learner- and faculty-centric services. The technical infrastructure is changing from modifications of existing management information systems and a suite of in-house applications to a relationship-management infrastructure and open source and commercial applications. The on-going *60YC* planning and development efforts involve shared work by learning engineers, IT developers, and administrators. HDCE's *60YC* infrastructure allows them to conduct experiments to test learning experiences, new infrastructure tools, and administrative processes in response to evidence of learner success, faculty satisfaction, and operational efficiency.

Following these two sections on *Challenges and Opportunities for Stakeholders* and *Current Models and Strategies,* a concluding chapter by Richards consolidates themes from all chapters, assesses the current state of *60YC* implementations, and proposes dimensions for research. Preparing for job changes and upskilling, and for successive shifts in careers, creates entirely different demands on learners, instructors, career counselors, employers, and all other stakeholders in building and sustaining adult capacity. As we have seen, the *60YC*, driven by the synergistic digital economy, extends the two- to eight-year university experience and other traditional forms of education and training to learning throughout a lifetime. The chapter identifies two dimensions for future research. First, students as consultants-entrepreneurs must accept responsibility for their own learning. They must learn to collaborate, to lead and follow, to be agile and resilient, and to learn how to continue learning. How are the transferable intrapersonal, interpersonal, and cognitive competencies that make this possible integrated into the instructional methods of the university? Second, the evolving relationship between the student and the university begins with first contact and extends through 60 years. How will universities adapt infrastructure and administrative processes to support this relationship?

The book ends with acknowledgements and the biographies of the authors.

Conclusion

Much remains to be understood about how the *60YC* might become the future of higher education and adult learning. Whatever models emerge, they must include strategies that help those now involved in adult learning—both providers and students—to transformatively change their behaviors. Porfeli and Vondracek (2009) emphasize that individual development is shaped both by organismic factors (biological predispositions and Piagetian developmental-psychological constructions) and by contextual factors (human history and social institutions). Bronfenbrunner's ecological model (1979) posits that social contexts are hierarchically linked to each other (i.e., developmental systems theory). Kegan and Lahey (2009) describe how these factors combine to make many adults immune to change.

In my opinion, the biggest barrier we face in this process of reinventing our current methods, models, and organizations for these activities is *unlearning*. We have to let go of deeply held, emotionally valued identities in service of transformational change to a different, more effective set of behaviors. This is both individual (an instructor transforming practices from presentation and assimilation to active, collaborative learning by students) and institutional (a higher education institution transforming from degrees certified by seat time and standardized tests to credentials certified by proficiency or competency-based measures). Unlearning requires not only novel intellectual insights and approaches but also individual and collective emotional and social support for shifting our identities—not necessarily in terms of fundamental character and capabilities but in terms of how those are expressed as our context shifts over time. I hope higher education will increase its focus on the aspirational vision of the *60YC* as an important step toward providing a pathway to a secure and satisfying future for our students.

References

Accenture. (2017). *New skills now: Inclusion in the digital economy.* Retrieved from https://www.accenture.com/_acnmedia/PDF-63/Accenture-New-Skills-Now-Inclusion-in-the-digital.pdf

Accenture. (2018). *It's learning. Just not as we know it: How to accelerate skills acquisition in the age of intelligent technologies.* Retrieved from http://www.g20yea.com/images/reports/Its-Learning-Just-Not-As-We-Know-It.pdf

Acemoglu, D., & Restrepo, P. (2018, December). The wrong type of AI? Artificial intelligence and the future of labor demand. *Toulouse Network for Information Technology News, 1–5.* Retrieved from https://idei.fr/sites/default/files/IDEI/documents/tnit/newsletter/newsletter_tnit_2019.pdf

Alexander, E. P. (1979). *Museums in motion: An introduction to the history and function of museums.* Nashville, TN: American Association for State and Local History.

Andrews, B. F. (1918). The Land Grant Act of 1862 and the land grant colleges. US Department of Interior, Bureau of Education. *Bulletin, 13,* 7–10.

Argyris, C., & Schon, D. (1978). *Organizational learning: A theory of action perspective.* San Francisco, CA: Jossey-Bass.

Aronowitz, S. (1990). The new labor education: A return to ideology. In S. H. London, E. R. Tarr, & J. F. Wilson (Eds.), *The re-education of the American working class* (pp. 21–33). Westport, CT: Greenwood Press.

Autor, D. H. (2019). Work of the past, work of the future. *AEA Papers and Proceedings, 109,* 1–32. doi:10.1257/pandp.20191110

Bakhshi, H., Downing, J., Osborne, M., & Schneider, P. (2017). *The future of skills: Employment in 2030.* London, England: Pearson and Nesta. Retrieved from https://futureskills.pearson.com/research/assets/pdfs/technical-report.pdf

Bates, R. S. (1965). *Scientific societies in the United States* (3rd ed.). Cambridge, MA: MIT Press.

Bode, C. (1960). *The anatomy of American popular culture, 1840–1861.* Berkeley: University of California Press.

Branon, R. (2018, November 16). Learning for a lifetime. *Inside Higher Ed.* Retrieved from https://www.insidehighered.com/views/2018/11/16/why-longer-lives-require-relevant-accessible-curricula-throughout-long-careers

Bronfenbrunner, U. (1979). *The ecology of human development: Experiments by nature and design.* Cambridge, MA: Harvard University Press.

Brookfield, S. (1986). *Understanding and facilitating adult learning.* San Francisco, CA: Jossey-Bass.

Bryson, L. (1936). *Adult education.* New York, NY: American Book Company.

Chafe, W. H. (1991). *The unfinished journey: America since World War II* (2nd ed.). New York, NY: Oxford University Press.

Clark, R., & Mayer, E. (2016). *E-learning and the science of instruction: Proven guidelines for consumers and designers of multimedia learning.* New York, NY: Pfieffer.

Cognizant. (2017, November). *21 jobs of the future: A guide to getting and staying employed over the next 10 years.* Retrieved from https://www.cognizant.com/whitepapers/21-jobs-of-the-future-a-guide-to-getting-and-staying-employed-over-the-next-10-years-codex3049.pdf

Cognizant. (2018, October). *21 more jobs of the future: A guide to getting and staying employed through 2029.* Retrieved from https://www.cognizant.com/whitepapers/21-more-jobs-of-the-future-a-guide-to-getting-and-staying-employed-through-2029-codex3928.pdf

Columbus, R. (2019, January). *Nondegree credentials, work-based learning, and the American working class.* Retrieved from American Enterprise Institute website: http://www.aei.org/wp-content/uploads/2019/01/Nondegree-Credentials-Work-Based-Learning-and-the-American-Working-Class.pdf

Cremin, L. A. (1970). *American education: The colonial experience, 1607–1783.* New York, NY: HarperCollins.

Cross, K. P. (1981). *Adults as learners.* San Francisco, CA: Jossey-Bass.

Cuban, L. (2013). *Inside the black box of classroom practice: Change without reform in American education.* Cambridge, MA: Harvard Education Press.

Daniels, G. H. (1971). *Science in American society: A social history.* New York, NY: Alfred A. Knopf.

Daugherty, P., & Wilson, H. J. (2018). *Human + machine: Reimagining work in the age of AI.* Cambridge, MA: Harvard Business Review Press.

Dede, C. (2013). Connecting the dots: New technology-based models of postsecondary learning. *EDUCAUSE Review, 48*(5), 33–52.

Dede, C. (2016). Social media and challenges to traditional educational models. In C. Greenhow, J. Sonnevend, & C. Agur (Eds.), *Education and social media: Toward a digital future* (pp. 95–112). Cambridge, MA: MIT Press.

Dede, C. (2018, October 19). The 60 year curriculum: Developing new educational models to support the agile labor market. *The Evolllution.* Retrieved from https://evolllution.com/revenue-streams/professional_development/the-60-year-curriculum-developing-new-educational-models-to-serve-the-agile-labor-market/

Dede, C. (2019). Improving efficiency and effectiveness through learning engineering. In C. Dede, J. Richards, & B. Saxberg (Eds.), *Learning engineering for online education: Theoretical contexts and design-based examples* (pp. 1–14). New York, NY: Routledge.

Dede, C., Grotzer, T., Kamarainen, A., & Metcalf, S. (2017). Virtual reality as an immersive medium for authentic simulations. In D. Liu, C. Dede, R. Huang, & J. Richards (Eds.), *Virtual reality, augmented reality, and mixed reality in education* (pp. 133–156). Hong Kong, China: Springer.

Dede. C., Ho, A., & Mitros, P. (2016). Big data analysis in higher education: Promises and pitfalls. *EDUCAUSE Review, 51*(5), 22–34.

Deming, D. (2017). The growing importance of social skills in the labor market. *Quarterly Journal of Economics, 132*(4), 1593–1640.

Deming, D., & Kahn, L. (2018). Skill requirements across firms and labor markets: Evidence from job postings for professionals. *Journal of Labor Economics, 36*(S1), S337–S369.

Dewey, J. (1938). *Experience and education.* New York, NY: Collier Books.

Eurich, N. P. (1985). *Corporate classrooms: The learning business.* Princeton, NJ: Carnegie Foundation for the Advancement of Teaching.

Fadel, C., Trilling, B., & Bialik, M. (2015). *Four-dimensional education: The competencies learners need to succeed.* Boston, MA: Center for Curriculum Redesign.

Forshaw, T., Rosas, S., & Maples, B. (2019, June). Closing the signaling gap. Paper presented at the MIT LINC Conference, How to thrive in a new learning society, Cambridge, MA.

Frey, C. B., & Osborne, M. A. (2013, September 17). *The future of employment: How susceptible are jobs to computerisation.* Oxford, England: Oxford Martin School. Retrieved from https://www.oxfordmartin.ox.ac.uk/downloads/academic/The_Future_of_Employment.pdf

Funk, C. (1998). The "Art in America" radio programs, 1934–1935. *Studies in Art Education, 40*(1), 31–45.

Gallagher, S. R. (2018). *Educational credentials come of age.* Boston, MA: Northeastern University. Retrieved from https://www.northeastern.edu/cfhets/wp-content/uploads/2018/12/Educational_Credentials_Come_of_Age_2018.pdf

Georgia Tech Commission on Creating the Next in Education. (2018). *Deliberate innovation, lifetime education.* Atlanta, GA: Georgia Institute of Technology. Retrieved from http://www.provost.gatech.edu/sites/default/files/documents/deliberate_innovation_lifetime_education.pdf

Goldin, C., & Katz, L. F. (2010). *The race between education and technology.* New York, NY: Belknap Press.

Gould, S. J. (1981). *The mismeasure of man.* New York, NY: Norton.

Grace, A. (1948). *Educational lessons from wartime training: The general report of the commission on implications of armed services educational programs.* Washington, DC: American Council on Education.

Granger, D. (1990). Open universities: Closing the distances to learning. *Change, 22*(4), 44–50.

Gratton, L., & Scott, A. (2016). *The 100-year life: Living and working in an age of longevity.* London, England: Bloomsbury Business.

Gutman, H. G. (1976). *Work, culture, and society in industrializing America.* New York, NY: Knopf.

IBM. (2005). On demand learning: Blended learning for today's evolving workforce. Retrieved from https://www-03.ibm.com/services/ca/en/mobility/documents/OnDemandLearning.pdf

ICDE Working Group. (2019, January). The present and future of alternative digital credentials (ADCs). Retrieved from https://icde.memberclicks.net/assets/ICDE-ADC%20report-January%202019%20%28002%29.pdf

Inkster, R. P. (1987). How do you know? Michael Polanyi and adult education. *Proceedings of the twenty-eighth annual Adult Education Research Conference.* Laramie, Wyoming: University of Wyoming, Conferences and Institutes.

International Labour Organization. (2019). *Work for a brighter future.* Global Commission on the Future of Work, Geneva, Switzerland. Retrieved from the International Labour Organization website: https://www.ilo.org/wcmsp5/groups/public/---dgreports/---cabinet/documents/publication/wcms_662410.pdf

Kegan, R., & Lahey, L. L. (2009). *Immunity to change: How to overcome it and unlock potential in yourself and your organization.* Cambridge, MA: Harvard Business Press.

Knowles, M. S. (1970). *The modern practice of adult education: Andragogy versus pedagogy.* New York, NY: Association Press.

Knowles, M. S. (1977). *A history of the adult education movement in the United States* (Rev. ed.). Huntington, NY: Krieger.

Lagemann, E. C. (1987). The politics of knowledge: The Carnegie Corporation and the formulation of public policy. *History of Education Quarterly, 27*(2), 205–220.

Lewin, K. (1947). Frontiers in group dynamics. *Human Relations, 1*(1), 5–41. doi:10.1177/001872674700100103

Maddux, C. D. (2001). *Educational computing: Learning with tomorrow's technologies.* Needham Heights, MA: Allyn & Bacon.

Marquis, A. G. (1986). *Hopes and ashes: The birth of modern times, 1929–1939.* New York, NY: Free Press.

Marsick, V. J., & Watkins, K. (1990). *Informal and incidental learning in the workplace.* London, England: Routledge.

Maskin, M. R. (1973). *Black education and the new deal: The urban experience* (Unpublished doctoral dissertation). New York University, New York, NY.

McLaurin, M. A. (1978). *The knights of labor in the South.* Westport, CT: Greenwood Press.

Mezirow, J. (1991). *Transformative dimensions of adult learning.* San Francisco, CA: Jossey-Bass.

Morrison, T. (1974). *Chautauqua: A center for education, religion, and the arts in America.* Chicago, IL: University of Chicago Press.

Muro, M., Maxim, R., & Whiton, J. (2019, January). *Automation and artificial intelligence: How machines are affecting people and places.* Metropolitan Policy Program. Retrieved from The Brookings Institution website: https://www.brookings.edu/wp-content/uploads/2019/01/2019.01_BrookingsMetro_Automation-AI_Report_Muro-Maxim-Whiton-FINAL-version.pdf

Nasseh, B. (1997). A brief history of distance education. *Adult Education in the News.* Retrieved from: http://www.seniornet.org/edu/art/history.html

National Academies of Sciences, Engineering, and Medicine. (2018). *How people learn II: Learners, contexts, and cultures.* Washington, DC: The National Academies Press. doi:10.17226/24783

National Research Council. (2012). *Education for life and work: Developing transferable knowledge and skills in the 21st century.* Washington, DC: The National Academies Press. doi:10.17226/13398

Neumann, W. (1979). Educational responses to the concern for proficiency. In G. Grant, P. Elbow, T. Ewens, Z. Gamson, W. Kohli, W. Neumann, … & D. Riesman (Eds.), *On competence: A critical analysis of competence-based reforms in higher education* (pp. 66–94). San Francisco, CA: Jossey-Bass.

Noffsinger, J. S. (1926). *Correspondence schools, lyceums, chautauquas.* New York, NY: Macmillan.

Organization for Economic Cooperation and Development. (2018). *The future of education and skills: Education 2030.* Retrieved from http://www.oecd.org/education/2030/E2030%20Position%20Paper%20(05.04.2018).pdf

Organization for Economic Cooperation and Development. (2019). *Trends shaping education, 2019.* Paris, France: OECD Publishing. doi:10.1787/trends_edu-2019-en

Perrett, G. (1985). *Days of sadness, years of triumph: The American people, 1939–1945.* Madison: University of Wisconsin Press.

Polanyi, M. (1967). *The tacit dimension.* New York, NY: Doubleday.

Porfeli, E., & Lee, B. (2012). Career development during childhood and adolescence. *Career Programming: Linking Youth to the World of Work, 134,* 11–22. doi:10.1002/yd.20011

Porfeli, E., & Vondracek, F. W. (2009). Career development, work, and occupational success. In M. C. Smith & N. DeFrates-Densch (Eds.), *Handbook of research on adult learning and development* (pp. 412–435). New York, NY: Routledge.

Prewitt, T. (1998). The development of the distance learning delivery system. *Higher Education in Europe, 23*(2), 187–194.

Rodrik, D. (2017). *Straight talk on trade: Ideas for a sane world economy.* Princeton, NJ: Princeton University Press.

Rohfeld, R. W. (Ed.). (1990). *Expanding access to knowledge: Continuing higher education, NUCEA, 1915–1990.* Washington, DC: National University Continuing Education Association.

Rossiter, M. W. (1975). *The emergence of agricultural science: Justus Liebig and the Americans, 1840–1880.* New Haven, CT: Yale University Press.

Schwab, K. (2016, January 14). *The fourth industrial revolution: What it means, how to respond.* Retrieved from World Economic Forum website: https://www.weforum.org/agenda/2016/01/the-fourth-industrial-revolution-what-it-means-and-how-to-respond/

Scott, D. (1980). The popular lecture and the creation of a public in mid-nineteenth-century America. *The Journal of American History, 66*(4), 791–809. doi:10.2307/1887637

Seybolt, R. F. (1925). *The evening school in colonial America.* Champaign: University of Illinois. Retrieved from https://www.ideals.illinois.edu/bitstream/handle/2142/27914/eveningschoolinc24seyb.pdf

Sizer, T. R., & Sizer, N. F. (1999). *The students are watching: Schools and the moral contract.* Boston, MA: Beacon Press.

Southern Regional Education Board. (2019, February). *Unprepared and unware: Upskilling the workforce for a decade of uncertainty.* Retrieved from https://www.sreb.org/sites/main/files/file-attachments/2019_adultattain_webversion.pdf

Stanford2025. (n.d.). *Open Loop University.* Retrieved from the Stanford 2025 website: http://www.stanford2025.com/open-loop-university/

Stevens-Long, J., & Crowell, C. (2002). The design and delivery of interactive online graduate education. In K. E. Rudestam & J. Schoenholtz-Read (Eds.), *Handbook of online learning: Innovations in higher education and corporate training* (pp. 151–169). Thousand Oaks, CA: Sage Publications.

Stubblefield, H. W., & Keane, P. (1994). *Adult education in the American experience: From the colonial period to the present.* San Francisco, CA: Jossey-Bass.

Tebbel, J. (1974). *The media in America.* New York, NY: New American Library.

Thompson, D. (2009). A brief history of research and theory on adult learning and cognition. In M. C. Smith & N. DeFrates-Densch (Eds.), *Handbook of research on adult learning and development* (pp. 463–483). New York, NY: Routledge.

Towner, L. W. (1966). The indentures of Boston's poor apprentices: 1734–1805. *Publications of the Colonial Society of Massachusetts, 43*, 417–468.

Van Hise, C. (1915). The university extension function in the modern university. *Proceedings from the first National University Extension Conference*. Madison, WI.

Verduin, J. R., & Clark, T. A. (1991). *Distance education: The foundations of effective practice*. San Francisco, CA: Jossey-Bass.

Wecter, D. (1937). *The saga of American society: A record of social aspiration, 1607–1937*. New York, NY: Charles Scribner's Sons.

World Bank. (2019). *World development report 2019: The changing nature of work*. Washington, DC: World Bank. doi:10.1596/978-1-4648-1328-3

World Economic Forum. (2018). *The future of jobs report 2018*. Retrieved from http://www3.weforum.org/docs/WEF_Future_of_Jobs_2018.pdf

World Economic Forum. (2019a). *Dialogue series on new economic and social frontiers shaping the new economy in the fourth industrial revolution*. Retrieved from http://www3.weforum.org/docs/WEF_Dialogue_Series_on_New_Economic_and_Social_Frontiers.pdf

World Economic Forum. (2019b). *The global risks report 2019* (14th ed.). Retrieved from http://www3.weforum.org/docs/WEF_Global_Risks_Report_2019.pdf

World Economic Forum. (2019c). *Leading through the fourth industrial revolution: Putting people at the centre*. Retrieved from http://www3.weforum.org/docs/WEF_Leading_through_the_Fourth_Industrial_Revolution.pdf

World Economic Forum. (2019d). *Strategies for the new economy skills as the currency of the labour market*. Retrieved from http://www3.weforum.org/docs/WEF_2019_Strategies_for_the_New_Economy_Skills.pdf

World Economic Forum. (2019e). *Towards a reskilling revolution: Industry-led action for the future of work*. Retrieved from http://www3.weforum.org/docs/WEF_Towards_a_Reskilling_Revolution.pdf

2

Education, Age, and the Machine

ANDREW SCOTT

Introduction

Human capital is usually ascribed a core role in models of economic growth (Lucas, 1988; Romer, 1990; Barro & Sala-i-Martin, 2004; Acemoglu, 2009). Although theoretically and empirically the magnitude and channels through which human capital affects growth vary (Mankiw, Romer, & Weil, 1992; Benhabib & Spiegel, 1994; Islam, 1995; Barro, 1997; Bils & Klenow, 2000), the consensus is that it is a key variable driving productivity growth. Goldin and Katz (2007) go as far as to argue that the 20th century was the "human capital" century. They also argue that the rise of the US as the world's largest economy was due to its educational exceptionalism and its "instituting [of] mass secondary schooling and then establishing a flexible and multifaceted higher education system" (p. 18).

If a historical analysis shows the strength of US educational achievement, a current and forward-looking assessment suggests major challenges. Two forces in particular will demand profound changes in the educational system. Given the increases in life expectancy that have occurred over past decades, children born in rich countries today have a realistic expectation of living into their 90s or even to 100 (Gratton & Scott, 2016). This, in turn, gives rise to the prospect of a 60-year career that will necessitate a focus on lifelong learning and greater resources dedicated to adult education. The second major driver of change is technology and the development of artificial intelligence (AI) and robotics (Brynjolfsson & MacAfee, 2014; Ford, 2015; Schwab, 2015; Bughin, Manyika, & Woetzel, 2017). This is expected to lead to major churn in the labor market and a shift in the skills needed to secure employment. As discussed in Chapter 1, "Reconceptualizing Lifelong Learning in the Era of the Synergistic Digital Economy," together longevity and technology, or age and the machine, represent major disruptive challenges to our existing educational system—at the beginning and throughout life.

Given the scale of the likely changes resulting from these trends, it seems no exaggeration to imagine that *what* we learn, *when* we learn it, *how* we learn it, and *who* we learn it from will all change. If the educational system successfully meets this challenge, then there is every reason to believe that Goldin and Katz's conclusion will hold for the 21st century too—education will help underpin sustained economic growth and support inclusive prosperity during a time of substantial social and economic change. A failure to respond will mean disappointing economic growth, widening inequality, and the prospect of increasingly dysfunctional political institutions. Much therefore hinges on the ability of the educational system to respond to the combination of longevity and technology.

The first part of this chapter looks at the challenges facing the educational system from an economic perspective. It then proceeds to examine the consequences for the educational system before moving on to consider what needs to be the main focus of the educational system and who has responsibility for providing it. It then outlines a number of difficulties to be faced in achieving this agenda, and a final section concludes.

Challenges

The US educational system has to deal with five major economic challenges in the coming decades: (a) a levelling off of human capital, (b) a declining return to purely cognitive skills, (c) overeducation, (d) AI and robotics, and (e) longer lives and working careers.

A Levelling off of Human Capital

As Jorgenson, Ho, and Samuels (2016) document, a continual increase in the average level of education of US employees is coming to an end. The education level of new entrants into the labor market remains high, but the process whereby each cohort entering the labor market has higher qualifications than preceding ones is ending. Currently 42% of Americans aged 55–64 have postsecondary education compared to 48% of 25–34-year-olds. The gap is, in other words, small and narrowing. Increases in educational attainment are therefore set to end as a source of trend US economic growth. Further educational improvements will require either an increase in postsecondary education or the spread of adult education deeper into older age groups.

The Great Reversal

According to Beaudry, Green, and Sand (2016), since 2000 there has been a decline in the demand for jobs involving purely cognitive tasks. The result has been "high skilled workers mov[ing] down the occupational ladder and increasingly displac[ing] lower education workers in less skill intensive jobs" (p. 199). This suggests a socially inefficient mix of outcomes from the educational system.

Skills Mismatch

As discussed by Cappelli (2014), the great success of the US educational system in achieving ever-rising numbers of qualifying students has led to "the prevailing situation in the US labor market, as in most developed economies, [being] skill mismatches where the average worker and job candidate has more education than their current job requires" (p. 46). This is not an argument against education per se but does point to a dislocation between the output produced by the educational system and the employment needs of the economy. As with the Great Reversal, this fact raises questions about what should be taught and when it should be taught. It also raises the issue of whether adult education might be a way of better matching the needs of the economy with the outcomes of education.

AI and Robotics

Considerable concern exists over the impact of AI and robotics on the labor market (Frey & Osborne, 2013; Arntz, Gregory, & Zierahn, 2016; Bughin et al., 2017). At one level this concern is simply a re-expression of a long-standing fear that technological progress leads to job losses. As far back as 1589 Queen Elizabeth I of England denied a patent to the inventor of a mechanical knitting machine over concerns of its impact on the employment of knitters and weavers (William Lee, 2019).

The standard economic analysis of such fears suggests they are misplaced. It is true that technological progress enhances worker productivity so that fewer workers are needed to produce a given level of output. However, precisely because workers are more productive firms are interested in hiring more of them and particularly in allocating them to more higher-value-added activities. These two effects are what Acemoglu and Restrepo (2018) call the "displacement effect" (workers are more productive and so fewer are needed) and the "productivity effect" (workers are more valuable so more of them are demanded). Famously, the introduction of ATMs did not lead to *fewer* but to *more* bank clerks, as freed from the need to dispense cash they could engage in more valuable customer service activities. Similarly, the invention of the first spreadsheet software package Visicalc, in 1979, led to the loss of an estimated 400,000 book clerk jobs in the US but also to the creation of 600,000 accounting jobs.[1]

The relative magnitude of the displacement and productivity effects will vary across sectors and regions. The mix will depend in part on the ability of firms to boost output in response to higher productivity and to substitute workers into more higher-value-added tasks. As mentioned in Chapter 3, "Are We Ready for the Jobs that the Digital Economy Will Offer to Us," given the speed at which AI and robotics are developing, there are genuine fears that the displacement effect could be more rapid than previously thought, and so we may see a surge in unemployment, especially in certain sectors and regions.

As emphasized by Acemoglu and Restrepo (2018), the overall impact of technology on unemployment will likely depend on a third channel—the "creation" effect. In response to new technology and higher incomes, a whole host of new jobs have previously been created in the wake of past technological revolutions. Some of these jobs will be involved in supporting the very digital industries that are bringing about the AI and robotics revolution. However, we will also see a proliferation of other service sector jobs as the economy reorients itself toward new sources of growth. For instance, jobs in caring for older individuals, life coaches, and so forth, are all likely to proliferate in the years ahead. This shift in the composition of jobs will obviously bring about a shift in educational demands and the rise of new courses to support these new jobs.

However, whatever the net impact of these three forces on unemployment, the greatest number of people impacted will come from those employed. As the nature of existing jobs and required skills shifts in response to new technology, there will be a need for those employed to reskill.

Initial estimates (as explained by Frey and Osbourne, [2013]) of the impact of automation from AI and robotics arrived at high levels of potential job losses but these have since been revised downwards. Key to these downwards revisions has been the task-based approach to jobs (Acemoglu & Autor, 2011). Any job is made up of numerous tasks, and automation will result in the loss of some of these tasks. According to Manyika et al. (2017) only 5% of jobs are made up of tasks that are fully automatable, and 60% of jobs consist of tasks that are at least 30% automatable. Therefore, for most workers the main impact of technological change will be not unemployment but a shift in the make up of tasks that define their job. Only those with jobs that are mainly automatable are under threat of unemployment from new technologies. According to the Organisation for Economic Cooperation and Development, this is around 9% of all jobs (Arntz et al., 2016).

This 9% of the workforce that would lose their jobs through automation will be looking to reskill in order to secure employment in new roles. However, the main way the majority of workers will be impacted by technology is through a shift in the tasks they perform. This in turn will lead to substantial needs to retrain and reskill in order for workers to benefit fully from these new technologies.

This has obvious implications for the educational system. Since at least the work of Jan Tinbergen (1974), the standard assumption in economics is that technology is complementary to skilled labor. Hence the workforce is in a race between education and technology. As technology advances, we need to increase our education to remain competitive with machines and to be productive in the workforce. Those individuals who do not increase their education in response to new technology either lose their jobs or see their wages decline.

This is precisely the story that Goldin and Katz (2007) tell about the US in the 20th century. In response to the Industrial Revolution, there was a major increase in education so that first primary and then secondary education became compulsory, and there was an ever greater enrollment in higher education. Crucially, the US made sure that this increase in education was broad-based and equal rather than meritocratic or focused only on higher income households. Given that 92.3% of the US population already have completed at least high school and 15% have completed post-secondary education, if education is to continue its race with technology it will need to focus more on what gets taught and when it gets taught (e.g., a shift to lifelong learning).

Longevity

As stressed in Gratton and Scott (2016), the 20th century saw the creation of a three-stage life—education, employment, and then retirement. When the Social Security Act of 1935 introduced a basic right to a state pension at age 65, in the US life expectancy at birth was 61.7 years.

However, as documented by Oeppen and Vaupel (2002), over the last 100 years best practice life expectancy (as defined by the country with the highest average life expectancy at birth) has increased at the rate of 2–3 years every decade. The consequence of this is that each generation has been living 6–9 years longer than the previous. That means, according to the UK government, a girl born in 2017 has a one in three chance of reaching a 100. While forecasting future life expectancy is inevitably uncertain, the gains already achieved mean that children born today need to prepare for a life that will stretch into their 80s or 90s with high probability.

This has the consequence that working careers will also need to extend. With a life expectancy of 85 and a savings rate of 10%, working careers need to extend into the early and mid-70s to finance a pension worth 50% of final salary. With a life expectancy of 100 and a similar savings rate and desired pension, then work extends until you are 80—a 60-year career. The implications of longer life for longer careers are already being felt in the workforce with sustained trend increases occurring in both the numbers and proportions of people aged over 55, 65, and 75 still working. Since 1998, the US has increased employment by nearly 22 million, and 20 million of that increase in employment has come about from workers aged over 55.

In response to the pressures on Social Security from longer lifespans, governments are increasing the state pension age, but if this is all that happens then it will be a poor response to increasing longevity. It will be crucial to focus on significant lifelong learning if 60-year careers are to be a productive and positive experience. It is pointless to push back retirement to enable a 60-year career if 40 years is spent in employment and 20 years in unemployment.

The need for lifelong learning is further enhanced by the shift to what Gratton and Scott (2016) refer to as a multi-stage life. Key to this idea is the realization that time is structured by social convention. The emergence of the three-stage life in the 20th century led to the creation of two new stages of life—adolescents and retirees. As life lengthens, we restructure time and construct new patterns of behavior at all ages and create new stages of life, many of which will raise new educational requirements. This is leading to new patterns of behavior at all ages and new stages of life being created, many of which will raise new educational requirements.

Gratton and Scott (2016) suggest this restructuring of the life course needs to be done with the idea of maintaining a healthy balance across four classes of assets—financial, productive, vitality, and transformational. Extending a three-stage life to accommodate a 60-year career ensures that an individual's financial assets remain strong, but over a 60-year career productive assets (e.g., skills and knowledge) will decline without further investment; vitality assets (physical and mental health, friends, and relationships) will also diminish, and no investment will be made in transformational assets (the individual's ability to instigate and navigate through periods of change).

So as life and careers lengthen, life becomes multi-staged, with each stage focusing on accumulating a different mix of assets. One stage may be mainly financially orientated; another may offer a better work/life balance; one may be more entrepreneurial or engaged with social purpose.

This emergence of a multi-stage life has many implications for careers and education. The first is that, compared to the three-stage life, a multi-stage life contains more transitions. These times of change will frequently be associated with the need to gain more education and develop new skills to prepare for the next career stage. It also points to the need for educational programs that support and encourage such transitions by providing a toolkit for change. The second major implication is that unlike a three-stage life, a multi-stage life can be sequenced in numerous ways. This has the fundamental insight that as life lengthens age and stage will become increasingly disentangled. For educational institutions, the punchline is that I may be an undergraduate at 20, 40, or 60. As firms respond to a multi-stage life through recruitment policies that offer multiple entry points, educational horizons will have to extend beyond traditional ages in a profound way.

Consequences

This collection of challenges has profound consequences for the educational system.

The Return on Education Has Likely Increased

The Tinbergern dynamic between education and technology means that as technology advances we need to invest more in education. Of course, this does not mean more of the same education. What we learn and when we learn it will need to change. The return to education has increased overall but not the return to all forms of education.

More Education at Older Ages

A greater focus on adult education seems inevitable as a result of these changes. First, given the already high levels of secondary and post-secondary education in developed economies, it is inevitable that further investment in education will come in adult years. Second, as life and careers lengthen, the horizon over which education pays back extends. If working life stops at 60, major skill investments at 55 have a low return. If careers last until your 70s, the return on reskilling is much higher. Third, AI and robotics will disrupt the existing workforce leading to the need to retrain and upskill. Crucially, technology impacts how education at an early stage will need to change to prepare students for different careers, but the impact of technology on currently employed workers makes this an issue very much about adult education.

Employment Focused

Education has many aims and purposes, and it is clearly a mistake to justify its role purely in terms of its contribution to GDP and employment. Given concerns over mass unemployment (Frey & Osborne, 2013; Ford, 2015) or the rising leisure time

(Brynjolfsson's "Digital Athens") that technology will support, it may even be that our future education system will be aimed ever more at helping us deal meaningfully with a life of leisure. However, the impact of technology on the workforce and the need for older workers to remain productive to finance longer lifespans all suggest that much of this increase in demand for education will be focused on later-life employment issues. This makes it post-graduate in a broader sense of the word and so is likely to be more extensively based around non-degree qualifications. It also means that education will be more specifically skills-based rather than focused on general education as discussed in Chapter 7, "Market-Driven Education: The Imperative for Responsive Design and Application."

Different Motivations

Older workers will have different reasons and motivations for seeking education than traditionally younger students have. Four broad categories can be distinguished: (a) reskill, (b) upskill, (c) transition, and (d) renewal. Each of these, in turn, links into whether the education is being sought to get a job, safeguard a job against automation, investigate options around future possible employment paths, or as part of a deeper transition. Each motive requires a different form of education and coursework and may be non-overlapping with traditional educational provisions to younger students.

Reskilling will be the case for someone who has lost their job or fears losing their job and wishes to earn a completely new skillset. The provision of new skills is of course a constant educational aim, but reskilling requires "unlearning" as well as learning and provides novel pedagogic challenges.

Upskilling is defined here as the case where an individual may have an existing stock of knowledge but needs to update this and take it to a new level (e.g., build on an existing skill base but update). For instance, coding and data analytics is a rapidly expanding field rife with technological obsolescence (Deming & Noray, 2018), meaning individuals have a constant need to reinvest in their skills. This is probably the closest of all to existing educational models but will need to take into account the existing stock and vintage of an individual's knowledge.

The previous two categories are very much about skills, but education is also about broader individual development, and a key part of a multi-stage life will be transitions where individuals dramatically change their work skills and identity and move into a new career path. As a consequence, educational courses that provide support and cohort mentoring for individuals experiencing transition will be extremely important. Gratton and Scott (2016) emphasize the importance of transformational assets and helping people rewire not just their skills but their identity; their aims and objectives will be an important component of lifelong learning in a multi-stage life.

University education brings together a group of young individuals at a formative time in their lives. They bring an existing set of values and beliefs, interact with a varied group of others, and reform their values, their ambitions, and senses of purpose. Providing a platform for your life has to be one of the great aspirations of successful education. As life expands, the need for a renewal or recasting of values and purpose becomes ever more apparent especially in mid-life. There is currently an under-institutionalization of support for midlife transitions, and this will be a fertile ground for experimentation. Encore.org's Marc Freedman remarks that it is not so much a "midlife crisis" as a "midlife chasm" that individuals face, and they lack the social norms and institutions to support midlife transitions (2011). Stanford has its Distinguished Careers Initiative, and in the UK a number of companies are experimenting with 'mid-life MOTs'—company provided opportunities to check finances, health, relationships, and career aims—but these are very much pilot projects.

Age Agnostic

Educational institutions are one of the most evident examples of how society has become segregated on the basis of chronological age. Ever since governments started to keep reliable birth records, society has started to use chronological age as a means to structure bureaucratic processes (Thomas, 1977), and this reached its apotheosis in college admissions and retirement.

As multi-stage lives lead to a disconnect between age and stage, educational institutions will need to think about breaking away from age segregation and becoming more age agnostic. Recognizing which types of education will benefit from intergenerational elements and which are best kept as age-segregated will be an important strategic choice for many institutions as covered in Chapter 9, "Implementing *60YC* Learning at the Harvard Division of Continuing Education." Reskilling and upskilling can probably benefit from intergenerational mixing especially given the employment experience that older students can bring to the classroom. Transition and renewal courses would undoubtedly benefit from some aspects of intergenerational mixing, but clearly different transitions may still require some age segregation.

Learning versus Education

Learning is a verb while education is a noun that usually involves some sense of completion, normally symbolized in the form of a certificate. Lifelong learning means that education is never completed but is always being built and constructed. This is very different from the three-stage life view which sees a career built on a finished educational base. This, in turn, places new demands on the educational system as it needs to create a more navigable system for both the individual and the employer.

When education is a linear progression based on a clearly defined hierarchy of qualifications then, for both the learner and the employer, progression is easy to plan and to observe. With the twists and turns of a multi-stage career—and the fact that much adult education is likely to be of a non-degree form and may be based around very specific skills or acquired in small slithers of time—the need to provide a coherent map for learners and employers will rise.

Different Base

Longer working careers and lifelong learning will also impact what we need to do in earlier stages of education. With a longer life, child development extends. The 20th century saw the creation of adolescence, and a similar period of exploratory adult development is currently developing for those in their 20s. Longer lives and working careers mean that early commitment is less attractive and options and exploration become more valuable. This suggests delaying specialization and opening up education to more experiential courses.

Technological change is bringing about a data-rich environment. The result is that education is shifting from a situation where facts are scarce to one where they are abundant. Combined with the emergence of multi-stage lives, this requires a shift from teaching how to recall facts to one where learning how to learn and evaluate become core. In the words of Eric Hoffer, "In times of drastic change it is the learners who inherit the future. The learned usually find themselves equipped to live in a world that no longer exists" (1973, p. 22).

Technology will also require changes in how things are taught. The Industrial Revolution ushered in factories, offices, and Taylorism. This was complemented by the development of schooling that focused on sitting down, processing assigned work, sticking to fixed hours, and being regularly assessed by a superior figure. All this was good training for factories and offices. A new technology that requires more independent-driven work and an emphasis on collaboration, investigation, and teamwork will require similar organizational shifts in how education is provided.

What to Learn?

In general, the increasing focus on lifelong learning will require two broad educational aims. The first is making sense of change and transition (what Gratton and Scott [in press] refer to as navigation, exploration, and relating). Longevity and technology lengthen our lives and careers but are likely to increase and shorten the individual stages that collectively define our life course. In this case, it will be imperative that education helps people form a narrative of their own path, provides opportunities to explore and consider options for their future, and enables transitions and change to be supported by a cohort and a community with an emphasis upon connectivity—whether face-to-face or mediated by technology.

The second focus will be on securing jobs and employment. If this is to be done in a forward-looking sense it requires insight into the likely skills that firms will want in the future. Given the uncertainty about the pace and direction of technological change, it is important to note that we do not know for sure what will be the key areas of demand. However, a consensus is beginning to form around Autor, Levy, and Murnane's (2003) task-based analysis of recent job changes.

Jobs can be considered as requiring either manual or cognitive skills and are made up of either routine or non-routine tasks. Autor, Levy, and Murnane's empirical work leads them to conclude that "within industries, occupations and education groups, computerization is associated with reduced labor input of routine manual and routine cognitive tasks and increased labor input of nonroutine cognitive tasks" (2003, p. 1279).

This framework suggests that, looking forward, the areas of skills that are least likely to be taken over by automation are those involving cognitive non-routine tasks. As AI and robotics develop further, manual non-routine jobs are likely to be automated (e.g., driverless cars), and rapid improvements in AI will lead to job losses through automation of high-value-added, routine, cognitive tasks (sales and marketing, accounting, legal advice, etc.). This leaves the area of non-routine cognitive tasks as the place where most employment will be centered.

These are areas where human comparative advantage is strongest. In general, the intuition is that as machines become ever smarter and better at being machines, then the human role in production will be based around exploiting areas where humans have a comparative advantage—that is being human. As Apple VP of Retail, Angela Ahrendts remarks, "The more technologically advanced our society becomes . . . the more we need to go back to the basic fundamentals of human connection" (TED, 2013).

The focus on growth in non-routine, cognitive jobs has obvious implications for education and also has worrying implications for inequality. Most analysis of where the greatest job losses will occur emphasize the impact on relatively low-skill and low-wage jobs. This suggests that the greatest educational challenge of all will be providing at scale retraining for older workers with perhaps limited previous education.

However, it should also be noted that human skills need not be cognitive—empathy and human understanding will become increasingly important and are poorly characterized as cognitive. This is important as, in general, education assumes that high skilled individuals are more intelligent or smarter students, but empathy and compassion are likely to be much more loosely correlated with intellectual ability than analytical skill building. For instance, most faculty meetings in academia display high levels of IQ but much lower levels of EQ. Some of the human skills that will be in demand as AI and robotics make their progress may be poorly aligned with the usual attributes of students that institutions select.

Evidence of these shifts in desired skill mix is already with us. Deming (2017) finds that between 1980 and 2012 jobs requiring high levels of social interaction grew by nearly 12% as a share of the US labor force. Math intensive jobs without a social dimension actually fell over the same period. Jobs that combined high levels of math skills and social skills grew particularly quickly in number and saw healthy wage growth.

This growing importance of "soft skills" suggests that educational institutions need to focus on increasing the proportion of behavioral traits relative to academic skills. This in turn raises two interesting questions. Is this a set of skills that existing educational institutions are well qualified for? And do we credential these softer skills?

Who Should Provide the Education?

There are two dimensions to the issue of who should provide the education of the 21st century. One is about the relative roles of the individual, the corporate sector, and the government. The other is about what type of institutions or companies actually delivers the education.

On the former, it is inevitable that the individual now bears greater responsibility for their own education. Historically, firms have often provided the majority of lifelong learning. They would recruit individuals based on general skill ability and then provide training and support to develop the skills needed for specific roles. However, as careers lengthen and turnover increases, firms show less and less interest in doing so and seem to demand "plug and play" levels of skills. As highlighted by Cappelli (2014), this in turn is leading to growing criticism by corporations of the skills mismatch. With the rise of the gig economy, the responsibility for training increasingly falls on the individual who will look to use small slivers of time to update themselves as well as to create longer periods of transition for more substantial investment in education.

This greater individual responsibility for investing in education will also change the relationship between educational institutions and their alumni. Alumni will look to their alma mater for guidance and support over possible pathways and for continual opportunities to invest.

Governments will also have a role to play. In the Industrial Revolution, governments increased the age at which students could exit education. Compelling adults to continue their education is unlikely to be a workable policy but providing inducements for lifelong learning through tax incentives, such as lifelong learning accounts or even providing income support for "skillbatticals," are measures that will help in the race between education and technology.

Further, while shorter job tenure and the rise of contingent working has diluted corporate interest in training, it has not eradicated it. Given the changing nature of careers, employers that can offer to employees a good salary and flexible working conditions that enable ramping up and down over the lifecycle, plus provide opportunities to learn, will have an advantage in securing the most productive workforce. They will also be interested in ensuring that gig economy workers possess up-to-date relevant skills and either individually, collectively with other firms, or in conjunction with labor organizations will look to provide key skills. This may be done through their own corporate training programs or through the creation of new "centers of excellence" that combine a variety of providers and courses for firms and individuals to choose and select from as explained in Chapter 6, "Known for Whom We Include: Designing Models for Lifelong Education at Arizona State University."

This leads to another feature of how the educational landscape will change. Longer lives and technological change will undoubtedly continue to increase demand for education in general and for the existing programs that the educational system offers. However, much of the above training is about short as well as long courses, using short as well as long periods of time, and a much more on-demand employment focus. In general, this is very different from the expertise that existing educational institutions possess, which is built around longer courses of full time study based on a younger population for some form of educational certificate.

Some existing institutions will be agile enough to move into new areas and new products, and most will be capable of some level of innovation, but new products, new providers, and new alliances and collaborations will also be formed. Some of the fixed costs that define important elements of existing educational institutions (research excellence, sporting facilities, etc.) will constrain pricing and affect their ability to compete in this marketplace. Further, many existing institutions excel in terms of providing an education rather than specific skills and in creating a firm boundary between work and education. These will remain valuable attributes but may be hard to combine with producing short, experiential, job-focused education that shifting fundamentals require without forming an alliance with different providers. Existing institutions will need to make key strategic decisions about which of these new educational markets they enter into and if they do so alone or with partners. Further, structural changes to the educational system will arise not just because of shifts in demand as to what education is needed. Just as AI offers the prospect of enhancing productivity across the economy it also holds the same promise for the educational sector. Incorporating technology into the existing range of teaching tools is an evolving agenda for educational institutions but, in turn, also opens up the opportunity for new providers and new products.

Problems

Given the substantial shift required in our educational institutions it is not surprising that a number of major problems present themselves.

How Do We Successfully Deliver Adult Education?

As covered in Chapter 1, "Reconceptualizing Lifelong Learning in the Era of the Synergistic Digital Economy," while there has been a long history of adult education that can provide many insights, the future need is very different both in terms of scale and purpose. Although there is a body of knowledge around andragogy, adult education has not been tested to the same degree or does not provide the same wealth of data as traditional first-stage education provides. What works and how to deliver it is still an open question.

Asymmetric Information and Mis-Selling

Investing in education has become more important, and the individual's responsibility for achieving this has increased. The educational landscape is changing with new providers and new products, many of which are of a non-degree form. This will create major regulatory challenges.

Education as a market is rife with asymmetric information (Akerlof, 1970). The prospective student may not know what they do not know and will have a problem determining whether what is on offer genuinely meets their needs. As we know from financial providers, the risk of mis-selling in such circumstances is substantial. The current system, based on academic credentials and a historical system of respectability, is already under threat as student fees rise in magnitude, but a whole new regulatory environment will be required as lifelong learning grows and much of this new regulation will be additional to existing academic credentials.

Credentialing

Educational achievement is usually measured by a form of accreditation—a certificate that measures the individual's achievement in passing a course, usually with a certain grade. Whether the credential recognizes general achievement in mastering a set of skills or a field of knowledge, or is a signal that indicates the underlying quality of the student (see Spence, 1973) is a matter of debate. But in either case the qualification forms a key indicator for individuals as they start in the labor market. Once embarked on their career, the role of educational credentials is usually lessened as there is more information for firms to use to assess the competence and skills of a potential employee. If part of the rising educational need in response to technological disruption and longevity is met by new products and new providers and potentially in the non-degree space, the issue is what role will credentials play.

Given the need for lifelong learning to be stackable and portable, some common understanding of what different courses achieve is needed both for students and employees. Given that reskilling and transitions will become more important, the need to acquire more recent credentials for older workers will be greater as CVs will provide less industry-relevant skills as individuals go through more career transitions. The problem is heightened by the fact that much of lifelong learning may be based on short courses; the focus will be on skills relevant for specific employment, and there will be a rising demand for soft skills. This triumvirate of characteristics creates an urgent need precisely in the areas where education finds credentialing hardest.

Some of this will be mitigated by the use of peer-to-peer referencing and the emergence of brand leaders in certain areas of provision. The other possibility is that AI itself may generate a way to measure and monitor skills independently of exams or courses. If this development happens, the effect on traditional educational qualifications will be substantial.

Inequality and Inclusiveness

As Goldin and Katz (2007) stress, one of the key distinguishing features of US education in response to the Industrial Revolution was inclusiveness. The educational system did not focus just on the meritocratic or financial elite but on broad-based education and provision of skills as well.

Already a range of educational opportunities are opening up for those with resources, but given the scale of the technological change underway it is crucial to come up with a cheap and scalable means of delivering lifelong learning. Some form of collaborative network between universities, community colleges, and potentially private providers will be needed to enable this as well as concerted policy efforts.

Conclusion

This chapter has focused on two particular aspects of education. The first is how the changing employment landscape will affect the demand for education. Of course, education is about far more than simply providing the foundations for a working career. These other motivations for education will also be affected by many of the changes we have discussed.

The second aspect of our focus has been on what is likely to change. However, it is important to stress that much will remain unchanged. The educational system will continue its focus on numeracy and literacy, science and the humanities, as well as successful character development and learning of advanced technical skills.

We have also focused on how the educational system can respond to changing educational needs. But there is also a deeper agenda for educational institutions to follow. As emphasized by Acemoglu (2019), technology alone does not determine what type of jobs are created. If there is an abundance of well-trained individuals with the human skills needed to work productively with AI and robotics, then firms are more likely to create "good" jobs providing decent wages and interesting working opportunities. If the educational system fails to provide individuals with the right skills, then the danger is that technology will be used to achieve mindless automation and provide poor jobs for workers. By providing individuals in large numbers with the skills needed to ensure that technology creates good jobs, the educational system can lead the way and not just respond adaptively to shifts in labor demand.

Technology and longevity are already transforming society and the economy and will continue to do so, and so it is inevitable that the educational system is on the verge of a major structural change. More education is needed, and for the first time this will not be front-loaded but distributed over a lifetime. The foundations of longer lives will also require learning different skills earlier in your career. This will lead to changes in when and how education is provided. The changing nature of jobs will also require a shift in emphasis on what skills need to be taught. As well as the when, how, and what, we are also likely to see changes in who provides the education.

The good news for the educational system is that the continued growth it has benefited from over the last 100 years looks set to continue. The more challenging news is that this expansion will manifest itself as a shift into new areas that are currently poorly served—adult education, skills, and employment-based learning and shorter cumulative programs.

Note

1 For a further investigation of the impact of spreadsheets in the workplace, consider the National Public Radio story at https://www.npr.org/sections/money/2017/05/17/528807590/episode-606- spreadsheets?t=1533803451907

References

Acemoglu, D. (2009). *Introduction to modern economic growth*. Princeton, NJ: Princeton University Press.

Acemoglu, D. (2019, April 26). Where do good jobs come from? *Project Syndicate*. Retrieved from https://www.project-syndicate.org/commentary/automation-vs-job-creation-by-daron-acemoglu-2019-04?barrier=accesspaylog

Acemoglu, D., & Autor, D. (2011). Skills, tasks and technologies: Implications for employment and earnings. *Handbook of Labor Economics, 4*, 1043–1171.

Acemoglu, D., & Restrepo, P. (2018). *Artificial intelligence, automation and work* (Working Paper No. 24196). Cambridge, MA: National Bureau of Economic Research.

Akerlof, G. (1970). The market for "lemons": Quality uncertainty and the market mechanism. *The Quarterly Journal of Economics, 84*(3), 488–500.

Arntz, M., Gregory, T., & Zierahn, U. (2016). *The risk of automation for jobs in OECD countries: A comparative analysis* (Working Paper No. 189). Paris, France: OECD. doi:10.1787/5jlz9h56dvq7-en

Autor, D., Levy, F., & Murnane, R. (2003). The skill content of recent technological change: An empirical exploration. *Quarterly Journal of Economics, 118*(4), 1279–1333.

Barro, R. (1997). *Determinants of economic growth: A cross country empirical study*. Cambridge, MA: MIT Press.

Barro, R., & Sala-i-Martin, X. (2004). *Economic growth* (2nd ed.). Cambridge, MA: MIT Press.

Beaudry, P., Green, D., & Sand, B. (2016). The great reversal in the demand for skill and cognitive tasks. *Journal of Labor Economics, 34*(S1), 199–247.

Benhabib, J., & Spiegel, M. (1994). The role of human capital in economic development: Evidence from aggregate cross country data. *Journal of Monetary Economics, 34*(2), 143–173.

Bils, M., & Klenow, P. (2000). Does schooling cause growth? *American Economic Review, 90*(5), 1160–1183.

Brynjolfsson, E., & MacAfee, A. (2014). *The second machine age: Work, progress and prosperity in a time of brilliant technologies*. New York, NY: W. W. Norton.

Bughin, J., Manyika, J., & Woetzel, J. (2017). *Jobs lost, jobs gained: Workforce transitions in a time of automation*. San Francisco, CA: McKinsey Global Institute.

Cappelli, P. (2014, August). *Skill gaps, skill shortages and skill mismatches: Evidence for the US* (NBER Working Paper No. 20382). Cambridge, MA: National Bureau of Economic Research.

Deming, D. (2017). The growing importance of social skills in the labor market. *Quarterly Journal of Economics, 132*(4), 1593–1640.

Deming, D., & Noray, K. (2018, September). *STEM careers and technological change* (NBER Working Paper No. 25065). Cambridge, MA: National Bureau of Economic Research.

Ford, M. (2015). *The rise of the robots: Technology and the threat of mass unemployment*. London, England: Oneworld.

Freedman, M. (2011). *The big shift: Navigating the new stage beyond midlife*. New York, NY: Public Affairs.

Frey, C., & Osborne, M. (2013). *The future of employment: How susceptible are jobs to computerisation?* (Working Paper). Oxford, England: Oxford Martin Programme on Technology and Employment.

Goldin, C., & Katz, L. (2007). *The race between education and technology*. Cambridge, MA: Harvard University Press.

Gratton, L., & Scott, A. (2016). *The 100-year life: Living and working in an age of longevity*. London, England: Bloomsbury Press.

Gratton, L., & Scott, A. (in press). *Social pioneers*. London, England: Bloomsbury Press.

Hoffer, E. (1973). *Reflections on the human condition*. New York, NY: Harper Collins.

Islam, N. (1995). Growth empirics: A panel data approach. *Quarterly Journal of Economics, 110*(4), 1127–1170. doi:10.2307/2946651

Jorgenson, D., Ho, M., & Samuels, J. (2016, July). *Education, participation and the revival of U.S. economic growth* (NBER Working Paper No. 22453). Cambridge, MA: National Bureau of Economic Research.

Lucas, R. E. (1988). On the mechanics of economic development. *Journal of Monetary Economics, 22*(1), 3–42.

Mankiw, G., Romer, D., & Weil, D. (1992). A contribution to the empirics of economic growth. *Quarterly Journal of Economics, 107*(2), 407–437.

Manyika, J., Chui, M., Miremadi, M., Bughin, J., George, K., Willmott, P., & Dewhurst, M. (2017, January). *Harnessing automation for a future that works*. San Francisco, CA: McKinsey Global Institute.

Oeppen, J., & Vaupel, J. (2002). Broken limits to life expectancy. *Science, 296*(5570), 1029–1031.

Romer, P. (1990). Endogenous technological change. *Journal of Political Economy, 98*(5), S71–S102.

Schwab, K. (2015, December 12). The fourth industrial revolution: What it means and how to respond. *Foreign Affairs*. Retrieved from https://www.foreignaffairs.com/articles/2015-12-12/fourth-industrial-revolution

Spence, M. (1973). Job market signaling. *The Quarterly Journal of Economics, 87*(3), 355–374.

TED. (2013, April 27). The power of human energy: Angela Ahrendts at TEDxHollywood [Video file]. Retrieved from https://www.youtube.com/watch?v=mZNlN31hS78

Thomas, K. (1977). Age and authority in early modern England. *Proceedings of the British Academy, 62*, 205–248.

Tinbergen, J. (1974). Substitution of graduate by other labour. *Kyklos, 27*, 217–226. doi:10.1111/j.1467-6435.1974.tb01903.x

William Lee. (2019). *Encyclopaedia Britannica*. Retrieved from https://www.britannica.com/biography/William-Lee

3

Are We Ready for the Jobs that the Digital Economy Will Offer to Us?

MICHEL SERVOZ

Introduction

My generation had an easy time: education was cheap, finding a job was super easy, keeping it was the norm. But what about now?

And indeed, if for the generation of my parents the norm was often the same job with the same company, and the family model was the male breadwinner, things started to shift with my generation. It has become common to hold very different occupations during a career and to take better account of the need to share family responsibilities with your spouse. But with our children, the change is major: they will face major career transitions; they will work longer; and it will be common to have several different occupations at the same time, combining self-employment and more traditional forms of employment. This is perhaps why, as described in the introductory chapter to this volume, Chris Dede advises his students to simultaneously prepare for their first two careers and to build skills that enable shifting to new work-roles in an uncertain future.

In fact, in my generation, the life sequence was straightforward: you get an education in your youth, and then, when you reach adulthood, you work continuously until the day you reach retirement. This sequence is broken now, as education, work, and career pauses will no longer be separated in different phases but will be integrated in a continuum. This integration reflects the impact of digitalization on the world of work and poses major challenges. Addressing these challenges will help us not only "solve" technological unemployment (long-term unemployment, in particular)—which should be the main societal goal of harnessing digitalization—but will also work in the new economy, where human-machine cooperation will increasingly be the norm.

Digitalization is the driver of major changes in jobs. In recent years, we have witnessed the transformation of travel agencies and retail banking increasingly replaced by online services. Banks have already seen a major transformation on the trading floors, where the profession of traders has been substantially replaced by algorithms, and now similar changes are affecting retail banking.

Digitalization also means that 90% of jobs now require IT skills, even traditional ones. As the work of secretaries, waiters, and drivers has become digitalized, their skills must keep up. Digitalization also implies that people can choose to work where labor and living costs are lower.

Successful participation in the economy may depend less on where people live and more on the speed and quality of their Internet connection. One of the best examples is the emergence of digital platforms. They are networks that coordinate transactions in a digital marketplace. Improved access to digital infrastructure enables complex services to be exchanged across countries.

The changes described above signal a profound transformation of the economy. The economy of the last century was dominated by strict work schedules, hierarchies, and repetitive tasks: a job meant a permanent contract attaching a worker to a firm. Today, work relations are becoming more fluid. They are based on peer-to-peer transactions and flexible work arrangements: they are driven not by tasks but by projects that unite groups of people until they are completed. This is giving a new bargaining power to individuals. It also gives power to those whose access to the labor market was previously limited by time constraints. People are also empowered to choose the project that they like best and that pays best. But there is one condition needed in order to benefit from these opportunities: to have the necessary skills and access to education.

This profound transformation is also impacting the architecture of firms. Vertical integration, which was the norm in the beginning of the previous century, has been replaced by a wide decentralization of companies to the extent that it is sometimes difficult to ascertain their boundaries or even their status.

The Ford Motor Company of the 1930s was fully integrated, owning the plants that manufactured the steel used in the cars. Until recently, the Japanese *zaibatsus* and Korean *chaebols* were integrated conglomerates dominating their national economies.

A new organization of firms emerged at the end of the 20th century, one that is more decentralized and is based on global supply chains. A telling example is IKEA, which procures its products from a global network of suppliers. It then sells these products, manufactured to its specifications, under its brand all around the world.

A more recent transformation is driven by the emergence of e-commerce and artificial intelligence (AI), leading to the meteoric rise of certain firms with a large online presence. They do not consider themselves as firms but as marketplaces; they see their role as connecting shoppers with vendors and collecting a fee for this. The Alibaba Group is a telling example of this new architecture. It became a global company in less than ten years (where it took IKEA more than 40 years to do the same). It has a limited workforce and diversifies its income to include various financial services (World Bank, 2019).

The above transformations have deep implications for the skills and competences required to perform as entrepreneur or as worker in this new economy. In a volatile, uncertain world, where disruption is the new normal, a hierarchical structure based on planning, prescription, and execution will not work well. This creates inflexible and inefficient structures incapable of keeping pace with rapid change and of reacting to disruption.

The integration of AI, robotics, and automation in organizations should cause them to become more collaborative and team-oriented—optimized for adaptability and learning in preparation for technological disruption as opposed to the traditional top-down hierarchical structures (Lindzon, 2017). This also implies multidisciplinary teams or networks collaborating in rapid learning and fast decision cycles.

Constantly adapting work allocation will be essential to make the most effective use of different qualifications and to develop them. Shifting tasks across workers raises company efficiency and creates more agility. A key to a new organization of companies will be introducing a culture of learning throughout the organization.

This new corporate learning culture is also made possible by technological advances. The office and the company can be increasingly dematerialized and new online education tools will be available to manage a fast-learning environment. In the field of education, this is reflected in the need to ramp up the academic institutions' student-centric focus—a student relationship management approach, as described in Ann Brewer's chapter, "Employing the *60YC* as a Strategic Approach," in this volume.

How can we prepare for jobs and careers dominated by disruptions? There are many estimates of the number of jobs that will soon be destroyed by technology. There are also estimates of new job creation: by 2030, according to predictions from McKinsey, technology spending alone will create 20 million to 50 million new jobs (Bughin, Manyika, & Woetzel, 2017). This sounds impressive, but it should be added that these jobs have strings attached: we will need to work longer, to have a strong skills foundation, to have access to cheap and effective re-skilling systems, and to be overall intellectually agile and open. As Andrew Scott describes in chapter two, "Education, Age, and the Machine," the ongoing digital transformations in the world of work mean that what we learn, when we learn it, how we learn it, and who we learn it from will all change.

The impact of automation on jobs implies the transformation of tasks that form a specific job. We are already witnessing some of these transformations. Other transformations that will affect jobs in the coming years are hardly possible to predict. Education is a long-term investment in knowledge, based on the information that we have at any point in time on labor market and societal needs. And it is a fact that today, by the time students graduate from university, a substantial part of the subjects they learn in year one has started to become obsolete. Most students receive information and knowledge about the world as we know it today not about what they need to do to successfully manage career transitions in case of radical changes. In fact, a very large percentage of children starting school today will have jobs that do not exist today (World Economic Forum, 2016).

Youth Education: Learning to Learn, the Essential Foundation

While most of the focus in this volume is on adult education, implementing the 60-Year Curriculum (*60YC*) must start with primary education. In order to make sure that students' skills have the resilience necessary to adapt to jobs, occupations, and organizations that are very different from today and mostly unknown, five elements are essential (Servoz, 2019): strong basic skills, a focus on transferable skills, digital proficiency, blurring the boundaries between vocational and general education, and supporting the school-to-job transition.

Strong Basic Skills

All young people must acquire a sufficient proficiency level in basic skills, that is, literacy, numeracy, and digital skills. It is not acceptable that in Europe today we have 61 million Europeans (the size of the population of one of the largest European Union Member States!) who do not have these basic skills. Looking at the scores from the Program for International Student Assessment (PISA), the picture is not reassuring for some of the most advanced economies: some are seriously lagging, and this will be a major stumbling block to their economic development if the percentage of low achievers continues.

The gaps in adult education are also a reflection of problems in primary and secondary educational systems. The share of underachievement of 15-year olds in basic skills in Europe and the US remains unacceptably high. According to the Organization for Economic Cooperation and Development's latest PISA data released in December 2019, 21.6% of European students underachieved in science, 21.7% in reading, and 22.4% in mathematics, and these shares increased since the previous testing period. This is an additional cause for concern in the age of AI, as low achievers cannot successfully complete basic tasks that are required in modern societies. Early school-leavers will become unemployable adults! For people with poor literacy and numeracy, let alone poor digital skills, finding a job in the new economy, and keeping it, might be an impossible task.

Indeed, as the Organization for Economic Cooperation and Development (OECD) points out, successfully equipping young people with basic skills is key to addressing the challenges of automation:

Young people leaving education with low basic skills may become trapped in low-skilled occupations at high risk of automation, with a large cost of moving to another occupation if they lose their jobs. As well as limiting the number of students who drop out, policies [to boost basic skills] can ensure that vocational education and training programs include a strong component of cognitive skills in addition to job-specific skills (2019, p. 119).

A Focus on Transferable Skills

As posited by Chris Dede in Chapter 1, "Reconceptualizing Lifelong Learning in the Era of the Synergistic Digital Economy," achieving the goals of the *60YC* requires rethinking the objectives of education. The curricula in secondary schools should focus more on skills that are transferrable across jobs and will not be subject to automation: these include general cognitive skills (the capacity to understand an environment that is increasingly uncertain), critical thinking, problem solving, creativity, and communication; there should be a minimum threshold of transferrable, cognitive skills provided in the programs of any secondary school and university. In fact, no student should leave school without adequate proficiency in these skills. This would provide an insurance policy for whichever technological disruption one faces: one can get back on their feet and move on to another occupation.

The curricula in secondary schools, and even more so in universities, are focused on knowledge and facts. Teaching creative thinking, problem solving, and teamwork are not considered as topics per se; they are regarded as educational methods that can improve the acquisition of knowledge. Students are not assessed on whether they perform well on any of these topics. Whereas, in fact, they are the skills which will be the most useful to any student in their professional (and social) life! Obviously, it is not suggested to reduce the level of proficiency of students on key knowledge, such as STEM. The shift to the competencies that will guarantee the resilience of students in a changing labor market should be achieved, *inter alia,* through a change of teaching methods that puts emphasis on creativity, problem solving, and critical thinking so that students are assessed on their capacity to learn to learn rather than on the knowledge they can find in textbooks.

In this context, the European Commission proposed a "Council Recommendation on Key Competences for Lifelong Learning" in January 2018.[1] Its objective is to improve the development of key competences (e.g., literacy, languages, civics, and digital skills) in educational systems, for people of all ages throughout their lives and to provide guidance to EU Member States on how to achieve this objective. The aim is to better prepare people for changing labor markets and active citizenship in more diverse, mobile, digital, and global societies through the following:

- focusing more strongly on basic skills (literacy, languages, and basic digital skills) as well as on horizontal competencies such as creativity, problem solving, critical thinking, and communication;
- focusing on promoting entrepreneurial education and experiences at all levels of education;
- focusing on improving the acquisition of science, technology, engineering, and mathematical (STEM) competence and making careers in these areas more attractive;
- updating the definition of digital skills to include coding, cybersecurity, and digital citizenship aspects; and
- strengthening citizenship, democratic values, and human rights in the civic competence.

Digital Proficiency

In addition, a new subject should be added to the secondary school curriculum, which could broadly be called computer science but would include more than just coding by teaching other aspects such as networks, algorithm development, and data science. The recent efforts to introduce coding in some secondary schools are not enough by themselves to help students navigating the digital economy. Learning a programming language is simple, especially as it is increasingly close to natural language: it is not so important as compared to understanding the intricacies of AI and robotics to which students will be exposed as workers, consumers, or citizens. And all students need to be fluent in using digital appliances, employing various software, and navigating the Internet; the time allocated to this subject in the curriculum should be equivalent to the time spent teaching physics, math, or biology, and it should be taught over several years. At present, about 85% of the machine learning workforce is male. Unless more balanced and diverse developer teams are actively encouraged, conscious or subconscious biases could sneak into algorithms, which will influence their output (Servoz, 2019). The introduction of such a subject could thus also help address gender biases in algorithm development.

An interesting approach in this context is the P-TECH 9–14 school in New York, designed to close the gap between young people's ambitions for college and careers and the specific skills needed by employers in digital industries. In a P-TECH 9–14 school, students earn a high school diploma, an industry-recognized associate degree, and gain relevant work experience in a growing field. The schools create a seamless program for students to acquire academic, technical, and workplace skills. Mentoring, workplace visits, job shadowing, and internships are integrated into each student's preparation for the identified jobs. Employer-partners commit to ensuring that graduates are "first in line" for jobs (Industry Partner, n.d.).

Blurring the Boundaries between Vocational and General Education

The organization of secondary educational systems needs to put more focus on skills combination and to give more flexibility to students to combine technical and general subjects in their studies so that they eventually have the capacity to blend STEM skills with traditional subjects such as business operations. The key is adaptability; the capacity to respond to unexpected circumstances; and learning new skills autonomously and quickly. In fact, the boundaries between vocational/technical education and general education should be blurred; there should be real bridges and flexibility between general and technical tracks to avoid the wrong perception that technical education is a second-rate path to a successful career and to avoid the situation where choosing the technical track of education prevents a student from going into general education later.

Australia's Technical and Further Education (TAFE) institutes are good examples in this regard. They are government-owned providers of vocational and technical education courses, which can lead to different types of qualifications, general or technical. The student pathways are not limited to these courses, as they also give access to general higher education by providing credits toward some higher education courses. The TAFE sector is the biggest education and training sector in Australia (Studies in Australia, 2019).

Another good example, this time from Europe, is the Swiss Vocational Education and Training (VET) system. The VET system is fully embedded in and connected to the country's overall education system (Accenture, 2017). At the age of 15 or 16, young people decide what to do for their post-compulsory degrees. Essentially, they choose between the general education and VET pathway. Two further options exist within each pathway: the academic baccalaureate and special baccalaureate in general education, and the two-year certificate or three-to-four-year federal VET diploma within VET. Thanks to Switzerland's nationally recognized credentials for all programs, graduates can be sure that VET diplomas will have currency with future employers or future educational institutions. The Swiss VET system's permeability enables young people to make up for less than ideal choices and changing preferences by providing progression routes among every educational level and type. For example, the federal VET diploma can be combined with the federal vocational baccalaureate for strong students who want to continue their education at a university of applied sciences. With the addition of the University Aptitude Test, the student can progress into a conventional university. This increases the flexibility of different educational paths, serves as a bridge between general and technical tracks, and, in effect, blurs the boundaries between vocational and general education.

Supporting the School-to-Job Transition

When looking for a first-time job, young people should be asked to demonstrate their skills and their competencies, not to show their diplomas. The process of matching labor market demand and supply should be reimagined by transforming the job application stage—job requirements should be reformed so that employers and public employment services list the skills required for jobs instead of degrees/diplomas for vacancies. This should also serve to encourage applications from a diverse skillset.

An example of this approach is Skillful, developed by the Markle Foundation as an initiative to help American workers and employers adapt to the digital economy (Markle, n.d.). Skillful facilitates transparency around the value of educational and training programs and fosters the adoption of skills-based talent management practices to give educators a clearer picture of which skills are in demand in their area, businesses a better way of recruiting and assessing applicants, and job seekers a better understanding of potential career pathways. Since its launch in Colorado, nearly 600 businesses have been trained on skills-based hiring practices and more than 200 career coaches have joined an online community to learn from Skillful and each other. Skillful recently expanded with the creation of the Skillful State Network, a collaboration of 20 governors from both major political parties, to transform the US labor market to become skills-based (Accenture, 2018a).

Re-Inventing Post-Secondary and Adult Education

Current educational systems are time-compressed in a way that may not be suited to current or future labor markets. They force narrow career and expertise decisions in early youth. The chronological divide between formal education and the labor market needs to disappear, as learning, R&D, knowledge sharing, retraining, and innovation take place simultaneously throughout the work life cycle, regardless of the job, level, or industry (World Economic Forum, 2017). And adult education is also not sufficiently adapted to adults who learn differently: shorter sessions are needed that are made simpler and with more repetitions (Accenture, 2018b). Chris Dede in Chapter 1 and Punya Mishra and Jacqueline Smith in Chapter 6 in this volume look into more details in the need to re-invent adult education as a central part of implementing the *60YC*.

Adult education (or lifelong learning) has been recognized for a long time as an important element to keep the employability of any worker at a high level. However, in practice, it does not work and is not adapted to the challenges of a fast-changing world of work: the statistics show that those who benefit from lifelong learning are often those who need it least (i.e., highly skilled workers), whereas vulnerable workers tend not to have access to it. Furthermore, employers tend not to anticipate and to prepare their workers systemically for major skills adaptations: the tendency remains to make workers redundant and recruit ones who have the right skills immediately when current workers are lagging in their skillsets. In addition, most of the lifelong learning programs are about providing very specific technical skills and not about the general cognitive skills that are essential for a labor market dominated by automation and innovation. Therefore, the following are essential elements of a solution: reforming post-secondary education, encouraging private sector involvement, and refocusing public employment services (Servoz, 2019):

Reforming Post-Secondary Education

In Chapter 7, "Market-Driven Education: The Imperative for Responsive Design and Application," Jason Wingard and Christine Farrugia point out that today's workers will find themselves in a state of continuous professional learning over their lifetimes. This continual adaptation necessitates the reform of post-secondary education so that it addresses the needs of the *60YC*.

The time sequence of post-secondary education should be revisited, with important implications for the curriculum; the norm for young people out of secondary schools should be bachelor's degrees revisited to be more focused on cognitive skills, but this initial curriculum should be completed by successive sessions or one or two semesters, for instance every five years, when students would enhance their initial education, focusing either on technical or general competences needed for their career progression. The notions of graduate and alumni would become irrelevant, as throughout their career the individual would remain a student of a given university, the latter being responsible for keeping skills up-to-date and completing them when necessary.

To overcome the practical differences this may entail, there is also a need to go beyond the current focus on a single institution (such as one's alma mater) providing lifelong learning opportunities. For example, coalitions of different schools could work together to provide lifelong learning, depending on their expertise in different fields/courses. This could be extended to higher education by creating regional coalitions. The current higher education system is organized as a conventional end point for acquiring knowledge in which students attend an institution for several consecutive years before graduating and starting work. This approach is problematic when it comes to acquiring and updating one's skills at key junctures in one's career. Some concepts have been developed to overcome this.

One interesting example is Stanford's "Open Loop University" concept, imagining how the university could change by 2025 (Stanford2025, n.d.). In the Open Loop system, students could start university whenever they feel ready (be it at 18 or 24). They would have a total of six years education over a lifetime to be used whenever and however they deem fittest. Students could start their studies, then leave university after two years to join a company, then come back in their 30s, 40s, or 50s for example. Having acquired some professional experience, they then come back not only to enrich their skills but also to teach about their experience. Knowledge could thus be obtained across classrooms and practical settings.

To make higher education fitter for the *60YC*, we also need to make it more personalized. A good European example in this regard comes from the Swiss Federal Institute of Technology in Zurich (ETHZ). ETHZ offers a program of customized continuing education focusing on advanced materials, process, and manufacturing technologies. Participants' expertise and skills are promoted and expanded in a targeted way, using a research-oriented approach that takes full account of their interests and needs. Participants design personalized study plans in cooperation with a mentor. Within the scope of their personalized study plan, they can take part in research projects, deepen and supplement their technical knowledge through courses, or share their expertise in seminars. The customized ETHZ program gives experienced professionals from technical industries an opportunity to deepen their expertise and extend their skills in their field in the broader area of advanced materials and processes. The program builds on the expertise of its participants and is designed to focus on a particular area that is specific for each individual. Current advances in AI technologies could be used to scale up such an approach to secondary schools as well and over a variety of educational programs.

Encouraging Private Sector Involvement

Companies should take more responsibilities in the training of their employees, not so much for current tasks but to help them to develop their potential beyond current tasks and to anticipate future changes. Looking at the relevance of lifelong learning systems, the OECD finds that the odds of participating in any type of training are significantly lower among workers in jobs at risk of being automated (Nedelkoska & Quintini, 2018). Workers in fully automatable jobs are more than three times less likely to have participated in on-the-job training, over a 12-month period, than workers in non-automatable jobs. Differences in training participation outside work are also striking, with workers with the highest risk of automation about twice less likely to participate in formal education and 3.5 times less likely to take part in distance learning. At present, when they provide lifelong learning opportunities, companies overwhelmingly focus on training their employees for current tasks. Besides a very small minority, employers are not preparing their companies and their employees for an economy shaped by AI. There is thus a larger role for companies to work with educational institutions as the AI revolution in the economy unfolds. One such area of collaboration could be the design of new curricula.

A good example of how business can help developing the potential of their employees is the partnership between Starbucks and the Arizona State University (Starbucks, n.d.). Starbucks is offering to its employees the possibility to undertake the preparation of a university degree in a field that employees can choose freely and which does not need to be formally linked to Starbuck's business operations. It is an interesting example, which may be related to the difficulties that Starbucks currently faces to retain employees in the long term at a time when unemployment is very low, but it is clearly designed to make the career potential of the worker the first priority. Punya Mishra and Jacqueline Smith describe the collaboration between Arizona State University and Starbucks in more detail in their chapter within this book.

Refocusing Public Employment Services

The above implies a rebalancing of responsibilities for workers between public employment services and companies. Currently, when the skills of a worker become outdated, the natural tendency is for the employer to make the worker redundant, hence shifting the responsibility and the financial burden to the public employment service, whose job it is to help the worker to get some training and get back to employment. Public employment services should not limit their role to helping the unemployed but should also help currently employed people to prepare transitions in cooperation with the companies that employ them. This is mutually beneficial as it reduces substantially the financial burden of paying unemployment benefits for all.

Indeed, as Accenture (2018a) points out, successfully addressing technological transformations would mean building upon the skills that workers have already learned rather than discrediting or discounting them. This would in effect mean focusing on *new skilling* rather than only on *reskilling*, thereby providing workers with new skills to supplement their existing expertise.

A good example in the area of personalizing employment services is the Skills Bank in Sheffield (UK) that supports employers in the Sheffield City Region to invest in the skills that their staff needs to help their business develop and grow. Advisors work with businesses to identify the skills needed, to connect with high quality training providers, and to provide funding of up to 70% of the cost of training staff to gain new skills or refresh existing capabilities (Sheffield College, n.d.).

Another good example of personalizing employment services from Europe is Bob Emploi. It is a digital service using algorithms based on data from the French Employment Agency to help job seekers find resources that best match their specific profiles. The services assess a jobseeker's individual situation before providing personalized recommendations on viable employment strategies. Within its first year, Bob Emploi had reached 130,000 users, 42% of whom say the platform contributed to their finding a job (Accenture, 2018a).

Where Is the Mid-Career School?

By observing the educational institutions that cater to the needs of workers in transition, the conclusion that comes to mind is that they are often ill equipped to provide general cognitive skills and not well organized to cater to the needs of adults who have socio-economic constraints. It is easier for people with university degrees to transition between occupations. Adult education thus needs to put more focus on those without basic education or university education; those are the individuals most at risk of being replaced.

Adult learning, whether provided through companies or the mid-career school, should be tailor-made to the needs of adult students: there should be a repair component in all the cases where the adult concerned has an issue with basic skills, literacy, numeracy, and digital skills. There should also be a strong component related to general cognitive skills that needs to outweigh any specific technical learning. Finally, the informal skills acquired by workers on their jobs should be evaluated so that a recognition/certification of these skills is equivalent to formal credentials provided by the educational system. In addition, flexibility is needed in the way teaching is delivered to avoid income losses for the workers and to provide flexible teaching hours and processes (on-line teaching can be an important element).

Becoming More Mobile

Mobility schemes should be introduced between employers to offer promising professionals the opportunity to learn in a different environment for a period of one year. Such mobility schemes have been proven to be very beneficial to individuals (e.g., learning different working methods or foreign languages, acquiring new technical expertise, etc.) and to the sending company that can use the scheme to send the trainee to one of its clients as well as providers to develop business-to-business relations.

Obviously, such a plan could be built on the model of the classic European Erasmus Programmes for students. Erasmus+ is the EU's program to support education, training, youth, and sport in Europe. Its budget of €14.7 billion provides opportunities for over 4 million Europeans to study, train, and gain experience abroad (Erasmus, n.d.). Financial envelopes would need to be made available by authorities to support companies in this effort, in particular on the practical aspects (i.e., language training, short-term housing, etc.). This would require agreements between the companies or organizations concerned by the mobility of a worker to set the terms and conditions of the secondment in a way which is mutually beneficial for them.

All of the above imply a deep transformation of our universities and third-degree education to become a fairer reflection of our societies across generations, lifestyles, and origins. The mix of students will become much more diverse with many ages represented and several generations on campus—populations traditionally underrepresented at elite institutions—gaining greater access. The infrastructure of universities will have to be reviewed to cater to the needs of a more dynamic and diverse population. This review process will also need to address the fact that young students may not any longer form a majority of the student population. Older students with professional experience will reconnect with their university and provide precious expertise based on their accomplishments. Are we ready for the changes that will ensue?

How Much Is This Going to Cost? Who Will Pay?

To successfully manage transitions over a longer career, workers need to have access to social safety nets that are adapted to the new realities of work. This also raises the question of funding—who pays for managing the transitions workers will need to undergo? With an increasing share of capital and a declining share of labor in income, how can governments fund these safety nets?

When one examines tax rules in different countries, it is obvious that they are not well aligned to the needs of supporting longer careers, incomes during career transitions, and costs of retraining or up-skilling. The broad assessment is that in many countries the current funding available from tax sources is largely insufficient to cope with the new education needs of a longer career and provides the wrong incentives.

Often tax systems treat labor and capital income differently, resulting in incentives to invest in physical instead of human capital, and they do not provide incentives to companies to invest in human capital. The tax system should, on the contrary, provide financial incentives for individuals to develop their skills efficiently, as better skill levels lead to higher wages and stronger employment prospects, higher productivity and profits for businesses, and higher growth rates and tax revenues for governments (Organization for Economic Cooperation and Development, 2017).

For instance, in the UK, where companies investing in R&D can claim generous tax relief on their investments, there are not the same incentives when it comes to training employees. In contrast, the Austrian tax system includes a full tax allowance for training expenses, and a further 20% of actual expenses is deducted from taxable income, implying a 120% tax allowance in real terms (Costa, Datta, Machin, & McNally, 2018).

Social protection is based on models established in the previous century, and all its components, as well as the measures designed to help career transitions, are linked to a labor contract not to the individual subject of this labor contract. Adult education and lifelong learning are essentially linked to labor contracts. If, as many analysts predict, we are going to see a substantial reduction of wage employment coupled with a move toward self-employment, then the safety nets should be attached to the individual in the form of a personal account.

Finally, it is interesting to note that recently social protection funding has increasingly relied on government funding, and the share of social contributions paid by social partners is declining, notably that of the employers. The emergence of non-standard forms of work as the norm is likely to put additional pressure on the financing of social protection in the future. Non-standard workers and the self-employed pay lower contributions than employees and accordingly have less access to social safety nets (European Commission, 2018). An additional important issue is the collective representation of the workers engaged in these non-standard forms of work: this has a direct impact on social protection, which in Europe is often jointly managed by the social partners.

New Solutions and Experimentations

In order to resolve the financing gap, to respond to the new training needs, and to align collective representation to the new world of work, some innovative suggestions have been made, and some new approaches are being experimented with.

BOOSTING COLLECTIVE REPRESENTATION

Social protection as well as active labor market policies, including lifelong learning, are managed or strongly influenced by, in Europe, social partners; employers' and workers' representatives come together to find common solutions to the challenges of the new world of work. It becomes thus essential that the emerging non-standard forms of work benefit from some form of collective representation. It is complicated, as the platforms are not formally employers and regard people who work for them as "service providers" rather than workers. But it is essential, as apprenticeship plans and dual education are often jointly managed by social partners in Europe.

In this context, an interesting initiative has been launched by Uber in the UK, UberEngage, that is based on the establishment of advisory groups of senior Uber drivers in each city where Uber operates; these groups are in charge of listening to the drivers' needs and ensuring their voices are heard by management (Uber, 2019). Another interesting initiative developed in Belgium is Smart, which operates as a cooperative active in several European countries providing services to freelance workers such as training, legal advice, and information (Smart, n.d.). In the same way, some existing trade unions have started to open their membership to self-employed and online platform workers: it is the case for instance with IGMetall in Germany (European Commission, 2018).

TAXING THE DIGITAL ECONOMY

To improve the funding of labor market transitions, one suggestion has been made to introduce a so-called "robot tax," taxing robots at a similar rate to the workers they replace. The proceeds would be used to fund the labor market transitions stemming from digital automation. Implementing such a tax would also prove very hard: there is a major risk of evasion and of companies using robots moving to tax-free jurisdictions that will stifle innovation in the countries where the tax is applied. Additionally, pure displacements will be hard to identify; the more common impact of digital automation is to assist workers in their tasks and augment their capacity.

In many ways, the current tax rules in most countries do not address a situation where companies are global, virtual, or have little or no physical presence. There is a growing demand to ensure that digital companies also contribute their fair share of tax. For example, in the EU, digital companies currently have an average effective tax rate half that of the traditional economy. In this light, given the difficulties to find a common European approach on the matter, France started to implement a digital tax as of January 1, 2019. The United Kingdom has already announced a 2% levy on revenues from the activities of UK users of search engines, social media platforms, and online marketplaces to be applied as of 2020. But to be effective, such reforms need to be part of a concerted global discussion to avoid distortions in international tax competition. The recent agreement of the OECD to reach by 2020 a multilateral long-term solution to the taxation challenges arising from digitalization is a welcome development in this regard.

TOWARD A UNIVERSAL BASIC INCOME?

In this context, some are arguing that a universal basic income (i.e., an unconditional stipend robust enough to maintain a dignified life) could be an effective way to compensate workers who are displaced and would support them in taking up studies and undertaking creative endeavors or entrepreneurial ventures. Some experiments in Europe have been launched. At the beginning of 2017, Finland launched such an experiment, which lasted until the end of 2018. The target group was composed of 2,000 people between 25- and 58-years-old, all of whom were recipients of the basic unemployment benefit. For two years, they were paid €560 per month, equal to the basic unemployment insurance. There was no means testing, and recipients could work without losing the benefit. While results from the first year of the experiment will be released later in 2019 and the final report in 2020, preliminary findings suggest that employment levels did not improve, but participants felt happier and less stressed (Servoz, 2019).

Even if we disregard the obvious issue of how expensive such a plan would be, it is not believed that this offers a sustainable solution to the challenge of a longer working life with several job transitions. On the contrary, it may have the unwanted effect of excluding those receiving the stipend by not providing incentives to upgrade skills toward new job opportunities, hence keeping them in the margins of society.

Moving to a Fairer Financial Burden Sharing

As we are moving to a new economy where the delineation between labor and the provision of services is blurred, it is important to ensure that the costs of social safety nets are better shared between individuals, companies, and the state. Today, the financing of social protection is gradually shifting to general taxes. This trend will accelerate with the rise of self-employment.

This requires innovative solutions providing more flexibility and access to individuals throughout their careers, which could, for example, be built on a concept of an individual portable account (Servoz, 2019).

A UNIVERSAL PERSONAL ACCOUNT...

Every individual could have a universal personal account providing insurance against the main risks covered by social protection and supporting career transitions. This means maternity, illness, pension, and unemployment, but also adult vocational education and training: this plan would be the main instrument to help individuals managing career transitions.

The funding could come from a generalized social contribution, a small amount levied on services billed by platforms (Uber, Airbnb, TaskRabbit, etc.) along the sales tax/VAT model. This would all be paid by the customer so that online platforms are not disadvantaged. Online platforms will remain responsible for collecting the contributions. At the same time, social contributions from "traditional" employers and employees with labor contracts will continue to be collected.

The universality of such an account implies the possibility for the individual to accumulate credits (for instance for training) and to use them at a certain point in time for a major requalification necessitating a long training period (for instance, a one-year program at a university). Obviously, there should be limits on how much can be transferred from one component to another so that the major social risks remain adequately ensured.

...WITH A DEDICATED FINANCING

This implies a major shift in the sources of financing for adult education and for social protection: indeed, a wider population would benefit from social protection and lifelong learning opportunities as they would be extended to self-employed and non-standard workers, and more and longer career transitions would be covered by the plan. This means more financial support from the government and from employers.

A financial instrument sponsored by governments could, for instance, be created to support reskilling by tapping financial markets and lending directly to workers. This instrument could be designed to provide incentives for companies to use the fund to train their workforce and to get financial institutions on board. Making such an instrument attractive to financial institutions could be achieved by loan guarantees provided by the US. The fiscal impact will be partially offset by decreased spending on unemployment benefits. This newly created instrument should fund training programs, which target occupations facing labor shortages and specific skills in high demand by companies.

In Europe, such a concept has been proposed by France Stratégie (2017). Their idea is to create a Spinelli Fund, which is targeted at those most in need: unemployed people and low-skilled young people; students already enrolled in higher education who want to finance an additional year of studies; employed and self-employed who want vocational training to change their career path or access a higher-skilled job; as well as refugees who need to acquire specific skills to enter the labor market.

Another interesting example focusing only on skills is Singapore's SkillsFuture Credit, which aims to encourage individual ownership of skill development and lifelong learning. All Singaporeans aged 25 and above receive an opening credit of $500 as of January 2016. The credit does not expire, and the Singaporean Government will provide periodic top-ups. Currently, employers are eligible for subsidies ranging from up to 50% to 90% of course fees for supported courses. Under the enhanced training support scheme for small to medium enterprises (SMEs), SMEs receive a course fee subsidy of up to 90% when they sponsor their employees for training. In addition to course fee subsidies, sponsoring employers will also receive absentee payroll support (My Skills Future, 2018).

Conclusion

In conclusion, we shall remember that time and again, we have faced major technological disruptions, and each time our societies did not manage these transitions well, which resulted in major difficulties, unrest, or crises. We should all the more be focused on managing the transition better now that there is a clear acceleration of technological changes and a need to ensure a longer working life. However, this requires:

- A major investment effort in research, education, IT infrastructure, and systems to be shared between public budgets and companies; some countries have already shown that they are prioritizing this.
- A major rethink of education; creating education aimed at adults, not simply a few retraining sessions scattered over the course of a career, giving young people the capacity to learn rather than feeding them with technical knowledge that can quickly become obsolete.

Note

1 The full council recommendation can be read here: https://eur-lex.europa.eu/legal-content/EN/TXT/?uri=uriserv:OJ.C_.2018.189.01.0001.01.ENG

References

Accenture. (2017). *Jobs now: Swiss-style vocational education and training. Voices from Companies, Governors and CEOs.* Zurich, Switzerland: Swiss-American Chamber of Commerce. Retrieved from https://www.accenture.com/us-en/insight-swiss-style-training

Accenture. (2018a). *Inclusive future of work: A call to action.* Retrieved from https://www.accenture.com/us-en/company-inclusive-future-work

Accenture. (2018b). *It's learning. Just not as we know it: How to accelerate skills acquisition in the age of intelligent technologies.* Retrieved from http://www.g20yea.com/images/reports/Its-Learning---Just-Not-As-We-Know-It.pdf

Bughin, J., Manyika, J., & Woetzel, J. (2017). *Jobs lost, jobs gained: Workforce transitions in a time of automation.* San Francisco, CA: McKinsey Global Institute.

Costa, R., Datta, N., Machin, S., & McNally, S. (2018, March). *Investing in people: The case for human capital tax credits* (Briefing Note 007). London, England: Centre for Vocational Educational Research, London School of Economics and Political Science. Retrieved from http://cver.lse.ac.uk/textonly/cver/pubs/cverbrf007.pdf

Erasmus. (n.d.). What is Erasmus+? Retrieved from https://ec.europa.eu/programmes/erasmus-plus/about_en

European Commission. (2018). *Employment and social development in Europe: Annual review 2018.* Luxembourg, Europe: Publications Office of the European Union. Retrieved from https://ec.europa.eu/social/main.jsp?catId=738&langId=en&pubId=8110

France Stratégie. (2017). *The Spinelli fund: A European compact for skills* (Note d'analyse No. 63). Retrieved from https://www.strategie.gouv.fr/sites/strategie.gouv.fr/files/atoms/files/fs-na-63-spinelli_fund_20171115_web.pdf

Industry Partner. (n.d.). *P-tech.* Retrieved from http://www.ptech.org/how-it-works/partners/industry-partners/

Lindzon, J. (2017, February 28). How AI is changing the way companies are organized. *Fast Company.* Retrieved from https://www.fastcompany.com/3068492/how-ai-is-changing-the-way-companies-are-organized

Markle. (n.d.). Skillful: Building a skill-based labor market. Retrieved from https://www.markle.org/rework-america/skillful

My Skills Future. (2018). Retrieved from https://www.myskillsfuture.sg/content/portal/en/header/faqs/skillsfuture-credit.html

Nedelkoska, L., & Quintini, G. (2018). *Automation, skills use and training* (OECD Social, Employment and Migration Working Paper No. 202). Paris, France: OECD. doi:10.1787/2e2f4eea-en

Organization for Economic Cooperation and Development. (2017). *Taxation and skills* (OECD Tax Policy Study No. 24). Paris, France: OECD. doi:10.1787/9789264269385-en

Organization for Economic Cooperation and Development. (2018). *PISA 2015: Results in focus.* Retrieved from https://www.oecd.org/pisa/pisa-2015-results-in-focus.pdf

Organization for Economic Cooperation and Development. (2019). *OECD skills outlook 2019: Thriving in a digital world.* Paris, France: OECD. doi:10.1787/df80bc12-en

Servoz, M. (2019). *The future of work? Work of the future! On how artificial intelligence, robotics and automation are transforming jobs and the economy in Europe.* Report for the European Commission. Retrieved from https://ec.europa.eu/epsc/sites/epsc/files/ai-report_online-version.pdf

Sheffield College. (n.d.). Sheffield city region skills bank. Retrieved from http://www.sheffcol.ac.uk/employers/skills-bank

Smart. (n.d.). Retrieved from http://smartbe.be

Stanford2025. (n.d.). Open Loop University. Retrieved from http://www.stanford2025.com/open-loop-university/

Starbucks. (n.d.). The Starbucks college achievement plan. Retrieved from https://starbucks.asu.edu

Studies in Australia. (2019). Technical and further education. Retrieved from https://www.studiesinaustralia.com/studying-in-australia/what-to-study-in-australia/types-of-education/technical-and-further-education

Uber. (2019). Retrieved from https://www.uber.com/en-GB/drive/resources/uberengage

World Bank. (2019). *World development report 2019: The changing nature of work*. Washington, DC: World Bank. doi:10.1596/978-1-4648-1328-3

World Economic Forum. (2016). *The future of jobs: Employment, skills and workforce strategy for the fourth Industrial Revolution*. Retrieved from http://www3.weforum.org/docs/WEF_Future_of_Jobs.pdf

World Economic Forum. (2017). *The global human capital report 2017: Preparing people for the future of work*. Retrieved from http://www3.weforum.org/docs/WEF_Global_Human_Capital_Report_2017.pdf

Employing the 60-Year Curriculum as a Strategic Approach

ANN M. BREWER

Higher education around the world is endeavoring to customize curricula and methods to match rapidly changing societal requirements and cultural shifts. Employing the 60-Year Curriculum (*60YC*) as a strategic framework is one such method to address these challenges and is the focus of this chapter. The *60YC* spans a person's life from the time of high school graduation through, and including, active life in retirement. Most people will have varied life and work experiences, career involvements, and understanding of success. Perceptions of self and identity—both felt and ascribed—will change over a 60-year life after high school. The 60-year journey will vary for each person, as will the markers of that life, such as employability and retirement. Given this, the predicaments that adult learners and educators tackle are subjective, multifaceted, diverse, and, at times, difficult to address. The *60YC* will need to be flexible enough to meet the challenges of adult learners as they negotiate changes and transitions as part of their identity and achievements.

Until a few decades ago, employers controlled the career paths of individuals. Today, career paths are in the hands of the individual (McDonald & Hite, 2008). Wingard and Farrugia's chapter in this volume outlines how today's workers confront endless professional learning throughout their lifespans, during which they will employ different strategies at different points.

People are faced with the prospect of sponsoring their own learning and all that entails—time, distance, costs, and outcomes. For some time, in the United States as well as in many countries around the world, degree costs have been escalating at a rate higher than the consumer price index (Faulk & Wang, 2013). Given this, short courses, and the credentialing of such, might prove to be a better value proposition aligned to the *60YC* than traditional undergraduate and postgraduate courses, not to mention the lower fee structure for the former (Schwartz & Hoffman, 2015). Steering a pathway through this uncertain and high-investment terrain is nearly impossible without some guidance. It is critical for educational institutions to understand how strategic and student-centric foci can support their efforts to achieve educational objectives and learning outcomes for students and educators alike.

It is a great irony that innovation in education, when applied to educational institutions themselves, is a controversial concept frequently prompting resistance from academics and governing bodies. Employing a learner perspective appears to unsettle academics, and there is often a resistance to develop curriculum that is based on interdisciplinary—let alone transdisciplinary—approaches such as design learning (Scheer, Noweski, & Meinel, 2012), a focus of the second half of this chapter.

There is no doubt that a transdisciplinary approach will be one of the necessary factors to allow the dynamism of the *60YC* to fulfil its value proposition. In the same way, most adult learners are pursuing innovative and cost-effective ways to enhance their learning and skill development, judging from the growth in short courses both on campuses and online. Many adults are highly motivated to learn, and they have the needs and the means to obtain these services. However, educational institutions also need to consider those adult learners without the means to do so. Mishra and Smith, in their chapter in this volume, discuss how the diverse nature of learners' stories throughout their lives necessitates educational institutions challenging the rhetoric–reality gap. They argue that the time has come to deliver courses that create a more inclusive learning domain to meet the needs of students and to help them live fulfilling lives. Moreover, learners want to take control of the preferences for their learning through a self-guided process. Adult learners want to and need to become more collaborative (co-learning) and to step outside of their comfort zones.

Despite this, the types of innovation that educational institutions are investing in are mainly in infrastructure, learning technologies, and research, particularly STEM. Elsewhere, innovations are largely incremental and insufficient to trigger the types of changes that will be necessary to bring about the *60YC* if left to educational institutions alone. It is not about developing a whole new mission, but instead it is about integrating student-facing services and functions to create novel educational models and approaches. This chapter offers two suggestions for applying the *60YC*, namely design learning and a "strategic student relationship management" (SSRM) approach (discussed below). Both of these strategies lead to contextualizing and personalizing learning, which is so important for adult learners given the changing needs and demographics of students, the dynamics of the global educational marketplace, and the need to build strategic relationships with prospective adult learners.

In Dede's chapter in this book, he discusses an array of models that might serve to meet "the more general need to equip and help all adults from any background at any stage of their lives" (Chapter 1, p. 4) and how institutions might partner with each other to achieve this outcome.

Design Learning for Co-Learning

An important model for educational institutions to consider is partnering with adult learners to facilitate their participation in curriculum design. In today's digitally connected, globalized world, didactic pedagogy is at variance with expectations from students and employers. Teaching-by-telling and learning-by-listening are insufficient for developing proficiencies capable of handling the challenges of students' futures in societies undergoing continuous changes with increasing muddiness and unpredictability. In the *60YC*, the learning journey is formed by the need to bridge the gaps between knowledge creation and understanding and then taking action to transform concepts into feasible realities. A design-learning approach is a way to step back and determine what the problem was in terms of dissatisfaction with the current approach so as to shape an empathetic, student-centric lens on what could be.

Human-Centric Learning

Design thinking is a human-centric process of learning that is making solutions (Kelley & Kelley, 2013). The process develops implicitly and intuitively drawing upon experiences with people participating in practice (Schön, 1984). Using this approach, educational institutions would engage prospective adult learners, employers, and others within a collaborative design process. This approach would also overcome the "problem of practice" (City, Elmore, Fiarman, & Teitel, 2009), convoluted conundrums with no simple solution.

Applying Design Thinking to Learning: Definition and Principles

The principles and methodology of design thinking (Simon, 1967; Rowe, 1991) can potentially guide and assist adult learners in assuming responsibility as well as shape and navigate their student journey no matter the destiny. Design thinking links learning principles (Ramsden, 1992) with more intuitive creative thinking to meet the needs of adult learners in ways that are technically feasible and viable in terms of sustainable outcomes. By applying design learning as a learning framework, it is considered "both a mechanism for learning . . . [and simultaneously] a learning process" (Dym, Agogino, Eris, Frey, & Leifer, 2005, p. 112). The methodical fusion of skills, knowledge, and practices of design learning exemplify "a systematic approach with rules based on evidence and a set of contextualized practices that are constantly adapting to circumstances. It is a skillful, creative activity that can be improved on with reflection and scholarship" (Beetham & Sharpe, 2007, p. 6). Courses would then be designed and implemented in a feasible and strategic way and evaluated by how they function in practice (Kelley & Littman, 2001). The value of design learning takes many forms including personal and online learning as well as the practice of measuring its outcomes (Dede, 2019).

Design Learning in Practice

Although action and experiential learning are not novel pedagogical methods, what is new is inviting students to play an active role, and hence to have a more collaborative relationship, with curriculum designers facilitating both a generation of knowledge and understanding "that lead to the acquisition of both disciplinary knowledge, personal and interpersonal skills; and product, process and system building skills" (Crawley, Malmqvist, Ostlund, & Brodeur, 2014, p. 29).

Design learning is a practice that integrates a sequence of connected and it-erative steps and is used to approach, reframe, and solve ill-defined, real-world problems across a varied collection of situations. Participants engaged in design learning contribute and form knowledge and gain emotional intelligence by trial and error using their senses and actions to facilitate the outcomes. Design learning involves a transformation in the learners' qualities within the design learning process—it is genuine, engaged learning. Designing a curriculum with adult learners necessitates a democratic, active, and stratified instruction that facilitates learning. Choices are unpacked to ascertain underlying assumptions, values, and beliefs that are critical for all designers engaged in the process.

Design thinking embodies a suitable preliminary prototype for shaping learn-ing and teaching strategy. It is more important than ever to enrich the design and subsequent implementation and operation of a more comprehensive, empirically validated and practical learning strategy for adult learners. Further, it is about working collaboratively to enhance the lives and well-being of learners and, in so doing, to draw from as many different perspectives as possible that bear on the complex matters of today (Vianna, Vianna, Adler, Lucena, & Russo, 2012).

The outcome of this approach would be that courses designed and delivered would be a closer fit to the needs of what students are grappling with—upskilled strategies for their working and professional lives. At the same time, this ap-proach would employ students' real-life experiences to rejuvenate and align learning to potential career paths and life journeys. An approach such as this would help educational institutions encourage academics to think like designers; to retreat from passive teaching approaches; and to focus on active, experiential, and problem-based learning (Glen, Suciu, Baughn, & Anson, 2015).

Implications of Learning for the 60YC

Student transition into a *60YC* context is an important aspect of curriculum de-sign, linking content, delivery, and assessment with prospective students' previ-ous learning experiences and knowledge bases. The reason for this is that "design [acts] as the 'glue'—the bridge, facilitator, protector, explainer, valuer, modeller, orchestrator, and advocate of all thinking types" (Kelley & VanPatter, 2005).

To date, the implementation of design learning into adult learning is sluggish and partial, even though conventional pedagogy falls short of assisting students in meeting the challenges of the 21st century. Pedagogy is a term applied in re-lation to the teaching of children. To differentiate the differences in the learning assimilation of adults in contrast to children, the term *andragogy* suggests that adults learn differently and hence require distinct approaches to learning and teaching. Dede's chapter in this volume outlines the diverse frameworks for adult learning and education.

Adults integrate and orient their learning in present and future contexts, drawing from their past life experiences. Embracing these principles, design learning focuses on understanding adult learners and developing curriculum and services to address their genuine needs rather than those assumed by educators on their behalf.

Just like other industries, higher education institutions need to consider that addressing individual student demands is a central way to differentiate themselves from their competitors. While the *60YC* can be viewed in terms of age cohorts, that alone would be missing the point, as people's lives, and hence learning journeys, do not necessarily align to demographics.

To be successful, the *60YC* assumes that the student is the dominant unit of analysis, with action learning as the guiding principle. When education is directed at the individual, interactive relationships can be forged by the educational institution with each student. To establish a good relationship and student experience, every touchpoint between the educational institution and the individual is important. This includes the first contact, while the student is still at school, as well as at various connection points with the institution throughout the student's career and through social media. Moreover, since the attention is on the individual, students will feel they have a greater stake in their learning journey and will become more committed and accountable for their learning. In turn, they are more likely to provide feedback to the educational institution and post reviews about their experiences on social media.

60YC Strategic Student Relationship Management (SSRM)

In the past, educational institutions assumed student loyalty, as did the banking industry and every other commercial sector. It was expected that students would engage in further study, accept the increase in course fees and personal debt, become active and loyal alumni, and encourage their children to attend the same educational institution as they had. A significant component of the *60YC* is recognizing diverse categories of students and designing strategies for addressing their various needs. Examples of such strategies include improving relationships with students, ramping up efforts to reach out to potential new students, and discovering appropriate approaches for addressing unanticipated learning needs, for example, just-in-time instructional design. The *60YC* helps to re-focus and change mindsets about student value, not only targeting specific individuals but also pursuing as yet unknown prospective students through their networks, referrals, information, and experience-sharing using social media.

Communicating and building strong relationships with students is important and is valued by all stakeholders (Florea & Duica, 2017). Attending to both student value and SSRM means that educational institutions need to ramp up their student-centric focus rather than rely on supply-driven approaches as in the past. It also means that there is greater *co-optician* potentially among educational institutions, taking on a marketing strategy similar to those in commercial organizations. The processes and systems of educational institutions need to be shaped by a student-centric focus. Marketing plays a significant part in building connections with students so that the educational institution can stay relevant to them and, at the same time, remain responsible to its stakeholders.

Strategic and Tactical Value Metrics

The concept of student value is critical to SSRM not only for the economic welfare of the institution but also as a metric for adjusting its marketing reach, which, if conducted successfully, contributes to the former. Apart from its operative worth, student value can be employed to provide a measure of the total student experience as long as the educational institution has a single-source view of students across all communication avenues and the capability to disseminate student intelligence to all student-facing services within the educational institution. As a result, student information management is relevant for both the internal and external demand chain.

The purpose of SSRM is consequently to gain a sustainable, competitive advantage by optimizing value and fulfilment for the student and mining institutional value from the relationship. Understanding, as opposed to assuming, what students need, and, hence, their choices, is vital for educational institutions to meet students' needs. Understanding and assuming are two different things. Understanding is not only about mere facts or knowledge, but it also builds on knowledge to discern what is relevant or not in specific contexts (Ritchhart, 2015). Facts are artefacts of understanding; this encourages further exploration to see what lies beneath what is visible on the surface.

Engaging external stakeholders to participate in curriculum design allows educational institutions to harvest and harness information from the most suitable sources and can lead to developing new ideas that return value to students and subsequently to the institution. Educational institutions, like other organizations, are relying on superficial data analytics at the expense of really understanding what is going on when students make choices about their learning (Christensen, Hall, Dillon, & Duncan, 2016). It is important to understand why students do what they do. For example, data analytics and student attributes alone do little to clarify why students are studying online at 2 a.m. or why they choose to come to campus rather than complete a course online or a self-paced course. Design thinking leads to deep learning and understanding about the needs of adult learners; it is a powerful tool given its student-centric approach building on both cognitive and emotional attributes. Creating options for student choice is central to design learning; this makes the design process empathetic and has the capacity to engage diverse thinking and emotions in curriculum design.

Case Study

At the Sydney campus of the University of Newcastle, a proposal for a group of courses was co-developed. The aim was to provide continuing professional education for individuals and organizations involved in the development, design, and delivery of new urban/city design and planning approaches to meet the needs of a changing urban environment in metropolitan/non-metropolitan New South Wales. Planners, architects, urban designers, legal professionals, engineers, and policy makers in New South Wales and indeed across Australia are faced with changing dynamics in city building and city management arising from increasing urbanization forces, including population increase, population mobility, demographic changes, and cross-cultural pressures on communities of all sizes in the nation. These forces are particularly acute given the fast-moving urbanization process in the core cities and suburbs across New South Wales.

The issues are so dynamic that the professionals who are attending to them have little time to react to the new policies and procedures or to design appropriate instruments to meet the challenges they face. Many of these instruments are not keeping pace with changes impacting social life and the undercurrents of the economy and communities. To address this, for example, housing policies and housing affordability need to be mixed with urban planning tools and other instruments that have not been part of most core curricula in these academic programs. Moreover, the intermixing of disciplines to meet the challenges is not currently available, but it is essential to meet the tasks with which lawyers, planners, urban designers, and other civic officials are faced as attempts to introduce new forms of housing, light rails, subways, air, and ground transportation systems are occurring very quickly in both urban and metropolitan New South Wales. Therefore, it is essential to provide this new network of policy leaders and policy implementers with the latest knowledge that they need so that they can be successful in meeting the needs of diverse communities.

The idea for this series, called Urban Innovations, is to fashion a set of masterclass studio-learning opportunities for professionals from diverse disciplines and career stages to update them on the latest national and international information about the ways to address challenges as easily and effectively as possible.

Urban Innovations will knit together a dynamic series of contemporary issues anchored in the latest scholarship and buttressed with field practice so that participants learn from current problems and share their wisdom. A set of core themes will be the prism through which Urban Innovation strategies and methods will be examined. In addition, the instructors will include international and national experts and practitioners to provide the most recent information that participants can immediately apply in their own contexts. Participants will use their learnings as a steppingstone in their own career development within a portfolio of professional short courses. A certificate of completion for the year-long series is evidence of learning and an important part of the continuing-professional-development credential portfolio.

The Benefits of the Student Value Management Approach

A successful, data-based SSRM system, with student value as its driving metric, empowers an educational institution to gain strategic advantages by integrating and consolidating student information: With relevant student information and participants' histories, the student services remain consistent across contact and service channels.

The entire educational institution needs to release communication in a timely and relevant manner with students, matching their needs with the most appropriate courses. This tactic is achieved by ensuring a single source of "truth" and ensuring that information is integrated across all communication channels.

Similar to precision medicine, the potential of utilizing a wide array of personal data to tailor services is enormous (Hood & Flores, 2012). If possible, personalization needs to span both the services and courses offered to each student to satisfy their special expectations. Similarly, managing student cases ensures that appropriate responses occur at the earliest time. Further, generating and managing campaigns require sufficient flexibility to adapt to changes in student information or behavior. Responding to student leads, referrals, and inquiries would be handled more effectively. Hence, managing all institutional processes in a distributed service model by introducing a central point of control ensures all institutional processes are implemented and performed with an agile response.

The development of new technological advances and the unprecedented reach of social media is characterized by the engagement of students—active and prospective—through the integration of the Web 2.0 and social media as well as by the use of data-driven insights to optimize the overall student experience. Educational institutions need to encourage active student participation online while also using software applications to track real-time social data. This information enables educational institutions to offer relevant content and personalized messages to specific students as well as to improve the student experience at each touch-point along their journey. Additionally, the combination of data across different social media platforms allows educational institutions to determine student value not only based on increasing enrollments but also based on their online behavior in terms of referrals, knowledge dispersion, and the influence of other members of the social media community.

In summary, SSRM is the strategic process of targeting the students that an educational institution can most beneficially support and shaping interactions between themselves and prospective students. The ultimate goal is to optimize the current and future value of students by balancing both parties' interests judiciously. With SSRM, an educational institution can design an environment and flexible support system to respond readily, including course innovation, student expectations, the convergence of traditional educational markets, the emergence of new technologies, privacy issues, and new student communication channels. There is still a major issue in SSRM of people not understanding its significance. For example, institutions must listen to and understand the feedback from students and, in turn, communicate with them in a way most likely to increase their satisfaction and achieve repeat enrollments and referrals.

The Demand for a *60YC*

The major factors that influence strategic SSRM and have significant consequences for all learners and educational institutions confronting enormous changes are as follows.

Trends Influencing SSRM

Just as the *60YC* is a global approach to learning for adults, all industries have implemented a global strategy to their businesses. In the education sector, for example, a student can enroll in a US-based university course online while residing in a different country. Students today are choosing the best courses from those offered worldwide that address their needs now. Educational institutions are no longer offering one-size-fits-all to a limited student base in their local area. They are delivering courses to an increasingly diverse and fragmented population of potential learners in flexible ways. The *60YC* is a way for educational institutions to anticipate and move this process forward, and, in so doing, satisfy unmet demand.

Adult learners wish to access to learning just-in-time, that is, learning that can be applied to their circumstances and that therefore must be modularized and relevant. This leads to the notion of micro-learning: facilitating adult learners to see learning as routine and track their progress as they proceed through their learning journey. Technological developments mean institutions also can offer genuine value to students through customized course and service propositions. For example, the University of Newcastle, Australia, as well as other universities, is investigating and investing in block-chain applications to track, register, certify, and enhance the utilization of acquired learning assets. Verifying learning is important for students, employers, and educational institutions. Block chain provides proof of completion and acquisition of learning that can be stored permanently and shared in a tamper-proof ledger by individual students.

To provide an analogy, the *60YC* is following a strategy increasingly used in the health sector: personalized medicine tailored to the patient's medical needs at the specific time that suits them. Personalized medicine is well established as being a significant part of the solution for providing better healthcare outcomes, and so it is too for the *60YC*.

However, in both domains there are multiple challenges to wide-scale implementation by providers and implications for education and healthcare stakeholders alike. In order for personalized learning to have its anticipated value, the focus of the learning needs must be human-centric and, as far as possible, relevant to each individual instead of abiding by generalities. Additionally, it is necessary that innovative models are developed. The problem is that providers and stakeholders have different motivations, largely driven by economic decisions. Nevertheless, empowering adult learners will also be a significant factor, as well as diversification and time scarcity, to increase the pursuit of more personalized courses and delivery methods. Lambert and Leitner's chapter in this volume discusses this personalization as a principle for designing educational services. Only then will a greater number of institutions respond accordingly. As can be seen from above, the learner's location is irrelevant and access to markets is no longer restricted, so demands for partnering with other educational providers is becoming not only a necessity for some institutions but also more readily achievable through integrating students and partners.

One of the main impediments to implementing a *60YC* is the lack of integration between the learning and digital strategies, mainly as one is controlled by academic staff and the other is not. Many academics have not met with their digital team and vice versa. Digital is very easy to involve students with directly, as technology makes real-time connectively possible, which allows building a strong relationship without a physical presence.

Through social media, apps, and real time data, word-of-mouth is now done via social media (Chaffey, 2016). Educational institutions utilize this as a way of learning about what students want and using this to design new courses, programs, delivery methods, communication strategies, as well as outcome metrics. Also, social media allows instantaneous responses. For example, Facebook has 1.72 billion active students per month that spend about 50 minutes on the website each day, often browsing educational, institution-run Facebook pages (Stewart, 2016). Institutions use social media designed by students to their advantage.

The shift from a one-sided, unilateral conversation between the educational institution and the student to a multilateral conversation between several students and the educational institution increases the complexity of the marketing function even further. Educational institutions need to listen carefully and monitor student reviews and feedback provided online. To engage students, educational institutions also have to be open to the new student role as an interactive part in the student relationship with the educational institution and to be willing to give up some of their control. Furthermore, they have to find new ways to interact with the student. Otherwise, they will take a back seat and effectively be restricted to advertising and media planning. Also, educational institutions need to adjust their marketing strategies to overcome the increased ad-skepticism and ad-avoidance of students by contacting the student through multiple channels and being more transparent and honest.

Given all these changes, the *60YC* scenario facilitates ways of identifying student preferences, value provision, and course and service customization. Course-centric strategies cannot address these advanced requirements, but student-centric strategies do. In exactly this environment, SSRM, if executed correctly, represents an impressive competitive means to satisfy new demands. Educational institutions need a management approach that realizes increasing student heterogeneity, puts available data to good use, and uses student engagement as a key objective function (i.e., strategic student value management).

There are a number of trends influencing SSRM augmenting the power of students' engagement. For example, the changing demography, including an ageing and ethnically diverse population, leads to greater student diversity. Employment trends demonstrate people are changing careers due to economic development and working differently—some longer due to good health, choice, or financial necessity—as well as changing work patterns with greater workplace flexibility. There is a rise in convenience and self-service awareness, increasing the demand for experience and authenticity.

Implications of the *60YC* SSRM for Course Design

Applying a strategic design to courses draws in collective values and interests; details actions by going step-by-step after implementing orientation from

Figure 4.1 Human-centered co-creation (based on Burkhardt, 2009)

scenarios; and centers on learning embedded in context rather than in a set of isolated procedures (Meroni, 2008). This approach provides a way for being distinctive while addressing student needs with a lower impact on the environment than the educational model (Mont, 2002). Some of the components which strategic design includes are depicted in Figure 4.1.

The *60YC* framework provides the impetus to co-design an innovation-inspired curriculum framework that affords adult learners the opportunity to engage in various types of learning across diverse environments that makes allowances for time, distance, and cost. It is a democratic, practical, and empowering process grounded in action-learning through interactive inquiry and focused on how to learn within the perpetual, co-creative learning processes of learning partnerships at both the institution and local levels.

A student-centric co-design is a good way for thinking, constructing, and implementing the *60YC*. The inclusion of various stakeholders and their active participation in this process is fundamental for transforming ideas into acceptable and feasible solutions. Considering not only the institution's demands and interests but also the importance of the student-centric approach implies a process of systemic change, both in the policy sense as well as in the relationships among the various stakeholders. In that sense, the concept of the *60YC* means expanding the scope of design and, for that reason, increasing the possibilities for diverse stakeholder interventions, revealing a greater focus on results and impact for learning and addressing learners' needs throughout their adult lives. The co-design process is thus transformed, requiring not only the creative development of ideas but also a high level of empathy derived from a student-centric focus ensuring that innovations are actionable and scalable.

References

Beetham, H., & Sharpe, R. (2007). *Rethinking pedagogy for a digital age: Designing and delivering e-learning.* London, England: Routledge.

Burkhardt, H. (2009). On strategic design. *Educational Designer, 1*(2), 1–49.

Chaffey, D. (2016). Global social media research summary 2016 [Web log post]. Smart Insights. Retrieved from https://cdn.ymaws.com/www.productstewardship.us/resource/resmgr/Phone_Books/Global_Social_Media_Statisti.pdf

Christensen, C. M., Hall, T., Dillon, K., & Duncan, D. S. (2016). *Competing against luck: The story of innovation and customer choice.* New York, NY: Harper Business.

City, E. A., Elmore, R. F., Fiarman, S. E., & Teitel, L. (2009). *Instructional rounds in education.* Cambridge, MA: Harvard Education Press.

Crawley, E., Malmqvist, J., Ostlund, S., & Brodeur, D. (2014). *Rethinking engineering education* (2nd ed.). New York, NY: Springer.

Dede, C. (2019). Improving efficiency and effectiveness through learning engineering. In C. Dede, J. Richards, & B. Saxberg (Eds.), *Learning engineering for online education: Theoretical contexts and design-based examples* (pp. 1–14). New York, NY: Routledge.

Dym, C. L., Agogino, A., Eris, O., Frey, D., & Leifer, L. (2005). Engineering design thinking, teaching, and learning. *Journal of Engineering Education, 94*, 103–120. doi:10.1002/j.2168-9830.2005.tb00832.x:103-120

Faulk, B. D., & Wang, Z. (2013). Undergraduates with employer-sponsored aid: Comparing. *Journal of Student Financial Aid, 43*(3), 1–17.

Florea, N. V., & Duica, A. (2017). Improving communication and relationship with customers using models to measure their value. *Valahian Journal of Economic Studies, 8*(22), 47–56. doi:10.1515/vjes-2017-0006

Glen, R., Suciu, C., Baughn, C. C., & Anson, R. (2015). Teaching design thinking in business schools. *The International Journal of Management Education, 13*(2), 182–192. doi:10.1016/j.ijme.2015.05.001

Hood, L. & Flores, M. (2012). A personal view on systems medicine and the emergence of proactive P4 medicine: Predictive, preventive, personalized and participatory. *New Biotechnology, 29*(6), 613–624. doi:10.1016/j.nbt.2012.03.004

Kelley, T., & Kelley, D. (2013). *Creative confidence: Unleashing the creative potential within us all.* New York, NY: Crown Business.

Kelley, T., & Littman, J. (2001). *The art of innovation: Lessons in creativity from IDEO, America's leading design firm.* New York, NY: Doubleday.

Kelley, D., & VanPatter, G. K. (2005). Design as glue: Understanding the Stanford D. School. *NextD Journal Conversation, 21*, 1–9.

McDonald, K. S., & Hite, L. M. (2008). The next generation of career success: Implications for HRD. *Advances in Developing Human Resources, 10*(1), 86–103. doi:10.1177/1523422307310116

Meroni, A. (2008). Strategic design: Where are we now? Reflection around the foundations of a recent discipline. *Strategic Design Research Journal, 1*(1), 31–38.

Mont, O. K. (2002). Clarifying the concept of product-service system. *Journal of Cleaner Production, 10*(3), 237–245. doi:10.1016/S0959-6526(01)00039-7

Ramsden, P. (1992). *Learning to teach in higher education.* London, England: Routledge.

Ritchhart, R. (2015). *Creating cultures of thinking: The 8 forces we must master to truly transform our schools.* New York, NY: Wiley.

Rowe, P. (1991). *Design thinking.* Cambridge, MA: MIT Press.

Scheer, A., Noweski, C., & Meinel, C. (2012). Transforming constructivist learning into action: Design thinking in education. *Design and Technology Education: An International Journal, 17*(3), 1360–1431.

Schön, D. A. (1984). *The reflective practitioner: How professionals think in action.* New York, NY: Basic Books.

Schwartz, R., & Hoffman, N. (2015, Summer). Pathways to upward mobility. *National Affairs, 31.* Retrieved from https://www.nationalaffairs.com/publications/detail/pathways-to-upward-mobility

Simon, H. A. (1967). The business school a problem in organizational design. *Journal of Management Studies, 4*(1), 1–16.

Stewart, J. B. (2016, May 5). Facebook has 50 minutes of your time each day. It wants more. *The New York Times*. Retrieved from https://www.nytimes.com/2016/05/06/business/facebook-bends-the-rules-of-audience-engagement-to-its-advantage.html

Vianna, M., Vianna, Y., Adler, I., Lucena, B., & Russo, B. (2012). *Design thinking: Business innovation*. Rio de Janeiro, Brazil: MVJ Press.

5

Creating the Next in Higher Education at Georgia Tech

STEPHEN W. HARMON AND NELSON C. BAKER

Introduction

In 2015, the Georgia Institute of Technology (Georgia Tech) undertook a multi-year effort to identify factors driving change in higher education with an eye to creating a vision of what higher education may be like in 2040. Independent of work at other institutions surrounding the 60-Year Curriculum (*60YC*), we undertook a two-year process, involving over 50 stakeholders, to identify factors driving change in education and to craft a response to this change. This response was published in 2018 as the report of the Commission on Creating the Next in Education and is titled "Deliberate Innovation, Lifetime Education" (Georgia Institute of Technology, 2018). Perhaps not surprisingly, many of the ideas in the report are congruent with those of other institutions working on the *60YC*. Or, if it is surprising, it is also a good sign that several independent thought leaders arrived at similar conclusions. Either we are all on the right track or we at least share the same delusions. This chapter details the work at Georgia Tech in creating our notion of the *60YC*, discusses the efforts we currently have underway to realize the vision of our commission, and explores possible alternative futures for higher education in general. To be fair, this chapter focuses more on the teaching mission of higher education. We know that many universities have other missions as well, such as the creation of new knowledge, but it is the mission of instruction and human learning as applied into action that drives the premise for this chapter and the ties to a lifetime curriculum.

The OMS CS

While Georgia Tech has always been invested in innovation, in some ways our current work on looking at the future of higher education gained a new focus with the success of the Online Master of Science in Computer Science (OMS CS). In 2014, a group of thought leaders at the institute partnered with key stakeholders at other academic institutions and in industry to address the growing shortage of skilled computer scientists. Seeing obvious bottlenecks in the way universities currently train computer scientists, this group asked whether there was some way to take advantage of the affordances of new and emerging technologies to remove those bottlenecks and offer high-quality education for a low price to a large number of people. The recent emergence of massive online open courses

(MOOCs) seemed a promising avenue to explore. Although Georgia Tech had been doing various forms of distance learning for over 40 years, it was possible to greatly expand our outreach and impact.

Success of the OMS CS

Today, the success of the OMS CS has been widely acknowledged. With over 9,000 students in the program and nearly 2,000 graduates to date, the program is currently producing about 10% of the Master of Science in Computer Science degrees in the United States. The program uses the same learning outcomes, and assessments of these outcomes, as the residential program at Georgia Tech. Students in the OMS CS consistently perform just as well as the students in the on-campus program. The OMS CS has been financially self-sustaining for a number of years. It has led to the creation of other Georgia Tech OMS degrees using the same model—one in analytics and one in cyber security. Both of these more recent degree programs are on track to be as successful as the OMS CS.

We currently have over 12,000 students in these three online degree programs. Far from being the case that having an online program diminishes the reputation of our on-campus programs, we have found the reverse to be true. While the computer science programs at Georgia Tech have enjoyed a strong reputation for some time—with all CS programs being ranked in the top ten in the United States—the OMS CS has spread this reputation to a much broader and more global audience. The pool of applicants continues to increase, and the quality of these applicants has not decreased. We are still unsure what the ceiling might be for these kinds of programs.

Building from existing curricula in our residential Master of Science in Computer Science, Analytics, and Cybersecurity programs, the OMS programs benefit from an extensive instructional design and development process before they are launched. Two critical ideas informed our approach as we created these programs. First, from the outset it was our contention that you could rarely, if ever, simply "put" an existing course online. Instead, courses must be intentionally designed for the online environment. One of the key differences between face-to-face instruction and online learning, especially asynchronous online learning, is that in face-to-face settings instructors can get immediate feedback from the students and adjust on the fly if they see that their lesson is not working. This capability means that although it is always preferable for instructors to enter their classrooms highly prepared, experienced and nimble instructors could get away with less preparation and could adjust their lessons as they gave them. This capacity for immediate adjustment does not exist in asynchronous online classes. Students and instructors are separated not only by distance but also by time. Instructors cannot look across the classroom and get a feel for students' comprehension just by looking at the expressions on their faces. Instructors cannot adjust on the fly. All of this means that the online lessons must be created from the beginning to be robust and highly effective. Any experimentation with formats or pedagogies must be completed long before the lesson goes live. Thus, the online lessons are heavily produced, modularized each with their own learning outcomes, and can take weeks or even months to develop.

The second critical idea was scale. Our desire for the master's degrees to be low cost could only be achieved if we found a way to offer the program to a large number of students. Through much careful analysis and the development of innovative business models, we determined that we could offer the entire OMS CS degree for under $7,000 if we were able to enroll at least 3,000 students. A discussion of how we developed these business models is beyond the scope of this chapter, but the fact that we were about to launch a single degree program with at least 3,000 students is very pertinent. Pedagogies and instructional techniques that work fine with a class of 15 or 20 students may not work at all when you have 500 or 1,000 students in a class. For one thing, just consider how difficult it would be to evaluate and provide meaningful and timely feedback (what some people call grading) for 1,000 coding projects. If each one averaged roughly 300 lines of code, you now have 300,000 lines of code to read through. And that is just for one assignment in a 15-week course. Just to manage the workload, we needed to rethink how most of our faculty taught. In the end, we created a structure of TAs and graders, and we specifically crafted assignments that allowed us to guide student learning at scale. We also broke our lessons down into meaningful and digestible chunks. Each learning objective is supported by a video that runs from five-to-seven minutes, followed by an activity that gives the students practice and feedback. TAs triage students learning difficulties, and faculty are free to analyze class trends and address broader issues. Since the courses are developed entirely before the semester begins, the OMS programs effectively take on a flipped classroom approach, where instructors are able to spend their time scaffolding student learning rather than merely delivering content.

Unintended Outcomes

There were several unintended outcomes from the success of the OMS programs. The first was a realization that other frameworks than the traditional model for a high-quality higher education experience were possible. Although we certainly were aware that these frameworks could be possible, there is always a certain timidity that inhibits one from thinking too boldly. The success of the OMS CS in a way gave us our freedom to consider change far more grandly then we had prior. It also brought along faculty and administration who might otherwise have been less interested, or even resistant, to the idea of drastic change in our higher education models. Virtually everyone who has been involved in the OMS programs has come away enthusiastic about them. They have had a significant impact not only on the number of students that we reach but also on how we teach our traditional residential students. Almost all faculty who have been through the instructional design process to create a course for the OMS programs have gone on to take those same techniques and apply them to their own residential programs. This body of faculty and administrators who experienced this success first-hand led us to realize that we now had on campus a cadre of individuals who were not only open to the new ideas but also were enthusiastic about the idea of reshaping higher education.

Along with this realization was another that had always lurked in the back of our minds but now began to come to the fore. Not only are other frameworks for higher education possible, it seems increasingly obvious that other frameworks are also necessary. The rapid pace of technological advancement, coupled with an increasing human lifespan, a more global interconnectivity, rapidly shifting demands for skilled workforce development, and ever-evolving patterns and means of social interaction, all combine to put increasing pressure on models of higher education that have gone largely unchanged for hundreds of years. As Chris Dede notes in Chapter 1, although higher education institutions have experimented profusely with emerging communications technologies and media over the years, they have tended to use the new tools in ways that essentially propagate poor pedagogy. They have been slow, and often unwilling, to adopt research-based, effective pedagogies and andragogies.

Additionally, public perception of higher education has been becoming more negative, particularly among Republicans. A report published by the Pew Research Center (2017) found that, although a small overall majority (55%) still had a positive perception of higher education, a majority of Republicans (58%) felt that higher education had a negative impact on the country. This was up from 45% a year earlier. Whatever the reasons for this shift in public perception, and there are undoubtedly many, the sector ignores it at its own peril. It seemed clear to us that the time was ripe for a broad-scale, long-term reimagining of the future of higher education.

The Commission on Creating the Next in Education

In 2015, Rafael Bras, Georgia Tech's Provost, convened a group of 50 to 60 stakeholders (comprising faculty; staff; students; administration; and external stakeholders including alumni, employers, and policymakers) and charged them with the mission to "take a look at the Institute's current educational principles and methodologies, benchmark best practices in higher education, and make recommendations about how the Georgia Tech of the future will serve new and different generations of learners" (Georgia Institute of Technology, 2018, p. 2).

Called the Commission on Creating the Next in Education (CNE), the group embarked on a one-and-a-half-year process of discovery, which led to a report entitled "Discovering the Drivers of Change in Higher Education" (Georgia Institute of Technology, n.d.). This report detailed five areas that may have the greatest impact on higher education going forward. These are: (1) demographic trends and shifts, (2) socioeconomic forces, (3) the changing nature of students and their learning needs, (4) advances in the science of learning and teaching that can be anticipated, and (5) how an institution organizes for deliberate evolution and development to meet the need for continuing innovation in higher education.

Factors Driving Change in Higher Education

The first phase of the Commission on Creating the Next in Education involved the gathering of data, context, and the current state of higher education. The Commission asked, "What is driving changes in higher education and what trends might continue to change higher education?" There were several factors on which the team focused.

DEMOGRAPHIC CHANGES

The group found from various local, state, and federal databases that there is a decline in the number of 18-year-old individuals who have historically made up many universities' student bodies. Other studies show that the average age of a college student has continually risen over the last two decades; therefore, many individuals are going to work or to community or local colleges rather than to four-year institutions. Certainly, there has been movement of people within the United States from the Northeast and Midwest to the Sunbelt states and West Coast, changing general population sizes and makeup. But so too are gender, ethnicity, age, and socio-economic distribution changes taking place. Each of these trends impacts those whom higher education needs to serve and perhaps the manner in which they seek to be served.

LEARNER NEEDS

As new knowledge is being created, so are new corporate organizations. These new entities, and even the existing corporate and government organizations, call for new skills and abilities across the workforce. Understanding the core competencies of these new roles should impact existing and future curricula and formal, as well as informal, learning activities. Due to the changes in demographics and new competencies, learners today and tomorrow have different mindsets. What is important to them may not be what was important before. Further, the motivations of the learners may be different than before—more job focused, perhaps even short-term focused on specific outcomes rather than on a more general education. How can higher education meet these demands yet provide the pathways to the future? Even with the creation of pathways, returning for more education is not a thought that many students seeking their first degree entertain, yet they need to start to realize the importance of this for the world in which they are entering.

NEW SCIENCE OF LEARNING AND ASSOCIATED PEDAGOGIES

With study and technology have come new insights on how humans learn and how they might best learn. Further, understanding how learning might differ from individual to individual is becoming possible. Various cognitive learning approaches are emerging, and we are making progress in developing the types of approaches that might be needed across the demographic changes that are taking place. Technologies such as artificial intelligence and virtual and augmented reality, coupled with data analytics, are driving new ways of meeting learning challenges and creating new pedagogies to improve learning. Most important, we believe, is that the confluence of research and technology on human cognition must be met with a culture shift toward education innovation. The ability for faculty to learn about new pedagogy and new technologies is going to be critical for universities, enabling them to succeed and allowing their learners to thrive in the future.

SOCIO-ECONOMIC FORCES

Increasing tuition and stakeholder concern have certainly been a main part of national dialogue. Despite many universities receiving less funding from the public sector, and therefore making up for that loss in tuition increases, the value of higher education, both perceived and perhaps real, is questioned daily. The political and societal needs for jobs are real. The ability to create and drive economic development for social well-being puts new pressures on higher education, and the creation of workforces to meet the needs addressed earlier further exacerbate these demands.

ORGANIZATIONAL STRUCTURES

How an institution of higher education organizes itself to meet the needs arising from these demographic changes will be a topic of further study likely for many years to come. For example, within many institutions adult education exists in separate and often independent units from the academic disciplines, while undergraduate education resides within those disciplines. This separation can have the effect of signaling to faculty that adult education is not a part of their responsibilities. Faculty focus on what they should teach the 18-year-olds, but rarely ask themselves what they should be doing for the 50-year-old learners. Or, consider the academic bureaucracies that often hinder the adoption of new curricula and teaching methods. With exponential growth in scientific knowledge, not only do new developments within fields occur more rapidly than curriculum committees can adjust, but entirely new fields also develop just as rapidly. Yet the old adage about academic change too often holds true: "It is easier to change the course of history than it is to change a history course." To meet these and similar needs, Georgia Tech believes that an institution must be deliberate in its intent and focused on its direction with academic planning. It must then innovate to change itself to meet these new demands.

POLICY IMPLICATIONS

From federal to state to local policy, a wide variety of external regulations impact higher education institutions. For example, from the limitations on and interpretations of what types of education credentials financial aid applies, to where and who can receive such aid, dozens of policy implications affect virtually every aspect of higher education. These implications are now global in scope with the advent of the General Data Protection Regulation (GDPR), export controls, tax structures, and other regulations. The direct costs, as well as the opportunity costs, of such regulation are not insignificant to higher education.

Ideation Process

Following the publication of the discovery report, the CNE reorganized itself to focus on responding to the challenges it identified. How could universities best position themselves to thrive in the future? From the outset, we had been focused on avoiding incrementalism. We instead wanted to think more boldly. To help accomplish this, we set our end point at the year 2040. We felt that looking ahead three-to-five years, as most strategic plans do, would probably push us toward smaller and less impactful types of outcomes. We acknowledge that it is difficult to predict what universities, or the country, will be like 20 years hence, but rather than worrying about being exact in prediction and planned actions, we are focused on being more directionally correct. We look at our process more as identifying options for the future rather than selecting and achieving a specific future. We may not get it exactly right, but we do feel that we can position ourselves to take advantage of whatever circumstances may prevail at that time with a focus on ideas we believe to be common and needed in a future state.

We followed a design-driven process to guide our work from this point. In addition to large-scale ideation processes that we conducted internally, we also co-sponsored two global challenge efforts with the Department of Education. From these, we got hundreds of participants from around the globe to give us their best ideas on reimagining higher education. We took great inspiration from some of these ideas and invited the winners of the challenges to join us on campus and participate in our effort.

We also held a week-long, campus-wide student engagement effort. As the culmination of this, we set up a display in a heavily trafficked area and asked the students to write down where they saw themselves and the university in the year 2040. Interestingly, many of the students were drawn in by the Polaroid camera we had out, and we encouraged the students to take a picture of themselves and put it next to their comments. Seeing this throwback technology was a first for many of them. The students gave us quite a few good ideas to pursue. Although it did not make it into our final report, one common theme that ran through the students' responses was that whatever they were doing, they would be doing it on the planet Mars.

From the ideation process, three working groups emerged dealing with near-, mid-, and far-term outcomes. Although our focus had been on the long-term, in our process we developed many good ideas that were instead short-term. Eventually, we formed separate groups to take advantage of these short-term opportunities. We consider the mid-term ideas as steppingstones that would lead us to the far-term outcomes. We morphed these into broader sections for a unified final report.

As we analyzed the dozens of possible directions we could take and the hundreds of project ideas we generated, it began to become clear that there were two overarching themes that seemed to predominate. These were "deliberate innovation" and "lifetime education."

Deliberate Innovation

We had an institutional need for cultural shifts to drive purposeful, non-incremental innovation. As mentioned above, it was important for us to take the long view and avoid a regression to the mean of small, easy-to-predict changes. Fortunately, we had access to the Georgia Tech Center for Deliberate Innovation (CDI, formerly known as Flashpoint), a startup incubator/business accelerator that could help us make these cultural shifts. Building on the work of Kegan and Lahey (2016) on deliberately developmental organizations, CDI encouraged us to consider three different types of innovation and tried to shift our thinking to focus more on the third one.

These three types of innovation are informative innovation, transformative innovation, and formative innovation. "Informative innovation" is the most common form of innovation and is what tends to happen naturally in most organizations. It informs, but does not change, your normal business. It is an incremental process of taking what you already do and adding to it. For example, if students can currently take two electives in a degree program, allowing them to take three electives would be informative innovation. This form of innovation can occasionally have real benefits, but perhaps just as often can lead to bloated, confusing, and siloed academic structures and programs.

"Transformative innovation" is what most institutions aspire to. This form of innovation actually changes your normal course of business. It transforms what you are already doing into something different. Our online master's of science programs are an example of transformative innovation. We were already offering MS degrees in computer science, but we changed the way we offered them by putting them online and at scale with a new business model. This had the effect of transforming not only that degree program but also the institution itself, as we then had to change the way we handled admissions, student services, and graduation, among a host of other things, to accommodate the program's success. Transformative innovation carries more risk than informative innovation but can also lead to bigger rewards.

But our primary goal in our deliberate innovation process focused on the third type of innovation, "formative innovation." Unlike informative and transformative innovation, formative innovation does not start from a position of seeking to add to or change what you are doing already. Instead it starts by looking at what you are *not* doing currently. It focuses on the formation of new activities, processes, or structures. It looks for adjacencies and synergies with an organization's goals and seeks to move the organization into heretofore unexplored territories. An example from the business world might be Xerox's move from a copier company to a document company. Rather than simply incrementally making better and faster copiers, Xerox realized that the thing being copied was the core of their business, not the copy machine. This shift in focus reinvented the company and allowed them to create entirely new lines of products and services. In higher education, we might argue that informal learning is an area ripe for formative innovation. In higher education, we tend to focus on formal learning environments and structures (e.g., classrooms and credit hours), but as Dede points out in Chapter 1, social media sites such as YouTube are now a more common way for adults to learn, with 73% of adults in the US using the platform (Pew Research Center, 2019). Formative innovation requires us to examine what business we are truly in. Is it just the university business? Is it education? Training? Workforce development? Or social transformation? This is not an easy question to answer, but it is the question with the greatest potential for positive change.

Lifetime Education

A number of factors drive Georgia Tech's view of lifetime education, some internally focused, but most external to all universities.

RATE OF KNOWLEDGE CREATION

From the advent of Moore's Law, technology is increasingly changing the work that we do. Whether through new processes, new tools, or new knowledge, individuals and employers alike are in a constant struggle to be both efficient and relevant to the needs of their products and customers. Increasingly, universities are seeking to put more into the traditional, four-year curriculum than time allows. This approach is at its breaking point for many disciplines. Further education beyond the traditional length of degree programs is often not practical, and in some cases this turns potential students of these fields away from the discipline.

INDUSTRY NEED

As technology is created and/or matures and new knowledge is created, new industries and business models are invented. These activities keep employers either seeking new talent or finding ways to upskill existing workforces. While industry can find new talent from graduates of higher education, the rate of new capabilities within the workforce drives demand faster than the supply of new graduates. (See Chapter 3 by Michel Servoz in this volume for more discussion of this topic.)

LONGER LIFESPAN

With modern health care and techniques providing better quality of living, people are living longer. As mortality rates decrease, people have to work longer in order to have their retirement funds last post-employment. This trend is amplifying the need for lifetime education as the constant need for new knowledge and skills has an even longer impact over one's career.

INDIVIDUAL DESIRES TO CHANGE JOBS/CAREERS

In recent years, individual preference has created the desire to change jobs and/or careers more frequently. The Department of Labor estimates now that the average individual will work 11–14 jobs over their working years and have 3–5 careers

(Bureau of Labor Statistics, 2019). These shifts cause individuals to need to obtain new knowledge so that they can either seek the transition or be capable of the new position after transitioning. Thus, a continual need exists for upskilling and re-skilling across the workforce.

EDUCATIONAL DEBT

Within our universities, students are taking on more debt to finish their education, causing changes in their lifestyle and career choices (among other impacts). In response, students are increasingly choosing to seek education in manageable chunks so that they can pay for the education and fit it into their already busy lives. The typical comments at graduation ceremonies that describe commencement being the "beginning" are taking on new importance as individuals cannot afford their schooling all at once.

All of these factors informed the CNE as we initiated the Georgia Tech commitment to lifetime education. We believe that higher education must be providing more than traditional degrees to traditional students. At the center of our thinking is what we call the "iron triangle" of quality, accessibility, and affordability in higher education. Our OMS degrees were based on this thinking. There was some fear that when we created the affordable degrees at scale, we would cannibalize our existing residential programs. That turned out not to be the case. Goodman, Melkers, and Pallais (2018) found that the OMS CS program satisfied otherwise unmet demand. Students who enrolled in the program would not have enrolled anywhere else if the program had not existed. We must take the results of our research and more broadly shape them into educational products. These endeavors will keep an individual informed about new knowledge but will more generally impact their employers and the economies in which they work and live.

Five Major Initiative Areas

In order to support the shift to a culture of deliberate innovation focused on lifetime education, we decided to focus on five emerging themes from among the hundreds of possible projects we could undertake. These are: (1) whole person education, (2) advising for a new era, (3) new products and services, (4) AI and personalization, and (5) distributed world-wide presence.

Whole Person Education

Merely having a depth of expertise in a particular field is even now not sufficient for the success for our graduates and almost certainly will not be sufficient in the future. Seen elsewhere in the concept of a t-shaped learner, we recognize that we need a renewed focus on the soft skills that supplement and enhance the strong, technical skills our students have currently. A t-shaped learner is someone who has a depth of technical expertise in a discipline but also has a broad base of other skills that allows them to use and communicate their technical knowledge in a wide variety of settings (Brown, 2005). These skills include such things as communicating, providing leadership, team-building, problem-finding, and demonstrating emotional intelligence. Efforts in this initiative area include the expansion of experiential learning, globalization at home, and professional development for graduate students. Additionally, we call for a reanalysis of the overall curriculum to focus on whole-person development. We have begun this process by attempting to coordinate existing work and centers at the institute in order to develop a systemic approach to whole-person education. Some of these efforts include The Atlanta Global Studies Center (https://atlantaglobalstudies.gatech.edu/), Georgia Tech's Serve, Learn, Sustain initiative (https://serve-learn-sustain.gatech.edu/), and Create-X (https://create-x.gatech.edu/), a program to build entrepreneurial skills in students by helping them create and launch their own startups.

Advising for a New Era

As we look to engage with our learners for life, we realize that new models for advising must also emerge. Simply deciding what courses an undergraduate should take each semester is not sufficient. Having access to some version of a lifetime coach seems advantageous. Efforts in this initiative area include prescriptive advising, intrusive advising, developmental advising, and predictive advising. Prescriptive advising is what most institutions do today. It involves helping students find and sign up for the right courses to meet the requirements of their degree programs. Developmental advising is focused on personal development. It helps students choose majors and careers through discovering their passions and what gives purpose to their lives. Intrusive advising uses learning analytics data to determine when students might be struggling in their studies and allows for interventions to help them succeed. Predictive advising is a new form of advising we are developing. Because we are a research-intensive university, our faculty often have a unique glimpse into the future of what may be coming in society and work. Predictive advising seeks to give students a chance to prepare for future careers in fields that may not yet exist. For example, at this point it seems likely that quantum computing will bring a major shift in computing and all the many sub-disciplines it comprises. We can use predictive advising to begin to prepare students now to work in a quantum computing world even though most quantum computing efforts are still experimental. Just as with buying future options on the stock market, there is some risk that the future bet will not pay out if the projected need does not materialize. But we believe we can manage that risk while at the same time providing potentially huge benefits for our students.

We also aim to address personalized advising for a lifetime through a variety of technology-enhanced efforts, collective data gathering, and data mining, enabling innovative options such as creating a personal board of directors for each learner. Rather than having a single advisor, each student will have a team of advisors, each specializing in certain aspects of advising, much like a corporation has a board of directors. The prescriptive advisor will help students manage the day-to-day requirements of the institute and degree programs. This advisor may well be an AI agent. The developmental advisors may include both traditional career counselors but also alumni who have career and life trajectories that are similar to where the student started and wants to end up. The intrusive advisors will include student-success coaches and study-skills experts. The predictive advisors will include faculty who are expert in the student's discipline and can make sure that the students are preparing for a variety of futures. This personal board of directors will meet with the student both individually and as a group periodically to jointly help guide the student to success. We are currently in the early stages of putting this approach together and are seeking to build the resources, both human and technical, to manage it.

New Products and Services

The traditional array of higher education options, largely focusing on courses and degrees, do not seem sufficient for the wide variety of skills our learners will need in the future and throughout their lives. We will need a broad array of new products and services to better suit the greatly diverse and ever-changing needs of our future learners. Some of these might include using micro-credentials, establishing a matrix of "minimester" classes, transcending the Carnegie unit as the sole credit for accomplishment, and using emerging technologies to better accomplish some of the things we do poorly now, such as using blockchain to reimagine how academic credentials can work. We have been running our own experiments in using blockchain technology for academic credentials for a couple of years and have recently joined a consortium with several other institutions to establish a common framework for the kind of digital credentials that will enable much greater flexibility and utility in what we offer.

AI and Personalization

Personalizing education has been a goal of educational technologists ever since Benjamin Bloom's 1984 landmark study showing that one-to-one tutoring in a mastery-learning format is two standard deviations more effective than almost all other group pedagogies. Unfortunately, one-to-one tutoring is not a technique that can scale. There are simply not enough tutors to go around. Now, however, it is possible that technology is beginning to allow us to change this and allow personalized learning at scale. We have already begun experimenting with using artificial intelligences as a part of our classes, most notably with the Jill Watson experiment (Goel & Polepeddi, 2019). We are looking to develop a suite of AI tools to better support our learners. We are currently expanding the Jill Watson experiment to work with a much broader array of classes and are in the early stages of creating AI-based research assistants and personal tutors.

Distributed World-Wide Presence

While maintaining a physical campus has been a hallmark of higher education for a thousand years, the success of our own online programs and our globalization efforts make it clear that the physical campus itself is not enough. How can we provide the Georgia Tech experience for the many learners we have that will never step foot on the campus? We are in the process of developing the Georgia Tech Atrium, a light-footprint space that is accessible to our learners wherever they may be. Although some of the Atrium projects will be actual, physical spaces, others may exist only in an augmented-reality environment. Within the Atrium project, we have the opportunities to support other types of distributed presences as well, such as a "human library" concept in which readers interact with people who have a particular set of relevant life experiences just the way they may have interacted with books in the past. We are in the process of establishing the governance framework for the GT Atrium project and funding it.

Model of Forecasting (Possible Futures, Probable Futures, Desirable Futures, Black Swans)

There are many models of forecasting, formerly known as future studies. In this final section of our chapter, we will present one such model and then examine possible scenarios within it for what higher education may look like in 2040. In the world of forecasting, futurists define four major types of future: the possible, the plausible, the probable, and the preferable. The possible encompasses every outcome that might exist, however unlikely, based on knowledge we do not yet have. The plausible includes every outcome that could exist, based on our current understanding. The probable future is what we think is likely to happen based on current patterns. The preferable is what we would most like to happen. These futures expand outward from our current time in a "Cone of Plausibility," in which each future is a subset of its predecessor (Taylor, 1990). The further out from the present we project, the less certain we can be, moving from the probable in the near term to the merely possible in the far term. One should note that the preferable future may not necessarily lie in the probable cone but could lie anywhere along the projected path. See Figure 5.1.

A key purpose of the projects we have described above and undertaken as a result of our Commission on Creating the Next in Education is to help direct us toward that preferable future. By taking certain actions now, we hope to create, or at the very least not rule out, the possibility for other actions in the more distant future. You may notice that the Cone of Plausibility also contains "wildcard" futures. These are futures in which unlikely and unforeseen events occur anyway and have a dramatic impact on what actually occurs. For example, the September 11th terrorist attacks drastically changed the course of human events, giving us the world in which we live today. Possible technological advances may have the same effect on the institution in the far future. In particular, advances in artificial intelligence, brain-computer interfaces, nanotechnology, neuroscience,

Cone of Plausibility

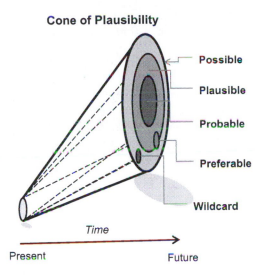

Possible

Plausible

Probable

Preferable

Wildcard

Time

Present

Future

Figure 5.1 The cone of plausibility

biogenetics, and robotics have the potential to radically change the way education can and will take place. But at this writing, it is impossible to know which, if any, of these will come to fruition with respect to learning. Therefore, we have consciously decided to leave these possible advances in the wildcard category and focus instead on what, at least today, seems probable.

As we consider the building blocks that form the foundation of Georgia Tech's options for the future, it is important that we recognize and account for the systemic nature of higher education. Like many systems, higher education has a tendency toward equilibrium. As we make a change to one part of the system, other parts react in order to keep the overall system in its original form. When we begin to design and implement projects positioning the Institute for the future, we must keep this systems-orientation in mind. Far too often technology has been introduced to educational systems as a one-shot panacea. The thinking has long been that technology by itself can solve all of education's problems. We repeatedly see thinking along these lines, such as, "If we give every student an iPad (or insert your favorite technology), scholastic performance will improve, dropout rates will go down, and costs will plummet." Long experience and a body of research spanning many decades has shown this mentality generally leads to failure. Instead, we know that technology is only one component of a complex, dynamic interaction among many stakeholders, goals, and processes.

Conclusion

We continue to learn about the future of higher education and the role higher education over a lifetime has, and needs to have, with regional and national economies and, most importantly, with people. For it is the people that benefit the most, and we want to do everything possible to improve the human condition as the Georgia Tech strategic plan outlines. For Georgia Tech as a public university, that means looking at how we can serve all Georgians, our region, and beyond along the lifetime of people using our academic and research strengths. We continually look to the future and what can be, and to how we might help shape that future. We also know that many things will continue to change, and we need to be prepared. Likely, that is the biggest piece of our thinking—how to prepare our teams for continual change, how to listen and listen intently to the needs of the many stakeholders, and how to put vision into action that can be nimble as change occurs. The creation of a university academic-master-plan will become the guiding, strategic, mobilizing agent for the university's own lifetime education.

References

Brown, T. (2005, June 1). Strategy by design. *Fast Company*. Retrieved from https://www.fast company.com/52795/strategy-design

Bureau of Labor Statistics. (2019, August 22). *Number of jobs, labor market experience, and earnings growth: Results from a national longitudinal study* (News Release). U.S. Dept. of Labor. Retrieved from https://www.bls.gov/news.release/pdf/nlsoy.pdf

Georgia Institute of Technology. (n.d.). Discovering the drivers of change in higher education. Retrieved from: https://provost.gatech.edu/discovering-drivers-change-higher-education

Georgia Institute of Technology. (2018). *Deliberate innovation, lifetime education* (Report). Retrieved from: https://provost.gatech.edu/sites/default/files/documents/deliberate_innovation_lifetime_e ducation.pdf

Goel, A. K., & Polepeddi, L. (2019). A virtual teaching assistant for online education. In C. Dede, J. Richards, & B. Saxberg (Eds.), *Learning engineering for online education: Theoretical contexts and design-based examples* (pp. 120–143). New York, NY: Routledge.

Goodman, J., Melkers, J., & Pallais, A. (2018). Can online delivery increase access to education? *Journal of Labor Economics, 37*(1). doi:10.1086/698895

Kegan, R., & Lahey, L. (2016). *An everyone culture: Becoming a deliberately developmental organization*. Boston, MA: Harvard Business Review.

Pew Research Center. (2017). *Sharp partisan divisions in views of national institutions*. Retrieved from https://www.people-press.org/2017/07/10/sharp-partisan-divisions-in- views-of-national-institutions/

Pew Research Center. (2019). *Facebook, YouTube continue to be the most widely used online platforms among U.S. adults*. Retrieved from https://www.pewresearch.org/fact-tank/2019/04/10/share-of-u-s-adults- using-social-media-including-facebook-is-mostly- unchanged-since-2018/ft_19-04-10_socialmedia2019_facebookyoutube_2/

Taylor, C. W. (1990). *Creating strategic visions*. Strategic Studies Institute, US Army War College, Carlisle Barracks, Carlisle, PA. Retrieved from http://www.dtic.mil/dtic/tr/fulltext/u2/a231618.pdf

6

Known for Whom We Include

Designing Models for Lifelong Education at Arizona State University

PUNYA MISHRA AND JACQUELINE SMITH

Introduction

Providing access to quality education across the lifespan of a wide swath of the population is not a new concern for educators. This idea was at the heart of the Open University in Britain in the late 1960s. Speaking at the inaugural meeting of the Open University, Chancellor Geoffrey Crowther said:

> The first, and most urgent task before us is to cater for the many thousands of people, fully capable of a higher education, who, for one reason or another, do not get it, or do not get as much of it as they can turn to advantage, or as they discover, sometimes too late, that they need.
>
> (1969, para. 3)

He continued that "the existing system . . . misses and leaves aside a great unused reservoir of human talent and potential" (1969, para. 3).

One could argue that this need has become even more salient with greater demands and greater uncertainty of access to education than ever before. No less important is the breadth of extant knowledge that learners today have to contend with, as the quote below suggests:

> The modern school is forced to meet the demands of a rapidly changing civilization. Today the world of the learner is almost unbounded. He must acquire facts relating to a bewildering variety of places and things; he must acquire appreciations of far-reaching interrelationships. The curriculum and methods of teaching must undergo a continuous appraisal. New subject matter and new devices for instruction are being scrutinized for their potential contributions to the learning process.
>
> (Devereux, Engelhardt, Mort, & Stoddard, 1933, p. 1)

This quote, resonant as it may seem today, is from a book published almost 90 years ago, back in 1933! These challenges persist, in part, because the design of our educational institutions has remained unchanged since the end of the 19th century (Crow, 2018), despite the fact that the scale at which we seek to address these challenges has increased dramatically. That said, we must approach innovation within the education system (and in the development of a 60-Year Curriculum [60YC]) with a sense of humility since these are deeply grounded systems and structures that can often be recalcitrant to change. It is also important to learn from previous experiments and interventions that attempted to increase access to a wider population than served by current educational institutions and offerings.

For instance, consider a more recent innovation—Massive Open Online Courses (MOOCs)—that was heavily touted as being the solution to education's vexing problems. MOOCs were *the* game changer. As Thomas Friedman wrote in *The New York Times*:

> Nothing has more potential to lift more people out of poverty—by providing them an affordable education to get a job or improve in the job they have. Nothing has more potential to unlock a billion more brains to solve the world's biggest problems. And nothing has more potential to enable us to reimagine higher education.
>
> (Friedman, 2013, para. 1)

However, as we know, MOOCs, for the most part, failed to live up to their expectations as multiple studies have demonstrated. For instance, a study by University of Pennsylvania showed that only about half of those who registered for a course ever viewed a lecture, and only about 4% completed the courses. More significantly, what remained unrealized was the potential for MOOCs to expand educational access to populations that have not been typically served before. For instance, students who took a series of low-cost online courses offered by San Jose State and Udacity actually performed worse than those taking the same classes on campus. In fact, only 12% of high school students taking an algebra class passed the course. Overall, it turned out that MOOCs were meeting the needs not of the under-privileged but rather of people who had already had some college education. The same UPenn study demonstrated that approximately 80% of students in the MOOCs that were studied already had a college degree.

As it turned out, the students who succeeded in these new environments were not necessarily the ones the MOOCs were designed for. MOOCs, curiously enough, appeared to be designed for self-motivated, self-regulated individuals who were willing to work independently. (Interestingly, and we suspect not coincidentally, this is a profile that would match that of many early MOOC designers and creators.) It is not surprising, then, that MOOCs were not effective in addressing the needs of students who needed it the most—despite the massive data sets on user behavior that were analyzed and used to design the system.

As we seek to develop plans within the 60YC, we need to see the case-study of MOOCs as a cautionary tale. At one level, these can be considered failures of design—where the design of the artifact took precedence over the broader systems and cultures within which they function (see Chapter 1 by Chris Dede, in this volume, for a more extended discussion of these issues). This suggests that we need a more expansive view of what we mean by design, particularly within educational contexts.

Understanding Our Blind Spots in Educational Design

One of the important factors we in higher education need to understand as we embark on this work are the biases inherent in how we (as members of existing educational systems) view the world. These hegemonic design biases can be seen as failures of design stemming from three different components of their design/production process. In MOOCs, for example, these components are (a) the source of MOOCs, the universities actually producing them; (b) the actual design of the MOOCs themselves, the user experience and pedagogical techniques within them; and (c) the research and development community around MOOCs (Meaney, 2019).

We focus on the hazards caused by iterating the design of MOOCs based on the behavior patterns of early users and adopters of the technology. These early adopters are not representative of the broader population whose needs MOOCs were attempting to address. Meaney calls this an "iteration inequity loop" where "data from existing courses, at present taken primarily by college educated users (~80% of users), is mined and used to optimize future design, tailoring MOOCs to fit the behavior patterns of those less likely to need help" (2019, p. 1). This would be a classic example of an unknown unknown, a blind spot as it were, where well-intentioned, data-driven strategies are undermined by an inherent bias in the data itself. What this means is that we cannot seek to learn just from those who show up, since these are not necessarily the ones we are trying to reach.

Addressing this blind spot requires us to think differently about the design of educational systems, approaches that emphasize the development of better strategies to get at data that would drive our strategies. And most importantly, it requires us to have an expansive view of what we say when we speak of educational design (as per the Five Discourses of Design framework presented below).

To address our blind spots, we must better understand the lived experiences of our potential learners and how they develop during their entire lifespans. We turn to prior research in two key areas: narrative identity formation and career development.

The Five Discourses of Design in Education

A systemic and sustainable impact of educational design interventions can emerge, we believe, only when we conceptualize design the right way. Design, as traditionally conceived in education, focuses on the designed artifact or occasionally on a designed scenario, process, or experience. Mishra, Scragg, and Warr (2018) and Warr, Mishra, and Scragg (2019) argue for a more expansive framework for design, taking inspiration from previous work in design theory (Buchanan, 2001; Lockwood & Papke, 2017). They call these spaces "discourses" to capture the multiplicity of ways of "combining and integrating language, actions, interactions, ways of thinking, believing, valuing, and using various symbols, tools, and objects to enact a particular sort of socially recognizable identity" (Gee, 2011, p. 201). This important idea of identity is something we will return to later in the chapter.

Figure 6.1, the Five Discourses of Design framework, represents the relationships among five spaces of design: artifacts, processes, experiences, systems, and culture (see Table 6.1 for added details of each). In this model, discourses are similar to Buchanan's "orders of design," in that they are "places of invention shared by all designers, places where one discovers the dimensions of design thinking by a reconsideration of problems and solutions" (1992, p. 10). Clearly the "dimensions of design thinking" (as Buchanan describes it) will vary as we rethink the very nature of the participants. As Dede and others have argued (in this volume and elsewhere), there is something fundamentally different about

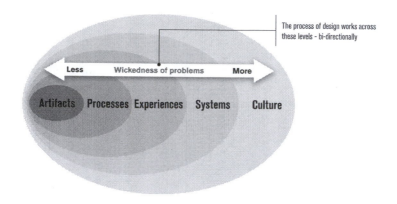

Figure 6.1 The five discourses of design in education

TABLE 6.1 The Five Discourses of Design, Explained

Discourse	Definition	Example
Artifacts	Stable objects that can be perceived through the senses	Curricular materials, tools, software, manipulatives, videos
Processes	A procedure or direction that can be used outside of the context it was created within achieve a goal	Lesson plans, curricula, schedules
Experiences	A piece of time with associated sights, sounds, feelings, and thoughts	Activities, celebrations (e.g., graduation), learning communities
Systems	An organized and purposeful structure of interrelated and interdependent elements	Registration, certification system, degree program, evaluation systems
Culture	A pattern of shared basic assumptions that allows groups to perceive and interpret the world in similar ways, to develop and communicate meaning, and to transmit values to new group members	Perceptions of technology, schools, or education broadly

the learner population we are seeking to connect with within the context of designing the *60YC*. This has to do with a range of factors (such as their personal histories, demographic identity markers, evolving narrative histories, and where they are in their careers).

Although all discourses are spaces for design, they differ in that they place the focus of the design in a different place. That is, they represent different communities of work (domains). Each discourse differs from others in terms of the judgment, elements, tools, practices, attitudes, and knowledge required to practice design. The designing of systems and culture requires very different forms of each of these domains than if one were focused on design artifacts or processes. This is not to say that the design of artifacts or processes is not important to the reimagining of systems and culture, just that they are not sufficient. Specifically, in the context of the *60YC* it is imperative that we frame these discourses within what we already know about adult learning and the history of institutions that have typically functioned in this space. (Again, this is described in greater detail in Dede's introductory chapter in this volume).

We suggest that one reason educational theorists have not been successful at changing education is because we have not developed a systems view of the problem at hand. The solutions we come up with are narrow, and we rarely consider the surrounding systems and cultures. We argue that developing a deeper understanding of design and design theory can help us begin to address the underlying systems and cultures of education, enabling more impactful approaches to designing and implementing learning technologies at scale.

A systems or cultural view of design allows us to identify and address some key biases that can color our approaches toward developing new educational interventions.

Narrative Identity

The field of narrative identity focuses on the stories we tell about ourselves. These stories evolve and change over time, as we grow, learn, mature, and adapt to the world around us, adding new experiences, emphasizing certain elements, and understating other ones. According to this framework, individuals are inherently seekers of meaning who use these narratives of self to develop identities and, through that, link plans and goals to behavior. As Singer writes:

> To understand the identity formation process is to understand how individuals craft narratives from experiences, tell these stories internally and to others, and ultimately apply these stories to knowledge of self, other and the world in general.
>
> (2004, p. 438)

Cognitive psychology has an extensive history of studying the nature of autobiographical memory and the narratives that develop from these memories (Baddeley, 2004). Relatively more recent is a focus on how these autobiographical stories or narratives inform our identities (i.e., the nature of narrative meaning-making) (McAdams & McLean, 2013). The key concern of this somewhat new discipline (also known as "narrative identity research") is "how individuals employ narratives to develop and sustain a sense of personal unity and purpose from diverse experiences across the lifespan" (Singer, 2004, p. 437). As Fivush, Booker, and Graci write:

> At the broadest level, narrative meaning-making refers to how individuals make human sense of experiences in ways that help them understand themselves, others, and their worlds. How individuals do this immediately and over time changes as individuals revisit and reconstruct the experience to meet new developmental challenges and is fundamental to understanding the narrative meaning-making process and how it is related to identity and well-being.
>
> (2017, pp. 128–129)

These stories play many important roles in our lives. We can employ stories to raise our spirits, guide our actions, or influence others as a tool of persuasion or rhetoric. We can draw inferences from stories with particular self-relevance in order to gain insight into our own nature, values, and goals. The accumulating knowledge that emerges from reasoning about our narrative memories yields a life story schema that provides causal, temporal, and thematic coherence to an overall sense of identity (Singer, 2004).

This sense of identity provides the context for understanding how individuals see themselves, address challenges, and develop goals and actions to achieve these goals. This, however, is not a static process—it evolves over one's lifespan through changes in biology and cognition, the demands of specific life stages, and the broader influences of culture and community. Thus, an individual's narrative is fluid, adaptive, and a genuine work in progress.

It is important also to realize that this is not an isolated process but rather is a social-cognitive developmental one. Narrative meaning-making is conditioned and mediated by the broader socio-cultural matrix we are embedded in and is grounded in specific cultural, communal, and historical contexts. As Singer writes:

> The stories individuals create draw from the existing repertoire of cultural narratives based in myth, fable, literature, popular entertainment, and ethnic family history that define the meaning making parameters of their lives. Their personal narratives, their "narrative identity" situates them meaningfully in their culture, providing unity to their past, present, and anticipated future.
>
> (2004, p. 445)

In other words, the domain of narrative identity or life-story construction seeks to understand how people make sense of their experiences and lives, both as individuals as well as bound within multiple social, cultural, and community contexts (such as race, ethnicity, membership in groups, and so on). It is important, as Ann Brewer argues in Chapter 4 of this volume, that we go beyond narrow demographic categories when we think of learners, since, as she writes "...people's lives, and hence learning journeys, do not necessarily align to demographics" (p. 63). Our approach to design focuses on the socio-cognitive developmental aspects of narrative identity, specifically on changes in individuals' sense of self and their consideration of possible futures. This clearly has implications for all of the five discourses of design—from how we think of the design of systems and culture to experiences, processes, and artifacts. A broader focus on narrative identity can inform how each of these discourses of design are to be constructed in order to best meet the needs of learners—each of whom has a deeply individual narrative arc as they enter the educational system and move on to their new future.

Career Development across the Lifespan

There is a significant body of empirical and theoretical work that looks at the nature of career development across the lifespan. This aligns with the broader discussion of these matters as described by Dede in Chapter 1. This line of inquiry goes beyond the psychological frames that guide the narrative meaning-making work described above and focuses more on the intersection of the self and work. This becomes particularly critical when we consider that the world of work is under significant transformation today. The world of work is rapidly changing with significant economic, environmental, and societal disruptions across the horizon. The economic pressures of machine learning and artificial intelligence (AI) will surely exacerbate the already accelerating rate of technological and economic transformation. This state of flux indicates that life in the decades to come cannot be grounded in traditional, steady occupational roles. The "de-jobbing" of individuals and the "re-engineering" of organizations suggest that we need to move away from a focus on occupations and "instead concentrate on the rainbow of life roles enacted in the theaters of home, school, work and community" (Savickas, 1997, p. 251).

This new focus of career development implies a shift away from supporting one goal of a career but rather to supporting and fostering the full development and well-being of the person even while being sensitive to the broader life structures and themes of the individual. Thus, any framework that seeks to understand career development needs to emphasize four key perspectives: individual differences, development, self, and context (Savickas, 1997). The argument here is for an adaptive, goal-driven, teleological framework that emphasizes the transactional relationship between an individual and the environment. Similar to the narrative identity approach, this way of thinking of career development focuses on not the individual but rather the individual-in-situation, since it is clear that individuals in different phases of their lives could have dramatically different goals.

This is a fluid, dynamic frame of view that emphasizes adaptability over readiness or maturity. In this context, career adaptability focuses on being ready to contend with not just preparing for and participating in work but also for being ready to deal with and adjust to the unexpected. Moreover, in this fluid context, it becomes increasingly important to consider the array of roles that an individual exists within rather than just the context of work. Life-planning becomes a critical component of this process, factoring in everything from work to family, leisure to worship, and individual needs to communal responsibilities.

An important aspect of career development literature is the twin ideas of exploration and commitment. In this context, exploration refers to "active consideration of alternatives," both ideologically (such as philosophical, religious, or political) and interpersonal (such as friendship, dating, and sex roles). Commitment, on the other hand, describes the achievement of a sense of self and identity across these domains. Thus, preparing oneself for life requires the individual to "look ahead and to look around, to develop the self, and, in due course, to choose suitable and viable opportunities to become the person she or he wants to be" (Savickas, 1997, p. 257).

Given that our narrative identities are deeply intertwined with broader social-cultural factors, any suggestion of intervention we develop for education needs to factor in the multiple influences of these aspects on narrative meaning-making and career development. Of critical importance are the work and other community-related contexts within which individuals exist as well as the broader cultural matrix that offers suggestions and opportunities as we explore and commit to particular paths. We suggest that we need to develop a better understanding of the range of identity formation processes across a wide spectrum of humans and their myriad anticipated futures if we are to truly meet the needs of the *60YC*.

Introducing Arizona State University as a Site for Educational Design at Scale

Arizona State University (ASU) is evolving a *Universal Learning*® educational model capable of being of service to all learners, at all stages of life, from all socioeconomic backgrounds, through educational, training, and skill-building opportunities. The *60YC*, with its emphasis on occupational changes and transitions, falls within ASU's Universal Learning framework. Since President Michael Crow's arrival at ASU in 2002, the university has used a design-build approach with rapid prototyping and iterating of new initiatives (consistent with the five Discourses Design framework presented earlier). ASU has launched several experiments that push the boundaries of its traditional degree programs—a systems-design approach toward educational transformation.

An important aspect of the systems-design approach has been focusing on the evolving narrative identities of students which has allowed ASU to design a suite of services and processes to serve degree-seeking students from their initial inquiry with the university to graduation. ASU is committed to continuous improvement through service-design processes such as the development of a journey map (i.e., a visual representation of the learner's experience with the educational service from start to finish). These maps enable us not just to break

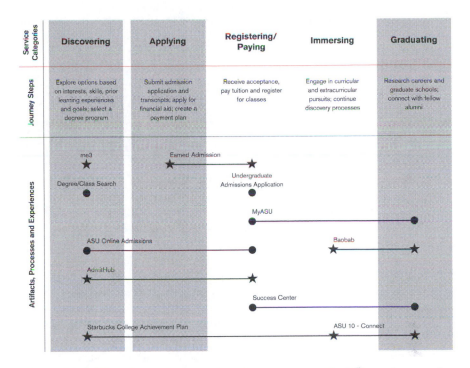

Figure 6.2 ASU undergraduate student journey map with direct to learner delivery (E to L)

down what is often a complex process into individual stages but also to identify problem points and obstacles which are getting in the way of a smooth and efficient learner experience. Thus, these maps help us recognize opportunities for innovation as well as the critical touchpoints where these innovations may connect with the learner. Demonstrated in Figure 6.2, ASU has developed artifacts, processes, and experiences to help undergraduate students explore their narrative identities and progress through their degree programs. Understanding the stages of a student's journey helps the administrators identify opportunities to modify existing artifacts, processes, and experiences and to develop new ones.

The focus on systems design in ASU's work has also allowed us to reimagine the systems that go into the delivery of education. For instance, the traditional model, which we call "direct to learner" or "E-to-L" (education-to-learner), involves an individual learner selecting a course, degree, or learning experience from the university, paying for that opportunity, and receiving that offering. In contrast, one could imagine an "E-to-B" (education-to-business) approach, when a company purchases training on behalf of their employees and plays a role in determining how and when the offering will be delivered. We believe that in response to the upskilling needs of adult learners, universities such as ASU will need to reimagine their E-to-L and E-to-B functions.

E-to-B approaches engage learners who are already working and who seek professional development for their career or to expand their career development options. Among the more innovative attempts in this regard are ASU's partnerships with businesses including Starbucks and Uber. The business partner's roles may include providing financial support (i.e., tuition), generating program awareness through marketing campaigns, or establishing incentive and reward structures for educational attainment.

The Starbucks College Achievement Plan, announced in June 2014, will graduate 25,000 Starbucks employees with undergraduate degrees by 2025. The idea is straightforward. Partners (Starbucks employees) in the United States working an average of 20 hours per week can earn a bachelor's degree with full tuition reimbursement without any obligation to remain employed at Starbucks after they graduate from ASU. As of May 2019, more than 3,000 Starbucks Partners have graduated with a bachelor's degree and another 12,000 are currently participating in the program.

Before starting classes, Starbucks Partners take ASU 10-Connect: ASU Orientation, a one-week, non-credit course. Partners learn about ASU's mission and policies, discover the value of a university degree from a research institution, explore tools used in online courses, and identify key components of a work/life/ school balance plan. In keeping with the systems-design approach—and learning from past experiences—the orientation was partly adapted from earlier orientations provided to online students and partly was custom designed specifically for Starbucks Partners, keeping their unique context in mind.

In a similar vein, in November 2018, ASU announced an education partnership with Uber. Uber drivers who meet the program's eligibility requirements can earn an undergraduate degree through ASU Online or can pursue nondegree courses about entrepreneurship and English as a second language through ASU's Continuing and Professional Education program. Learners in the nondegree modules receive a completion certificate for achieving a minimum score on assessments. The modules are self-paced with an expected duration of 4–6 hours each. The nondegree topics were selected in response to a survey that revealed that many drivers choose to drive with Uber in order to support their goals as entrepreneurs and small business owners.

To further advance its E-to-B strategy, ASU recently launched InStride, a for-profit, learning services company. As President Crow said in an interview, InStride was launched in order to accelerate the E-to-B movement and to "partner with more employers who seek to provide flexible learning options for employees no matter what stage of their career they are in" (as cited in Green, 2019, para. 3). The partnership with InStride seeks to provide educational attainment to 35 million adults who are currently in the workforce but have not completed their college education. The goal is to meet the needs of these adults "who work for a company and have no pathway [back] to college" (as cited in Green, 2019, para. 8). In that sense, InStride operates as an intermediary organization to recruit corporate partners and manage corporate relationships and is thus an example of how E-to-B can be expanded and systematically integrated into the structures of a university.

Moreover, universities have an opportunity to identify new pathways to learners (E-to-X) in partnership with a range of organizations including but not limited to voluntary associations and nonprofit, direct-service organizations. These distribution partners can reach learners who are connected through existing social capital and shared identities. Although social (or human) capital has several definitions (see Andrew Scott in Chapter 2 of this volume), this approach to reaching universal learners relies on the Organisation for Economic Cooperation and Development's definitions of "networks together with shared norms, values and understandings that facilitate co-operation within or among groups" (OECD, 2001, p. 41).[1] Distribution partners may also help the university reach groups of learners who share a circumstance such as individuals who are living in refugee camps or who are currently incarcerated.

As ASU broadens the scope of learners it engages and supports beyond degree seekers, the linear journey map in Figure 6.2 will shift to a cyclical design. The graduating stage may become a certifying stage that leads to more discovering. Below we describe some of the artifacts, processes, and experiences that signal how ASU is preparing for this shift. We focus on the three service categories where ASU has made the most disruptive progress: discovering, applying, and graduating.

Discovering

With ASU's suite of educational offerings evolving and expanding, learners will need new ways to explore which options best meet their needs and goals.

ASU has already embraced technology to aid prospective and current undergraduate students' discovery processes. Me3 is a mobile-enhanced website that helps prospective undergraduate students explore their ongoing, evolving narrative identity by assessing their career interests, exploring college majors, and planning which high school classes they should be taking now to reach—what they currently believe are—their future goals. Me3 offers an interactive, image-based interest assessment. Based on responses to the assessment, me3 recommends three career paths and three college majors for each career. Me3 then suggests a list of high school courses a student should take toward those goals and helps them track their academic progress. By charting a pathway through high school, me3 helps students understand what they need to do to complete all the crucial requirements and be academically college ready. In other words, me3 helps students explore future versions of themselves and, at least tentatively, plan toward that goal.

The broad educational system is often made of sub-systems (universities, colleges, corporations, etc.) that need to align in their goals to meet the needs of potential learners. One example of systems that seek to work together is the manner in which ASU incorporates third-party products such as AdmitHub into its processes. AdmitHub responds to students' questions and guides them through enrollment processes (from discovering to applying). AdmitHub uses AI chatbots and connects students with human advisors. The AdmitHub intelligent, mobile-messaging platform enhances how enrollment administrators advance and evaluate messaging campaigns to prospective students. Nearly 99% of inquiries can be handled by the AdmitHub virtual assistant because students share similar frequently asked questions. This means staff can focus on inquiries that are best suited for human intervention.

ASU is designing additional tools (and exploring partnerships with others who have developed tools) related to skill and interest assessment. For example, the learner with immediate upskilling and employment needs will want to understand how their skills match with job opportunities in their geographic area. Presently, our career exploration tools refer students to job outlook projections from the US Department of Labor. Moving forward, we want learners to be able to make education choices with an understanding of job opportunities by zip code instead of relying on national data. Improving how our resources are designed must be coupled with efforts to shift student, faculty, staff, and employer mindsets. Specifically, universities must help learners develop a lifelong learning mindset that embraces the concept that their narrative identities will evolve over time (Smith & Meaney, 2016). The tools must represent the mindset by representing the short-term curricular pathway as part of a lifelong educational journey. We are beginning to work with ASU alumni to identify their preferred type of learning (academic courses, personal development, professional skill building) and delivery methods. Because professionals are already members of several online communities, we are exploring how to create an engaging learning environment that seamlessly integrates with their lives.

In the E-to-B delivery model, the employer may influence the discovery process by prioritizing particular credentials or learning pathways in an effort to eliminate current or potential skill gaps and prepare for emerging opportunities. This means the discovery tools may include search filters from the employer and/ or the algorithm that generates search results may be informed by the employer's hiring needs.

In the E-to-X model, learners' shared norms, values, and understandings may be reflected in the design of the discovery and, ultimately, learning tools. The Baobab tool, described below, provides an example of this approach.

Applying

ASU's aspiration is to provide learning opportunities to any learner. This means learners' abilities and past experiences will range greatly. Me3 recommends high school courses that will set up the student for success in a desired undergraduate degree program. As we seek to expand access, we are faced with a range of non-traditional learners. For instance, learners entering university several years after high school completion will have dramatically different narrative identities, career development pathways, and learning styles. (Dede in Chapter 1 and Michel Servoz in Chapter 3 of this volume provide deeper context for these issues.) This requires the development and communication of new pathways within the discovery and application tools. (See Huntington Lambert and Henry Leitner in

Chapter 9 of this volume for examples of educational offerings and services that support adult-learner-centered approaches to a lifetime of learning.)

An example of a disruption in the application process is ASU's launch of Earned Admission (EA), which offers a pathway into the university regardless of prior educational experience or location. The EA offering serves as an on-ramp for learners who need additional support in order to qualify for admission to ASU Online. Students prove their academic readiness by taking a rigorous set of open-scale, online courses and earning a 2.75 GPA or above. Students (or their sponsors) pay for credit only when they successfully pass the course (with a C or higher). The credits from the EA pathway can be transferred to any accredited higher education institution in the US and are stackable for credit in ASU's degree programs.

The design of the system has to provide flexibility to the learner (or the organizations that are sponsoring the learner) to meet them where they are in terms of their evolving narrative identity. EA students will not be permanently defined by their prior academic performance. Preliminary data as of March 2019 indicates that students who enter ASU on the EA on-ramp have the capacity to succeed. Research based on 186 EA students indicates that EA students have higher first term GPAs than other ASU Online students. Moreover, "EA students show higher completion rates" of courses in their first term as compared to other ASU Online students (T. Fikes, personal communication, May 18, 2019). The initial results from Earned Admission are a positive indication of the manner in which ASU has broadened its reach to engage and support non-degree seeking learners.

The examples above describe a few of the innovations that ASU has initiated in keeping with this mission of being inclusive and accessible. These have included new models of reaching learners directly (E-to-L) as well as of partnering with organizations to sponsor learners toward courses that fit their current career development context. One unexplored area of innovation that ASU is actively looking into is an E-to-X pipeline wherein the university would partner with groups that are defined more by their shared identity rather than professional affiliation. This is an exciting area for future development (one example is given below).

Graduating

ASU is advancing several experiments to engage alumni in continuous learning beyond a degree program. Baobab, the Mastercard Foundation Scholars community platform, is an E-to-X approach that connects thousands of recipients of the Mastercard Foundation Scholarship to noncredit learning modules, collaborative workshops, career preparedness coaching, and networking experiences. Scholars gain access to the platform while enrolled in degree programs and then, most importantly, maintain access throughout their lifetime.

The Mastercard Foundation Scholars Program … allows students whose talent and promise exceed their financial resources to complete their education. With a vision that education is a catalyst for social and economic change, the program focuses on developing leaders [primarily from sub-Saharan Africa] who are transformative, encouraging them to be active contributors in their communities.

(Scholars, n.d.)

For the postsecondary scholarships, the foundation selected universities across the globe to serve as Scholars Program Partners. University partners commit to enabling student success and exposing Scholars to the foundation's transformative leadership skills and mindsets. Thus, participants build "on a foundation of integrity" and, "driven by self-awareness and a sense of purpose," address issues related to inequity and seek to help by "improving the lives of others and making or influencing positive change" (Novy-Marx, 2014).

The Mastercard Foundation asked ASU to design learning experiences that would emphasize the Scholars Program's commitment to transformative leadership skills and mindsets and its ethos of giving back. The skills include adaptability, self-awareness, critical thinking, collaboration, creativity, communication, ethical action, and professional skills. The mindsets are courage, empathy, vision, integrity, resilience, humility, inclusiveness, and curiosity. ASU created a series of experiences on Baobab related to each skill that stack into badges. To exemplify that a learner's journey is never truly complete, the badges are designed in continuous levels. Each level is signaled visually by changing color and level title for the badge. For example, as a learner moves from consuming content on a particular skill to actively contributing to the discussion, the badge changes color from blue to brown and the level title changes from "scholar" to "catalyst." Figure 6.3 below demonstrates the badge progression. Conceptually, a learner could complete infinite levels, each one progressively taking more effort. Pragmatically, the content team will continue to update the modules (and levels) as the needs of the learners change over time. Presently, the Baobab users are postsecondary students and recent alumni. However, platform use will change once all of the users are professionals and, by design, Baobab will evolve with the alumni's emerging needs.

Figure 6.3 Badge progression on the Baobab platform for the adaptability skill

As a social learning network, the platform crowd-sources and shares resources and opportunities such as articles, videos, digital tools, scholarships, internships, jobs, and seed funding sources, across the community. As alumni progress in their careers, we anticipate that their contributions to the platform will evolve. For example, the ASU team who develops and curates the content on Baobab will seek out alumni who are experts in various fields to share their expertise with the Baobab community by engaging in the one-to-many mentorship program or posting job and entrepreneurship opportunities. Aspirationally, Baobab will offer additional modules that confer certified microcredentials related to in-demand skills such as data science, digital marketing, computer programming, and graphic design.

Developing a lifelong learning platform to fit the needs of thousands of Scholars required in-depth design preparation. ASU received a planning grant from the Mastercard Foundation to engage Scholars in the design process of this virtual community in 2014 resulting in a clickable prototype that was ultimately developed. In the summer of 2016, the platform was beta tested with 200 Scholars and ultimately released to all Scholars and scholarship alumni a few months later. There are more than 7,000 learners on Baobab with approved plans to expand the platform to all of the Mastercard Foundation's program alumni (currently estimated at 50,000 young people).

ASU assembled technical, content, and research teams to design, develop, launch, and operate the Baobab platform in partnership with technical vendors. The technical team manages the development of the platform including the advancement and testing of new features. The content team develops the learning experiences and manages collaboration with subject-matter experts. Content development includes the design and delivery of visual, multimedia, animation, sound, and graphic features. Moreover, the content team manages the Baobab Ambassadors and Community Managers who serve as advocates for the platform. The research team leads the monitoring, evaluation, and learning research to understand the impact of Baobab on the Scholar network. Short term, user-experience research is also conducted to inform the refinement of the platform's functionality and look and feel.

This is an important example of some of the themes developed earlier in the chapter—identifying the narrative identity of learners entering the system and seeking to go beyond the hegemonic design bias that often plagues such initiatives. The continual iterative approaches taken toward the development of the Baobab system—the idea that Scholars would be members for life, that the program would continually evaluate and evolve over time—are all key components of preventing programs from getting ossified over time.

Conclusion

We began the chapter with some examples of how educational tools and interventions can fail due to design flaws. We encourage university administrators to advance new systemic designs across all five Discourses of Design with a student-centered

102 • Punya Mishra and Jacqueline Smith

approach. Moreover, step-wise (linear) processes for student success will be insufficient in the context of the *60YC*. Shifting the system to allow for iterative learning cycles will empower the learner to evolve their narrative identities (including their work and personal interests) and enable the university to respond in turn. We have provided examples of how ASU, in keeping with its mission of being known for whom we include rather than whom we exclude, is engineering new artifacts, processes, experiences, and systems to meet the needs of a broad spectrum of 21st-century learners.

Note

1 The OECD notes that students without a prior connection or shared norms may develop social capital as a result of sharing the educational experience. This concept is not explored in this chapter. According to the OECD,

> Schools can foster values for social co-operation as well as providing 'meeting places' where various social networks can intersect. More broadly, institutions of higher education, adult learning and professional associations can foster networks crossing different sectors of learning, enterprise and voluntary initiative. To the extent that teaching methods and organisation [sic] of learning encourage shared learning and teamwork as well as openness to new ideas and cultural diversity, the more schools can underpin social capital which bridge across different groups in society.
>
> (2001, p. 46)

References

Baddeley, A. D. (2004). Chapter 1: The psychology of memory. In A. D. Baddeley, M. D. Kopelman, & B. A. Wilson (Eds.), *The essential handbook of memory disorders for clinicians* (pp. 1–14). Chichester, England: John Wiley & Sons.

Buchanan, R. (1992). Wicked problems in design thinking. *Design Issues, 8*(2), 5–21.

Buchanan, R. (2001). Design research and the new learning. *Design Issues, 17*(4), 3–23. doi:10.1162/07479360152681056

Crow, M. M. (2018). *National service universities: Arizona State University and the fifth wave of American higher education* (Working Document). Retrieved from https://president.asu.edu/sites/default/files/national_service_universities_2018.pdf

Crowther, G. (1969). Lord Crowther's inaugural address. BBC Open University. Retrieved from https://www.open.ac.uk/library/digital-archive/pdf/script/script:5747089b4a53f

Devereux, F. L., Engelhardt, N. L., Mort, P. R., & Stoddard, A. J. (1933). *The educational talking picture*. Chicago, IL: University of Chicago Press.

Fivush, R., Booker, J., & Graci, M. (2017). Ongoing narrative meaning-making within events and across the life span. *Imagination, Cognition, and Personality, 37*(2), 127–152. doi:10.1177/0276236617733824

Friedman, T. L. (2013, January 26). Revolution hits the universities. *The New York Times*. Retrieved from https://www.nytimes.com

Gee, J. P. (2011). *An introduction to discourse analysis: Theory and method*. New York, NY: Routledge.

Green, K. C. (2019, April 18). Introducing InStride, ASU's for-profit, preferred provider strategy for growing online enrollments. *Inside HigherEd*. Retrieved from https://www.insidehighered.com/blogs/digital-tweed/introducing-instride-asu%E2%80%99s-profit-preferred-provider-strategy-growing-online

Lockwood, T., & Papke, E. (2017). *Innovation by design*. Wayne, NJ: Career Press.

McAdams, D. P., & McLean, K. C. (2013). Narrative identity. *Current Directions in Psychological Science, 22*(3), 233–238. doi:10.1177/0963721413475622

Meaney, M. (2019). *The future of social mobility? MOOCs and hegemonic design bias* (Faculty of Education Working Papers Series). England: University of Cambridge.

Mishra, P., Scragg, B., & Warr, M. (2018). The 5 discourses of design in e-learning. In *Proceedings of E-Learn: World Conference on E-Learning in Corporate, Government, Healthcare, and Higher Education* (pp. 1362–1365). Las Vegas, NV: Association for the Advancement of Computing in Education.

Novy-Marx, M. (2014). *Women's transformative leadership in Africa*. The MasterCard Foundation. Retrieved from https://mastercardfdn.org/wp-content/uploads/2018/05/Womens-Transformative-Leadership-2014-accessible.pdf

OECD. (2001). *The well-being of nations: The role of human and social capital*. Retrieved from http://www.oecd.org/site/worldforum/33703702.pdf

Savickas, M. L. (1997). Career adaptability: An integrative construct for life-span life-space theory. *The Career Development Quarterly, 45*(3), 247–259.

Scholars Program for Africans. (n.d.). Retrieved from https://mastercardfdn.org/all/scholars/

Singer, J. A. (2004). Narrative identity and meaning making across the adult lifespan: An introduction. *Journal of Personality, 72*(3), 437–460.

Smith, J., & Meaney, M. (2016). *Lifelong learning in 2040*. The Roosevelt Institute. Retrieved from http://rooseveltinstitute.org/lifelong-learning-2040/

Warr, M., Mishra, P., & Scragg, B. (2019). Beyond TPACK: Expanding technology and teacher education to systems and culture. In K. Graziano (Ed.), *Proceedings of Society for Information Technology & Teacher Education International Conference 2019* (pp. 2558–2562). Chesapeake, VA: Association for the Advancement of Computing in Education (AACE).

Market-Driven Education

The Imperative for Responsive Design and Application

JASON WINGARD AND CHRISTINE FARRUGIA

Introduction

Today, the higher education sector faces the imminent challenge of how to prepare students with the applicable skills and abilities necessary to secure a job after graduation and continuously adapt to ever-changing workplace demands throughout their careers. Unfortunately, evidence suggests that many newly minted graduates are unable to find jobs that match their academic training and credentials (Abel, Deitz, & Su, 2014; Pianin, 2014; Garcia-Navarro, 2018). Employers also face consistent barriers identifying and recruiting graduates with the appropriate skills that align with their business needs (Bessen, 2014; Restuccia, Taska, & Bittle, 2018). Though a gap between the skills employers need and those possessed by graduates has long existed, this chasm is widening due to the accelerated pace of innovation and business change, the increasing complexity of the workplace, and the globalization of business operations (as described in Chris Dede's introductory chapter in this volume). As Mara Swan, an executive vice president at Manpower Group, states, "There's always been a gap between what colleges produce and what employers want, but now it's widening" (as cited by Tugend, 2013). In light of the current misalignment between higher education and employers, academic institutions are being called upon to better match the outcomes of higher education with what employers need (Wingard & Farrugia, in press).

Although higher education is not the only sector responsible for furnishing graduates with the skills and abilities needed for the workforce, it has an outsized role in educating students for professional work and leadership roles. Absent higher education embracing its role in creating a pipeline of skilled talent, there are trending indications that employers will instead create other solutions to identify talented workers for professional jobs—largely or completely bypassing higher education. For example, there is a growing movement toward skills-based hiring that focuses on identifying talented employees by their demonstrated skill sets rather than relying on their degrees as a signal of their employability (Lohr, 2017; Glassdoor, 2018). Google, Hilton, Ernst and Young, and IBM are examples of companies hiring with job descriptions that do not require a college degree for many professional positions (Glassdoor, 2018; Purtill, 2018). Many of these companies find that on-the-job training and vocational short courses provide comparable, or even superior, training compared to a four-year degree. Likewise, students and families are increasingly receptive to the notion of moving directly from high school to professional work, or combining work with higher education studies (Kaplan University Partners, 2019).

In this chapter, we describe the existing gap between higher education and employers and discuss the relative implications of this disconnect for workers and employers alike. We then present a framework to delineate our approach to higher education-employer engagement and its connection to employability. Finally, we apply this framework to the case of the Columbia University School of Professional Studies, focusing on how the school approaches employer engagement throughout its academic and co-curricular activities in service of maximizing the employability of its graduates.

Higher Education's Inadequate Engagement with Employers

Currently, higher education falls short of expectations in producing market-ready, employable graduates. Inadequate employer engagement is the principal culprit for this failure. Weak employer engagement by higher education materializes in three key ways: (1) employer perspectives are often sidelined during curriculum development; (2) higher education curricula are typically too stagnant to adapt to the rapid pace of change in industry; and (3) higher education focuses too narrowly on classroom-based learning rather than fostering the development of skills that are transferable to the workforce.

Employers Absent from Curriculum Development

Academic curricula are typically designed by college and university faculty, with occasional involvement of other staff such as instructional designers. Because curriculum design is primarily faculty-driven, employer perspectives on the skills and knowledge that graduates will need for the workplace are largely sidelined, with the result that graduates enter the workplace with skills and knowledge that are often too theoretical and impractical.

There are notable exceptions to this mode of curriculum development, particularly by schools that are designed to serve the needs of employers or that prepare graduates to work in a specific industry. For example, business schools commonly seek input from companies on how to better prepare graduates to meet their corporate needs (De Novellis, 2019). Military academies serve government armed forces and closely align their curriculum to serve the needs of the military-as-employer (Columbia SPS, 2019). Other pockets of strong employer engagement include schools or programs that prepare graduates for licensed professions, such as nursing, the medical fields, and accounting. The curricula of such programs are designed around prescribed standards for those professions, typically established by a professional association or aligned to state standards. Cooperative education programs have robust interaction with employers through structured work placements that are deeply integrated into the academic curriculum (Kochan, Finegold, & Osterman, 2012). These exceptions provide instructive examples of the many higher education programs that incorporate employer input into their curriculum development.

Our current educational system in the United States aligns graduate education with the professions, such as law, medicine, business, and so on, while generalized liberal education is the province of undergraduate studies (Davidson, 2017). This structure largely relegates the focus on employability to graduate-level programs, leaving undergraduate education with a relative deficit of employer input into the overall orientation, instructional approach, or desired outcome of undergraduate education.

Static Curricula

Higher education curricula are generally designed to be the culmination of a faculty's collective expertise on a subject in which they have invested considerable time learning and researching in order to master the knowledge of their discipline. Under this model, governed by faculty expertise, curricula are expected to remain largely consistent over time, which provides limited opportunity to adapt courses and programs to fast-paced changes in the business world. Cathy Davidson (2017), a leading expert in curricular innovation in higher education, describes how the current model of US higher education was developed in the late-19th to early-20th centuries and has remained largely the same since. The risk of this deficit is that when curricula do not adapt quickly higher education produces graduates with outmoded knowledge that is no longer applicable to the working world.

Too Narrow a Focus on Classroom Learning

Although there is clear value in immersing students in classroom-based instruction, a greater focus on experiential learning activities can provide a bridge between the classroom and the workplace. Classroom-based instruction is valuable for building students' baseline knowledge of theories, concepts, and contexts among a community of learners focused on the same task and without outside distractions. However, effectively translating that knowledge to the workplace requires an approach that integrates outside contexts and provides the opportunity for students to apply their growing knowledge and strengthen their skills (Khan & Ahmed, 2018). Work-based learning activities involving experiential learning, such as internships and capstone projects, provide such an opportunity by bringing the student to the workplace to engage in a practical project driven by the employer's needs and by requiring the student to apply their newfound knowledge in a real-world context (Lipka, 2019). Effective experiential education provides both a rich learning opportunity for students to actively engage in their learning experience through hands-on participation that is situated in context and a purposeful, pragmatic opportunity to solve a real-world problem.

The experience must also entail some risk by presenting a novel problem that stretches the learner beyond their comfort zone and involves critical reflection (Kolb, 1984; Morris, 2019).

Why Is Lack of Employer Engagement a Problem for Higher Education?

Some in higher education do not view the lack of employer engagement as a problem, their view being that higher education should rightly be focused on advancing learning and scholarship, which may not always align with the needs and interests of employers (Mulholland, 2015; Gutkin, 2019). Proponents of such ideas critique the notion that higher education should directly serve the needs of the labor market and argue it should instead focus on developing content knowledge and critical thinking skills. While these views have merit, in short: "Getting a job and being employed matters" (Walker & Fongwa, 2017, p. 1). Students and their families invest time and money in higher education with the expectation that they will receive a return on that investment and that the degrees they earn will prepare them for productive work and meaningful careers (Holmes, 2013). Employers, too, have an interest in their ability to make use of the skills that graduates bring to the workplace.

When employers are unable to make use of the skills that college and university graduates acquire through their schooling, unemployment and underemployment is the result, and, indeed, this has been a critical problem in recent years (Abel et al., 2014). Unemployment has dire implications for graduates, their families, and society overall (Abel et al., 2014; Burning Glass Technologies, n.d.; Garcia-Navarro, 2018). A recent survey found that only half (47%) of parents feel that US colleges prepare students well for the workplace, and 57% report that the cost of college does not justify its value (Kaplan University Partners, 2019), suggesting that higher education as a whole needs to do more to strengthen its value proposition for students and their families.

Current learning structures have firm boundaries between learning on the job and learning in the classroom. The rise of the corporate Chief Learning Officer (CLO) role provides evidence that on-the-job learning is growing in importance and is becoming more intentional, structured, and integrated into many companies' operating models (Wingard, 2015). From the employer perspective, employer-based training programs are often preferred because companies can capture learners early in their careers and mold them to the organization in ways that are hyper-focused on the needs of the organization, their products, and their customers. In the minds of employers, higher education institutions offer a broader view of the landscape and train students in a wide array of analytical skills and leadership competencies that may not be relevant to the employer. Even though these kinds of competencies position students for career advancement, they often fall outside of the narrow technical skills that employers hire for. For learners, this situation presents them with the dilemma of having to choose either employment or education; if they leave a job to pursue education, they miss out on learning skills valued by their employer, but if they forego education in favor of employment, they likely miss out on developing the leadership competencies that enable them to advance professionally. More robust engagement between employers and higher education mitigates this dilemma by making the learning boundaries between the two worlds more porous.

Greater employer engagement by higher education provides a pathway to integrate academic learning goals with employability goals. This applies to students' abilities to secure a first job following their undergraduate studies as well as to developing learners throughout their careers. In the United States, job training, professional development, and adult education have historically been provided by employers and not through a robust, integrated lifelong learning system leading to a shortfall in meeting the training and development needs of adults (LaPointe & Wingard, 2016). As discussed in Dede's introductory chapter, once learners move into the workforce, they will continue to revisit higher education throughout their lives, as their careers evolve and their learning objectives change. With lengthening lifespans, the ability to pivot careers is growing in importance for working professionals (Lipka, 2019). As learners continually engage with higher education throughout their careers, a range of higher education-employer engagement strategies can help academic programs meet the varied needs of different learners.

Framing an Educational Approach to Address the Higher Education-Employer Gap

The current disconnect between higher education and employers has significant implications for the employability of college graduates and their ability to adapt to career changes over their lifetimes. As Punya Mishra and Jacqueline Smith describe in Chapter 6 of this volume, the traditional model of education as a direct transmission of education to the learner is now evolving to include business as a mediating actor that can potentially play a role in shaping educational offerings to meet the skill needs of their workers. In this section, we describe what is meant by employer engagement and its relationship to employability, skill development, and career adaptation.

Employer Engagement

Relationships between higher education and employers take many forms including recruitment, training, research, market development, and corporate social responsibility (Seagraves, Kemp, & Osborne, 1996). According to Hogarth et al. (2007), employer engagement with higher education encompasses the following:

- Recruiting college and university graduates;
- Serving as an employer themselves (higher education institutions are often large employers in their locales);
- Providing lifelong learning and professional development;

- Supplying research and development relevant to industry; and
- Participating in economic development initiatives, which are typically government-funded.

For the purposes of this chapter, we focus on the components of employer engagement that pertain to the preparation of learners for the professional workforce. Thus, we concentrate on recruitment and lifelong learning. Although college and university engagement with employers is significant for research and development, and higher education institutions serve an important role as employers themselves, these components do not explicitly focus on the effective development of skills and abilities that are needed for professional careers and, thus, are outside of our scope.

The concept of employer engagement in higher education has gained firm traction with community colleges, and these provide a valuable example for four-year institutions (Head & Polk, 2019). For example, in New York State, a typical community college engages with more than 100 local employers (Abel, Davis, Deitz, & Reyes, 2018). Most community colleges in the state include employers on curriculum advisory committees, host employers on campus for guest lectures, and participate in site visits of employers' workplaces. They also facilitate opportunities that bring students and employers together, including work experiences, career fairs, and mentoring. Despite their prevalence in the community college sector, the adoption of extensive employer engagement at four-year institutions in the US is lacking. Employer engagement should be embraced by a broader swath of higher education to produce better employment outcomes for graduates and more effective talent development for employers. (In this volume, Chapter 3 by Michel Servos and Chapter 6 by Mishra & Smith provide insight on this topic.)

Employability

The ultimate aim of employer engagement is to improve both the employability of graduates through the development of career-related competencies as well as the ability of graduates to adapt throughout their careers. There are many conceptions of what employability means, and no clear consensus has emerged on its definition (Forrier & Sels, 2003; Suleman, 2018). Definitions range from a set of qualities that individuals possess to a type of social position that make college graduates "acceptable" to employers (Holmes, 2013). Forrier and Sels (2003) conceptualize employability as both a process that safeguards job security by thinking more expansively than just being hired into a first job as well as the ability to move into subsequent jobs throughout the worker's lifetime. In their model, employability is a function of an individual's position in relation to the labor market as well as the individual's characteristics and competencies that enable them to change jobs throughout their careers. Based on this conception, employability can be understood as the ability to secure, maintain, and change a job.

Regardless of the scope of the specific definition of employability that is under consideration, what is common is the role of employers in employability.

Suleman (2018) contends that employability is determined by employers who are the ultimate deciders on whether an individual possesses the characteristics that qualify them for employment. Workers learn skills and competencies throughout their lives in formal education settings and in the workplace. Indeed, because of this fluid learning process, a more purposeful collaboration between higher education and employers is required to meet employability goals.

Skills and competencies are terms frequently used in connection with employability. Despite the ubiquity, confusion about these two concepts abounds. Competencies differ from skills in that competencies indicate how someone performs their job successfully; while skills indicate what an employee has learned how to do (Beckett, 2018). Competencies encompass skills and the knowledge and abilities needed to achieve job success (Beckett, 2018). An example of a skill is the ability to write a report or to manage a database, while a competency would be attention to detail or the ability to think strategically (Human Resource Systems Group, n.d.). Both skills and competencies are important contributors to employability as both factor into an individual's ability to secure work throughout their life.

Because careers change and evolve throughout a worker's lifetime, career adaptability is a necessary component of employability. Career adaptability is a psychosocial construct concerning an individual's ability to cope with changing work conditions and occupational transitions (Super & Knasel, 1981; Johnston, 2018). Career adaptiveness is necessary both for individuals to cope effectively with external factors that instigate significant career changes as well as changing personal interests and career goals.

Career adaptability theory distinguishes readiness, resources, responses, and results as dimensions of adaptability (Savickas & Porfeli, 2012; Johnston, 2018). Though career adaptation can encompass numerous and varied strategies for contending with transition, the literature on lifelong learning suggests that higher education is expected to play a prime role in the retraining of workers for multiple careers over their lifetimes (Dede, 2018). Indeed, many individuals currently pursue continuing education programs at higher education institutions in order to advance in their current professions or to navigate transitions to new careers (Sabria-Bernado, Llinas-Audet, & Isus, 2017).

Addressing the Higher Education-Employer Gap: The Case of the Columbia University School of Professional Studies

The Columbia University School of Professional Studies provides a case study of a school that strategically and purposefully engages with employers as part of its core mission. The School of Professional Studies (SPS) is one of 20 schools affiliated with Columbia University. The school spans the educational continuum, from pre-college through graduate and executive programs, but the bulk of students pursue master's degree programs. SPS delivers 16 master's degrees and 17 certificate or certification programs that target current and aspiring professionals who want to advance their knowledge to accelerate their careers.

The school's philosophy is rooted in the idea that both established and emerging markets face disruption on all fronts, and few organizations are equipped to lead through change. To meet the demands of the new world of work, SPS's mission is to innovate market-forward programs to close the gap between what employers demand and what graduates can deliver. By bringing together industry-leading practitioners, innovative models, interdisciplinary problem-solving, and impact-driven leadership, SPS frames the value of a professional education to meet the most pressing needs of students, markets, and society. With deep ties within and across industry sectors, the school's goal is to harness real-time insights for real-world impact. SPS's educational offerings are guided by leaders and innovators in business who serve as advisors to senior leadership, partners, and employers of the school's graduates.

The Columbia SPS Approach to Employer Engagement

Columbia SPS takes a multi-pronged approach to engaging with employers in service of strengthening the ties between education and the workplace. Employer engagement at Columbia SPS occurs within the framework of academic governance structures to ensure the delivery of a rigorous education that is overseen by the school's faculty, tenured faculty from across the university, and the university. The school incorporates employer perspectives in the classroom through its scholar-practitioner faculty model, industry input into curricula and program development, and partnerships on experiential learning activities such as capstone projects. Employers are also engaged outside the classroom through the school's Executives in Residence program, lecture series, and career-design programming.

Scholar-practitioners in the classroom serve as a crucial link between the school and employers. Our faculty includes both educators and practitioners who are active leaders in their fields. The school's scholar-practitioners feature an average of 15 years of experience in corporate and nonprofit organizations, and 50% have doctorate degrees—many from Ivy League and similar caliber institutions. This model enables our students to learn from both research-focused, full-time faculty as well as from executive experts who are directly engaged in the imminent challenges and opportunities facing leading organizations across sectors, including finance, pharmaceutical, media, technology, and others.

Columbia SPS believes that experience working in industry is important for properly preparing students for their careers, and the school relies on its faculty to provide their expertise as practitioners. A large majority of our faculty are part-time and working in industry while they are teaching, which gives our students valuable connections to their fields and access to relevant context about how to apply the skills and knowledge they are acquiring to the real world.

To balance this extensive industry experience among our part-time faculty, SPS appoints full-time faculty who fulfill the scholar-practitioner model, which includes both academic scholarship and industry experience. The full-time faculty serve as anchors for the school's academic quality through their participation in school-wide governance committees, policy review, curricular oversight, advising, admissions, and professional network development with employers and other organizations in their industries. Over the past three years, full-time faculty appointed to the master's degree programs have doubled in order to provide expert leadership at the programmatic level. The school's full-time faculty have extensive experience either in industry or in academia and are dedicated to interdisciplinary scholarship that connects theory and practice. Full-time faculty are active members of their fields and are engaged in publishing, presenting at conferences, consulting, and more. In 2016, the school introduced full-time Professors of Practice in addition to the school's full-time and part-time lecturers. Professors of Practice come to the school with substantial professional CVs and real-world experience and deepen the scholarly connections to industry.

Beyond the school's embrace of scholar-practitioners in the classroom, SPS also incorporates business leaders into the school's co-curricular programming, most notably through the Executives in Residence program and the Talks@Columbia series. Executives in Residence are senior executives from world-class companies across industries. Recent executives hail from companies such as BlackRock, Boston Consulting Group, Duane Morris, Hyatt Hotels, IBM, and Pfizer. They enrich the school's academic mission by bringing diverse, real-world experiences to students through a range of activities, including student mentorship, instruction, lectures, and engagement.

The Talks@Columbia series, launched in 2015 as a presentation series by industry leaders, researchers, and faculty, takes place through live events and as digital content that is distributed through the school's YouTube channel. The content of the Talks@Columbia series includes a diverse array of topics and speakers such as Chelsea Clinton and Randi Epstein discussing the science and ethics of marketing wellness; a conversation on leadership with Gloria Steinem and Gayatri Devi; and Mark Bertolini, former CEO of Aetna, sharing his insights on purpose-driven leadership. With a tagline of "learn for life," this public speaker series aims to reach all learners—from those enrolled at the university to the general public through digital delivery.

Crafting *flexible, dynamic curricula* that are easily adaptable to changing business needs is one of the key ways that SPS lives its mission of providing industry-driven education. SPS takes a market-forward approach to education driven by a commitment to deliver academic programs that meet the needs of industry. Through our deep ties with employers across sectors, we gather insights about where industries are heading and harness those insights to adapt existing academic programs and to innovate new program formats that address evolving market needs. These industry insights inform the university-driven processes for curriculum development and ongoing academic program review that reinforce the academic depth and rigor of the school's programs. The school's agile approach to curricula development exemplifies our commitment to advancing knowledge with purpose in order to meet rapidly evolving global market needs.

An example of the school's responsiveness to the needs of the marketplace is the recent development of a new master's degree program in Wealth Management, whose first students are scheduled to begin in fall 2020. The program was developed with robust input from employers through an advisory board consisting of leading asset management firms who examined the need for the program, including Deloitte Wealth, Goldman Sachs, Merrill Lynch, Morgan Stanley, and Wells Fargo. The wealth management sector is growing, with an expected $30 trillion in generational wealth that will be transferred to millennials in the coming years and a projected growth in personal finance managers of 16% by 2028 (Bureau of Labor Statistics, 2019). Based on the advisory board's assessment and the projected growth of the profession, it was determined that the program would fill an expected need in the marketplace and that Columbia SPS is well positioned to develop an innovative, online program to fill this need.

The Certified Financial Planner (CFP) Board served as the guide for the curriculum, and the program is a CFP Board Registered Program. The program is delivered through an online-only format, which provides flexibility to attract current professionals and career-changers seeking to transition into the growing field of wealth management. The program actively engages employers as either recruitment partners or career partners. Corporate recruitment partners co-host in-person or online recruitment sessions for prospective students to provide information about the program to their affiliates, which potentially benefits the corporate partner by deepening their pool of talent trained in the field of wealth management. Recruitment partners also collaborate with Columbia on thought leadership activities in the field, including research and speaking opportunities. Career partners focus on connecting students to opportunities through activities such as hosting webinars for enrolled students to provide information about careers in the field. They also sponsor applied research projects that help students connect their learning to real-world contexts, and they provide externships for students to shadow wealth managers at their companies. These formal opportunities for employers to partner with the program enhance the academic experience for students and support the alignment of the program to the needs of the industry.

A hallmark of Columbia SPS's educational approach is the integration of *interdisciplinary problem-solving* into the curriculum in the form of capstone projects for its master's programs. Capstone projects advance students' creative problem-solving skills in an applied setting by providing an opportunity to work on actual business problems being faced by industry partners. Examples include a project with the New York Public Library to apply data analytics to improve customer satisfaction, another project with Celebrity Cruises to uncover opportunities in luxury retail to attract passengers, and a project with the city of Flint, Michigan to empower the community to overcome its water crisis. By advancing and applying theoretical and practical knowledge across disciplines, SPS students, faculty, and alumni make a significant impact on real-world business problems like climate change, cybersecurity, and the evolution of medical care.

While there is some variation in the management of capstone projects across Columbia SPS programs, the capstone project of the Nonprofit Management Master's Degree Program provides a representative example of the school's approach to engaging employers through capstones. In accordance with the focus of the nonprofit management program, capstone clients are nonprofit organizations. The nonprofits that serve as capstone clients are faced with an organizational challenge for which they would like the students to research, analyze, and recommend strategic solutions. Through the course of the capstone project, which is carried out over an academic semester, representatives from the student group regularly interface with organizational representatives as they work to address the organization's needs. Specifically, the capstone clients commit to interacting with the university in the following ways:

- Providing a point-of-contact who serves as the primary owner of the project and interfaces with the capstone course instructor;
- Participating in two meetings or calls with the program director or faculty in advance of the capstone semester;
- Providing materials, proprietary information, and other resources pertinent to the project;
- Providing student and faculty access to key personnel throughout the semester as needed; and
- Engaging in two in-person meetings with students.

At the initial meeting at the beginning of the semester, clients provide an overview of the organization and its needs, and, at the end of the semester, they attend the final presentation and provide direct feedback to the students.

Care is taken to carefully integrate the goals of the nonprofit organization with the pedagogical goals of the program in order to provide a capstone experience that serves both the business needs of the nonprofit as well as an in-depth educational and professional experience for the students. This process begins before the capstone project takes place via a collaborative, consultative process involving the academic director and faculty from the nonprofit management program, the nonprofit's executive director, and other key, senior personnel.

Capstone projects provide ongoing interaction between the employer—a nonprofit organization in this case—and the program's students and faculty. This sustained engagement over the course of a semester provides the learning conditions necessary for students to apply their theoretical knowledge to a practical, real-world case, which ultimately serves the larger goal of making students more employable and producing graduates with both the in-depth knowledge and practical skills needed by employers. Kermit Kaleba of the National Skills Coalition recently stated that employers are often challenged to engage in work-based learning opportunities for students because they are already strapped to train their own employees and do not have the capacity to train students as well (as cited in Lipka, 2019). Kaleba contends that higher education has a valuable role to play in this equation by serving as the intermediary between students and employers to facilitate the achievement of the desired learning outcomes.

As students craft their career pathways, a key component of SPS's robust support for *career readiness* is the Career Design Lab (CDL). At SPS, the Career

Design Lab strengthens ties between SPS and industry partners to help foster learning, networking, and career building. The approach of the CDL is to guide students and alumni throughout their careers, not merely to a job following graduation. The mission of the CDL is to "aim to be the career and life compass for SPS students and alumni—a hub of informed connectors, helping them to find their true ambition by exploring career options and motivating them to pursue a meaningful career path" (Career Design Lab, n.d.). The CDL philosophy is to serve as a hub connecting students and alumni with employers and with each other, as the student and alumni network itself includes numerous industry leaders prevalent in the San Francisco area. This connector model provides the information and resources necessary for students to design their career paths, both upon graduation and throughout their careers.

With two locations—New York and San Francisco—as well as an online presence, the CDL provides a range of activities that connects employers with students and alumni. The CDL's signature event is its annual career week, held on campus in New York, which includes panels with industry leaders, a school-wide career and networking fair, "Career Talks" information sessions, management workshops, webinars, hot spots, a Virtual Business Card Program, and other career-related events. In addition to this annual event, the CDL provides a number of online and in-person events throughout the year spanning industry-insight panels, on-campus interviews, and corporate and organizational information sessions. In November 2018, SPS opened a second CDL in San Francisco to enhance the school's ties to San Francisco-based industries, particularly those focused on technology and innovation. The SPS Master of Science in Applied Analytics and Master of Science in Technology Management are most closely aligned with these industries as well as programs in strategic communication and bioethics.

Conclusion

Robust engagement between higher education and employers can take many forms. In the realm of professional education, the connection between the academy and industry has elevated importance because of the role of schools of professional studies in providing career-related education. As lifespans lengthen and career structures morph from the old model of linear pathways through a single career to a more flexible model where professionals routinely alter their professional pathways throughout their life stages (Andrew Scott, Chapter 2 in this volume), it will be increasingly imperative for all higher education units to incorporate elements of employer engagement into their academic approach. Doing so does not detract from academic quality; rather, it adds to a quality educational program and enhances the employability of its graduates. The case of Columbia University's School of Professional Studies offers an example of how a comprehensive approach to employer engagement can be undertaken.

The School of Professional Studies has a core commitment to align its programs to the market needs of employers and, in service of this goal, engages with employers in myriad ways through our academic and co-curricular programming. In addition to engaging with employers, higher education must also partner with coordinating agencies such as governments and nonprofits to develop multi-sector partnerships in support of workforce development and lifelong learning (Wingard & Farrugia, in press; Wingard & LaPointe, 2016). To deepen our commitment to employer engagement even further, we are developing an agenda in the Center on the Future of Work that will focus in part on the question of how employers are adapting to current and future changes in their industries and in workplaces more generally. Automation, the rapid evolution of technology, changing demographics, and the globalization of business operations are accelerating the need for companies to adapt to changes quickly and to anticipate new developments that have yet to occur. Professionals, too, are faced with the challenge of how to understand the large-scale shifts that will impact their careers, so they can develop a strategy to adapt and not be left behind. These changes in the future of work precipitate the need for new strategies for talent development, new modes of credentials, and learning innovation.

References

Abel, J. R., Davis, T., Deitz, T., & Reyes, E. (2018). *Employer engagement by community colleges in New York State*. New York, NY: Federal Reserve Bank of New York. Retrieved from https://www.newyorkfed.org/medialibrary/media/outreach-and- education/workforce-development/NYS-Employer-Engagement-Community-Colleges- Report.pdf

Abel, J. R., Deitz, R., & Su, Y. (2014). Are recent college graduates finding good jobs? *Current Issues in Economics and Finance, 20*(1), 2014. Retrieved from https://papers.ssrn.com/abstract=2378472

Beckett, S. (2018, March 14). What's the difference between skills and competencies? [Web log post]. Retrieved from Human Resource Systems Group (HRSG) website: https://resources.hrsg.ca/blog/what-s-the-difference-between-skills-and-competencies

Bessen, J. (2014, August 25). Employers aren't just whining: The "skills gap" is real. *Harvard Business Review*. Retrieved from https://hbr.org/2014/08/employers-arent-just-whining-the-skills-gap-is-real

Bureau of Labor Statistics. (2019). Occupational outlook handbook: Financial managers. Retrieved from U.S. Department of Labor website: https://www.bls.gov/ooh/management/financial-managers.htm

Burning Glass Technologies. (n.d.). Underemployment: The long-term impact on careers. Retrieved from https://www.burning-glass.com/research-project/underemployment/

Career Design Lab. (n.d.). Columbia University School of professional studies. Retrieved from https://sps.columbia.edu/students/career-design-lab

Columbia SPS. (2019, June). *Higher education: Still the solution for a workforce in flux?* [Video file]. Presented at the Forum on the Future of Work, Columbia University, New York, NY. Retrieved from https://www.youtube.com/watch?v=vFBZ_-kd8pk

Davidson, C. N. (2017). *The new education: How to revolutionize the university to prepare students for a world in flux*. New York, NY: Basic Books.

Dede, C. (2018, October 19). The 60 Year curriculum: Developing new educational models to support the agile labor market. *The Evolllution*. Retrieved from https://evolllution.com/revenue-streams/professional_development/the-60-year- curriculum-developing-new-educational-models-to-serve-the-agile-labor-market

De Novellis, M. (2019, January 8). What do employers want from business schools? *AACSB Blog*. Retrieved from https://www.aacsb.edu/blog/2019/january/what-do-employers- want-from-business-schools

Forrier, A., & Sels, L. (2003). The concept employability: A complex mosaic. *International Journal of Human Resources Development and Management, 3*(2), 102. doi:10.1504/IJHRDM.2003.002414

Garcia-Navarro, L. (2018, July 15). How underemployment is affecting the job market. National Public Radio. Retrieved from https://www.npr.org/2018/07/15/629212924/the-call-in-underemployment

Glassdoor. (2018, August 14). 15 more companies that no longer require a degree: Apply now [Web log post]. Retrieved from Glassdoor website: https://www.glassdoor.com/blog/no-degree-required/

Gutkin, L. (2019, July 12). Elite schools are national treasures. Their elitism is what makes them such. *The Chronicle of Higher Education*. Retrieved from https://www.chronicle.com/article/Elite-Schools-Are-National/246657

Head, L., & Polk, B. (2019, July 19). Inside college-employer partnerships: The importance of trust. *The EvoLLLution*. Retrieved from https://evolllution.com/revenue- streams/corporate_partnerships/inside-college-employer-partnerships-the-importance-of- trust/

Hogarth, T., Winterbotham, M., Hasluck, C., Carter, K., Daniel, W. W., Green, A. E., & Morrison, J. (2007). *Employer and university engagement in the use and development of graduate level skills* (Research Report RR835A). Institute for Employment Research. Nottingham, UK: University of Warwick.

Holmes, L. (2013). Competing perspectives on graduate employability: Possession, position or process? *Studies in Higher Education, 38*(4), 538–554. doi:10.1080/03075079.2011.587140

Human Resource Systems Group. (n.d.). Behavioral competencies. Retrieved from https://www.hrsg.ca/behavioral-competencies

Johnston, C. S. (2018). A systematic review of the career adaptability literature and future outlook. *Journal of Career Assessment, 26*(1), 3–30. doi:10.1177/1069072716679921

Kaplan University Partners. (2019). *Destination college: Exploring new routes to success* (Summary Report). Retrieved from https://kaplan.com/wp- content/uploads/2019/04/Destination-College-Report-Kaplan-UP-4.19.pdf

Khan, M. M., & Ahmed, M. E. (2018). Capstone project based experiential learning-case of Institute of Business Management. *Journal of e-Learning and Higher Education, 2018*, 1–23. doi:10.5171/2018.412705

Kochan, T. A., Finegold, D., & Osterman, P. (2012, December 1). Who can fix the "middle-skills" gap? *Harvard Business Review*. Retrieved from https://hbr.org/2012/12/who-can-fix-the-middle-skills-gap

Kolb, D. A. (1984). *Experiential learning: Experience as the source of learning and development.* Upper Saddle River, NJ: Prentice-Hall.

LaPointe, M., & Wingard, J. (2016). How did we get here? A history of education and training in the United States. In J. Wingard & M. LaPointe (Eds.), *Learning for life: How continuous education will keep us competitive in the global knowledge economy* (pp. 3–9). New York, NY: American Management Association.

Lipka, S. (2019). Preparing students for 21st-century careers (Roundtable Report). *The Chronicle of Higher Education*. Retrieved from http://connect.chronicle.com/21stcntrycrs?cid=CHE_HA_MKTO_21STCNTRY_ALL_0

Lohr, S. (2017, June 28). A new kind of tech job emphasizes skills, not a college degree. *The New York Times*. Retrieved from https://www.nytimes.com

Morris, T. H. (2019). Experiential learning—A systematic review and revision of Kolb's model. *Interactive Learning Environments*. doi:10.1080/10494820.2019.1570279

Mulholland, J. (2015, December 10). Academics: Forget about public engagement, stay in your ivory towers. *The Guardian*. Retrieved from https://www.theguardian.com

Pianin, E. (2014, January 29). The surprising reason college grads can't get a job. Retrieved from CNBC website: https://www.cnbc.com/2014/01/29/the-surprising-reason- college-grads-cant-get-a-job.html

Purtill, C. (2018, August 23). Apple, IBM, and Google don't care anymore if you went to college. *Quartz at Work*. Retrieved from https://qz.com/work/1367191/apple-ibm-and-google-dont-require-a-college-degree/

Restuccia, D., Taska, B., & Bittle, S. (2018). *Different skills, different gaps: Measuring & closing the skills gap* (Report). Retrieved from Burning Glass Technologies website: https://www.burning-glass.com/wp-content/uploads/ Skills_Gap_Different_Skills_Different_Gaps_FINAL.pdf

Sabria-Bernado, B., Llinas-Audet, X., & Isus, S. (2017). Determinants of user demand for lifelong learning in institutions of higher education. *International Journal of Training and Development, 21*(2), 145–166.

Savickas, M. L., & Porfeli, E. J. (2012). Career adapt-abilities scale: Construction, reliability, and measurement equivalence across 13 countries. *Journal of Vocational Behavior, 80*(3), 661–673. doi:10.1016/j.jvb.2012.01.011

Seagraves, L., Kemp, I., & Osborne, M. J. (1996). Are academic outcomes of higher education provision relevant and deliverable in the workplace setting? *Higher Education, 32*, 157–176.

Suleman, F. (2018). The employability skills of higher education graduates: Insights into conceptual frameworks and methodological options. *Higher Education, 76*(2), 263–278. doi:10.1007/s10734-017-0207-0

Super, D. E., & Knasel, E. G. (1981). Career development in adulthood: Some theoretical problems and a possible solution. *British Journal of Guidance and Counselling, 9*(2), 194–201. doi:10.1080/03069888108258214

Tugend, A. (2013, June 28). What it takes to make new college graduates employable. *The New York Times*. Retrieved from https://www.nytimes.com

Walker, M., & Fongwa, S. (2017). *Universities, employability and human development*. London, England: Palgrave Macmillan.

Wingard, J. (2015). *Learning to succeed: Rethinking corporate education in a world of unrelenting change*. New York, NY: Academy of Management.

Wingard, J., & Farrugia, C. (Eds.). (in press). *The future of work: Optimizing the talent pipeline*. Stanford, CA: Stanford University Press.

Wingard, J., & LaPointe, J. (2016). What might an effective system of lifelong learning look like? In J. Wingard & M. LaPointe (Eds.), *Learning for life: How continuous education will keep us competitive in the global knowledge economy* (pp. 219–223). New York, NY: American Management Association.

8

The Role and Potential of University-Based Executive Education and Professional Development Programs in the 60-Year Curriculum

A Case Example of an Intensive Residential Program for Higher Education Leaders

JAMES P. HONAN

Introduction

In his overview in Chapter 1 of the various driving forces and contextual factors pointing toward the need for a 60-Year Curriculum (*60YC*), Chris Dede high-lights several high-level themes, including reinvention; ongoing occupational change; and continuing, professional, adult, and lifelong learning.

Building on this helpful set of framing issues, the focal point of this chapter is a specific type of teaching and learning experience that usually takes place in the middle or later stages of the overall arc of a *60YC*, typically when an individual is well-along in their career, professional, and academic trajectory—university-based executive education and professional development programs. An example of a long-standing, university-based version of this type of offering will be highlighted in depth in this chapter—The Institute for Educational Management (IEM) at the Harvard Graduate School of Education, a residential, executive education program for senior higher-education leaders. This chapter considers the role and potential that university-based executive education and professional development programs such as IEM may play in the *60YC* continuum.

Executive Education and Professional Development Programs in Context: Their Role in the Broader Higher Education Ecosystem

Numerous colleges and universities offer a wide range of executive education and professional development programs as an important element of their mission and overall strategy. In most cases, these programs are offered through graduate and professional schools. As noted by Rasmussen and Callan (2016),

> Schools that have active executive education programs display a strong understanding of the needs of practitioners and they work hard to convey the impression that they are integrating the experiences of practitioners into the executive education programs that they offer.
>
> (p. 406)

They also observe that "a strong brand, particularly a strong university brand" (p. 401) is an important success factor in the executive education arena.

At Harvard University, numerous executive education and professional development programs are offered by Harvard Business School, Harvard Kennedy School, Harvard Graduate School of Education, Harvard Law School, Harvard T. H. Chan School of Public Health, Harvard Graduate School of Design, Harvard Extension School, Harvard Medical School, and Harvard Divinity School. These programs vary in length from a few days to several weeks and cover a wide range of professions and fields.

The audiences for these types of short-term, intensive teaching and learning experiences tend to be leaders, managers, and professionals in existing roles who are interested in next-level learning opportunities, new content, tools, and frameworks, all of which are linked to emerging challenges and upskilling needs for them as individuals and/or within their own organizations. Factors in the rapidly changing external environment such as globalization, digitalization, and fundamental changes and advances in the technology sector (including artificial intelligence and robotics) are highlighted and discussed in other chapters of this book. These broader contextual developments will require university-based executive education programs to evolve in the coming years to meet new learning needs effectively.

The senior-level executive education audience has very particular and distinctive teaching and learning needs and interests, such as expectations for new and innovative content, high-quality pedagogy, and applicability to and relevance for work and professional settings. Executive education audiences are self-directed in terms of their interest in taking part in such programs. As noted by Suutari and Viitala (2008), managers and leaders are "increasingly being encouraged to take responsibility for their own learning" (p. 381). Having an appreciation for this perspective on learning is a key element of designing and delivering effective executive education programs to experienced leaders.

Kets de Vries and Korotov (2007) provide additional insight into the various factors motivating this particular audience of learners:

> Participants in executive education programs often go back to school to explore how to best use their strengths and talents, how to avoid unproductive allocation of their time and energy, and how not to miss out on emerging opportunities. The motivation for taking the program is often an excitement about one's capacities and new horizons or, in some cases, anticipatory anxiety of possibly not being successful and missing one's chances.
>
> (p. 376)

In a study of executive education programs at schools of public policy, Rasmussen and Callan (2016) add additional detail to the type of learning executive education participants expect programs to deliver:

> There is more demand for practical applications of theory, and more time spent on exploring participants' challenges and experiences and less on basic skills and foundational issues. . . . There are more connections to cases, simulations, and similar pedagogical tools, to students' background and work experiences, and more effort generally to draw out experiences from students.
>
> (p. 400)

Many university-based executive education programs, including those offered at Harvard, commonly utilize case-method teaching as part of their design and delivery. Case teaching works particularly well with experienced, senior-level leaders. This pedagogical approach can help identify alternative ways of framing and identifying complex leadership and management problems and assist participants in identifying alternative leadership approaches and techniques for addressing these problems. Case teaching also is quite effective in tapping into the wide range of experiences senior-level leaders bring to their participation in executive education programs.

University-based executive education and professional development programs represent a niche in the overall higher education ecosystem, including the evolution of the 60YC, and are designed to meet the specific learning needs of skilled and experienced leaders and managers.

The Institute for Educational Management (IEM) at the Harvard Graduate School of Education

An example of a long-standing, university-based executive education and professional development program is the Institute for Educational Management (IEM) at the Harvard Graduate School of Education (HGSE). First offered in 1970, IEM began as a six-week, residential, executive education program developed by faculty at Harvard Business School and HGSE. It has evolved over 50 years to a nine-day, face-to-face program led and delivered by faculty at HGSE; it now also includes two online follow-up components. More than 4,700 senior leaders from colleges and universities around the world have participated in IEM over the past five decades.

By design, the program takes a cross-role approach in terms of both audience and program curriculum, inviting participants to take an institution-wide perspective on their work as opposed to a purely functional viewpoint. This approach enables participants to integrate their functional role with those of other cabinet-level, senior leadership positions. IEM participants engage individuals in other roles from campuses other than their own in ways that might be more challenging than similar discussions among members of their own leadership teams.

IEM attracts individual participants from a wide range of roles as opposed to entire cross-functional teams. Programs with the latter focus exist in the executive education ecosystem and have a different design and format than programs such as IEM, which attracts individual participants.

A Profile of IEM Participants—Senior Higher-Education Leaders

Each year, IEM enrolls approximately 100 participants, all of whom are senior leaders of colleges and universities. IEM participants represent a range of titles, roles, and institutions. All IEM participants hold jobs that are challenging and complex. The participant group represents a range of personal, professional, and academic backgrounds. The cross-role approach is intentional; participants can spend time with and learn from individuals they would otherwise not interact with.

Participants identify a range of reasons for applying to and enrolling in IEM—a spectrum of ways of fitting the program into one's personal and professional world. Among the reasons applicants identify for wanting to attend IEM are to spend time thinking about their work as senior higher-education leaders; to explore current and emerging challenges and opportunities in the higher education sector; to take some time away from day-to-day work for reflection, rejuvenation, and inspiration; and to develop new perspectives on one's leadership approach. Myrsiades (2001) observes that participants in executive education programs expect to "capitalize on the breadth and experience of talent present as well as to work on issues of immediate interest and concern to the participants" (p. 799). IEM aspires to meet both expectations regarding the content and design of the program and its curriculum.

Participating in an intensive executive education program such as IEM is, in many cases, a once-in-a-lifetime opportunity for professional development and personal learning. Enrolling in a residential executive education program such as IEM represents a nontrivial commitment to one's learning; it can take many years to find the time or make the time to attend the program. Taking advantage of such an opportunity requires financial resources, time away from work and family, and support from colleagues, family, and friends.

Identifying a Leadership Challenge as a Focal Point for Professional and Personal Learning in IEM

In advance of the IEM program, all participants are asked to prepare a brief, written summary of one-to-two pages in length of a leadership challenge or problem of practice they are currently facing in their work as senior leaders of colleges and universities. The idea is to identify a professional or personal challenge that participants want to think more deeply about, are willing to discuss with fellow IEM participants, and are hoping to make progress on during the program. As such, the leadership challenge constitutes a key aspect of a participant's learning agenda for the program. As a result, it is important to note that the 100 participants each come with a learning agenda that is both personal and meaningful.

During the IEM program, participants' leadership challenges are used and referenced in the context of the theories, frameworks, and tools that are presented and discussed throughout the program curriculum. In addition to serving as a focal point for professional and personal learning, participants' leadership challenges serve as the basis of small discussion-groups in which participants receive counsel, consultation, and feedback from their peers. A summary of the leadership challenges identified by participants is shared with the IEM faculty to help deepen their understanding of the issues that are important to the participants. In addition, the key themes of the leadership challenges are shared with the participants in the opening session of the program. The curricular focus of IEM evolves over time according to the most important leadership challenges that participants identify.

Leadership challenges reflect a wide range of topics relevant to senior-level higher education leaders—challenges are both personal and institutional, and sometimes these dimensions interact. Personal leadership challenges include developing new skills and approaches to leadership and management, managing time, meeting expectations for delivering results, and being an effective team leader. Institutional challenges, not surprisingly, represent some of the current and emerging issues facing colleges and universities and their leaders: undertaking presidential transitions; adapting organizations to cope with and support innovation and change; developing effective diversity, equity, and inclusion strategies; addressing enrollment management trends; launching new initiatives; responding to budget and business model constraints; supporting technology-related disruption; dealing effectively with faculty and trustee governance matters; and developing tuition and financial aid policies and strategies.

IEM Curriculum and Faculty

The formal IEM curriculum and various sessions and modules in the program are intentionally designed to be aligned with leadership challenges as well as current and emerging issues in the context of college and university leaders and their institutions. A study of in-house, executive education programs designed for college and university leaders at a state university identified several key characteristics of an effective education offering:

> that it be intimately tied to anticipating and causing industry change, that it focus on the centrality of active distributive leadership, and that it engage participants in activities that translate into action plans linked to actual organizational outcomes desired by the institution.
>
> (Myrsiades, 2001, p. 795)

These elements of effective program design are reflected in IEM's curricular development and are consistent with several the key points made by Chris Dede in his introductory chapter in this volume regarding adult learning and education.

Topics in the formal IEM curriculum include personal/authentic leadership; budgeting and financial planning; enrollment management; financial aid and admissions policies; diversity, equity, and inclusion strategies; faculty and trustee governance; leadership transitions; external relations; big data; strategic planning; and presidential leadership. Program sessions are designed to incorporate multiple teaching and pedagogical formats including presentation and discussion, case studies, interviews, panels, and small group workshops. On any given day, there are typically three to four 90-minute teaching sessions with scheduled breaks and meals. Time is also allocated each day for small discussion group meetings, optional affinity group meetings, and social events. The goal is to create a sequence of varied types of engagement that build on each other to maximize participant learning, both individual and collective.

As is the case with other executive education and professional development programs for experienced leaders, faculty who teach in IEM need a combination of content expertise, well-developed pedagogical skills, practical experience in the field, and a nuanced theory and practice perspective. In their analysis of the primary characteristics of successful, university-based executive education programs, Margulies and Gregg (2013) note the fundamental role that the quality of the faculty plays:

> From the student (customer) perspective, it is all about quality of instruction. In effect, the instructor *is* Executive Education as far as the student is concerned. Faculty quality is the single most important factor in the attractiveness of Executive Education. Managers and leaders are keenly interested in current developments, best practices, new research into management processes, and emerging knowledge and process that might aid in their decision-making.
>
> (p. 5)

The IEM faculty keep these interests in mind as they design and deliver program sessions. Targeting their efforts to the specific learning needs and interests of senior-level leaders is essential to program success. Whereas programs and courses designed for graduate students have fundamental characteristics (e.g., focus on introductory or foundational content and/or core courses, etc.), executive education programs and modules must be tailored to reflect the extensive experience senior-level leaders bring to the program.

Incorporating a Range of Teaching and Learning Modalities in the IEM Program

IEM utilizes a variety of teaching and learning modalities, each of which provides participants with a range of opportunities for learning. These include classes, formal curriculum, and large group discussions; small discussion groups; affinity groups; individual preparation and reflection; meals and social events; and free, unstructured time.

Classes, Formal Curriculum, and Large-Group Discussions

The formal IEM curriculum consists of three-to-four faculty-led sessions with the large group each day of the program. Faculty utilize a range pedagogical approaches to these sessions—case study teaching, interactive lectures and discussions, panels, interviews, etc.

Small Discussion Groups

Participants are assigned to small discussion groups (usually 8–10 participants per group), which provide many learning opportunities that are not possible in the larger participant group of 100. Groups meet daily and remain intact for the duration of the program. Small groups serve multiple purposes that enable personalized and individualized learning: they are a venue for receiving feedback and advice on individual leadership challenges; they can play a sounding board role for a problem or challenge an individual is experiencing in their work; and they are a mechanism for sharing experiences and expertise. There is not a designated facilitator or leader for the small discussion groups. Participants are encouraged to rotate the convening role, to set an agreed-upon learning agenda for the group, and to identify a process for achieving the small group's learning agenda during the program. The purpose of the small discussion group is learning; small discussion groups are not task oriented, and there is no required final report, presentation, or product. There is not a one-size-fits-all approach to effective, small-discussion-group learning—each group sets its own course and strategy. The IEM program team does a brief mid-program check-in with a member of each discussion group to get a sense of strategies and techniques that are working particularly well.

Affinity Groups

Executive education program participants come with significant experience, expertise, and knowledge. Since it is not possible to cover all topics and issues that participants might be interested in as part of the formal IEM curriculum, affinity groups represent a flexible, nimble, responsive mechanism to meet participant-identified learning needs. Participants interested in connecting with colleagues with common interests in a topic or challenge can nominate and convene small affinity groups to pursue this type of peer learning. Affinity groups are typically convened at lunch during the program; in some cases, groups hold follow-up meetings and conversations.

Individual Preparation and Reflection

IEM participants are encouraged to set aside time for individual preparation (reading) and reflection before and after all the formal classes and sessions during the program. The persistent day-to-day demands of high-level leadership and administrative roles in colleges and universities make this learning modality important and, unfortunately, all too rare. Many participants report that they seldom have time to read and think in their roles. They are encouraged to find and take the time (daily) to read and prepare for teaching sessions throughout the program. IEM faculty assign case studies and readings that are essential components of their work with participants.

Meals and Social Events

IEM participants have numerous and frequent opportunities for informal interactions and conversations with each other at daily meals (which they have together) and several social events. In this regard, participants are encouraged to try to meet and speak with everyone in the program before it ends. The program is residential in nature (participants are housed at a single location and spend all their time together during the day in the classroom and at meals). As such, it is fair to say that "the program is always on" and that opportunities for informal conversations and discussions are quite plentiful.

Free and Unstructured Time

Although the IEM schedule is intensive, there are multiple opportunities and possibilities to leverage free and unstructured time for reflection and learning throughout the duration of the program. This element of the program is quite different from the complex and fully booked schedule participants experience in their professional roles.

Participants are encouraged to think about how they can best use each one of the mechanisms above to facilitate and support their learning throughout the program.

Creating the Conditions for High Quality Teaching and Learning for Experienced Leaders

The primary job and role of the leadership and staff team of IEM is to create, optimize, and sustain the conditions for participants to focus on their own learning and to fully engage each teaching and learning modality.

One of the more complex and challenging tasks to carry out during an intensive, residential executive education program such as IEM is reorienting and shifting the pattern of time, attention, and mindshare from day-to-day, high-level, complex leadership and administrative work to focused, engaged, high-intensity teaching and learning. It can take a few days for this transition to take place. It is important to give participants permission to focus on their learning as opposed to the default position they have usually been in to accomplish things on a large and never-ending to-do list. The advice that is given to the IEM participants at the initial session of the program is counterintuitive: "You do not need to be in charge of anything or anyone except your own learning." It is important not to underestimate the challenge that this shift can present for busy, high-level professionals who may not have had the chance to prioritize learning at this stage of their professional and personal lives.

Participants are told that all logistical details (schedule, transportation, meals, classroom details, curricular materials, faculty, etc.) will be taken care of throughout the program. It can take a day or two for participants to trust the program team and to trust themselves to not think about logistics and day-to-day tasks and instead focus on learning. Once they make the shift, many participants observe how much they appreciate being a student again. (It is worth noting that, since the program participants are from the higher education sector, this is a very valuable shift in perspective.) Program participants are also reminded that the program is finite: the analogy of a pop-up store or restaurant is sometimes used to describe IEM. Participants are encouraged to stay in the moment as best they can and not to try to plan or think too far ahead as the program unfolds.

Developing an Action Plan

In addition to identifying a leadership challenge before attending the program and working with it in various ways during the program, IEM participants conclude the program by identifying action steps they will take when they return to their institutions. Given the various learning experiences that each participant leaves the program with, action steps can range from personal leadership changes to institution-wide initiatives. Participants share their action steps with members of their small discussion group on the final day of the program and identify ways in which small-discussion-group peers might offer support and advice moving forward.

Pursuing a Variety of Post-Program Outcomes

At the end of the IEM program, participants have used a variety of similes to describe the type of intensive, professional, and personal learning experience they have just taken part in. One participant noted that taking part in the program felt like "hitting the reset or restart button on a computer." Another noted that it felt like "pulling a car off to the side of the road to rest and refuel." One participant once poignantly observed that IEM was like "a campfire" that provided a powerful opportunity to think, reflect, enjoy the company of others, and "slow time down" (personal communication). There are multiple dimensions of potential post-program outcomes that IEM participants can leave the program with once they return to their organizations, and many participants experience one or more of them once they return to their work:

- Aligned with their pre-program desire for new knowledge, tools, frameworks, and approaches to leadership and management, some participants experience several "aha" moments that can lead to changing their minds and/or practices around a topic or issue. They literally think about situations and challenges differently, and this can lead to doing things in a better or new way.

- Working with individuals who bring decades of leadership experience and extensive academic or professional training makes it unsurprising that another outcome of participating in an intensive executive education program can be affirmation of one's current leadership practices and approaches. Some participants leave the program thinking, "I know how to do this work and I am good at it," an important insight for a leader at any stage of their development.
- After being away from their institutions and family and friends, some participants leave the program with a new (or renewed) and different perspective on their work and institution. Many participants note a deeper appreciation of and connection to their institutions, their colleagues, and their work.
- Because of spending a significant amount of time and engaging deeply with 100 other leaders, most participants leave the program with a significantly larger, wider, and deeper professional network, an asset for leaders at any stage of development, but particularly helpful for senior leaders. Being able to call on trusted colleagues for support, resources, and counsel is an important byproduct of taking part in IEM and similar programs. Participants are reminded that they are not alone and that they have many new friends and allies to assist them in their work as leaders.
- One of the most powerful post-program outcomes that some IEM participants experience relates to the issue of discovering, rediscovering, or renewing one's understanding of and connection to the purpose and focus of one's work. Some participants come face-to-face with the question *why* do I do this work?" Experienced leaders such as IEM participants must inevitably grapple with the question of whether what one is doing professionally (and what one has done for many decades in some instances) is a job, or role, or calling, or one's life's work. In some cases, the takeaway on this question is renewed commitment to the work and an interest in moving forward to higher levels of responsibility. In other cases, the outcome is a change of heart (some participants decide they want to go back to teaching and research rather than continue in a leadership or administrative role)—needless to say, this shift or pivot represents a fundamental and powerful learning outcome on both a personal and professional level.

Future Considerations

Over its 50-year history, IEM has evolved from a six-week program to one that is now nine days in length. Looking ahead, it will be important to consider how this trend might continue. Among the strategic questions that need to be considered in the coming years are the following:

- How long does an intensive, university-based, residential executive education and professional development program need to be to optimize the various learning experiences and outcomes that have been described above?
- What impact might technology-mediated teaching and learning play in program design before, during, and/or after an intensive, residential executive education program?

- How should one think about the theory and assumptions of intensive, university-based, residential, executive education programs in the future given the various changes and factors described above?
- What is the value proposition of bringing people together (literally), facilitating structured and intensive face-to-face interaction, and requiring participants to spend time away from work, family, and friends to focus on their personal and professional learning?

Answers to these fundamental questions will serve to inform and guide future IEM program design and delivery decisions.

There may also be implications for programs designed to address leaders' needs earlier in their careers and at other points in the 60-Year Curricular arc. For example, future programs and learning experiences for early-career leaders might have more hybrid or blended features or could leverage technology in more extensive ways. By contrast, one of the core design principles of a program such as IEM is providing an intensive and personalized learning experience to busy senior-level leaders by bringing them together and offering a varied set of face-to-face learning experiences. Looking forward, this might continue to be reflected in IEM's design and delivery structure and value proposition.

Lessons and Insights for the *60YC*: Potential Roles for University-Based Executive Education and Professional Development Programs

The IEM example provides some possible ways to look at the potential roles that university-based executive education and professional development programs might play in the *60YC*. For example, perhaps these types of programs can serve as a capstone or culminating learning experience in one's overall professional trajectory as a leader, providing helpful insights and serving as a catalyst for engaging in the next stages of one's leadership journey. In addition, participating in these types of programs can help to clarify and affirm one's core commitments and purposes as a leader—an important learning outcome for leaders at this stage.

In considering the types of executive education/professional development programs that might be offered to leaders at this point of the *60YC* continuum, it is important to consider what specific program design and experiences best meet the particular learning needs of individuals who might enroll in such programs. Consistent with this idea, McCarthy, Sammon, and O'Raghallaigh (2016) have developed a program design matrix that seeks to incorporate the perspectives of various executive education program stakeholders (participants, participant sponsors, faculty, higher education institutions, and academic partners) into program planning conversations (p. 567).

It seems clear that well-designed, university-based executive education programs that will effectively meet the learning needs of leaders at this stage of their development will need to reflect stakeholder input and counsel and will necessarily continue to be intensive, responsive to individual challenges, and highly interpersonal.

It is worth noting that that intensive, residential executive education programs such as IEM are somewhat difficult to scale for a range of reasons, including the fundamental design of such programs. Looking forward, it is likely that the development of technology-mediated teaching and learning in the design and delivery of these types of programs might help address scaling challenges. Incorporating more hybrid/blended program designs may lead to more ongoing and widespread connection and learning opportunities among program participants as well as potentially linking participants to larger and broader networks of like-minded learners at this stage of the 60-Year Curricular arc. Communities of practice supported by various technology-mediated platforms and structures are also supported by various national and regional professional associations and organizations as well as other executive education providers. It is possible that such mechanisms designed for senior-level leaders might be developed and become more widespread in the coming years.

Leaders with an interest in taking part in intensive, university-based, residential executive education programs as part of their lifelong learning agenda would benefit from improved advising, support, and counsel for choosing a program that would best meet one's learning needs. Perhaps, networks of peers and prior participants in such programs could serve as a mechanism for facilitating and improving access to such learning opportunities and would be more robust than existing word-of-mouth channels for such connection.

As noted by Dede, the driving forces and contextual factors pointing toward the need for a *60YC* create significant opportunities for university-based executive education and professional development programs to help leaders cope with rapid and fundamental workplace and occupational changes.

Rasmussen and Callan (2016) highlight this point, observing that governments and other public sector organizations face a range of emerging learning and professional development challenges, including

> the need to develop leadership talent; the stress associated with financial pressures and 'doing more with less;' the need to innovate in the development of public policy and the delivery of programs; and the need to ensure that citizens are satisfied with service delivery.
>
> (p. 407)

They express optimism about the potential and possibility of university-based offerings to address these challenges, concluding

> Because leadership is seen to be the wellspring for dealing with all these problems, successful executive education programs are likely to focus on leadership issues, including political acumen, organizational performance, people skills, developing junior staff, and making decisions based on public service values and ethics. In all of this, university-based executive education has obvious strengths compared to other providers and competitors.
>
> (p. 407)

If these types of programs are going to fulfill their promise and potential, it will be important to describe and account for tangible learning outcomes and to communicate this information to key stakeholders. In this regard, Seidle, Fernandez, and Perry (2016) examined ways in which leadership training and development programs in the public sector improve the performance of leaders and their organizations. They observe, "While knowledge gleaned from leadership research is often used to help screen and select candidates, scholars have rarely explored whether leadership training and development programs are effective, and the limited empirical evidence that is available paints a mixed picture" (p. 603). They add:

> Leadership training and development continue to grow as leadership has become increasingly important because of the complexity of the workplace and persistent calls for innovation and continuous improvement. Simply put, it is critical that we learn more about the effectiveness of leadership training and development programs to determine whether these massive investments are paying dividends.
>
> (p. 604)

Leaders and organizers of university-based executive education and professional development programs can strengthen their role in the *60YC* by continuing to identify and disseminate data on the impact that their programs have on both leaders and organizations.

References

Kets de Vries, M. F. R., & Korotov, K. (2007). Creating transformational executive education programs. *Academy of Management Learning and Education, 6*(3), 375–387. doi:10.5465/amle.2007.26361627

Margulies, N., & Gregg, J. R. (2013). Strategic planning for university-based executive education programs: Success factors and design alternatives. *Journal of Executive Education, 1*(1), 1–11.

McCarthy, P., Sammon, D., & O'Raghallaigh, P. (2016). Designing an executive education programme: Towards a program design matrix. *Journal of Decision Systems, 25*(S1), 566–571. doi:10.1080/12460125.2016.1189640

Myrsiades, L. (2001). Looking to lead: A case in designing executive education from the inside. *Journal of Management Development, 20*(9), 795–812. doi: 10.1108/EUM0000000006161

Rasmussen, K., & Callan, D. (2016). Schools of public policy and executive education: An opportunity missed? *Policy and Society, 35*(4), 397–411.

Seidle, B., Fernandez, S., & Perry, J. L. (2016). Do leadership training and development make a difference in the public sector? A panel study. *Public Administration Review, 76*(4), 603–613. doi:10.1111/puar.12531

Suutari, V., & Viitala, R. (2008). Management development of senior executives: Methods and their effectiveness. *Personnel Review, 37*(4), 375–392. doi:10.1108/00483480810877561

9

Implementing 60-Year Curriculum Learning at the Harvard Division of Continuing Education

HUNTINGTON D. LAMBERT AND HENRY H. LEITNER

The Socio-Economic Context

Learner Longevity and Rapid Change

In Chapter 1 of this volume, Chris Dede points out that today's learners will live longer, adapt repeatedly to evolving job requirements, and change careers several times as they pass through multiple stages in a lifetime of learning. Even now, these learners live in a society where 65% of the jobs that a typical middle-schooler will fill do not yet exist (Lambert, 2019). Many post-secondary learners are not residential four-year students; instead, they participate in flexible forms of education (UPCEA, 2019) because a virtualized two- or four-year education or a formal apprenticeship program, while arguably necessary, does not provide enough learning to last through or match the pace of the change encountered in a lifetime. As Figure 9.1 illustrates, a variety of education and training services will have to be available across several stages of a learner's life at the times and places they are needed.

Done well, a *60YC* education, delivered in modalities that are matched to learners' needs and pedagogical requirements, will maximize their ability to learn, equip them with the skills and knowledge they need for creating valuable work products in yet-to-be invented jobs and unforeseen careers, and enable them to fulfill civic and social responsibilities in an ecosystem of rapidly changing technology, global economic disruption, and environmental crises.

INSTITUTIONAL REORIENTATION

However, the education industry is in upheaval. The synergistic digital economy to which Dede refers is compelling suppliers of education to become ever more flexible, ever more responsive to customer needs, and ever more efficient in meeting those needs. Wasted credentials, impractical outcomes, unnecessarily long completion times, and failures to complete [National Center for Education Statistics (NCES), 2017, 2019] must be reduced. Administrative barriers between and within institutions that frustrate learners, faculty, and employers must be eliminated.

132

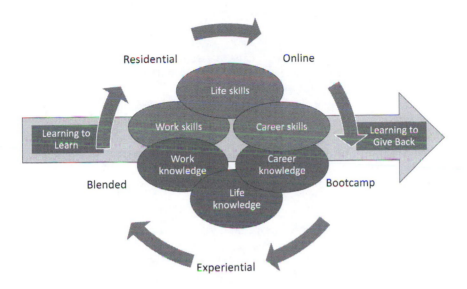

Figure 9.1 Modalities and objectives of 60YC learning

Higher education institutions are beginning to reorient their services to reduce these inefficiencies and integrate lifelong support for learners with modernized courses and degree programs.[1] Their aim is to establish and manage long-term learner relationships. Otherwise, those long-term relationships are likely to be captured and monopolized by a few global organizations or private companies such as Amazon, Apple, Microsoft, or Alphabet. That outcome likely would leave only marginal local or specialized markets for higher education institutions and ultimately provide society at large with much less diversity in knowledge creation and transmission.

Ann Brewer, in Chapter 4 of this volume, advocates for a "design learning" process for institutions developing *60YC* educational systems and services that are capable of sustained "strategic student relationship management." In her view, the challenge is not developing something new, but integrating student-facing services and functions to deliver innovative educational models and approaches. For higher education institutions, implementing Internet-era courses and programs is easy. Great institutional brands with decades of progress in teaching and learning continue to provide leadership in the science, engineering, and practice of delivering education. Educational information is cheap and easily available. Buildings, libraries, and even faculties no longer limit access to or delivery of that information. Many institutions now package and personalize their services for learners at all stages of life and deliver them in on-campus, online, workplace, and hybrid modes that match the individual learner's current situation and goals.

The hard part for institutions that are implementing the *60YC* is integrating dynamically evolving curriculum and changing delivery channels with revivified advising, credentialing, and other "alumni" services.

The Scope of the *60YC*

To appreciate the scale of the new academic, administrative, and information systems infrastructures and extended educational services that the Harvard Division of Continuing Education (HDCE) is developing to support *60YC* learning, first consider the operational make-up of HDCE.

HDCE is an educational outreach unit within Harvard's Faculty of Arts and Sciences. It consists of Harvard's Extension School, the Summer School, the Professional Development Programs (PDPs), and the Institute for Learning in Retirement. Its programs currently serve over 30,000 part-time and summer learners annually. HDCE is financially self-sustaining, and it draws on and contributes to the larger Harvard community in a variety of ways.

- The Harvard Extension School (HES) is designed for adult, part-time learners. In 2018–2019, it offered more than 900 on-campus, online, and hybrid courses to 17,000 students in fall and spring. It enrolls about 1,000 students in the undergraduate Bachelor of Liberal Arts (ALB) program and 3,000 in the graduate Master of Liberal Arts (ALM) program. Another 4,000 enrollees are doing coursework to earn admissions. 4,000 are enrolled in stackable graduate certificate courses, and the remaining 5,000 are taking advantage of the open-access admission to for-credit courses.
- The Harvard Summer School (HSS) offered 500 courses, including 100 pre-college and 21 study abroad courses, to 9,800 students. 3,000 of these students were high school aged; 2,500 were college-aged learners from other schools; and 4,300 were Harvard Extension students.
- The Professional Development Programs (PDPs) offered 83 open-enrollment programs to 2,917 participants.
- The Harvard Institute for Learning in Retirement (HILR) offered 144 peer-taught study groups to its 550 members.

Developing HDCE's *60YC* Implementation[2]

Objectives

Implementing the *60YC* at HDCE began with strategic plans for changing from lecture pedagogy and administration-oriented processes to online and hybrid pedagogies and learner- and faculty-centric processes. As we now are implementing hybrid online and in-person courses and program offerings and modifying our programs and system infrastructure to support lifelong engagement with learners, we are seeing change in demand and institutional reorientation play out dynamically. We have integrated *60YC* services that range from advising students who are planning and navigating career and job changes to fostering community connections. Instructional experiences themselves are changing to employ new means for learning and thinking. In short, our infrastructure, offerings, and relationships are evolving continuously to address the following strategic requirements.

VIRTUALIZATION

60YC educational solutions now assemble curriculum and select educational services to match individual learner's needs. Not only must boundaries of time and place go away, but the services provided also must be made administratively flexible and technically interoperable across institutions through the use of customer relationship-management-systems and the exchange of rich data for both human and AI analysis.

PERSONALIZATION

Only a *60YC* learner—not an institution—knows what kind educational solution will fulfill that individual's needs as they present and change over a lifetime. Therefore, the design of educational services and solutions must be fundamentally learner-centric and adapt to changing needs across the many phases of careers and lives. This applies to all forms of education, even though personalization is not expected to lead to the replacement of more formally organized residential experiences for the 15% of undergraduate and graduate students for whom that modality is appropriate.

CREDENTIAL HARMONIZATION AND MANAGEMENT

60YC credentials consist of a portfolio of life and job experiences, degrees, grades, certificates, badges, etc. For an employer or an institution to trust such a record and rely on the reputation of the granting authority, the credentialing process must formally validate attainment and competence, as well as ensure the accuracy and integrity of the data. To serve *60YC* learners' needs to provide their records of accomplishment and potential in a variety of unpredictable circumstances requires democratized access to credentials.

INSTITUTIONAL COLLABORATION

Both learners and *60YC* institutions must combine prior achievements, current capacities, learning objectives, and the capabilities of multiple institutions in order to make available and deliver the particular educational experiences and program outcomes that work best for the learner as well as for the institutions involved. Assessment of readiness, validation of programs, and delivery by multiple providers requires a degree of intra- and inter-institutional collaboration and customization that is new to higher education.

Tasks

HDCE learning engineers, IT developers, and administrators collaborate in *60YC* planning and development efforts. They use three types of information—evidence of learner success, faculty satisfaction, and operational efficiency gathered from instrumented systems and processes and extensive student and faculty interviews, as well as results from experiments with learning experiences—to guide development in the following specific areas.

INTEGRATING A META-CURRICULUM

HDCE offers key components of a *60YC* curriculum now. Its extensive range of courses, degree opportunities, certificates, executive education, and study groups serves high school students, degree completers, mid-career professionals, and retirees. We are working to reduce conflicting features among individual curricula in order to provide consistency among courses and programs.

ENGINEERING PEDAGOGICALLY INFORMED, EVIDENCE-BASED
LEARNING EXPERIENCES

We continue implementing and improving our learning engineering capabilities (Leitner, Nesson, & Walker, 2019) in order to continuously improve the quality of all of our offerings, as well as to grow our teaching and learning unit and its level of expertise. Our objective is to engineer great learning experiences that have outcomes satisfying both faculty and student objectives. This requires building data collection and real-time, evidence-based decision-making into all of our learning platforms. HDCE is organizing a Digital Teaching and Learning group and consolidating IT resources under a Director of Architecture, Software Development, Systems Integration, and Learning Platforms. This will enable sharing expertise and collaborating on course design and pedagogy, course production, instructional technology, and administrative infrastructure.

INTEGRATING LRM, FRM, AND SIS SYSTEMS

We are upgrading a heavily customized Student Information System (SIS) to place Learner Relationship Management (LRM) and Faculty Relationship Management (FRM) at the center of the learning paradigm and the institution's administrative processes. Readiness assessments, functional/technical analyses, and several business-process analysis exercises are guiding the modification and development of policies, practices, and workflows. The resulting integrated LRM, FRM, and SIS systems will enable us to strategically manage both the demand for and the supply of HDCE learning services during a student's learning life and across a variety of types of engagement with HDCE.[3]

Modelling Learner Value

The lifelong path of a *60YC* learner involves multiple and sometimes radical job and career changes that, in turn, entail learning in a number of educational modalities. A learning pathway might include courses, an internship, apprenticeship, or work-study experience; episodes of continuing education on campus and online to re-skill to earn a degree or training certificate; participation in a coding or management bootcamp; or several intensive professional or personal development exercises. To better understand the needs of such mid-career professionals, we used a semi-structured survey to conduct telephone interviews with two groups of learners who completed HDCE courses over the past five years.

Both groups were mid-career professionals who enrolled because they were either in an exploratory or planning stage for advancing or changing careers.

The responses of these learners are summarized in the descriptions of four general categories below. We believe that these descriptions are representative of the larger population of lifelong learners and that the individual responses that are included illustrate specific programmatic enhancements for instruction oriented to a lifelong, long-term, and continuous engagement.

RESULTS

These responses emphasized outcomes that have specific, short-term job utility, impart long-term adaptability and resilience, and sustain employability in the face of change across a range of unpredictable job roles and career changes, together with easily exchanged credentials that are competency-based, school validated, and secure.

- "If it's about employability, I think it's relationships and networking opportunities."
- "It is important for people to identify key spaces and . . . people need to find cross functional skill sets that would be beneficial . . . having multiple skill sets—as opposed to being specialized in one track."

CONNECTIONS

These emphasized services that support participation in communities of learning and practice, as well as long-term, but episodic, access to instruction, program planning, and career and life coaching.

- "A stronger career resource center and more networking events, especially for someone changing careers. . . . It would have helped to have some career networking events, and on an ongoing basis, not just ad hoc."
- "LinkedIn has been revolutionary. I want to be able to build my network: worked with this person at that institution etc. It is a vetted version of my resume and for references it is also important."

EFFICIENCY

Other responses focused on courses that are easy to recombine or stack into flexible "degree" programs coupled with credentialing processes that can be completed and used without wasted time, effort, and cost.

- "There is a lot of stuff out there, but hard to figure out what to choose and what to commit to. Would be really nice to have a formalized program, degree etc.—someone has crafted [a] program: here are the key skills you will need right now based on the industry so you can just jump in."
- "Integrate certifications within programs (e.g., LEED certified in sustainability program) and . . . certifications, badges etc."

PERSONALIZATION

Responses also emphasized tailored pedagogy and administrative processes that exploit multiple modalities, authentic evaluation, customized learning paths, and flexible entry and exit points, coupled with support services that preserve credit and accommodate ordinary life events.

- "Best/worst thing? Remote classes. But this comes with territory, Capstone . . . was a wonderful experience."
- "I could have made better course decisions; I cobbled things together, could have used more guidance."
- "Getting 'real world experience'—the most useful thing. Any experiential part the course incorporated was very valuable when it comes to trying to get employed."

Measuring Success and Performance

No curriculum or pedagogy has value if learners do not finish courses and degrees or fail to achieve their re-skilling or career-change objectives. Surveys and interviews provide foundational findings that can confirm or disconfirm general hypotheses about what learners want. But a deeper and more actionable understanding of the concrete needs of the population of *60YC* learners and the specifics of how to address those needs requires nuanced tools for research and learning engineering.

Fortunately, instrumented platforms, digitized content, and analytics are making it possible to provide tools beyond those based on measures taken before or after instruction. At HDCE, we are collecting data during the process of learning as well as longitudinally in order to better understand which constellations of metrics matter for detecting and responding to real-time instructional opportunities and shortfalls and for improving outcomes such as:

1. Attained or demonstrated competency;
2. Initial and long-term employability;
3. Resiliency to change in job, career, and environment;
4. Access to learning, records, and support services;
5. Cost relative to benefit and quality;
6. Connections with communities of learners, practitioners, and advisors;
7. Minimal time and effort to complete learning, to obtain employment, and to respond to new challenges; and
8. Convenient fit with personal qualifications and capabilities and with events of life and work.

Similarly, HDCE cannot sustain an implementation of the *60YC* that is not administratively and financially viable. We also are developing evidence-based criteria for assessing our organizational performance and effectiveness and for planning and decision-making to address the following strategic objectives:

1. Long-term relationships with learners, workers, and partners;
2. Individual and collective faculty and staff satisfaction;
3. Auditable processes with analytics for continuous improvement and accountability; and
4. Sustainable return from investments in practices and outcomes.

Conclusion

The *60YC* movement proposes that higher education institutions, which are best in the world at designing curriculum, expand their concept of curriculum from preparing a learner for one career to supporting a learner on a 60-year journey through a five-to-seven stage working life.

The infrastructure is shifting toward Customer Relationship Management (CRM) systems that integrate Learner Record Stores (LRS), expanded assessment and credentialing systems, and AI and analytics systems to enable and inform learners, their instructor/coaches, and administrators. Harmonized services and flexible data transfer are the keys to streamlining and integrating the several kinds of programs from several institutions or other providers that are implementing infrastructures to support the *60YC*.

Features of *60YC* implementations include high-engagement, technology-rich pedagogical modalities; hybrid online and residential learning experiences; faculty-driven quality control and curriculum development; learner-controlled credentials based on validated assessment and trusted exchange of credentials across systems and institutions; and dashboards for learners, instructors, and administrators that allow real-time situation assessment and support continuous improvement of teaching and learning. Institutions typically employ multiple platforms and exploit interoperability standards such as Learning Tools Interoperability (LTI) in order to reduce institutional risk and ease procurement of such platforms, as well as to support a variety of pedagogical approaches.

The *60YC* movement is growing rapidly and globally. It is now supported by a collaboration of deans, teaching faculty, authors, researchers, industry partners, and non-profits.[4] These *60YC* peers work together to increase understanding of key research issues and develop *60YC* educational solutions that embody a precise understanding of learner demand and institutional supply.

Three models for implementing the *60YC* promise to have global civic, social, and economic impact similar to that of the location-based educational infrastructure from which they arose. They increase institutional efficiency and learner value, provide open access to reliable and useful outcomes, and facilitate transfer of both learners and credentials among institutions—all the while expanding and informing choice by consumers.

The Elite/Ivy Model

This model is exemplified by HDCE. It provides specialized competency and deep expertise as well as access to exclusive social and economic networks.

The curriculum focuses on very high-quality and long-term results. Limited availability is leveraged to attract premier faculty, students, and institutional investment. Operations are not cost driven. Market estimates suggest that as many as 50,000 high-achieving learners is a realistic size of the demand for the Elite/Ivy model.

The Flagship Institution Model

This model is exemplified by Georgia Tech (as described by Stephen Harmon and Nelson Baker in Chapter 5 of this volume). Georgia Tech provides field- or profession-oriented competency and access to career-related networks. The curriculum is focused on expertise, quality control, economic return, and career progression. Institutional brand and reliable quality are leveraged to attract excellent faculty and high-quality students, as well as partnerships and funding for R&D. The market is estimated to be 100,000 to 500,000 profession-oriented learners (per field).

The Public University System Model

This model is exemplified by Arizona State (as described by Punya Mishra and Jacqueline Smith in Chapter 6 of this volume). It provides applied competency and expertise and access to job-related networks. The curriculum is focused on breadth, comprehensive services, and programs with near-term return on investment and very wide availability. Brand and availability are leveraged to attract competent faculty and motivated learners, as well as to sustain high-volume operations and private and public partnerships for programs and R&D. The demand is estimated to be at least 500,000 to 1,000,000 learners with applied goals.

There will be many instances and variations of the archetypes described above. Some will succeed; some will fail (Schejbal, n.d.). More importantly, no single institution will satisfy more than a fraction of an individual learner's lifetime needs from its own courses and degree programs. To win the loyalty of faculty and learners in the *60YC* ecosystem, each institution will not only have to qualify its educational services with respect to its own and industry-wide criteria for brand and integrity, but also will have to operate in a collaborative environment that enables learners to access a suite of offerings from multiple institutions.

Notes

1 For further information, see details of the University Professional & Continuing Education Association's (UPCEA's) 2019 annual conference at http://conferences.upcea.edu/annual2019/index.html
2 The authors wish to acknowledge seminal contributions to the development of the *60YC* concept and to the implementation strategy that we discuss in this chapter by Rovy Branon, Gary Matkin, and Nelson Baker, as well as by many others.
3 This development effort is receiving global support and funding because many others believe that a need-centered relationship management infrastructure and democratized control of earned credentials are essential features of the IT infrastructure for higher education.

4 For details of this growing collaboration, see the University Professional & Continuing Education Association's (UPCEA's) 2019 annual conference at http://conferences.up-cea.edu/annual2019/index.html

References

Lambert, H. (2019, March 20). Redefining norms critical to sustained relevance in the changing postsecondary environment. *The Evolllution*. Retrieved from https://evolllution.com/revenue-streams/market_opportunities/redefining-norms-critical-to-sustained-relevance-in-the-changing-postsecondary-environment/

Leitner, H., Nesson, R., & Walker, E. (2019). From artisanship to learning engineering: Harvard Division of Continuing Education's framework for improving teaching and learning. In C. Dede, J. Richards, & B. Saxberg (Eds.), *Learning engineering for online education* (pp. 71–89). New York, NY: Routledge.

NCES. (2017). First-time postsecondary students' persistence after 3 years. *The Condition of Education*. Retrieved from Institute of Education Sciences website: https://nces.ed.gov/programs/coe/indicator_tsc.asp

NCES. (2019). Undergraduate retention and graduation rates. *The Condition of Education*. Retrieved from Institute of Education Sciences website: https://nces.ed.gov/programs/coe/indicator_ctr.asp

Schejbal, D. (n.d.). Not all initiatives succeed and that's okay. The University Learning Store Initiative, *Unbound Spring 2019*, UPCEA. Retrieved from https://unbound.upcea.edu/leadership-strategy/continuing-education/not-all-initiatives-succeed-and-thats-okay-the-university-learning-store-initiative/

UPCEA. (2019). Hallmarks of online leadership. Retrieved from University Professional and Continuing Education Association website: https://upcea.edu/resources/hallmarks-online/

10

Assessment of the Current State of the 60-Year Curriculum and Research Agenda for the Future

JOHN RICHARDS

Societal Trends Are Changing the Dynamic of Work

Throughout this volume, the argument that deep technological changes, coupled with organizational adaptation (reengineering), are impacting the global, socio-economic environment is taken as given. The forces of change and adaptation have produced what Dede (Chapter 1) refers to as the "synergistic digital economy."

Students and workers in the synergistic digital economy no longer expect that their jobs will represent a progression through a single career during a lifetime. They expect their current job or career to disappear or disruptively evolve, forcing them to prepare for novel jobs in several new careers at unpredictable points throughout their lives. The requirement to prepare for a lifetime of changing employment is not optional.

Almost all chapter authors in this volume argue that this is a consequence of technological advances (see also McAfee & Brynjolfsson, 2017):

- AI and robotics are currently replacing workers in the production process and are projected to assume roles ranging from self-driving trucks and taxi services to medical diagnosis and legal research (Dede, Chapter 1; Scott, Chapter 2; Harmon & Baker, Chapter 5; Mishra & Smith, Chapter 6; Honan, Chapter 8); digitalization is changing the institutional structures as a consequence of these and other technologically driven advances (Servoz, Chapter 3).
- Globalization (Dede, Chapter 1; Harmon & Baker, Chapter 5) or interconnectivity (Mishra & Smith, Chapter 6) is altering the dynamics of marketplace competition. Many jobs are shifting to countries with lower standards of living and consequently lower wages.

The task of preparing learners for multiple careers over a lifetime completely alters the dynamics of the university and its relationship to its students. The catchphrase "lifelong learning" is merely suggestive. Students must develop competencies and attitudes that support the transition among jobs and careers. Universities must consider in depth how to prepare students for upskilling to meet the challenges of radically evolving jobs and multiple careers.

The chapter authors of this book envision the university adapting its structure and processes to supply continuous educational engagement and services in order to support lifelong learning driven by demands for the educational system to provide:

- A higher skilled workforce (Harmon & Baker, Chapter 5);
- Universal learning (Mishra & Smith, Chapter 6); and
- Ever-changing workplace needs (Wingard & Farrugia, Chapter 7).

As the title of this book and the term "60-Year Curriculum" (*60YC*) suggests, the need for maintaining a lifelong relationship with a student raises the expectation that there is, or ought to be, a methodology for evolving curriculum dynamically as the learner progresses through career shifts. We approached this methodology from the perspective of learning engineering, emphasizing the applied nature of adapting instructional methods and infrastructure (see Dede, Richards, & Saxberg, 2019). The term "curriculum" in the *60YC* refers to the full educational experience, including andragogy or instructional methods, educational content, and support services. As will become apparent, it is important to approach these elements separately rather than holistically or collectively.

This final chapter addresses implications for lifelong learning and identifies areas in which research and development are required.

From a Lifetime Career to a Lifetime of Careers

One-Career Learning

CAREER PREPARATION

Large parts of a university were designed to prepare students for one, well-defined career with the liberal arts being a notable exception. As described in Chapter 1, higher education assumed the task of career preparation, and the university evolved so that individual departments or schools could establish requirements for degrees, provide structure for internships and other field experiences, and prepare students for certifications or for pursuing advanced degrees. Though some departments have provided support for internships, practicum, and co-op programs, these have been focused on initial preparation for one specific career. Within departments or schools, there are explicit career services for (first) job placement, including internships leading to job offers, career fairs, and on-campus recruiting. However, lifelong coaching or mentoring, to the extent that it exists, is informal and based on a personal relationship between a student and professor. This is a picture of the one-career university as it currently exists.

ADVANCEMENT

From the perspective of the one-career university, planning for job and career growth is largely the responsibility of the student or the employer. There is little-to-no systematic support of alumni as they progress through their careers. The single exception is the granting of some advanced degrees. For example, in K–12 education, ongoing certification is generally maintained through continuing education credits (CEUs). These credits can be obtained in a variety of ways that are approved by the school district, such as conference attendance, participation in workshops, in-service training, or graduate courses. In situations of ongoing certification, wages are generally a function of years of service and participation in graduate courses. For example, pay-scale "lane changes" are typically linked to master's degrees; master's plus 30 credit hours; master's plus 45 hours; master's plus 60 hours; or a PhD or EdD. Education graduate schools have evolved to anticipate that large groups of students will follow such a progression during their careers.

Similarly, professional organizations like the American Medical Association (AMA), bar associations, and the American Institute of Certified Public Accountants (AICPA) certify their respective professionals and provide regular (i.e., quarterly, yearly, etc.) courses to fulfill re-certification requirements and to maintain currency.

Elsewhere in the university, support for career advancement is largely ignored by departments and, if done at all, is left to the continuing education division, extension schools, or executive education (see Honan, Chapter 8, this volume).

On-the-job training ("upskilling") is often provided by independent contractors. Job training and career counseling is a $15 billion market (IBIS, 2019). Large corporations and the military routinely rotate managers and promising leaders to provide broader experiences within the corporation and the armed forces.

JOB CHANGE

Job change and career advancement typically take place without direct university involvement. There are well-developed, first-job placement services, and there is some alumni networking, the latter particularly at large or exclusive universities. But the initiative for getting support depends heavily on the job seeker or the employer. Sample support services at a university with deep pockets include[1]:

- Alumni job boards connect alumni to opportunities posted directly from employers and fellow alumni.
- Alumni "advisor's hub" facilitates career conversations with alumni volunteers online. This also includes meet-up events.
- Alumni "employer's showcase" provides exclusive access to company receptions that take place in major alumni areas including Boston, Northern California, New York, and Washington, DC.
- Career "lunch and learns" inform alumni through live, online webinars featuring selected career experts. Topics are presented live and followed by real-time Q&A.

- The Office of Career Advising and Professional Development empowers MIT alumni, students, and postdocs to explore their life and career goals by helping them develop core competencies and build professional networks.
- The Alumni Association itself offers a list of recommended career professionals who can help with career development and career management.

Note that these are, at best, networking opportunities and highly location dependent.

Career Change

It is with respect to career change that the need for learning in the synergistic digital economy is most critical. Yet, there are virtually no services in the one-career university that directly support radical shifts in jobs or careers—either for identifying a potential new career or for education directly relevant to making the transition. Extension schools or divisions of continuing education do provide access to appropriate courses and even to new degrees. But, there is no involvement in these courses from the department that granted the original degree. Little formal mentorship for making a change is available, and there is scant support for maintaining ongoing relationships after graduation. In the sections below, we examine two attempts to identify viable transition paths for workers facing career changes.

PATHWAYS

The World Economic Forum (WEF) has produced a set of reports under the series title "Towards a Reskilling Revolution" (WEF, 2018, 2019). Reskilling captures the notion that the skills required for one career can translate to a different career. The difficulty in identifying potential viable and desirable jobs is substantial (see Smiley, 2015). WEF (2018) analyzed 958 job types using big-data methodology that identifies what are called "reskilling pathways" and "job transition opportunities" (p. 1). These pathways and opportunities are based on the similarity of the requirements for any two jobs in combination with the desirability of the target job.

The "good-fit" opportunities for transition must maintain the level of desirability of a potential job from the perspective of the worker. Desirability is determined by long-term employment stability, as well as by maintaining the current standard of living (2019, p. 4). According to the WEF, this standard of living goal would "require approximately two years of additional education and two years of additional work experience" (2018, p. 10). The nature of the additional education is left unexplored. The report recommends that companies develop targeted reskilling programs where digital experts provide "on-the-job training to their colleagues" (WEF, 2019, p. 22). As with upskilling, this approach feeds into a large, existing training industry.

Following a second approach, a group at Stanford established a database of over 15,000 skills (see Forshaw, Rosas, & Maples, 2019), then created a skills visualization tool that analyzes an individual's resume and other data. The tool creates a structured view that improves a person's ability to "see and self-explain their skills and competencies" (p. 4). The Stanford group's approach assumes that an individual who has participated successfully in the workforce already has skills, competencies, and knowledge that can indeed be applied to a new situation.

Both the WEF and Stanford approaches address the problem of identifying a viable path forward, but they do not address the need for altering or replacing a one-career program to anticipate multiple careers and empower transition among them.

Competencies for Multiple Careers

Domains of Competence

In Chapter 1, Dede identifies intrapersonal, interpersonal, and cognitive capacities as three "domains of competence" drawn from the US National Research Council report, "Education for Life and Work: Developing Transferable Knowledge and Skills in the 21st Century" (NRC, 2012). These domains are referred to in various terms in the NRC report and more broadly elsewhere as "21st-century skills," "college and career readiness," "deeper learning," and "higher order thinking" among others. While there may be differences among such categories, we will refer to them below as "21st-century skills."

The NRC report was focused on the K–12 curriculum. The value of extending the consideration of these three domains of competency and their implications to the university, as well as to the *60YC* curricula, is apparent.

INTRAPERSONAL COMPETENCIES

> Our intrapersonal domain, like Bloom's affective domain, involves emotions and feelings and includes self-regulation—the ability to set and achieve one's goals.
>
> (NRC, 2012, pp. 21–22)

Demand for a variety of intrapersonal competencies has been identified throughout this volume as resulting from a need to adapt to the synergistic digital economy. Thus, it is critical to incorporate these specific intrapersonal competencies into the *60YC*. Dede (Chapter 1) points to the need for flexible adaptation and cognitive flexibility. Scott (Chapter 2) identifies the need for an individual's ability to instigate and navigate through periods of change, as well to make sense of change and transition. Both Mishra and Smith (Chapter 6) and Wingard and Farrugia (Chapter 7) call for career adaptability. Honan (Chapter 8) stresses the importance of taking responsibility for your own learning. And Lambert and Leitner (Chapter 9) identify resiliency to change as a key metric. These intrapersonal competencies of flexibility, adaptability, and taking responsibility for, or orchestrating, one's own learning would seem to be developed independently from subject matter and, therefore, are inherently transferable, although substantiating this conclusion will require further research.

The second NRC report, "How People Learn II," identifies three ways that people orchestrate their own learning: metacognition, executive function, and self-regulation.

> Metacognition is the ability to monitor and regulate one's own cognitive processes and to consciously regulate behavior. . . . Executive function . . . involves the overall regulation of thinking and behavior and the higher-order processes that enable people to plan, sequence, initiate, and sustain their behavior toward some goal, incorporating feedback and making adjustments. . . . Self-regulation . . . is seen as involving management of cognitive, affective, motivational, and behavioral components that allow the individual to adjust actions and goals to achieve desired results.
>
> (NRC, 2018, p. 70)

A variety of K–12 curricula target the intrapersonal competencies. These range from mindfulness training to social-emotional learning. Art Costa and Bena Kallick have elaborated 16 habits of mind that provide a resource when an individual is faced with uncertain or challenging situations. "Habits of [m]ind are the characteristics of what intelligent people do when they are confronted with problems, the resolutions to which are not immediately apparent" (2008, p. 15). Costa and Kallick also argue that habits of mind transcend all subject matters (p. 39).

Again, the relevance of this work within K–12 education for higher education and the *60YC* is clear. Learning to learn requires that the learner orchestrates their own learning by establishing habits of mind that strengthen metacognition, executive function, and self-regulation. Higher education should move toward explicitly deepening these generalizable competencies.

INTERPERSONAL COMPETENCIES

> Interpersonal competencies are those used both to express information to others and to interpret others' messages (both verbal and nonverbal) and respond appropriately.
>
> (NRC, 2012, p. 22)

A range of interpersonal competencies have been identified in this volume. Dede (Chapter 1) emphasizes social perceptiveness. Scott (Chapter 2) talks about collaboration, investigation, and teamwork. Servoz (Chapter 3) refers to teamwork and communication. Brewer (Chapter 4) targets collaboration, or "co-learning." Honan (Chapter 8) identifies leadership challenges as one of the primary goals of the Executive Education program, and Lambert and Leitner (Chapter 9) have established a goal of their online programs to reinforce connections with communities of learners, practitioners, and advisors.

The Interpersonal Domain includes two clusters of competencies: team-work and collaboration and leadership. These clusters include competencies, such as communication, collaboration, responsibility, and conflict resolution.

(NRC, 2012, p. 4)

Within K–12 education, social emotional learning (SEL) focuses on both intrapersonal and interpersonal competencies. The Collaborative for Academic, Social, and Emotional Learning (CASEL) defines SEL as "the process through which children and adults understand and manage emotions, set and achieve positive goals, feel and show empathy for others, establish and maintain positive relationships, and make responsible decisions" (CASEL, 2019). Once more, the relevance of work done in K–12 to 60-Year Curricula is clear.

COGNITIVE COMPETENCIES

Following Bloom, we view the cognitive domain as involving thinking and related abilities, such as reasoning, problem solving, and memory.

(NRC, 2012, p. 21)

Cognitive competencies are closely tied to deeper learning and usually involve specific subject matter. Dede (Chapter 1) specifies judgment and decision-making, long-term capacity building, and systems thinking. Dede (Chapter 1), Scott (Chapter 2), and Servoz (Chapter 3) identify creativity or creative thinking. Servoz (Chapter 3) focuses on critical thinking. Servoz (Chapter 3) and Wingard and Farrugia (Chapter 7) emphasize problem solving. Mishra and Smith (Chapter 6) identify exploration.

Pedagogical techniques such as collaborative problem solving and project-centered learning—in which students work in teams—provide authentic experiences in collaboration, leading, following, and listening. Collaborative problem solving integrates interpersonal competencies for collaboration with cognitive competencies for problem solving (Organization for Economic Co-operation and Development, 2017, p. 9). Solving problems involves such collaborative competencies as "establishing and maintaining a shared understanding, taking appropriate action to solve the problem, and establishing and maintaining team organization." Problem solving competencies are "exploring and understanding; formulating a representation of the problem; planning and executing the plan; and monitoring and reflecting on the problem solution" (NRC, 2012, p. 222). As such, these instructional methods are teaching strategies that do not necessarily require changes in the curriculum.

Other Classifications of 21st-Century Skills

As described in Chapter 1, multiple taxonomies and classification schemas focus on 21st-century skills (see NRC, 2012, Chapter 2) as the skills and competencies required for learners to be prepared for the impending career shifts as outlined above. Many of these efforts to incorporate 21st-century skills into the classroom have focused on professional development for K–12 teachers. We describe two efforts to make corresponding alterations of the curriculum for higher education and for workforce training below.

Aoun (2017) argues that societal changes entail the need to add a new discipline, "humanics," to the curriculum. Within this new discipline are a new set of literacies and cognitive capacities. There are three literacies (data literacy, technological literacy, and human literacy) and four cognitive capacities (systems thinking, entrepreneurship, cultural agility, and critical thinking). The call for explicitly teaching these literacies and capacities plays a prominent role throughout Aoun's book.

Fadel, Bialik, and Trilling (2015) situate the 21st-century learner at the intersection of a four-dimensional scheme of knowledge, skills, character, and meta-learning. Although this scheme has mostly been applied to K–12, there have been some efforts to extend its application to the university. The authors argue, "Each knowledge discipline has a responsibility to include the learning of the skills, character qualities, and meta-learning strategies that are most aligned with it" (p. 45).

Both Aoun's (2017) and Fadel et al.'s (2015) approaches are fundamentally correct in their analysis of the situation. Certainly, disciplines will evolve as new discoveries and new approaches are uncovered, and big data and other emerging technologies will require new courses in their own right. But I am concerned that the solution to preparing students for 21st-century skills requires fundamental changes in andragogy, and preparing for a lifetime of learning requires the development of a capacity for long-term support. The fundamental need for new instructional methods and systematic lifelong support are at the heart of the *60YC*.

Curriculum or Andragogy?

Students' capacity to cope with rapid, unpredictable change in the workplace and in society throughout six decades of working life depends on educators' addressing each of the three domains of competency, not just from the beginning of and throughout the university experience, but in the pre-K–12 curriculum as well. The subtitle of one NRC report focuses on the need to develop transferable knowledge and skills. Servoz summarizes the skills and the requirements for educators as

...general cognitive skills (the capacity to understand an environment which is increasingly uncertain), critical thinking, problem solving, creativity, and communication; there should be a minimum threshold of transferable cognitive skills provided in the studies' programs of any secondary school and university.

(This book, Chapter 3, pp. 44–45)

Transfer is "the ability to extend what has been learned in one context to new contexts" (Byrnes, 1996, p. 74; see also NRC, 2000, Chapter 3). Transferable cognitive skills are notoriously difficult to teach. NRC (2000) points to the research that transfer is "affected by the degree to which people learn with understanding" (p. 55). In other words, for transfer of cognitive skills to occur, deep learning must take place.

According to the NRC, this "deeper learning" requires deliberate practice, an understanding of when, where, and why to use the knowledge, and an underlying motivation to apply what has been learned. Research conducted in the K–12 arena should apply to adult learning. Moreover, one would expect that individuals who have been engaged in their first career must have done deliberate practice; must have developed an understanding of when, where, and why to use their knowledge; and must have been motivated to apply what has been learned. The extent to which this first career experience applies to career shifts is an important area for research.

In other words, the *60YC* calls for new instructional methods that support learning how to be flexible and agile, learning how to learn continuously, and learning how to be resilient and adaptable. For example, Brewer (Chapter 4) applies design thinking to enrich the learning strategies for adult learners. We turn now to looking at this proposed new andragogy.

Changing the Andragogical Model

While participating in a 1990s K–12 school reform movement, I created a chart to capture the argument underlying the transition that education should undertake in order to serve a society that had left the Industrial Era with its predominance of factory work and machinery, and become the Information Processing Era with its focus on knowledge work. The model for reforming teaching and learning, so the argument went, should reflect the shift from the factory to the office as represented in Table 10.1, columns 1, 2, and 3.

I want to reconsider the arguments surrounding this earlier transition in order to underscore the on-going transition to what I am calling the "Digitalization Era" that is remarked on throughout this book. Marketplace demand has changed from being for workers who were essentially clerks, to workers who are consultants and entrepreneurs.

The Industrial Era worker in a factory was engaged in manufacturing and production. Preparation for work required basic arithmetic and literacy. J. M. Stephens (1967) found schools in mid-20th century America to be following a factory model. From this framework, Cuban (1993) explains how the image of schools-as-factories "exalts rational decision-making, suggesting that schools are mechanical; each part of the machine is connected to the others by an assembly line and can be fixed or improved" (p. 12; see also Collins & Halverson, 2009).

The brain model was a warehouse. Learning involved information transfer to place items in the warehouse. The student was a clerk working in isolation, and the teacher was a lecturer delivering the product. Multiple choice assessment determined whether the facts had been stored properly. The factory model required an eight-year, grade school curriculum (i.e., grades 1 through 8).

In the Information Processing Era, the worker is a clerk in an office engaged in knowledge work. Preparation for work requires such intellectual skills as problem solving, linear algebra, modeling, as well as rudimentary competence in using mechanical or electronic tools. The brain model is a processor. Learning involves collecting, analyzing, and representing data. The student is a symbolic-analyst (see Reich, 1991, pp. 177–180) with a specialized role within a hierarchy of teams. The teacher is a facilitator supporting and empowering the team. Authentic or portfolio assessment provides evidence for individual contribution to the effectiveness of the team. The information processing model requires a college, or 14-to-16-year, curriculum.

Education reform movements that began in the 1980s took the factory and office metaphors seriously. (For a critique of the accuracy of the factory model, see Watters, 2015.) These reform movements explored pedagogy, brought in research on learning from cognitive science, and have embraced the notion that a learner must construct his or her own knowledge.

We now need a new metaphor for learning and teaching that serves a life-long curriculum. As Scott argues in Chapter 2, "A new technology that requires more independent-driven work and an emphasis on collaboration, investigation, and teamwork will require similar organizational shifts in how education is provided" (p. 33). With multiple careers and many jobs within each career, this requires concomitant shifts from a centralized to a distributed model of work and from a role-based to a consultant model of the student.

This metaphor for the 21st-century workplace is the global network, in which multiple careers and many "gigs" within each career reflect the shift from a centralized to distributed organization and from role-based to ad hoc models of work. The shift from era to era parallels the shift in consumer behavior from shopping downtown to shopping in a mall to shopping online. The network worker is not just a poet or a member of a startup team but an Uber or Lyft driver; a telecommuting professional; graphics and layout artists supporting multiple companies; freelance writers, authors, and copyeditors; or an adjunct faculty member working for multiple universities.

This "network" model is illustrated in the fourth column in Table 10.1. The student, as a network worker, consults in a variety of roles on multiple projects of the moment in a distributed environment. The brain model is an agile network of data and processes. Learning is just-in-time, depends on transferable skills, and has ready access to endless content and processing tools. The student is an entrepreneur-consultant working on multiple ad hoc teams with changing membership. The teacher is a coach who provides continuity, perspective, and methods. Performance assessment focuses on the project deliverable. Preparation for a lifetime of work requires the ability to learn continually and adapt to new and unpredictable situations. Education in the Network Era requires a *60YC* that embraces an andragogy that includes collaborative problem solving with the objective of developing transferable competencies.

TABLE 10.1 Models for Education

1	2	3	4
Metaphor:	*Factory*	*Office*	*Network*
Curriculum:	Grade School	College	60 yr.
Nature of Work:	Manufacturing/ Production	Knowledge Work	Consulting Entrepreneurship
Era:	Industrial	Information Processing	Digitalization
Cognition Model:	Warehouse	Process	Agile Network
Learning:	Information Transfer	Thinking Skills	Transferable Skills
Student Role:	Clerk	Symbolic Analyst	Consultant Entrepreneur
Unit:	Individual	Team	Dynamic Teams
Content:	Curriculum	System	Project-deliverable
Teacher Role:	Lecturer/Information Resource	Facilitator/Process Resource	Mentor/Coach/ Advice Resource
Assessment Method:	Test/Time in job	Authentic/Degree	Performance Deliverable/ Portfolio
Pedagogy:	Telling	Enabling	Empowering

60YC *Andragogy*

Our approach to reorganizing higher education is to satisfy the demand for life-long learning by integrating the new andragogies enabled by the technologies and processes of the synergistic digital economy. The literacies and capacities that result do not in themselves form a new discipline or a novel curriculum. There clearly could be, and are, courses explicitly dedicated to aspects of the synergistic digital economy. However, it is the change in instructional methods to establish and support habits of lifelong learning that drives reorganizing the existing curriculum of every course and program. This is a change in pattern rather than substance.

Dimensions of Research

> Although there is a body of knowledge around andragogy, adult education has not been tested to the same degree or does not provide the same wealth of data as traditional first-stage education provides. What works and how to deliver it is still an open question.
>
> (Scott Chapter 2, p. 36)

The synergistic digital economy is impacting what, when, and how we are learning. Online learning has removed the residential restrictions on courses, and the hybrid potential of a *60YC* raises the possibility of a six-decade relationship with a learner (see Sarma, 2019). What does that look like? What are the emerging roles of the learner and the university?

Andragogy

How do we incorporate Network Era andragogy into university courses and programs? This fundamental question requires that we build a more sophisticated understanding of Network Era andragogy, particularly as it applies to the university. With respect to our three domains of competence: Interpersonal and intrapersonal competencies appear to transfer to new careers; however, it has been a challenge to teach cognitive competencies in the first place, and more importantly for our purposes, they have been resistant to transfer.

What are our options for learning engagement? Lectures, labs, independent studies, seminar-style interactions, tutoring, and internships are established formats for delivering university education. Of these, only lectures have been scaled massively by using lecture halls or distance learning technology. Now, institutions like the Harvard Graduate School of Education, Georgia Institute of Technology, and Arizona State University are exploiting the Network Era model to augment lecture capture. They are leveraging new infrastructure, online information, and simulations as well as adding interactive hybrid course formats in order to increase engagement and learning and eliminate, or reduce, the constraints of time and distance. There are open questions about the best methods for incorporating new technologies such as virtual, augmented, and mixed realities to bridge space and time for the learner (see Liu, Dede, Huang, & Richards, 2017). Research is needed to inform the implementation of these emerging andragogies and evaluate their impact on instructors and students (see Lambert & Leitner, Chapter 9).

This growing importance of "soft skills" (see Scott, Chapter 2) suggests that educational experiences need to increase emphasis on the development of transferable behavioral competencies to complement developing specific, practical, and intellectual skills. This suggestion raises several interesting questions. Assuming that existing educational institutions are, in fact, qualified to impart such competencies, how do they integrate intrapersonal and interpersonal competencies into university courses? How do they evolve andragogies for developing 21st-century skills into residential, online, and hybrid courses and programs? What sort of professional development is appropriate for faculty and staff?

Sustaining Lifelong Engagement

Sustaining lifelong engagement for learning raises important research questions. These are untested waters. Alumni relationships have been sustained in service of maintaining loyalty and promoting donations, but there has not been an extension of the learning contract beyond graduation. How does the university establish a relationship with a student that begins with first contact and extends through 60 years?

Who at the university is responsible for maintaining this relationship? How can mentoring and coaching extend through a career, or more to the point, through multiple new careers? How are mentorship or coaching transferred when alumni change careers? How does the university create a network effect among alumni, or to turn this around, how can each alumnus provide value to other alumni?

The easy part of developing long-term engagement, conceptually, is providing additional courses in hybrid environments. This is what universities know how to do. But how much and what kind of personal contact can we expect over 60 years? What are the protocols of lifelong engagement? Who is responsible for initiating contact?

What are the implications for infrastructure and administration? As Huntington Lambert asks in the foreword, "What is the higher education strategic information system of the future?" (p. xi). This is a critical component of Ann Brewer's Strategic Student Relationship Management system (Chapter 4).

Next Steps

In this final section of the chapter, we have summarized two dimensions of research that are critical to creating the *60YC*. First, how do we implement a Network Era andragogical approach across the university? Second, how do we distribute and sustain the learning relationship between students and faculty and the university across a lifetime?

We propose undertaking applied R&D projects as opposed to basic research. Creating a *60YC* is a learning engineering project, as described in Dede et al. (2019). However, developing the components of a *60YC* requires cycles of building, testing, measuring, and learning to discover—as well as to apply—engineering principles and practices.

These applied R&D projects should measure the short-term and the longitudinal impact of innovation on the quality and efficacy of andragogical paradigms, on the efficiency and effectiveness of course design and delivery processes, and on the capability and cost of technical and administrative infrastructure for creating and conducting courses that serve students' lifelong needs.

In addition to learning outcome metrics such as multiple factors of student success and instructor satisfaction, projects should be evaluated on organizational metrics such as the utility of replicable frameworks for planning and conducting R&D projects and the efficiency and scalability of the technical or administrative tools and processes that are developed.

We hope that higher education will rise to these challenges in order to ensure a desirable, sustainable global civilization over the next half-century.

Note

1 This particular sample of alumni support services comes from MIT. For a more detailed description of each of these services, see the career services page on the MIT alumni website: https://alum.mit.edu/careers/career-resources

References

Aoun, J. (2017). *Robot-proof: Higher education in the age of artificial intelligence.* Cambridge, MA: MIT Press.

Byrnes, J. (1996). *Cognitive development and learning in instructional contexts.* Boston, MA: Allyn and Bacon.

CASEL. (2019). Retrieved from the Collaborative for Academic, Social, and Emotional Learning website: https://casel.org/what-is-sel/

Collins, A., & Halverson, R. (2009). *Rethinking education in the age of technology: The digital revolution and schooling in America.* New York, NY: Routledge.

Costa, A. L., & Kallick, B. (Eds.). (2008). *Learning and leading with habits of mind: 16 essential characteristics for success.* Alexandria, VA: Association for Supervision and Curriculum Development.

Cuban, L. (1993). *How teachers taught: Constancy and change in American classrooms 1890–1990* (2nd ed.). New York, NY: Teachers College Press.

Dede, C., Richards, J., & Saxberg, B. (Eds.). (2019). *Learning engineering for online education: Theoretical contexts and design-based examples.* New York, NY: Routledge.

Fadel, C., Bialik, M., & Trilling, B. (2015). *Four-dimensional education: The competencies learners need to succeed.* Boston, MA: The Center for Curriculum Redesign.

Forshaw, T., Rosas, S., & Maples, B. (2019, June). Closing the signaling gap. Paper presented at the MIT LINC Conference, *How to thrive in a new learning society,* Cambridge, MA.

IBIS. (2019). Job training and career counseling industry in the US: Market research report. Retrieved from https://www.ibisworld.com/united-states/market-research- reports/job- training-career-counseling-industry/

Liu, D., Dede, C., Huang, R., & Richards, J. (Eds.). (2017). *Virtual, augmented, and mixed realities in education.* Singapore: Springer.

McAfee, A., & Brynjolfsson, E. (2017). *Machine, platform, crowd: Harnessing our digital future.* New York, NY: W. W. Norton.

National Research Council. (2000). *How people learn: Brain, mind, experience, and school.* Washington, DC: The National Academies Press.

National Research Council. (2012). *Education for life and work: Developing transferable knowledge and skills in the 21st century.* Washington, DC: The National Academies Press. doi:10.17226/13398

National Research Council. (2018). *How people learn II: Learners, contexts, and cultures.* Washington, DC: The National Academies Press.

Organization for Economic Co-operation and Development. (2017). *PISA 2015: Draft collaborative problem solving framework.* Retrieved from https://www.oecd.org/pisa/pisaproducts/Draft%20PISA%202015%20Collaborative%20P roblem%20Solving%20Framework%20.pdf

Reich, R. (1991). *The work of nations.* New York, NY: Vintage Books.

Sarma, S. (2019). Rethinking learning in the 21st century. In C. Dede, J. Richards, & B. Saxberg (Eds.), *Learning engineering for online education: Theoretical contexts and design-based examples* (pp. 194–209). New York, NY: Routledge.

Smiley, L. (2015, Nov. 18). Can you teach a coal minor to code? *Wired.* Retrieved from https://www.wired.com/2015/11/can-you-teach-a-coal-miner-to-code/

Stephens, J. M. (1967). *The process of schooling: A psychological examination.* New York, NY: Holt, Rinehart and Winston.

Watters, A. (2015). The invented history of "The Factory Model of Education." *Hacked Education.* Retrieved from http://hackeducation.com/2015/04/25/factory-model.

World Economic Forum. (2018). Towards a reskilling revolution: A future of jobs for all. Retrieved from http://www3.weforum.org/docs/WEF_FOW_Reskilling_Revolution.pdf

World Economic Forum. (2019). Towards a reskilling revolution: Industry-led action for the future of work. Retrieved from https://www.weforum.org/whitepapers/towards-a- reskilling-revolution-industry-led-action-for-the-future-of-work

Notes on Contributors

Nelson C. Baker is the Dean of Georgia Tech Professional Education. He is a professor in Civil Engineering and is president of the University Professional and Continuing Education Association (UPCEA) and Secretary General of the International Association for Continuing Engineering Education (IACEE).

Ann M. Brewer's research interests include leadership, change, and careers, all of which focus on equity- and inclusion-driven strategies. Her research on leadership focuses on knowledge and skills transfer, empowerment, and equity. Ann has deep experience in higher education leadership in Australia and applies her research in diverse sectors: corporations, private and government, universities, and diverse industry sectors.

Christopher J. Dede is the Timothy E. Wirth Professor in Learning Technologies at Harvard's Graduate School of Education (HGSE). His fields of scholarship include emerging technologies, policy, and leadership. He co-chaired two invitational research workshops on the 60-Year Curriculum (*60YC*) in June 2018 and June 2019. His co-edited book, *Learning Engineering for Online Education: Theoretical Contexts and Design-Based Examples* (2019), is about the infrastructure needed to support *60YC*.

Christine Farrugia is Director of Research Initiatives at the Columbia University School of Professional Studies where she leads research on the future of work, lifelong learning, and educational access. Previously, she was research director at the Institute of International Education (IIE) where she led Open Doors, a large-scale annual survey of international educational exchange in the United States. She has collaborated and consulted extensively with higher education institutions, associations, and national governments on students' educational and career pathways, international academic mobility, and data-driven planning.

Stephen W. Harmon is Associate Dean of Research in Georgia Tech Professional Education and Associate Director of the Center for 21st Century Universities. He is a professor in Industrial Design and past-president of the Association for Educational Communications and Technology (AECT).

James P. Honan is a Senior Lecturer at the Harvard Graduate School of Education. His teaching and research interests include financial management of nonprofit organizations, organizational performance measurement and management, and higher education administration. He is Educational Co-Chair of the Institute for Educational Management (IEM).

Huntington D. Lambert (Hunt) is Dean of the Division of Continuing Education and University Extension at Harvard University. The Division grew from 100 to over 900 online open access courses and from 18,000 to 30,000 learners students annually over the past six years. Previously, Lambert served as Associate Provost of OnlinePlus at Colorado State University (CSU), where he helped grow the research faculty's online programs. Prior to this, Lambert was a founder and interim CEO of CSU Global Campus, a new, fully online public university that has grown from zero to over 25,000 adult learners in a decade. He was also Associate Vice President of Economic Development at CSU, the former Director of the Colorado State University Entrepreneurship Center, and a member of the faculty at the CSU College of Business. During his business career, he planned and created 25 data communications and wireless startups in 12 countries, helping build a portfolio of companies valued at over $32 billion. He teaches strategy, entrepreneurship, and business plan development.

Henry H. Leitner is Associate Dean and Chief Innovation Officer for Harvard Division of Continuing Education (HDCE). He provides vision and leadership in the development and implementation of technology-based initiatives that serve both the administrative and academic areas, including online teaching and learning. He oversees the Master's of Liberal Arts degrees in IT at Harvard Extension School—graduate programs of study in which adult learners are exposed to modern software engineering methodologies; theoretical and formal areas of computer science; advanced topics in cryptography, nanoscale science, digital media arts and sciences, and enterprise computing; as well as the latest trends in IT management. Since 1986, he has been a Senior Lecturer on Computer Science for the School of Engineering and Applied Sciences at Harvard, where he has taught a number of large courses.

Punya Mishra is Associate Dean of Scholarship & Innovation and Professor in the Mary Lou Fulton Teachers College at Arizona State University. He also has an affiliate appointment in the Herberger Institute for Design and the Arts. He is internationally recognized for his work (punyamishra.com) in technology integration in teaching, the role of creativity and aesthetics in learning, and the application of design-based approaches to educational innovation. He is an award-winning teacher, an engaging public speaker, as well as an accomplished visual artist and poet.

John Richards is a Lecturer on Education at the Harvard Graduate School of Education teaching courses in entrepreneurship in the education marketplace. He is Founder and President of Consulting Services for Education, Inc. (CS4Ed), providing strategy, marketing, and business development services to the education industry. His co-edited book, *Learning Engineering for Online Education: Theoretical Contexts and Design-Based Examples* (2019), is about the infrastructure needed to support 60YC.

Andrew Scott is Professor of Economics and former Deputy Dean at London Business School having previously held positions at Harvard, London School of Economics, and Oxford University. His academic research focuses on the economics of longevity and he is the author of *The 100 Year Life – Living and Working in an Age of Longevity*. He has advised a range of governments including serving as Non-Executive Director for the UK's Financial Services Authority. He is currently on the advisory board of the UK's Office for Budget.

Michel Servoz is the Senior Adviser to the President of the European Commission on the digital transformation of the economy. Beforehand, he held different posts, in particular, Deputy Secretary General of the European Commission, Director-General for Employment, and trade negotiator. Prior to joining the European Commission, Michel had experience working as a law professor and judge in France.

Jacqueline Smith, J.D., has designed and launched university-wide initiatives at Arizona State University since 2009. She currently serves as Vice President at the ASU Foundation for a New American University. She is a Professor of Practice in ASU's Mary Lou Fulton Teachers College, where she focuses on university design and higher education and the law.

Jason Wingard is a leading executive, academic, and consultant in the areas of organizational strategy, leadership development, and the future of work. He currently serves as Dean and Professor of the Columbia University School of Professional Studies. He previously served as Managing Director and Chief Learning Officer at Goldman Sachs, a multinational investment bank. Dr. Wingard has published widely on the topic of strategy and leadership, including *Learning to Succeed: Reinventing Corporate Education in a World of Unrelenting Change* (2015) and *Learning for Life: How Continuous Education Will Keep Us Competitive in the Global Knowledge Economy* (2016). His forthcoming books include *The Future of Work: Optimizing the Talent Pipeline* (in press 2021) and *Kill the Degree? Disrupting Education for the New World of Work* (2021).

Index

Note: **Bold** page numbers refer to tables; *italic* page numbers refer to figures and page numbers followed by "n" denote endnotes.

Psychoanalysis Outside the Clinic

Also by Stephen Frosh:

For and Against Psychoanalysis
Hate and the Jewish Science: Anti-Semitism, Nazism and Psychoanalysis
Critical Narrative Analysis in Psychology: A Guide to Practice (revised edition;
    with P. Emerson)
Key Concepts in Psychoanalysis
After Words: The Personal in Gender, Culture and Psychotherapy
Young Masculinities: Understanding Boys in Contemporary Society (with A.
    Phoenix and R. Pattman)*
*The Politics of Psychoanalysis: An Introduction to Freudian and Post-Freudian
    Theory* (second edition)*
Sexual Difference: Masculinity and Psychoanalysis
With Glaser, D. Child Sexual Abuse (second edition)*
Identity Crisis: Modernity, Psychoanalysis and the Self
Psychoanalysis and Psychology: Minding the Gap
The Politics of Mental Health (with R. Banton, P. Clifford, J. Lousada and J.
    Rosenthall)

* *Published by Palgrave Macmillan*

Psychoanalysis Outside the Clinic

Interventions in Psychosocial Studies

STEPHEN FROSH

First published 2010 by
PALGRAVE MACMILLAN

Palgrave Macmillan in the UK is an imprint of Macmillan Publishers Limited, registered in England, company number 785998, of Houndmills, Basingstoke, Hampshire RG21 6XS.

Palgrave Macmillan in the US is a division of St Martin's Press LLC, 175 Fifth Avenue, New York, NY 10010.

Palgrave Macmillan is the global academic imprint of the above companies and has companies and representatives throughout the world.

Palgrave® and Macmillan® are registered trademarks in the United States, the United Kingdom, Europe and other countries

ISBN 978–0–230–21031–8 hardback
ISBN 978–0–230–21032–5 paperback

This book is printed on paper suitable for recycling and made from fully managed and sustained forest sources. Logging, pulping and manufacturing processes are expected to conform to the environmental regulations of the country of origin.

A catalogue record for this book is available from the British Library.

A catalog record for this book is available from the Library of Congress.

10   9   8   7   6   5   4   3   2   1
19   18   17   16   15   14   13   12   11   10

Printed in China

Contents

Acknowledgements

I would like to thank my colleagues in the Department of Psychosocial Studies at Birkbeck College, University of London, for their support over the past few years. I am particularly grateful to Lisa Baraitser for her generosity in allowing me to develop for this book a number of articles originally written jointly with her.

Some sections of this book have previously been published in different forms, as follows.

Part of the section of Chapter 3 entitled 'The Destructive Element: Kleinianism and its Literary Resonances' appeared in S. Frosh (2003), 'Psychoanalysis in Britain: The Rituals of Destruction', in D. Bradshaw (ed.), *A Concise Companion to Modernism*, Oxford: Blackwell.

Chapter 4 is based on S. Frosh (2010), 'Psychoanalytic Perspectives on Identity: From Ego to Ethics', in M. Wetherell and C. Mohanty (eds), *The Sage Handbook of Identities*, London: Sage, and on S. Frosh and L. Baraitser (2009), 'Goodbye to Identity?', in A. Elliott and P. du Gay (eds), *Identity in Question*, London: Sage, both reproduced by permission of SAGE Publications, London, Los Angeles, New Delhi and Singapore.

Parts of Chapter 5 are based on S. Frosh (2008), 'Elementals and Affects or On Making Contact with Others', *Subjectivity, 24*, 314–24, reproduced with permission of Palgrave Macmillan; S. Frosh (2009), 'What Does the Other Want?', in C. Flaskas and D. Pocock (eds), *Systems And Psychoanalysis: Contemporary Integrations in Family Therapy*, London: Karnac; and on S. Frosh and L. Baraitser (2009), 'Goodbye to Identity?', in A. Elliott and P. du Gay (eds), *Identity in Question*, London: Sage, reproduced by permission of SAGE Publications, London, Los Angeles, New Delhi and Singapore.

Chapter 7 is based on S. Frosh and L. Baraitser (2008), 'Psychoanalysis and Psychosocial Studies', *Psychoanalysis, Culture and Society, 13*, 346–65, reproduced with permission of Palgrave Macmillan.

I would like to thank Kelly Noel-Smith for the reference to Freud's account of Empedocles in Chapter 1. I am grateful to the members of the Freud Reading Group at Birkbeck College in 2007–9 for insights into Freud's literary and artistic writings, reflected in the discussion in Chapter 2.

Chapter 1

The Applications and Implications of Psychoanalysis

Psychoanalysis in and outside the clinic

Psychoanalysis arose at the end of the nineteenth century as a practice rooted in the 'clinic'. This clinic had a specific location in Freud's consulting room in his home in Vienna, but it rapidly became a metaphorical space referring to the setting for an encounter between a patient, defined as someone in a certain amount of psychological distress, and an analyst, who, through listening and interpreting, could alleviate that distress. Borrowing the terminology of medicine, both because this gave it prestige and also because most of the early analysts were doctors, the consulting room became the model for psychoanalysis thought of as a *treatment*. The procedures developed therein – for example, the use of a couch for the patient to lie on, the regulation of the duration of sessions to 50 minutes, the 'abstinence' of the analyst from undue emotional involvement with the patient – drew on the practices of medicine and came to govern the activities of psychoanalysts as professional therapists. As time went on, increasingly sophisticated theories about mental life arose from the work carried out along these lines, and these in turn influenced further developments in clinical work. In a very concrete sense, therefore, the therapeutic clinic became the source of psychoanalysis' vitality, and its theories and practices were developed to apply in the clinic.

This clinical focus is still characteristic of psychoanalysis, as is the locus of its theories as applied to the speech of individual 'patients' (technically, 'analysands'). In an important sense, this makes psychoanalytic knowledge 'artificial', in that it arises from, and refers back to, a very particular situation specially created to be different from the normal environment of everyday life. In few other places does a person have the opportunity to engage in a largely uninterrupted flow of talk with an attentive listener whose role it is to try to understand what is being said and to help the speaker make sense of it. Everywhere else, transactions of this kind are pedagogic (one person speaks in order to teach the other something), or instructional in a 'performative' sense (for example, giving orders or making or responding to requests), or conversational. In the psychoanalytic setting, however, what transpires

1

is at least an exaggeration of, and possibly radically different from, any other situation in which someone might speak. The analyst does not aim to teach or to make the patient do something; and when the analyst does speak, it is usually with considerable caution about revealing too much about her or his own life. *Reciprocity* of a certain kind exists, as the analyst tries to engage with integrity in the conversation with the patient; but *mutuality* in the sense of equivalence of contact does not. The 'clinic' therefore is a physical space (a bounded zone relatively free from inter-ruption), but it is also a description of a kind of relationship, in which one person makes her or himself available to interpretation by another, and both obey a set of procedural rules recognisable as psychoanalytic practice. This means that the expertise of psychoanalysts is primarily in how to deal with patients in a peculiar situation, and there is no obvious reason why that expertise should generalise to any of the other, very different, circumstances in which people might interact with each other.

Of course, this is nowhere near the whole story of psychoanalysis. The clinic has often been extended significantly to refer, for example, to group situations, to hospital wards, schools, therapeutic communities and learning environments. In each of these cases, some core aspects of the psychoanalytic setting are retained, but others are varied. Sometimes, what is retained is little more than a theoretical orientation that accepts a notion of the 'unconscious' as crucial for understanding motivation and behaviour; at other times, for instance in psychoanalytic group therapies or play-oriented therapy with children, the processes involved may closely mimic the traditional practices of dyadic psycho-analysis. The clinic, in this sense, is *portable*; its key element is the speech of the analysand or analysands, interpreted according to the principles of psychoanalysis by an analyst who is present in that live encounter but occupies a different position – that of the one who is available to think about what is going on, without speaking (too much) of her- or himself. The metaphorical status of the clinic is thus more important than its physical location because it operates as an organising structure for the relationship between any persons who engage with one another in this peculiar, but powerful, way.

If the clinic can be thought of like this, then what becomes central to psychoanalysis is not only a set of specific theoretical constructs (crucially, the existence of a dynamic unconscious, but also including notions such as free association, transference and interpretation), but also a live encounter between people, albeit of a special kind. This 'live-ness' seems absolutely crucial to the practice of psychoanalysis. This is because the capacity of the analyst to understand the patient, and of the patient to benefit from that understanding, depends on the two of them being locked into a visible relationship which can be tracked and

reflected upon. What analysts focus on are often tiny moments of emotional exchange, small slips or revelations, slight changes; similarly, patients are ever-alert to the timing and nuance of comments and interpretations. Psychoanalysis is a kind of microscopic examination of patterns of speech enacted in a relationship of often long duration (sometimes years of meeting several times a week), and hence of considerable depth. In its clinical form it depends on the actual presence of the people concerned, who can explore their interactions with one another as a way of understanding the 'dynamics' that are at work. This is why, for example, psychoanalytic interpretation is much more than just an intellectual affair in which the analyst explains to the patient what the reality is of her or his unconscious wishes or conflicts. As I have discussed in some detail elsewhere (Frosh, 2006), interpretation depends on the *context of the relationship* between analyst and patient. At the core of this – and what makes the relationship distinctively *psychoanalytic* – is the *transference*, understood as the unconscious way in which the patient relates to or 'uses' the analyst, and usually coupled with the reciprocal *countertransference*, referring to the analyst's response to this. In its strongest version, for example in the work of contemporary Kleinian psychoanalysts, the interpretation arises from the analyst's ability to reflect on her or his countertransference feelings, which are generated by the patient's transference; and the patient's response to the interpretation is in turn governed by the state of the transference. Even without unpacking all the niceties of this complex interchange, it is immediately obvious that interpretation depends on the co-presence of analyst and patient in relationship with one another and cannot take place reliably at a distance. Conventionally, it is even *defined* in terms of such an interpersonal relationship. For example in Sandler, Dare and Holder's (1973) influential account of psychoanalytic concepts, interpretation is referred to as 'all comments and other verbal interventions which have the aim of immediately making the patient aware of some aspect of his psychological functioning of which he was not previously conscious' (p.110). This quotation shows how what is being envisaged is a situation in which the 'verbal intervention' of the analyst draws out a response from the patient that is 'immediate', implying the presence of the two protagonists together. Without analyst and patient both being there, locked into their transferential relationship, interpretation in the psychoanalytic sense cannot take place.

The clinic out of which psychoanalysis has developed, the crucible for its concepts and its practices, is thus a metaphorical space surrounding a live encounter. This liveness is necessary for it and integral to the processes that go on within it. Anything else, therefore, is not psychoanalysis, however much appeal there is to the language or theoretical

constructs of psychoanalysis. So when a literary author's work is inter-preted in terms of childhood trauma, it is not psychoanalysis; or when a political commentator draws on ideas about unconscious national impulses, it is not psychoanalysis; or when a social psychologist or philosopher uses ideas about intimacy and stability of selfhood to understand identity conflicts, it is not psychoanalysis. None of these intellectual activities (including the writing of books about psychoanaly-sis), however carefully they employ psychoanalytic ideas, are in fact psychoanalysis, because they lack the specific kind of encounter that constitutes the psychoanalytic clinic. This seems clear, if not necessarily to everyone's taste. However, it leaves open another set of questions. If the practice of psychoanalysis depends on the clinic, what happens when it is *in fact* taken outside, and psychoanalytic ideas are used to make sense of non-clinical phenomena? Even if one agrees that this is not the same thing as being involved in, or conducting, a psychoanaly-sis, one might still claim that it offers a distinctive and productive approach to interpreting human actions, social phenomena and cultural products 'outside' the clinic. If the theoretical constructs generated inside the clinic by psychoanalysis have any robustness, why should they not be at least suggestive aids to comprehension of complex events that in their unexpectedness or emotional intensity seem to show the traces of the unconscious? Why vacate the field and have nothing to say just because the context is not exactly the same as the core psychoana-lytic setting? Or is it actually the case that moving outside the clinic strips psychoanalytic concepts of their meaning, so that when they are applied in this way they actually produce a kind of nonsense? There is in this a challenge to those who would apply psychoanalysis in social and cultural spaces outside the clinical sphere, for example to literary texts, films, or biographies, without access to psychoanalysis' character-istically detailed processes of intersubjective contact. If psychoanalysis is a specially staged live event, as claimed, then it loses its potency and legitimacy in being applied outside its conditions of emergence, the clin-ical encounter itself. On the other hand, perhaps psychoanalysis' capac-ity to theorise moments of irrationality and eruptions of fantasy is just too great to be ignored when such moments are visible outside the clinic; and if this is the case, then the challenge becomes not that of *justi-fying* psychoanalysis, but rather of deploying it creatively and yet with integrity. Perhaps the way in which psychoanalysis embodies an encounter provides a model for understanding and promoting all occa-sions on which 'something happens', so long as one recognises the possi-ble consequences of the leap being made from the clinic to its outside.

As it happens, psychoanalysis has had a contentious but productive history of engagement with the intellectual world outside the clinic,

specifically with the humanities and social sciences, since its inception; and it is still a widely used yet also controversial element in the critical armoury of those working in these disciplines. Early forays into literary and artistic theory by Freud and his circle (e.g. Freud, 1907, 1910a) had a significant impact on biographically-oriented work and also in opening out a domain of interpretive activity that was new in its orientation and its possibilities. In some areas, such as art history, literary criticism and film studies, the effect of psychoanalysis has been profound, provoking rich seams of research that touch on fundamental questions of structure, motivation, representation and response (e.g. Stokes, 1955; Ehrenzweig, 1967; Mulvey, 1989; Stonebridge, 1998; Žižek, 1991, 2006a). In philosophy, politics, history and law, psychoanalysis has at times provided a set of tools for conceptual work (e.g. Hirst, 1979; Wolfenstein, 1981), and offered a vocabulary and set of perceptions that have troubled or channelled major areas of social debate such as 'sexual difference' in gender studies or feminist philosophy (Brennan, 1989; Irigaray, 1985), 'otherness' in the context of racism (Kovel, 1995; Frosh, 2006) and various notions of personal and political emancipation as applied in social and political theory (Marcuse, 1955; Habermas, 1968; Whitebook, 1996). Despite fluctuations in the extent to which psychoanalysis is regarded as having cultural currency, it continues to be a significant intellectual resource in the humanities and social sciences, with especially influential recent deployments in some major works on art and politics, sexuality, violence and war (e.g. Žižek, 2006b; Rose, 1996, 2003; Butler, 2008). In part this attests to the cyclical pattern of repudiation and resurrection that psychoanalysis seems to undergo within academic settings. But it also shows very cogently that whatever the force of the argument that psychoanalysis really belongs only to the clinic (albeit in the broad sense described here), it has actually migrated elsewhere and become one of the most significant tools available to those who wish to understand the social world. This being so, the issue of whether psychoanalysis 'belongs' outside the clinic or not is of less significance than questions about the *effect* of this migration: what happens when psychoanalysis is used in this way, what are its benefits for the domains in which it is applied, what are the dangers, what insights are gained and what distortions are introduced? And if this is not to be a one-way street, in which the only thing considered is the *use* of psychoanalysis, one should also ask, what difference does it make *to* psychoanalysis itself when it is used in this way? Does it learn anything, does it change, are its own gaps in understanding revealed, is it added to in constructive ways? All this is to say that psychoanalysis may have something to offer, and it may benefit from this engagement with the outside world; but there is a great deal to unpick here, and many dangers to skirt.

Psychoanalysis as social critique

There is an important characteristic of psychoanalysis that should be noted at the outset of this examination of questions of translation and impact as psychoanalysis moves outside the clinic. This concerns the tension that it repeatedly enacts between what might be thought of as its *critical* capacity and a tendency to back away from what this criticism reveals, and instead fall into what one can only term a 'conformist' way of dealing with its own discoveries. What is meant here is that one part of the psychoanalytic tradition is to 'unsettle' situations by revealing the unconscious elements that feed into them; this unsettling capacity becomes *socially* critical when it seeks to expose power situations that rely on the denial of opposition and the pretence that it is necessary to maintain existing patterns of domination. 'Critical theory' in the tradition of the Frankfurt School, which from the middle of the twentieth century was a significant influence on politically radical social theorists, knew this well and explicitly drew on psychoanalysis to inform its insights (e.g. Adorno, 1967; Marcuse, 1955). Similarly, many contemporary writers of the left have been very inclined to see psychoanalysis as a route for a continued critique of power (see Frosh, 1999). There is an obvious reason for this, based on the idea that psychoanalysis has the capacity to disrupt the complacent acceptance of the status quo by revealing both the disturbance that lies behind it, and the way *nothing* is stable because there is always a pressure towards change, whether this be as a consequence of an excess of love or of destructiveness. This idea of the disturbing nature of psychoanalysis can be traced back to Freud, whose startling originality lay in identifying an underside to knowledge –how the unconscious subverts and disrupts whatever one thinks of as certain or clear. What Freud discovers is the unsettledness of psychic life, in which the tendency to rest at ease with oneself is undermined by the appalling capacity of unconscious elements to introduce something fantastic and full of desire. Whenever we believe we know something – even psychoanalysis – we are tripped up uncomfortably by our *wish* to know it. This wish always has unconscious components; it is spoken from a place within us about which we have little understanding, and over which we have even less control. Even this terminology, which makes the unconscious a 'place' and implies a modicum of stability, is of course wrong: what Freud emphasises is the *fluidity* of psychic life, in which the apparent concreteness of objects and thoughts is undermined by the appalling capacity of unconscious life to seep into it, to make of what should be 'real' something which is 'in reality' fantasy, with a life of its own. This kind of fantasy flows oddly along the riverbeds of the nocturnal and the dreamlike, the infantile and the wishful. *Nothing* is

solid; there is nowhere to run to, no real 'container' for anxiety, no firm holding that can totally relieve worry. Everything fades as one comes close to it. The dreamscape is the dominant motif of Freudian life: we may bump into things all the time, they may hurt; we may feel the knives and caresses of other humans; we may seek certainty and believe we have found it, for instance in religion or in the material solidity of home, or in the wiring of the brain; we may feel that love, or death, are ultimate foundational boundaries for being, and make it meaningful. In each case, however, not only does fantasy inhabit these things, translating them into wishful entities with blurred boundaries, making them indecipherable at least to some degree, and incommunicable to an even greater extent; but unconscious impulses always impishly trip us up as we approach them.

This is the joy and challenge of psychoanalysis: it populates the world with fantasies, and in so doing it dissolves all certainties. As Freud himself noted, it is an attack on the narcissism of the individual because it displaces each one of us from the centre of our own agency. Famously aligning psychoanalysis with the scientific advances of Copernicus and Darwin, which damaged the 'self-love' of humans by showing that they are not the centre of the universe, Freud argues that society's resistance to psychoanalysis is in part produced by the way it decentres the individual still further. Not only are we not the centre of the universe, we are not even in control of ourselves.

> But human megalomania will have suffered its third and most wounding blow from the psychological research of the present time, which seeks to prove to the ego that it is not even master in its own house, but must content itself with scanty information of what is going on unconsciously in its mind. We psychoanalysts were not the first and not the only ones to utter this call to introspection; but it seems to be our fate to give it its most forcible expression and to support it with empirical material which affects every individual. Hence arises the general revolt against our science, the disregard of all considerations of academic civility and the releasing of the opposition from every restraint of impartial logic. (Freud, 1917a, p.285)

We are spoken by, and enacted through, something else or *other* that is more 'real' than the reality we think we know, something which gives rise to resistance yet is scientifically irrefutable. This something is not to do with identity, or a 'true self' that one then spends one's life seeking out; it is rather the precise opposite of this, insisting that there is no such 'self' – an insistence that is now a routine legacy of poststructuralism and postmodernism. The language of the self still has a hold, of course, in ordinary speech and in the technical lexicon of many psychotherapeutic and social psychological enterprises, including much that passes

for psychoanalytic psychotherapy, but this does not make the self *real* in any meaningful sense. What psychoanalysis insists on, with its fundamental displacement of the locus of subjectivity away from anything that can fulfil the functions of selfhood, is that there is always something else speaking *in the place of the subject*. This means that there may be a fantasy of selfhood, but it is undermined, dispersed, even mocked by the relentless pressure that comes from unconscious life. It is as if the human subject is plugged into something else that gives it its energy 'from outside', yet presents the fiction that this comes from within. The shock occurs when the source of this power makes itself directly felt.

The problem – one which resonates through this book – is that the 'shock' of the unconscious is often too much to bear. One of the difficulties psychoanalysis has always had is in sustaining the clarity of its vision about the way unconscious life disturbs the scenery. Freud refers to the resistance to psychoanalysis that comes from its critics ('the general revolt against our science'), but even in his lifetime there were *insiders* whose deviations from psychoanalytic orthodoxy were interpreted as resistance to its major discoveries – notably Jung and Adler, both of whom tried to significantly reduce the emphasis on sexuality. In Freud's view, this move was mainly in order to make their own theories more easily acceptable to outsiders. However, it could also be seen as a symptom of a more general resistance amongst analysts themselves towards accepting the implications of their own discoveries. Throughout the history of psychoanalysis, this resistance has been expressed in a mode of conformity that seeks theoretical and social respectability and professional status, as against the more subversive and 'radical' position which questions the possibility of incorporating psychoanalytic knowledge into conventional academic and professional structures. Both these tendencies begin with Freud's own work, for instance in the encounter with hysteria, in which what is revealed is a split between Freud as 'man of science' and as disrupter of the rationalist assumptions of science itself. In an observation that has always seemed particularly astute, Toril Moi (1989) notes:

> Psychoanalysis is born in the encounter between the hysterical woman and the positivist man of science. It is in this reversal of the traditional roles of subject and object, of speaker and listener, that Freud more or less unwittingly opens the way for a new understanding of human knowledge. But the psychoanalytical situation is shot through with paradoxes and difficulty. For if Freud's (and Breuer's) act of listening represents an effort to include the irrational discourse of femininity in the realm of science, it also embodies their hope of extending their own rational understanding of psychic phenomena. Grasping the logic of the unconscious they want to make it accessible to reason. (pp.186–7)

In the context of femininity, always a fraught area for psychoanalytic work, Moi's reading suggests that psychoanalysis was founded in a gap between what could be known and what one might wish to know. The former requires an acknowledgement of lack: there are limits to what can be known; perhaps even nothing can be known reliably, given that the unconscious disrupts everything. The latter, however, represents a repression of this understanding, built up into the claim that an expert (the 'man of science') might get to know everything, a position later named by Lacan (1991) as 'the discourse of the Master'. This tension between knowing and disrupting knowledge is a key one for current debates about how psychoanalysis might be deployed outside the consulting room. Does it contribute to knowledge understood as a cumulative project in which things are waiting to be discovered, or can it be used to query such claims to knowledge, and if so, in the name of what does it do that? Perhaps the dilemma here is that although the project of bringing psychoanalysis into the 'academy' (to put it at its most theoretical) is an important one both for complementing and for challenging other approaches within the disciplines it encounters there, psychoanalysis tends to lose its socially critical power once it is appropriated as a mode of institutional knowledge (Frosh, 2006). This is, of course, a familiar dynamic in other 'critical' areas such as feminism and Marxism: when they enter into common use they can be appropriated or colonised in the interests of the thing they might have been set up to criticise. Adorno (1967) pointed out, and Althusser (1971) elaborated in a rather different theoretical language, that this is exactly how the 'administered society' operates: it co-opts its critics. As Freud himself knew (e.g. Freud, 1925), *accepting* a disturbing thesis can be a way of denying its truth: it can become defanged, a norm, just like any other knowledge.

The suggestion here is that if the co-option of an apparently critical discourse into a normalising one is a widespread phenomenon (for instance, it is visible in the continuing vitality of capitalism as it manoeuvres its dissidents into being sources of profit), there may be something specific, or at least exemplary, in the way in which this happens with psychoanalysis. Despite a great deal of historical optimism that it might have something important to offer as a critical approach to sociality, psychoanalysis has at least equally often been portrayed as a bureaucratising and conformist practice, in which adaptational and wishfully integrationist thinking is primary, trouble and trauma are individualised, and social relations are either ignored or made visible in a way that leaves them undisturbed (e.g. Jacoby, 1975). This accusation has usually been focused on ego psychology, the dominant form of psychoanalysis in America after the Second World War,

but this is now an old and perhaps partial appraisal. Indeed, whilst ego psychology concentrated on that side of psychoanalysis that stresses the necessity for control of unconscious impulses and adaptation to society and hence seems clearly at odds with the radical critique of society articulated by the 'Freudo-Marxists' (e.g. Marcuse, 1955; Frosh, 1999), it can also be understood as an honest response to the destructive explosion of *irrationality* embodied in fascism and Nazism. That is, despite its many and obvious limitations, one should not be too single-minded about pillorying ego psychology's attempt to reinstate rationality as a moral force, given the historical context out of which it emerged. However, something more general is at stake here: not just ego psychology as a mode of conformist psychoanalysis, but the tendency for the most demanding, most difficult ideas of psychoanalysis to give way to a kind of conformist moralism, a common sense which one might argue it is precisely the task of psychoanalysis to disrupt. Moi (1989, p.197) comments in relation to sexual difference and the tendency of psychoanalysis to 'colonise' in the sense of imposing a grid of rationality on the unconscious, that 'When the colonising impulse gains the upper hand, psychoanalysis runs the risk of obliterating the language of the irrational and the unconscious, repressing the threatening presence of the feminine in the process.' Writ large, this refers to an overwhelming trend in much psychoanalytic work to *normalise*, to create another edifice that mimics all the edifices of the disciplines and professionals around it, with grades of seniority and legitimate and illegitimate credentials, with graduation ceremonies and evaluation criteria, and with true and false knowledge.

Laplanche (1999) calls this psychoanalysis' tendency towards 'going-astray' from its own most radical insights. Using Freud's idea about being akin to Copernicus in decentring the human subject, Laplanche comments:

> If Freud is his own Copernicus, he is also his own Ptolemy. The revolution in astronomy lasted nearly two millennia, with some intuitions of the truth almost from the start, but also with an initial going-astray. In psychoanalysis everything, essentially, is produced by a single man – *simultaneously: the discovery*, affirmed at a very early stage, and which is conjointly (and for me indissociably) that of the unconscious and that of seduction – *and the going-astray*, the wrong path taken each time there was a return to the theory of self-centring, or even self-begetting. (p.60)

Laplanche's reference to the 'wrong path' refers to loss of the radical awareness of the causal nature of otherness that psychoanalysis makes possible. However, it has another resonance: one in which 'self-centeredness' is a *political* act that backs away from engagement with

the other and in doing so loses its principles. The starkest instance of this in the history of psychoanalysis is its failure in Germany to appreciate the implications of Nazism and to take a stand against it; as a consequence, psychoanalysis lost its moral valence, and can be thought of as taking a 'wrong path' that was very much a 'going astray' (Frosh, 2005). In language that serendipitously parallels Laplanche's vocabulary, the Mayor of Hamburg, Klaus von Dohnyani (1986), introducing the 1985 International Psychoanalytic Association Congress there, made some powerful accusatory comments about German psychoanalysis. These comments suggest a potential link between the kind of theoretical abandonment described here, and the loss of moral direction that can have significant political consequences:

> It therefore is my opinion that your colleagues who have described the weaknesses of psychoanalysts and their associations in the years leading up to and during National Socialism have helped to free us from historical entanglements by showing us how it really was – with respect to psychoanalysts, too, even Sigmund Freud. For fear of losing everything, bit by bit was sacrificed, every step being rational – and yet at the same time always in the wrong direction. Here a compromise concerning persons, there a compromise of principles, but always in the pretended interest of preserving the whole – which in the end was lost. (p.4)

Not all compromises lead to collaboration with Nazism, of course, and to accuse psychoanalysis of always having lost its way like this would be a gross calumny. Nor is it the case that psychoanalysis is any worse in this regard than other professions – law and psychiatry immediately come to mind. But if one is trying to hold onto what might be called the 'critical tradition' in psychoanalysis, which pays its full dues to its capacity for resisting conformist pressures (the opposite kind of resistance from that outlined by Freud when describing social responses to psychoanalysis itself), one has to ask about the connections between theoretical 'going astray' and the wandering down blind, or at least morally questionable, political alleys. This is one of the issues taken up by Jacoby (1983) in his account of the fate of European psychoanalytic radicalism (embodied especially by Otto Fenichel) once transplanted into America, so the point here is not only about Nazism, but about all occasions on which psychoanalysis fails to withstand the bureaucratising and conformist pressures placed upon it.

For Laplanche, the key issue is the extent to which *otherness* can be engaged with as the source of psychic life, his argument being that Freud's appreciation of other-centredness is both radical and precarious, always retreating back into claims for egoic mastery. More generally, this relapse into the hope of mastery is a retreat from recognition of the

essential alienness of human subjectivity, a retreat that is not accidental, but inherent in the material. As John Fletcher (1999) writes in his introduction to Laplanche's *Essays on Otherness*:

> To this dialectic between a decentring to which Freud officially aligns himself and a recurrent recentring, Laplanche joins the diagnostic notion of a wandering or going-astray of Freudian thought. . . . The covering over and occlusion of the discovery of the radical otherness of the unconscious and sexuality in Freud's thought, Laplanche suggests, trace out the movements of just such a covering over in the human subject itself. (p.3)

Awareness of the extent to which what is other dominates our existence is too painful, too terrifying, to be maintained; instead, both the subject and psychoanalysis itself 'wander' back from the momentary vision of this truth, to the fantasy of completeness, of narcissistic selfhood. There is something to be alert to here in reflecting on the impossibility of acceptance of the other, or at least on how painful such an acceptance can be. Laplanche comments (1999, p.67), 'One could endlessly demonstrate how the domestication of the unconscious never ceases to operate in Freudian thought, and this with regard to each of the foremost aspects of its alien-ness.' *Politically*, as well as 'scientifically', one might then say that each of its most profound inventions or discoveries is a threat to ease-of-mind, whether personally (as each individual analysand comes across something troubling in their speech to the analyst, for instance the racism that slips out, or the unwanted wish) or ethically/morally, as one comes across a claim made by psychoanalysis that disturbs the vision of human subjecthood that one would rather have. In each case, individually or institutionally, there is a tendency to 'wander', to back away from the insight that might itself have been painfully won, and take refuge instead in the safety of a knowledge that seems whole and reassuring, but instead is based on a damaging self-willed blindness towards what has already been seen.

This section has addressed a second theme of this book, which complicates the broader questions around what happens to psychoanalysis when it moves outside the clinic. The claim here is that psychoanalysis has an intrinsic link to radical social critique, because its concern is with unconscious impulses understood as destabilising and subversive of social as well as personal norms. In particular, psychoanalysis' positing of something 'alien' at the core of the human subject – an unconscious that somehow speaks 'through' the subject without being completely under the subject's control – draws attention to the central importance of *otherness* in personal and social life. Preserving this critical function of psychoanalysis is an important step in keeping

psychoanalysis alive and preventing it from ossifying into a form of expert received knowledge that can be easily accommodated into technologies of social control. However, not only is psychoanalysis subject to the same pressures towards bureaucratisation as are critical movements in other disciplines, but it also has its own internal momentum towards conformism derived from the disturbing nature of its discoveries. This suggests another set of issues which need to be addressed as one moves away from the clinic: can the direct engagement of psychoanalysis with social and cultural phenomena lead to a renewal of psychoanalysis itself, as it lays itself open to critical scrutiny in a more 'public' domain?

Normalising tendencies inside the clinic

Although this book is concerned with psychoanalysis outside the clinic, it is important to note, albeit briefly, criticisms of psychoanalytic clinical work that parallel the account of its drift into moralism and conformism as an academic discipline. Psychoanalysis is not divided into a radical clinical practice that sometimes loses its sharpness when it directly addresses culture or society. Rather, the tension between critique and conformity is *endemic* to psychoanalysis in all its manifestations – which is the point of Laplanche's previously quoted claim that 'the domestication of the unconscious never ceases to operate in Freudian thought.' Psychoanalysis as a clinical discipline has often demonstrated normalising approaches to patients. This has occurred most obviously in the case of homosexuality, where psychoanalysis has only recently, and partially, emerged from a long night of explicit and often highly damaging homophobia (Frosh, 2006; Isay, 1985). It also arguably applies generally in its adherence to models of family life based on an Oedipal norm that makes the relationship with the mother 'narcissistic' and that with the father (representing the prohibiting voice of the social law) the emblem of 'reality'. Issues here include the postulation of a normative developmental trajectory in childhood, giving a kind of 'teleological' feel to psychoanalytic theory (i.e. that there is a predictable developmental sequence resulting in mental health and that departures from this sequence are pathogenic); the promotion of particular familial organisations as if they are universal and necessary, especially in the context of gender relations; and ethnocentric assumptions about 'race', ethnicity and culture that may acknowledge the allure of 'other' cultures but neglect consideration of their specific characteristics when met with in treatment, and which also underplay the impact and historical cogency of racism and colonialism. The conservatism of the

psychoanalytic profession itself has also frequently been commented upon. This is evidenced in the tight regulation of acceptable versus unacceptable practice (the standardised 'fifty-minute hour' of treatment, for example); the compromises wrought by private practice; training regimes that reward conformity and militate against creative and critical thinking; and an aura of stiffness, fear of spontaneity and social conservatism that seems to pervade psychoanalytic societies. It does not take much imagination to see this as another manifestation of Laplanche's 'wandering'. Faced day-to-day with the slipperiness and determined challenge of the unconscious as it manifests in speech, with the disturbance it engenders and the erotic or aggressive embarrassments it perpetrates on, against, or in collusion with the analyst (not to speak of the *analyst's* unconscious and what it acts out in the clinical situation), perhaps it is not surprising that a covering-over and turning-away is provoked, so that there is not too much evidence left behind that something extreme happened here, something worrying and discomfiting. Living their professional, bourgeois lifestyle, perhaps it is too much to require of analysts that they should remain permanently plugged into the life-energy so delicately and waveringly uncovered by Freud. Is it really possible for their world to be restlessly populated by desire in all its peculiarities, without judgement or moralism, without platitude or denial? How does one go home to one's spouse and children, how does one remain a respected member of the community of doctors, lawyers and teachers, after a day spent so relentlessly grubbing around in the dirt? Perhaps it is only by dressing conservatively, metaphorically as well as literally, that this can be managed, that the veneer of respectability can be maintained, for oneself as well as the world. The sheer *effort* involved in remaining attuned to the surprises, insults and affections of the unconscious – again, one's own as well as one's patients – is exhausting and personally potentially damaging, as one struggles to withstand the assaults on one's identity and sense of coherence, on one's *integrity* in every sense of the word.

This is no excuse, of course, for the crass normalisations one sees in so much psychoanalytic clinical writing, let alone for its repeated failure to really address issues to do with the grounding of its clinical claims and the effectiveness of its treasured techniques (Frosh, 2006). Nevertheless, there is also something gallant about the continued willingness of these labourers of the soul to put themselves in the firing line, to take on the task of subjecting themselves to the daily assaults of unconscious missiles, day in day out, week after week, month after month, year after year (often with the same patient). Not only do they have to have a phenomenal capacity to withstand boredom (or to daydream), but they need to combine skins sufficiently thick to deal

with the constant assaults on their narcissism from patients who repeatedly tell them how useless they are, with a capacity for relatively calmly imbibing tales of terror and disgust, and with a further ability to ignore or parry overtly as well as implicitly erotic advances. All this has to be managed alongside retaining some alertness to the sensitive handling of deeply unhappy people. A close read of current clinical literature and exposure to clinical presentations suggests that many analysts carry this difficult feat off remarkably well, even allowing for the likely rewriting of reality that such unaudited accounts suffer from. Interestingly, there is also a heroic tradition of reporting therapeutic *failures*, from Freud onwards, that is perhaps even more impressive than the more conventional way in which a successful piece of analytic work is presented (in anonymised, hence distorted form) as a vignette supporting analytic theory. Freud's efforts in this vein, for example in the 'Dora' case history (Freud, 1905) in which his work came to an abrupt end by the patient walking out on him, show him trying both to learn from the events and also to legitimise his actions. No failure is truly a failure, but rather the manifestation of a resistance, or the consequence of a choice of patient known to be impermeable to treatment from the start (e.g. Freud, 1920a). This is often regarded, probably correctly, as a defensive response on Freud's part. However, the wish to make sense of failure is in itself not a malicious one, whether or not Freud was open enough about his own shortcomings, a point which also applies to later analysts. What is less common in the clinical literature is reflection on the assumptions underpinning analysis. Success or failure tends to be given in terms of an undeconstructed notion of therapeutic progress (albeit characteristically with caution about use of the troubling term 'cure'), using at best rather conventional notions of mental health. These often reference Freud's idea that improvement in a patient's capacity for love and work should be the goal, or possibly that 'The business of psychoanalysis is to secure the best possible psychological conditions for the functioning of the ego; when this has been done, analysis has completed its task' (Freud, 1937, p.402). It is far less common to find reference to the *critical* potency of the analytic process as something relevant to analytic aims.

An example might be useful here. Ann Smolen (2009) reports a case of child analysis with an adopted son of two gay male parents. This case went on for some years and was eventually broken off by one of the fathers, evidently against the wishes of the boy and his analyst. The case is beautifully described, with rich examples of the clinical encounter with the young boy and one of the fathers, and is followed by three respectful and insightful commentaries by other analysts. These commentaries are predominantly technical. One includes a parallel case

of a daughter of a lesbian couple (Herzog, 2009) and there is also interest in the 'new family form' involved, giving rise to some cautiously balanced comments about the importance of maintaining 'a strict analytical attitude', defined as 'what I mean is that it is necessary to try to observe and tend to reflect' (Ungar, 2009, p.28). There is much to be learnt from the case presentation and commentaries, and much to admire in the sensitivity of the work and the simple care and patience demonstrated by the analyst. Indeed, as regards the professional ethics of psychoanalysis the case is exemplary: despite all pressures to the contrary, the analyst does her best to stick with the patient whilst he tries to work things out and through for himself. There seems no question of a contracted period of time in which the therapy has to be concluded, but rather a recognition that what might often be needed is a pacing of work that reflects the reality of an intimate encounter, that is, that it has to unfold, that it has its ups and downs, that it can be difficult, and that much of its meaning resides simply in its durability. What is *not* visible, however – and, in a way, why should it be in an account that aims to promote professional practice, rather than question the assumptions of the profession itself? – is a mode of reflexivity that moves beyond the unquestionable capacity of the analyst to think about herself in relation to the boy, to further consider what *becomes of* psychoanalysis in such circumstances. What does this case do to the normative assumptions on which psychoanalysis is premised – not just in the sense of demanding liberal tolerance of 'new family forms', which still are seen as requiring special 'explanation' to the children who grow up within them (Ungar, 2009, pp.28–9)? What expectations are disrupted, what new thing is learnt, what assumptions about adulthood and childhood and the relations between them, as well as the relations between adults and children, are put into question; what, in a word, is there by way of *surprise*? My point here, as should be clear, is not that the work described is bad, neglectful, deceitful or retrograde; it is, rather, that it is *bureaucratic* in the sense evoked by Lacan's (1991) 'discourse of the university': it makes knowledge into technology, rather than exploring the way in which it can be explosive. How might psychoanalysis, as the discipline of the disruptive unconscious, maintain its capacity to shock? Only by itself being open to newness, to discovering something that it did not previously know existed. This is hard, in clinical work as elsewhere, though there is something to be said for the possibility that the clinical environment is more rather than less promising for this to happen: at least the patient is always present, to refuse to comply with the analyst's pre-existent schema. But when this is written about, in the case studies that comprise much of the analytic world's internal communication system, it is rare to find instances that say, 'my theory failed, I learnt something new.'

Constructions of psychoanalysis as a colonising science

The question of how to renew psychoanalysis so that it continues to be a shocking discipline, to itself as well as to others, is perhaps especially paradoxical in relation to applications of psychoanalysis outside the clinic. These applications reflect the ambition of psychoanalysis to be a 'general' theory, seeking out the materialisation of the unconscious in all areas of human activity. They also reproduce a specifically modern imaginary of the scientist as moralist, as the person (in fact, the man) who might be called upon to pronounce on the great issues of life and death. For Freud, the temptation to enact this role was too strong to be resisted. Psychoanalysis, he thought, was more profound than philosophy in that it dealt with the same issues, but in a way that was scientific – which also contrasted it with that other contender for the governing of human passions, religion, dismissed as an 'illusion' (Freud, 1927). Philosophy, Freud claimed to his friend Fliess, had been his first love: 'As a young man my only longing was for philosophical knowledge, and now that I am changing over from medicine to psychology I am in the process of fulfilling this wish' (Freud, 1896/1961, p.241); but once psychoanalysis emerged, he no longer respected the armchair creations of the philosophers. The key difference in his mind was the material, empirical foundation of psychoanalysis compared with the speculative nature of philosophy. For example, discussing the relationship between the ideas of the Greek philosopher Empedocles and his own theory of the life and death drives, Freud (1937, p.245) comments, 'But the theory of Empedocles which especially deserves our interest is one which approximates so closely to the psychoanalytic theory of the instincts that we should be tempted to maintain that the two are identical, if it were not for the difference that the Greek philosopher's theory is a cosmic phantasy while ours is content to claim biological validity.'

In this light, it is a well-known irony that a major criticism of psychoanalysis is over its *lack* of empirical grounding and its wobbly relationship to biological reality. Contrariwise (a good term for psychoanalysis in general), it is the great imaginative sweep of the discipline as well as its focus on questions of meaning rather than cause, that endears it to so many followers who are less than impressed with scientific reductionism. As often noted (e.g. Frosh 2006), this was not Freud's preferred path; for him, the scientific 'Weltanschauung' was the one that psychoanalysis should follow. But what can be termed the 'colonising' tendency in psychoanalysis has its origins in Freud's own proselytising activities, his claims for the universal validity of psychoanalysis, or at least its relevance to all fields in which people tread. How can one write on literature and art, on religion and war, on social structures, dreams

and daydreams, on jokes and sex, without exciting those who wish to make psychoanalysis a universal critical schema; and at times without drawing in the lost souls who want to make it a way of life? The clinical setting provides some of the frisson of psychoanalysis, with its opportunity for intense immersion in the lives of others – but as already noted, this is opposed by the responsibility entailed in this kind of contact, not to mention its repetitive and mundane quality, its sheer boredom and difficulty. 'What do they want from me?' might be the call of the experienced, honest analyst or therapist, facing her or his schedule of patients for yet another day. This mundanity grounds the speculative thrill of psychoanalytic theory, so that it is less likely to float away. 'Applied' psychoanalysis, using that term to signify the use of psychoanalytic theory outside clinical settings, has no such obvious grounding; there is nothing intrinsic to it to hold it in place. Hence its excitement and its risks: for those attracted to speculation, it is an open invitation to indulge. Freud himself claimed aversion to wildness in imagining psychoanalytic truths, yet also showed a tendency to engage in it, as he admitted in one of his most ambitious and important texts, *Beyond the Pleasure Principle* (Freud, 1920b, p.295): 'What follows is speculation, often far-fetched speculation, which the reader will consider or dismiss according to his individual predilection. It is further an attempt to follow out an idea consistently, out of curiosity to see where it will lead.' This is not to say that *anything* goes: constraints are imposed by the theory of psychoanalysis, by the traditions of the specific disciplines into which the psychoanalytic thinker might wander, and by the restrictions of common sense; but as will be seen, these constraints are not always effective in tethering psychoanalytic ideas to something resembling plausibility. And the contrary argument, of course, goes as follows: why should they be so tethered? If psychoanalysis is not simply an expression of whatever is already known and commonsensical, is not in league with normativeness and regulation, is not therefore, a bourgeois discipline, the work of which is simply to confirm the everyday in its greyness; then why should it not multiply fantasies, provoke breaks in the ready-made and received, the *obvious*? That is, why bother to deploy psychoanalysis if all it does is reproduce what everyone already accepts as true? Again, there is some danger in following this logic in the clinical situation, where one might do harm with one's mad speculations; but perhaps outside it, such madness can be indulged.

It is not difficult to see problems with this argument, notably that ideas have consequences even without the immediate danger of the misuse of power in the clinical situation. People go to war for ideas; ideas maintain conflicts between and within nations, in families and

groups; people liberate themselves and enchain themselves in the service of what they think and believe. The notion that ideas are harmless, or else that they are merely froth, bouncing about on the surface of economic and political waves, is no longer seriously maintained by anyone. In the specific case of psychoanalysis, the impact of ideas is especially pronounced, and is observable in the saturation of contemporary culture with psychoanalytic notions (Parker, 1997). This is not only a statement about the *marketing* of psychoanalytic ideas, for example in advertising or in novels. It is, additionally, a comment on the extent to which the reflexive self-understanding of contemporary western societies draws on psychoanalysis as a prominent 'discourse'. It might even be claimed that if psychoanalysis was only *partly* 'true' when Freud invented it, it is much truer now, at least in the cultures in which it has had high levels of intellectual penetration. The unconscious exists, even more than in Freud's day: it is a routine way in which people understand themselves and others, a discourse they draw on to make sense of their experiences, a tool to be used when struggling to manage their own behaviour and that of other people. Elementary notions in everyday life, such as that a person might be lying to her or himself, posit the existence of an area of unconscious mental functioning that draws implicitly on Freudian premises; displacement, projection, denial and repression are all widely used explanatory ideas, with or without their technical vocabulary. The broad psychologisation of culture is rife, and the contribution of psychoanalysis to that trend is highly pronounced. Hence, the interpretive claims that are made – especially if they are repeated endlessly – make a difference; at times, they might even be a matter of life and death.

This all puts some responsibility on those who apply psychoanalysis to find ways to constrain their activities that might parallel the procedures governing the clinical freedom of psychoanalysts to imagine all sorts of impossible things. How can these constraints be developed? One problem with the notion of 'applying' psychoanalysis is that it suggests that one well-formed discipline is going to be used to elucidate the obscurities of another – for example, that psychoanalysis has insights into art history that the historians themselves may not have – and that as a general theory it can be stretched across widely disparate areas of intellectual activity. Not only does this neglect the specifics of *psychoanalysis'* conditions of emergence and the question of the limits of its applicability; more to the point it neglects the specifics of the disciplines to which it is being applied. For example, can psychoanalysis speak of literature without using literary tropes? Is it fair to import it into music or art without deep knowledge of the conventions and technical apparatuses of those two immensely rich terrains? Is social

research the same as clinical activity when it comes to questions of inter-pretation and reflexivity? What do sociologists and political theorists know of group relations and conflicts that psychoanalysts know not? Did psychoanalysis 'cause' cinema, which grew up at exactly the same time, or was the direction of effect the other way around, or mutual?

This last example is a particularly apposite one, as it reminds us of the extent to which psychoanalysis is itself a modernist construction, with porous boundaries in relation to other such constructions. Like psychoanalysis, cinema burst on the scene from nowhere; like cinema, psychoanalysis has always dealt with illusions, fantasies and dreams. Gabbard (2001) describes this mutuality well:

> In 1895 there were two auspicious births. The Lumière brothers invented a rudimentary film projector, signifying the birth of the cinema, and *Studies in Hysteria* appeared, inaugurating the new science of psychoanalysis. Throughout the twentieth century the two new disciplines have been inextri-cably linked. As early as 1900 a writer would describe his psychotic episode in terms of 'the magic lantern' effects of the nickelodeons... In 1931 the American film industry was already being called a 'dream factory' ... reflect-ing the close resemblance between film imagery and the work of dreams. (p.1)

Given this context, the idea that psychoanalysis could hold the truth of cinema seems far-fetched; Gabbard (pp.4–5) notes that, 'Obviously, when one applies a psychoanalytic lens to the text of a film, one cannot hope for a definitive reading. A more modest goal is to emphasise how clinical psychoanalytic theory can illuminate what appears to be happening on the screen and the manner in which the audience experi-ences it.' The term 'illuminate' here reveals the complexities of the situ-ation. 'Illumination' (even 'Lumière') is precisely the activity of cinema, and one might argue that the vocabulary and technology of film is exactly what is needed to help us understand psychoanalysis itself. That is, maybe it is only amongst a population that is used to the play of images on a screen, out of which a narrative is made, that the distinc-tion between conscious perception and unconscious significance makes sense; or perhaps it requires familiarity with the kinds of visual glimpses and auditory hints to be found in the cinema before one can be completely comfortable with the way psychoanalysis finds meaning in small gestures and slips. The major shift of psychoanalytic film criticism towards Lacanian psychoanalysis in the 1970s (e.g. Mulvey, 1975; Metz, 1977) revealed the potency of the latter's focus on the imaginary and on representation; but perhaps it is also the case that Lacanian psychoanalysis *needs* cinema to ground it, to enable its concepts to make sense. The same might be true of psychoanalysis more generally –

its dreamscape is cinematic, and perhaps without film we could neither imagine it so thoroughly nor find it so convincing.

The argument unveiled by this example is that psychoanalysis itself is a cultural construction, a modernist project, and hence that whenever it seeks to establish its expertise, its mastery in other areas, it is exposed to a querying process in which its own conditions and assumptions are placed under scrutiny. Indeed, Rustin (1999, p.106) understands psychoanalysis as the 'last modernism', defining modernism as 'a movement which sought to understand, and develop new languages and cultural forms to represent the intractable obstacles which remained to human freedom and the powers of reason' (p.108) – a notably broad definition that incorporates most of the principled activities of the disciplines contemporary with psychoanalysis. Zaretsky (2004) similarly places its development in what he terms the 'second industrial revolution', Fordism and subsequent twentieth-century movements. If this is the case, psychoanalysis has no special position that it can exploit in order to grant it expert status in relation to other entities. It is, simply, one of a class of intellectual activities – perhaps a powerful one because of the protean nature of its concepts and the potential rigour of its methodology – itself produced by, and in the context of, other historical forces. As has many times been commented upon, psychoanalytic imagery and assumptions reflect a range of notions that were around at the time of its emergence (Frosh, 1991). Specifically, the claim that there is some interpretive depth reality which is truer than surface appearances is central to modernist views of creativity and resistance just as it is crucial to traditional psychoanalysis. It can also be detected in Freudian-based analyses of the socio-political situation, which classically emphasise the perpetual contradiction between personal desires and social necessity, with the attendant restrictions on full human happiness (Freud, 1930). *Underlying* psychological stability are unmet desires; social stability is built on the renunciation of instinctual impulses. This model of the surface threatened by 'unconscious' impulses that have been historically suppressed supplies the connection between the advent of psychoanalysis between 1895 and the 1920s and the many contemporaneous modernist images (in art, literature, music and politics) of revolution, of how what lies underneath can break through and overturn the established order. Freudian psychoanalysis spoke fully to this, and offered a route through, a way of thinking about how such elemental forces might be expressed without wiping out everything in their way. A consequence of this, however, is to *relativise* psychoanalysis: as a product of its time and locality, it too is ripe for examination and cannot be used as a sure ground on which to stand and from which others can be put in their place.

Areas of psychoanalytic influence in the arts and social sciences

That said, the impact of psychoanalysis on the arts, humanities and social sciences has been enormous. Sometimes this has transpired as a relatively straightforward and accepted mode of colonisation, but more often as a resisted practice (against which the natives take up arms), with problems and benefits both for the putative colonised group and the psychoanalytic imperialists themselves. Much of the early work was in essence crude psychobiography – for example, Freud's (1910a) own famous mis-analysis of Leonardo da Vinci, in which the artist's creativity is seen as a manifestation of his repressed homosexuality, itself linked to the speculative history of his relationship with his mother. Given the fascination of psychoanalysts with 'creativity', Freud's admiration for cultural heroes, and a rather general tendency for psychoanalysts to see themselves as kindred spirits to creative artists; and given the receptivity of artists, especially in the first half of the twentieth century, to those who might be able to speak seriously about dreams and nightmares; it is perhaps not surprising that a kind of mutual admiration should grow up between the two groups, though perhaps rather less obvious that the artistic community would appreciate the reductive interpretive propensities of the psychoanalysts. In retrospect, it is perhaps predictable that this reductionism, focusing analysis on 'personality' or 'character', should be the psychoanalytic tendency. Partly this is because psychoanalysis was an element in a psychological revolution that, far from displacing the human subject as the centre of all things (as Freud thought), rather developed or invented the *individual* as the locus of scientific and (particularly) literary concern. The emergence of the novel as the most popular literary form, for example, significantly predates psychoanalysis, but it is also part of the same movement towards individualisation that was a consequence of the industrial revolution, the 'long' period of modernity, and the gradual differentiation between private and public that was a characteristic of capitalist society (Berman, 1983). That the individual psyche should be seen as the source of artistic meaning is therefore predictable from the character and conditions of emergence of psychoanalysis itself. It was a reflection of, and a way of expressing, the pressure towards individualisation and the construction of an autonomous human subject, however self-contradictory this task should eventually turn out to be. Moreover, the push in psychoanalytic literary and art criticism to find roots for creativity in the artist's developmental history is not just a reflection of the specifics of psychoanalytic theory, but of its structure: the discipline was founded on the premise that meaning is made retrospectively, that looking back-

wards to childhood is necessary if one is to understand what has come 'next'. Indeed, this concept of backwardness or '*Nachträglichkeit*', translated in French as 'après-coup' and in English as 'deferred action' has become a key notion in contemporary cultural appropriations of psychoanalysis, perhaps because of its 'rediscovery' by Lacan (1953). As Eickhoff (2006) points out, these two translations actually emphasise two somewhat different senses (retroactivity and after-effect) implicit in the term coined by Freud. The former references the way meaning is conferred on an event from the standpoint of a later event that brings it to consciousness; while the latter describes the impact of early experiences on that which comes later. Despite the contradictory implications of these two ideas – the first of which emphasises the constant rewriting of the past from the situation of the present, whilst the latter has a more traditional and linear 'developmental' focus – the primacy given to a view of *history* in formulating explanations for human action is symptomatic of a specifically modernist consciousness. Yet this historical outlook also has some critical possibilities embedded within it. In its most widespread and 'classical' form, the developmental thrust of psychoanalysis promotes a backward-looking approach, in which the past is mined as the source of a linear sequence that is taken to be explanatory of the here and now. Yet clearly this is not the only way to develop notions of causality: *circular* explanations, in the sense of recurrent, repetitive time, are also rife in Freud. They are, for example, key to the notion of the death drive as summarising a universal tendency to repetition, and the unconscious has *timelessness* as one of its chief characteristics. So the reductive, linear approach is not only problematic from the point of view of art, which sees it as neglecting the specifics (formal properties and so on) of art traditions themselves; it is also very partial from the point of view of *psychoanalysis*. Whilst biography matters enormously, it only takes its meaning retrospectively, hence cannot be used unproblematically as a formula for interpreting the present (with a patient) or the produced work (in art).

What has made a profound difference to the reception of psychoanalysis in art and literary criticism, and to a lesser extent in the social sciences, has been the poststructuralist interest in the way in which knowledge is constructed *in the relation between* the material itself and the reader or viewer. This has, for example, rendered obsolete the solely biographical approach (however inviting it may be because individualism still exists) and has promoted examinations which explore the manifold ways in which meanings might be attributed to art works – that is, what they *produce*, rather than what they *reveal*. Psychoanalysis has come up with its own parallel approach, especially amongst those who have drawn on Lacanian theory, which is concerned with 'chains of

signifiers' and representational practices that refuse (or intentionally fail) to pin down meaning but instead focus on opening it up. This has to do again with retroaction: Lacan holds that sense is always made post hoc, being produced by the interpreter re-reading the subject's discourse in order to even it out, to find anchor points for it and consequently to make it safe and orderly, however complexly and aesthetically this may be done. Sense-making is therefore carried out from the standpoint of something that has already happened and can be molded into shape in the light of where one now finds oneself, a process of 'après-coup' if one is to use the distinctions within *Nachträglichkeit* mentioned above. As it unfolds, however, the chain of signifiers has no particular meaning, it just moves on, throwing out shards from which retroactive sense is then made. The role of psychoanalysis is to stay connected to the signifying process itself; it aims not to make narrative sense in which the unconscious is drawn on as an 'explanation', but rather to *disrupt* sense, to examine the building blocks out of which sense is being produced as a kind of epiphenomenon. This means that there is no specific 'truth' of the work of art to be uncovered; instead, interpretive – or, better, *reading* – strategies continuously revolve the art work to reflect different moments of connection and resonance, of light, off its surface. If one is concerned with this kind of productivity, with what amounts to the *effects* of an art work, then interpretation will shift moment by moment, and its purpose will be to fix meaning for only so long as for it to have an impact, and then to move on, disrupting the meaning that has just been found. Such an approach reduces the risk of psychoanalysis presenting itself as a master discourse that can uncover the truth, and sustains at least some element of its subversiveness. It seeks continually to undermine the temptation to take refuge in the belief that one has mastered the complexities of the art work, that one knows what it is about; in this way, it retains a link with the unpredictable seditiousness of the unconscious. But this is at a price: just like critics said about the excesses of postmodernism, psychoanalysis may become more playful and fluid, but less satisfying, less capable of taking a stand.

The examples of law and sexual difference

Many of the issues that arise in relation to the arts also emerge in social science disciplines such as social psychology, philosophy, politics, history and law. These particularly involve the use of psychoanalytic interpretations and concepts to make sense of social phenomena; that is, psychoanalysis is deployed as a way to augment the explanatory power of the disciplines concerned. For example, there is a long history of

discussion in law of how psychoanalytic accounts of the superego and the Oedipus complex can contribute to understanding legal authority and its transgression, and of the power of the law to 'inhabit' its subjects so that they regulate themselves, feeling guilty when they transgress law's injunctions, even at the same moment as experiencing enjoyment. This tradition really starts with Freud's (1913a) *Totem and Taboo* and his (1921) *Mass (or Group) Psychology and the Analysis of the Ego*, both of which deal with the way in which groups and societies enhance their control over their subjects through psychic regulation, particularly in the form of internalised constraints derived from external authority. The development of the concept of the superego, which is articulated fully in *The Ego and the Id* (1923), made it possible for Freud to theorise the route taken to this internal policing system, which he presents, in *Civilization and its Discontents*, through a simile of colonisation. 'Civilization ... obtains mastery over the individual's dangerous desire for aggression by disarming it and by setting up an agency within him to watch over it, like a garrison in a conquered city' (Freud, 1930, p.316).

Prior to this, there had already been legal discussion of the place of the superego in preserving social order, for example in a long paper by the jurist Hans Kelsen that appeared in the *International Journal of Psycho-Analysis* in 1924, which constituted an important and erudite partial refutation of Freud's own views on mass psychology. The significant point here is that psychoanalysis provides an explanatory account of how the seemingly arbitrary rules developed by a society to manage its activities can be *experienced* by its members as binding; and conversely, how there can be pleasure in transgressing these rules even when that transgression produces anxiety and guilt. This explanation is given primarily in developmental terms (Frosh, 1999): the Oedipal encounter with the father generates aggression and the fear of aggression, materialising as castration anxiety; this is dealt with by being incorporated into the psyche and appears 'institutionalised' in the superego. This internalised aggression is experienced as guilt, the most obvious price of civilisation; guilt which does not depend on actions, but which is plugged into wishes and unconscious life. 'Whether one has killed one's father or has abstained from doing so is not really the decisive thing. One is bound to feel guilty in either case, for the sense of guilt is an expression of the conflict due to ambivalence, of the eternal struggle between Eros and the instinct of destruction or death' (Freud, 1930, p.325).

Guilt arises as the external threat of punishment and is 'taken in' and given structural permanence in the superego, where it is free to judge wishes with the same sadistic vigilance with which it would previously

have judged actions. Nothing can be hidden: the psyche is set against itself, hedging in the thoughts and behaviours of the individual with proscription and punishment. Thus guilt has two origins, first a fear of authority, second a fear of authority internalised, the superego. Of these two, it is the latter that is more destructive to the happiness of the individual. 'The first insists upon a renunciation of instinctual satisfactions; the second, as well as doing this, presses for punishment, since the continuance of the forbidden wishes cannot be concealed from the super-ego' (Freud, 1930, p.319).

Ironically, the super-ego is an escalating phenomenon: created by instinctual renunciation (of Oedipal desire), it demands more and more renunciation as its aggression is turned against unconscious wishes; the stronger the repressions, the stronger the sense of guilt. Society needs this to happen, according to Freud. Obeying an erotic compulsion to form people together to protect them against nature and each other, it demands harnessing of externalised aggression and its replacement with this internal agency of control.

One can perhaps see why this is an attractive set of ideas for legal theorists interested in the hold that law has over people even in the absence of strong constraints, and conversely in the reasons why transgression occurs even when it seems not to be in the interests of the transgressor. In the superego and in the Oedipal scenario, there is a mechanism proposed that can explain these phenomena, and can in particular provide a language for expressing the intensity of feeling that accompanies legal events – ranging from playground complaints of unfairness to complex judicial questions of culpability and punishment. 'Inside' the mind there is an agency that judges; this agency has a life of its own, and is fuelled both by inner, wishful impulses and by external constraints, by the rigours and irrationalities of the social order. This theory has the added advantage of linking social and personal, and hence different kinds of law – from actual physical enforcement through to the subtle and formative manoeuvrings of ideology (Hirst, 1979). Law becomes infested with emotion, bought into by the human subject as she or he wrestles with conscience and the unconscious, with ideals and reprimands all experienced as deeply personal and hence carrying more weight than if they were 'merely' external. And as psychoanalysis never tires of showing, each prohibition exists *because* there is an impulse towards transgression (the incest taboo is universal because incestuous desires are universal) but also as an *invitation* to transgression – for example, a social taboo on miscegenation actually promotes it as exotic and exciting. Thus it becomes easier to understand why crime pays, emotionally if not always in reality, as people only do wrong because there is wrong to do. The law has its perverse underside, both

in the way it operates (Kafka being the great chronicler of this), but also in the temptation, even encouragement, it offers people to break it: in formulating prohibitions, it names their desire.

These are genuinely profound insights and liberate law from a rationalism that can only address subjects in mechanistic terms and will always remain confused by the failure of people to behave according to simple cost-benefit analyses. Law invites transgression, not only structurally (a law defines what lies outside it) but emotionally too. Moving away from the specifics of the Freudian theory of the superego, psychoanalysis here offers a considerable amount of further leverage on legal issues through its interest in what the Lacanians term 'imaginary' and 'symbolic' orders. The former relates to the illusion provided by the law, that human behaviour can be perfectly regulated and hence is perfectible. It is imaginary, in the sense of idealising and illusory, to think of anything in this way; and in the case of human behaviour, it is downright dangerous. The idea that law can provide answers to everything leads to repressive states, using that term to reference both social orders and states of mind; it is also 'regressive' in the sense of aspiring to something imagined to be early and utopian, a state of narcissistic oneness in which there is no contradiction, in which nothing disturbs the surface of bliss. The symbolic, on the other hand, follows on from the discussion of the superego: it asserts the primacy of the signifying chain in which the individual subject is placed. Whilst it is more familiar to understand this as a linguistic issue – Lacanian psychoanalysis being concerned with the practice of language – the rich description that Lacanian theory offers of how the symbolic works reinforces the notion of an external law that is crucial to psychosocial being. That is, law regulates, and within it the subject finds its location.

This account stresses the benefits to legal studies of using some elements of psychoanalytic theory, but there are also ways in which law has challenged psychoanalysis, particularly in terms of the structural relationship between social contracts and subjectivity. For instance, psychoanalysis' propensity to postulate universal psychic mechanisms that become formulated as legal injunctions (the incest taboo as a universal outcome of incestuous desire being the primary case) is punctured by evidence that radically distinct legal systems exist, and that they can and do shift as a consequence of social change. In addition, classical psychoanalytic identification of the Oedipal triad as the forum for the encounter with 'reality' is challenged by legal theory that sees law as itself arbitrary and contractual – not 'real' at all – though this criticism can be offset by the Lacanian rendering of the symbolic as a non-naturalisable 'order' that always, in important ways, fails.

The challenge to psychoanalysis can also be seen in some other areas

of social scientific application of psychoanalytic thinking, where the role of psychoanalysis has been questioned even when its concepts are being deployed. The clearest examples here are where psychoanalysis has mapped across to areas of political as well as intellectual struggle, in particular being used as a resource to 'explain' or at least help theorise the motivations of political actors. Sometimes this has led to psycho-analysis being attacked as a bourgeois, oppressive discipline; at other times psychoanalysis has been turned back upon itself, so that its own investment in the troubles it is analysing becomes a topic for considera-tion and concern. The most important instance of this kind is that of gender and sexual difference, to which psychoanalysis has attended from the start, when received notions of heteronormativity were chal-lenged by the formulation of sexuality as inherently bisexual, but supported by other psychoanalytic concepts such as penis envy. For Freud, as is well known, sexual difference was the 'bedrock' of psycho-analysis, beyond which it could not go, and this took the specific form of the refutation of femininity and the pursuit of masculinity. This was contested from very early on, in the work of psychoanalytic writers of the 1920s and 1930s, and the general sexual normativeness of psycho-analysis has continued to be the object of critique, both from feminists and from gay and lesbian writers (see Frosh, 1999, 2006). However, especially since the publication in 1974 of Juliet Mitchell's book, *Psychoanalysis and Feminism*, psychoanalysis has also been drawn upon by many theorists in a search for theoretical leverage on gender and sexuality. This does not mean that Mitchell's promotion of psycho-analysis as a sexually progressive discipline has gone unchallenged. Indeed, psychoanalysis' conservatism in this area is well documented: in theory and in clinical work it has rarely supplied convincing recruits to the radicalisation of gender politics or to the ranks of sexual revolution. More importantly, however, there is now a sense of banality about many of the psychoanalytic claims concerning gender and sexual difference. Freud's phallocentrism and misogyny, as well as his confusion over feminine development and sexuality, is so clearly documented as to require no detailed repetition. Virginia Goldner (2003), in a paper exploring the relationships between contemporary psychoanalytic thinking on gender and on sexuality, points out how gender is now commonly discussed in an ironic tone, to accentuate the way in which its taken-for-granted status has been thoroughly undermined. With the exception, she claims, of 'a band of Euro-Lacanians and a few surviving True Believers, Freud's theoretical contrivances on behalf of the penile phallus are now taken as prima facie evidence of his ambivalent homo-phobia, casual misogyny, and traditional family values' (pp.113-14). The issue of 'penis envy' no longer has much resonance outside stand-

up comic routines, and even the object relational idea that girls, because of their close ties with their mothers, struggle with issues of autonomy and separation whilst boys trip up over intimacy, can now be seen both as a truism and as a tautology, describing a socially induced state of affairs without grasping hold of the complexities of the psychological mechanisms at its root. To say that girls reproduce feminine stereotypes because of their identification with their mothers, and boys become 'masculine' because of their repudiation of their mothers, is not a specifically psychoanalytic formulation: it could just as easily have been derived from social learning theory. What has replaced all this has been, as Goldner (ibid.) lists it, the work of 'Contemporary feminists, gay and lesbian scholars, queer theorists, and generations of psychoanalysts looking for better ideas about sex and gender,' which has produced what she describes as 'theories that refuse to sit still, retaining the density of the analytic perspective while digging up the ideological infrastructure of normativity, objectivism and biologism'.

Despite this healthy critique of psychoanalytic platitudes, contemporary gender theory is almost unimaginable without psychoanalytic input. Serious writers such as Judith Butler and Lynne Segal, both deeply embroiled in the political and philosophical understanding of gender, routinely deploy notions of unconscious life, albeit showing care to avoid reductiveness and individualism in so doing. Indeed, in Butler's case, the centrality of psychoanalysis to her recent thinking has been very marked, even though her highly influential early book *Gender Trouble* (1990) showed few hints that this would happen. Importantly, the key concepts she uses are not those put forward by Freud and later analysts as explaining sexual difference; it is rather the psychoanalytic formulation of more general mental mechanisms, particularly the identificatory ones described in Freud's (1917b) *Mourning and Melancholia*, that give shape to her continuing interrogation of identity and identity politics. This tendency is also visible in Jessica Benjamin's detailed psychoanalytic explorations of gender (e.g. Benjamin, 1995), which again focus on identification, and rather parallel the situation in the humanities, where the most constructive engagement with psychoanalysis has not been through its specific claims about literature or art, but rather through the tools it makes available for conceptualising psychological and psychosocial phenomena. Psychoanalysis thus enters the fray and holds its own not so much because of widespread adoption of its specific theories of sexual difference, but rather because it offers a framework for thinking through ways in which subjecthood resonates to the beat of social divides, and in particular for dissolving the simple separation between social and individual that bedevils other social psychological approaches. It is the sophistication of the psychoanalytic

lexicon and its capacity for extension and disruption that attracts gender theorists, not its specific proposals about psychic development. This is even true of the Lacanian element: whilst there are aspects of Lacan's account of 'sexuation' that have had an impact on psychoanalytically inspired work in the area, it is more the general Lacanian approach that has mattered, particularly because of the centrality given to analysis of the 'phallus' in its imaginary and symbolic manifestations. It is almost as if psychoanalysis loses its liveliness in these areas when it resolves itself into a specific theoretical account, and retains it when it pumps out ideas about the symbolic mechanisms at the heart of psychosocial life.

As will be clear from this, gender theory has had a striking impact on psychoanalysis itself, querying its allegiance to a dull and normative model of heterosexuality, disputing the homophobia that seems to be close to the heart of its musings on homosexuality, and demanding that it renew itself in the context of contemporary understanding of sexuality, sexual orientation and gender politics. This has been received positively in some psychoanalytic circles, even though in the dogged work of the clinic there is perhaps less evidence of novel thinking. However, the influx of feminists into psychoanalysis (Julia Kristeva, Juliet Mitchell, Nancy Chodorow and Jessica Benjamin are all psychoanalysts, as are Muriel Dimen, Virginia Goldner and other influential figures in the gender field) has meant that there is a way of speaking to psychoanalysis from within, whatever the difficulties of holding onto one's radicalism without being co-opted, and this has resulted in some genuinely transgressive thinking. This is now extending into arenas such as mothering (Baraitser, 2009), historically the bastion of the most regressive psychoanalytic theorising, though also an area hard fought over by feminist writers. Perhaps here more than anywhere there is evidence of a reciprocal relationship between psychoanalysis and those who mine it for its insights outside the clinic; and this is despite the fact that it also contains some of the most conservative elements of the psychoanalytic approach, which see normative models of family life as sacred and treat diversions from the received heterosexual path and bourgeois family arrangements as pathological and pathogenic.

Types of psychoanalysis

This last point raises another large issue. Psychoanalysis has so far been described here mostly as if it is a homogeneous entity, albeit one riddled with tensions over what I have termed 'critical' and 'conformist' tendencies. However, as I have described in detail elsewhere (especially in

Frosh, 1999), this apparent homogeneity is far from the truth. Psychoanalysis is a very diverse field, constituted by numerous 'schools' which have certain basic ideas and practices in common (the main one being commitment to the centrality of the unconscious as an explanatory notion) and which overlap importantly with one another, but which also have significant differences. In some cases, these differences are so substantial that there is little common ground and instead a great deal of mutual antagonism; in others, the differences are so slight as to be almost invisible to an outsider, even if they are deeply felt by adherents of the different groupings. Broadly speaking, however, it is possible to discern three main approaches that have had important effects in the applied world 'outside the clinic'. The first of these is classical Freudian psychoanalysis, obviously visible in Freud's own work and in that of the early psychoanalysts, but also informing the writings of a wide range of critics in the arts and humanities, social theorists and applied social researchers. For example, the critical theorists mentioned earlier, alongside other traditional 'Freudo-Marxists', worked with Freudian notions of repression and sublimation to articulate their understanding of the machinations of society in managing the desires of its subjects. Similarly, a number of important literary and cultural critics of the mid-twentieth century (including Lionel Trilling, whose work is referenced in Chapter 3) rooted their sympathetic understanding of psychoanalysis mainly in Freud's writings. In contemporary social theory, this position is less visible, but it is extremely important in revised forms in current work that combines psychoanalysis and attachment theory, in applications of psychoanalysis to child development, and in the controversial emerging field of 'neuropsychoanalysis' (e.g. Fonagy and Target, 2007; Mayes, Fonagy and Target, 2007). In some ways, what seems to have happened is that after quite a long period of being under pressure from object relations theories to accommodate growing evidence of the social orientation of children alongside an increasingly powerful clinical literature focused on transference from a relational perspective, Freudian psychoanalysis has reinvented itself. This has involved casting off some of the more rigid perspectives of the old 'ego psychology', accepting the centrality of object relationships, and configuring its interests to be closely aligned with the more biologically oriented developmental sciences. This is producing a revitalised empirical psychoanalysis with a great deal to say about human development and with an increasingly powerful theoretical lexicon that is also influencing clinical practice, for example in the form of research-based 'mentalisation' therapies that combine brief psychoanalytic psychotherapy with some of the principles of cognitive therapy (e.g. Allen and Fonagy, 2006). However, whilst the contemporary Freudian school is making considerable contributions to

the application of psychoanalysis in developmental psychology and related areas, there is relatively little evidence of impact in the wider fields of social and political theory, or in the arts and humanities.

The second broad group of psychoanalytic positions can be gathered together in what might be termed the 'relational' school of thought. This is a very large grouping with some significant differences between sub-groups – for example, some of the American 'intersubjectivists' are highly critical of Kleinian approaches to clinical work (e.g. Benjamin, 2004). Nevertheless, there is one very important factor that unites everyone, from object relations theorists and Kleinians in Britain, through to the interpersonal and intersubjectivist analysts in the United States. This is adherence to a model postulating that *relationality* is the primary concern of psychoanalysis, and also the major motivational and explanatory concept to be used both in clinical work and in broader theorising involving psychoanalysis. Psychoanalysis from this perspective involves a focus on the quality of the contact between analyst and patient as a way of addressing unconscious features of the patient's relational practices. How such unconscious features are theorised and exactly how psychoanalysis addresses them varies considerably. For example, Kleinians focus on 'inner world' features of the patient, understood to be built up out of a complex mixture of psychological drives and relationships with internal 'objects' (crudely, representations of people or parts of people). For them, the way in which unconscious phantasies attached to objects operate within the patient is demonstrated through transference-countertransference exchanges in therapy, and the analyst's task is to utilise these exchanges to help the patient recognise and work through the conflicts produced by these phantasies (e.g. Waddell, 1998; Frosh, 1999). For other analysts of the British object relations school (e.g. Casement, 2002) and the American intersubjectivists (Benjamin, 2004, 2009), there is relatively more interest in the 'reality' of the relationship between patient and analyst, in which new modes of what Benjamin and others call 'recognition' can be articulated so that the patient gains an experience of being treated as a *subject* whose needs can be understood and possibly met (Benjamin, 1995).

In Britain, Kleinian psychoanalysis in particular has a long history of use in artistic and sociological work (e.g. Stokes, 1963; Segal, 1991; Rustin, 1991), which in the early years of the twenty-first century has been strengthened by the emergence of a field of psychosocial studies drawing on Kleinian ideas for empirical as well as social investigations (Hollway and Jefferson, 2005; Roseneil, 2006). In the work of Wilfred Bion in particular it has a strong applied dimension dealing with the development of a theory of thinking (Bion, 1962, 1963, 1967) and of

groups (Bion, 1959). Bion is also an example of a psychoanalyst very appreciative of the difference between analytic practice in the clinic and the process of writing about it and hence using it outside. The influence of the broader object relations tradition, particularly stemming from the work of Donald Winnicott, can be seen in much thinking on creativity and also in social democratic theorising on political processes. For example, the writings of Anthony Giddens (1991) and Axel Honneth (Fraser and Honneth, 2003), discussed briefly in Chapter 6, use this kind of psychoanalysis to help theorise the conditions of social life in late modernity. The Winnicottian perspective, which emphasises the primacy of human relationships in the construction of secure selves, has also heavily impacted on American intersubjectivist theory, which in turn has contributed to bringing psychoanalysis into an active engagement with the philosophy of ethics, an issue that will be returned to in detail in Chapter 5.

There are, however, a couple of critical points about the relational stance 'outside the clinic' that will recur in this book. The first relates to a debate about politics, inner worlds and psychoanalytic purity and reflects a tendency amongst psychoanalysts to pursue orthodoxy in the form of debates about what is 'genuinely psychoanalytic' in their own and others' work. For instance, in the context of Benjamin's account of recognition, Juliet Mitchell (2002) queries whether the non-Kleinian relational approach loses the central psychoanalytic concern with the unconscious:

> The direction in which Benjamin takes it [i.e. the notion of recognition] however, moves it away from psychic conflict, away from sexuality and destructiveness to give us a rich phenomenology of processes of recognition of sameness and difference in which the psychic world reflects the social world. This move excludes the fact that dynamically unconscious processes are different from conscious ones, that dreams and symptoms have meanings that can be deciphered but that are not reflective. Benjamin's injunction is made within a psychosocial, not a psychoanalytical framework. (p.227)

This point about the 'psychosocial' versus the 'psychoanalytic' will be returned to in Chapter 7, but it is notable here that Mitchell is holding onto a concept of 'psychic conflict' that is seen as *autonomous* in relation to social processes, whereas, she claims, the more 'psychosocial' approach of the intersubjectivists is one which understands psychic life as 'reflecting' the social world. Importantly, this critique is offered in a response from Mitchell to attacks on her own work by some who see her as having lost the political edge that characterised her feminist interventions in earlier writings (Mitchell, 1974; Segal, 2001). This tussle over what is and is not legitimately 'psychoanalytic', as well as what is

and is not 'political', is characteristic of both areas. What is interesting here is that it also reflects a debate within the broad field of relational psychoanalysis about what the connections might be between the postulated 'inner world' and its outer determinants and reflections.

A second point about relational psychoanalysis is more focused on applications of Kleinian theory. Much of this work is rich and enticing, but it also demonstrates a tendency to take psychoanalytic concepts and translate them for use in the cultural and social sphere without worrying about whether this translation is actually legitimate. For example, key clinical concepts such as projective identification, transference and countertransference are entrusted with explanatory weight in investigations of phenomena such as racism (Frosh, 2006) or war (Segal, 1995). The potential problem with this, already hinted at and discussed in more detail in Chapter 7, is both that this risks reduction of social processes to psychoanalytic categories and that it significantly alters the psychoanalytic concepts being deployed, without acknowledgment that this has happened. It is arguable, for instance, that neither projective identification nor transference mean the same thing inside as outside the clinic – indeed, as will be described later, some analysts argue that transference only exists as such in the psychoanalytic encounter. Using these terms to 'give meaning' to social analysis is thus a speculative, metaphorical process, but in some work at least it can harden into an explanatory identity.

This leads into the third group of psychoanalytic approaches in this very broad classification – the Lacanian and post-Lacanian schools. Despite there being a very strong international tradition of Lacanian clinical work, it seems fair to say that the major impact of Lacanian psychoanalysis on the arts, humanities and social sciences has derived from its theoretical machinery, often as if it has nothing much to do with the clinic at all. For example, the original impact of Lacanianism in the British and American academies stemmed mainly from its position within the general pantheon of poststructuralist theories (Coward and Ellis, 1977) as well as its being part of what in the 1980s was a very fashionable wave of 'French theory' that included the work of Foucault, Derrida and Althusser as well as a variety of French feminists, some of whom drew on Lacanian theory for their own writing (Marks and de Courtivron, 1981). This meant that applied Lacanianism did not have to make the move from the clinic in the same way as did other psychoanalytic theories; rather, it was worked out, usually by non-analysts, in the context of the 'outside', for example in film theory, literature, politics and feminism. This history has attractions and problems from the point of view of the current book. On the positive side, Lacanian psychoanalysis and its derivatives and even some of its antagonists are

fully incorporated into the academy and do not rely (or not solely) on the credibility given them by their clinical activities. This means that the strengths and limitations of Lacanian thought in the applied sphere can be judged in the same way as one might judge any other social or cultural theory, with less danger of an appeal to the expertise of the psychoanalyst as the one who knows the 'secrets of the unconscious' because of her or his clinical experience. There is also a specific element of Lacanian theory to add to this, which will be worked on extensively in this book. This is its own suspicion of claims to mastery, something Lacan expressed in his account of the transference as well as in his description of the 'four discourses' (Lacan, 1991), in which the 'discourse of the Master' is specifically registered as not identical to – or even opposed to- that of the Analyst. What this provokes is an approach geared not to uncovering unconscious meaning, but to repeated questioning of claims to knowledge, rather along the lines argued at the beginning of this chapter. Partly for this reason, the Lacanian stance is appealing as a way of utilising the psychoanalytic understanding that the unconscious *is disruptive* in the social and cultural field, without pinning this down to a position in which the analyst alone knows the 'truth' of what is going on.

The drawback to this is that in being set free of the clinic, Lacanianism is also highly prone to abstraction in a way that is much less true of other psychoanalytic schools. In some respects, precisely because it does not often highlight its clinical status, it also loses the specific grounds of its authority, and instead has to share a position as one amongst many potential vocabularies for theorising social phenomena. Perhaps the discomfort this produces is one reason why some Lacanians have insisted on the clinical locus of psychoanalysis and on the *illegitimacy* of straightforward translation of its concepts to the wider sphere of knowledge (e.g. Nasio, 1992). It may also be a motivation for the tantalising way in which Lacanianism often seems to undermine its own knowledge claims by expressing them in abstrusely paradoxical, technical or enigmatic ways (including mathematical formulae that may not stand up to scrutiny). The message here seems to be both that there is a superior form of abstract knowledge available in Lacanianism, and that the lesson of psychoanalysis is that no-one can ever know anything at all.

Many of the details of these schematically presented distinctions between different psychoanalytic schools will be returned to in the course of this book. What will become clear is that despite its difficulties, the primary engagement here is with the Lacanian perspective because of the way in which it highlights the disruptive potential of psychoanalysis and hence works against the ossification of psychoanalytic thought as an

expert system that somehow knows the truth of the unconscious and can explain it to the world outside the clinic. However, there is also a strong presence of relational psychoanalysis in this book, particularly in the discussions on ethics and on social identity, and also use of some theorists who do not stand within any one psychoanalytic school, notably the French analyst Jean Laplanche. None of these approaches are being presented as unproblematic, for it is part of the task here to examine how they work in order to identify what they offer to the field of social criticism, and some of what they lack.

Psychoanalysis in the social sciences: a psychosocial approach

In summary, more than a hundred years after the founding of psycho-analysis, it is apparent that the influences and controversies surround-ing it continue. The locus of psychoanalytic knowledge is in the clinical situation, so what is being enacted when it moves 'outside' is a transla-tion across and extension of psychoanalytic ideas and practices, raising issues about the distortions and possibly creative alterations that take place along the way. Of particular concern is the extent to which the limitations on 'wild' analysis (Freud, 1910b) that are produced by the clinical situation (meaningless or wrong-headed interpretations might, one hopes, be constrained by the presence of an actual analysand who can speak back to the analyst) are lost once the restrictive boundaries of that situation are removed. There is also the danger of psychological reductiveness, in which the specific disciplinary constraints of the humanities or social sciences are displaced by a tendency to reduce everything to personal psychodynamics, often with a pathological slant. Nevertheless, it is arguable that psychoanalysis holds something signif-icant for all the other disciplines – specifically, a capacity to theorise subjectivity in a way that is provocative and unique, through reference to the unconscious. In addition, the fertility of its applications reflects back on psychoanalysis itself. Some of the most important critical work applied to psychoanalysis has come from outside the clinical situation, as if the freedom to think without being concerned with the require-ments of therapy is a necessary condition for theoretical development.

This book takes up these themes through a number of engagements with applied psychoanalysis. It is by no means comprehensive: part of the argument is that psychoanalysis fails when it is used without detailed knowledge of the area under discussion, and trying to cover everything would simply replicate this failure. My own interests produce a bias towards social and political issues rather than the arts

and humanities. Applications of psychoanalysis in the fields of sexuality, gender and 'race' come into this in an especially powerful way, but I have written about these extensively elsewhere (Frosh, 1994, 1999, 2005, 2006) and want to focus the present discussion on some newer areas of concern. These include particularly the emergence of a psychoanalytically-inflected literature around relational ethics, linked to questions of recognition, violence and 'otherness'. Nevertheless, the reality of sexual and racial oppression haunts the current text as a kind of undercurrent that constantly questions the way psychoanalytic ideas traverse the space of the social world.

The focus of the book is therefore on the applications of psychoanalysis in what can be loosely termed the 'social sciences', though even here I am consciously selective. For example, apart from the brief discussion in this first chapter, there is little more on law and nothing on the imaginative uses of psychoanalysis that have impacted upon recent human geography (Kingsbury, 2007) or on some controversial attempts to incorporate psychoanalytic thinking into social history (e.g. Pick, 1995). There is also no account of the use of psychoanalysis in developmental theory (see Frosh, 1989, for an early discussion of this), despite its growing importance, and nothing on the clinical uses of psychoanalysis in non-analytic settings such as psychiatry or psychodynamic counselling (Spurling, 2009). On the other hand, I do offer some coverage of the engagement of psychoanalysis and literary studies with one another, even though this lies outside the arena of the social sciences. This is because I shall argue that some classical debates over the literary uses of psychoanalysis are in important respects paradigmatic for the concerns of 'applied psychoanalysis' as a whole, and can offer a template and source of ideas for the social science discussion that in particular relieves it of the temptation to descend into a controversy over psychoanalysis' 'scientific status'. Whilst this question of 'scientificity', which I have previously discussed (Frosh, 2006), has its own interest, I suggest that the example of literary studies reveals more strongly some key pointers to enlivening the encounter between psychoanalysis and another discipline. These include how to keep both protagonists open to the other and reflexive enough to change as a consequence of contact, and how to ensure that the uses to which psychoanalytic ideas are put are sufficiently grounded in the kind of evidence that is relevant to the other discipline. Freud's own 'literary' works are therefore considered early in the book, as is the vexed and thrilling issue of 'psychoanalysis and literature', to produce a kind of model in which what is advocated is a reciprocal influence of each discipline on the other – what Felman (1982a) calls the 'implication' of each discipline in the other, rather than the 'application' of psychoanalysis to

a field outside itself. This demands a certain degree of openness and reflexivity within psychoanalysis, as well as modesty in its claims; but it also suggests that there are real gains to be had when psychoanalysis is brought into the sphere of activity of other disciplines, that it may help open them up or disrupt their own received wisdoms. The rest of the book proceeds through explorations of the social psychological and ego psychoanalytic notion of 'identity', which also draws on the massive interest in identities that pervade the social sciences (including ethnic, racialised and sexual identities); to debates on 'relational ethics' and examination of what it means to 'recognise others'; and to explorations of psychoanalysis in political theory. The final substantive chapter, on psychoanalysis and psychosocial studies, takes up particularly strongly the question of what psychoanalysis can offer to this attempt to think the 'social' and 'psychological' subject as one entity, and what happens to psychoanalysis along the way.

The logic of inclusion and argument here depends on an understanding of one so far unacknowledged element of my own disciplinary perspective, that of 'psychosocial studies'. The specifics of this in relation to psychoanalysis are discussed in Chapter 7, but in general what is being explored in this emerging field is the possibility of developing an approach to human subjects that manages to theorise together what are usually taken to be separate: the 'social' and the 'personal' or 'individual'. This requires an engagement with theories of subjectivity –hence, psychoanalysis – and also with theories of the appearance of the subject in the social. That is, using a term popularised by Althusser (1971), we are dealing particularly with questions of 'interpellation', which means considering how the human subject is both formed as an entity through the social order, and yet has agency within it. This paradox, that one can be both 'subject to' the workings of society and yet also be a 'subject' in the sense of being an agent with power to act on the world, is a core issue for psychosocial studies, as it is for many in the broader field of social theory. For example, Judith Butler (1997) expresses the dynamic well in her account of how power both constructs the subject and is available to the subject for use; that is, the same processes that make the human a 'subject' of power also constitute what is often taken to be the 'essence' of human subjectivity itself. She writes (p.14), 'Power acts on the subject in at least two ways: first, as what makes the subject possible, the condition of its possibility and its formative occasion, and second, as what is taken up and reiterated in the subject's "own" acting.' Written more simply and generally, the issue here is how one can describe the human subject in a way that accounts for the richness of what is usually taken to be 'inner life' (fantasies, desires, affects and the like) yet also recognises how each of

us is constituted first and foremost as a social being. Psychosocial studies is a generic term for this project, and also refers specifically to a set of theories and studies that try to bring these two aspects of the subject together.

A recurrent question in this book, then, is how to approach psychoanalysis not as possessing a 'truth', but rather as opening out some questions and perceptions that enable us to think the social and the psychological together in a manner that genuinely offsets the reductive pressures that work to hold them apart. The choice of topics in the chapters that follow can be seen as an attempt at various 'interventions' to support this goal of advancing psychosocial understanding through the use of psychoanalysis. From its historical contextualisation in Freud's work in Chapter 2 to the explicit consideration of psychoanalysis in psychosocial studies in Chapter 7, the interventions I have chosen are those which combine psychoanalysis and social or cultural theory in an attempt to break down traditional society-individual differentiations. Earlier, two questions were posed for this discussion. The first was what happens to psychoanalysis when it moves outside the clinic. The second was how, when the move is made, psychoanalysis can preserve or enhance its value as a critical approach, able to challenge and disturb the disciplines with which it comes into contact, and also able to renew itself in the process. A third, related issue, is now at stake. This revolves around the 'project' of psychosocial studies, distilled into a specific question of whether psychoanalysis 'outside the clinic' can be a force through which the divide between social and personal, 'external' and 'internal', can be overcome.

Chapter 2

Freud on Art, Culture and Society

Although this book is concerned with contemporary trends in psycho-analysis as applied in the social sciences, there is, as ever, no escaping Freud. For one to understand why and how psychoanalysis has moved out of the clinic, it is important to realise just how ambitious was the psychoanalytic project from the start, and also just how much energy was spent by the early analysts in arguing over the use of psychoanaly-sis as an instrument of cultural study. In particular, Freud and his followers were intensely interested in ways in which artistic and cultural phenomena could act as evidence for psychoanalytic theories. The study of mythology, for example, which was a focus for many late nineteenth-century scholars, was seen as a rich hunting ground for the psychoana-lysts, particularly because of the apparent parallels between myths and dreams. Indeed, as Kerr (1993) has shown, for Freud and his early follower Jung it was so central that it became a space for disputation, expressing the growing personal and professional dissension between them. Jung developed work on myths earlier and more extensively than Freud, who initially regarded the younger man's research in this area as advancing psychoanalysis' credibility and field of application. However, once their relationship had soured, the study of myth became a site for recrimination and barely coded antagonism. Freud emphasised the sexual and paternal motifs to be uncovered in mythological structures, whilst Jung immersed himself in what Freud thought to be spiritual and maternal illusions. By the time of the publication of the Freud's main text on the subject, *Totem and Taboo* (Freud, 1913a), Jung had already left the psychoanalytic fold, but Freud's book was as much a polemic against him as it was a contribution to the anthropological literature. In this way, the study of mythology became a political tool for the advancement of different versions of psychoanalysis.

This brief example flags up some of the issues to be dealt with in this chapter. 'Applied' psychoanalysis has several aims, all of which are registered in Freud's own work. One is to seek to extend the reach of psychoanalysis by showing its utility in fields outside the clinic. This 'political' advancement of psychoanalysis is coupled with a genuine curiosity about what psychoanalysis might add to understanding social and cultural materials, and an irritation with those in other disciplines

40

who cannot comprehend the difference that the unconscious might make to their studies. Conversely, as Freud and his followers believed they were uncovering universal features of mental life, they also looked to the wider world for evidence to support their claims. Art and literature would be especially valuable here, given the supposed parallels between artistic creativity and dreaming; but broader social and cultural phenomena such as mythology would also be important sources of such evidential support. These two main purposes of applied psychoanalysis – to extend the reach of the discipline and to provide support for its claims – continue to be central motives for psychoanalysis outside the clinic. Their political significance in establishing the credentials of psychoanalysis also remains, as it was for Freud, a primary cause of the intensity of much of the succeeding debate.

This chapter explores some of Freud's own contributions to the extension of psychoanalysis outside the clinic, focusing first on what he had to say about artistic creativity, and then moving to a more central issue for this book, his views on society and some of its major features. The examples presented here show a few things quite clearly: that Freud was deeply committed to this extension of psychoanalysis; that he was often aware of its limitations and of the problems it might create; and that he was mostly engaged in an *application* of psychoanalysis where the advantage lay with his own approach, seen as casting light on phenomena that could otherwise only be partially understood. All these issues recur in later work and so contribute to the framing of the discussions in this book, but the last of them, what might be termed the 'colonialist project' of psychoanalysis, is of particular importance.

Culture on the couch

From early on in his psychoanalytic work, Freud was on the lookout for ways in which psychoanalysis might draw on evidence from outside the consulting room in order to establish itself more firmly, as well as for opportunities to use psychoanalysis for wider cultural and scientific ends in the service of knowledge in general – as part, that is, of a broader process of scientific enlightenment. The 'social', 'cultural' and 'psychological' were not fully distinct domains for Freud. Anthropology, religion, art and politics were areas in which the unconscious could be observed at work, and consequently had things to say to psychoanalysis and, even more significantly, things to learn from it. As early as 1912, Otto Rank and Hans Sachs had founded a journal, *Imago*, which was 'concerned with the application of psycho-analysis to non-medical fields of knowledge' (Freud, 1926, p.269). This journal had considerable

success until the Nazis seized the psychoanalytic publishing house, the *Internationaler Psychoanalytischer Verlag*, in 1938, after which it was reinvented in America as *American Imago*. *Imago* was entertaining from the start, and involved some of the early psychoanalysts in exciting cultural speculations of a kind that, as widely read bourgeois, they immensely enjoyed. Gay (1988) comments:

> The nonclinical writings of the inner circle generated opportunities for round robins of good will and mutual congratulations. Freud welcomed Jones' weighty contribution to *Imago* on the symbolic significance of salt; Jones told Abraham that he had perused his 'charming study' of Segantini 'with the greatest interest'; Abraham for his part read Freud's *Totem and Taboo* 'twice, with ever-increasing relish.' Admittedly, some of the pathographies of artists and poets produced in the Vienna circle were naïve and slapdash, and at times they aroused Freud's outspoken irritation. But whether well done or bungled, applied psychoanalysis was a cooperative venture almost from the start. Freud found this widespread interest agreeable, but he needed no urging from others to put culture on the couch. (p.312)

Gay argues that Freud's principles when moving from the couch to culture were 'few in number, easy to state, but hard to apply: all is lawful, all is disguised, and all is connected' (ibid.). Psychoanalysis reveals how culture operates to gratify or frustrate 'hidden wishes'; hence, psychoanalysis opens out new areas of cultural understanding, and advances human knowledge in all its fields of application. 'What mattered to him,' writes Gay (pp.312–13), 'was less what he could learn from art history, linguistics and the rest than what they could learn from him; he entered alien terrain as a conquistador rather than a supplicant.' As will be seen, this is not completely true: Freud was in considerable awe of what he termed 'creative artists', who he thought had an intuitive grasp of the unconscious that could be used to provide evidence for psychoanalytic claims. But it is the case that, for better or worse (mostly the latter), applied psychoanalysis has tended to mean an attempt at conquest rather than partnership. This is perhaps justifiable for Freud and his immediate followers, who were working in a context in which what mattered most was the establishment of psychoanalysis as a discipline with something unique to offer, and for whom psychoanalysis was a revolutionary activity that overturned all traditional authority and ways of understanding the world. But even then, the complexity of the relationship between psychoanalytic knowledge and the specialised knowledge produced by the disciplines with which it is in dialogue (or with which it interferes) is considerable. Freud seems to have had more than an inkling that, whatever his own pleasure in cultural speculation, there might be limits to what his new approach could do.

These early applications of psychoanalysis came in a number of areas, but with the possible exception of mythology they were more focused on art and literature than on what might now be termed the social sciences. Later on, not just in *Totem and Taboo* but even more in the great texts on religion and society of the 1920s and 1930s, Freud turned powerfully to consider social phenomena, but in this case the application of psychoanalysis was very much one-way. Psychoanalysis was a tool to make fuller sense of social and 'civilisational' concerns than the existing (e.g. political and anthropological) and emerging (e.g. sociological) social science disciplines could do on their own. However, in considering art and literature, Freud knew he was engaging with modes of intellectual practice that had their own considerable history and potency, and whilst the 'conquistador' was very much in evidence in his attitude towards them, he also realised that there might be something psychoanalysis could learn. For this reason, if one is to seek an open psychoanalysis that can speak with other disciplines without too much arrogance and appropriative desire, a place to start might be with the problematic but also provocative musings of Freud on creative artists and their products. Before turning to some of the social applications of psychoanalysis, therefore, this chapter looks at some examples of his work on art and literature as a way of beginning to sketch something of a methodology. What emerges is a tale that will become familiar of psychoanalysis stating too much too firmly about its own knowledge, but nevertheless participating in a dialogue that has intriguing effects.

Pillaging art

Freud's approach to art and literature was that of a pillager, taking from it whatever he could to support his work. However, this was not done out of disrespect: he was steeped in admiration for literature, which formed much of the background to his thinking. His writings are peppered with literary allusions and references, marking him out as solidly within the traditions of European thought, a romantic in his belief in the power of the creative imagination. More significantly, Freud believed that the psychological processes fuelling artistic creativity were identical to those revealed by psychoanalysis in the clinic, and hence that exploration of the former would advance and deepen general psychological knowledge. A seminal example of this reasoning can be found in his paper, *Creative Writers and Daydreaming*, which presents the 'assumption' that 'a piece of creative writing, like a day-dream, is a continuation of, and a substitute for, what was once the play of childhood' (Freud,

1908a, p.139). In this short piece, Freud undertakes both to outline the sources of the creative writer's work and also its impact on readers, arguing that the continuity with childhood play reveals that the phantasies appearing in literature (especially romantic literature) are expressions of unconscious wishes, either erotic (in young women) or both erotic and ambitious (in young men). Freud acknowledges that much creative writing seems to be at a considerable distance from this kind of reductive scheme, yet states that he 'cannot suppress the suspicion that even the most extreme deviations from that model could be linked with it through an uninterrupted series of transitional cases' (p.138). But the key argument is one which directly parallels the account given in *The Interpretation of Dreams*, which postulates that dreams arise when a 'day residue' activates a childhood experience that has become wholly or partially repressed:

> A strong experience in the present awakens in the creative writer a memory of an earlier experience (usually belonging to his childhood) from which there now proceeds a wish which finds its fulfilment in the creative work. The work itself exhibits elements of the recent provoking occasion as well as of the old memory. (p.139)

Freud takes this 'wish-fulfilment' to be a very general phenomenon, explaining both the work of the writer and the response of readers to literature. According to Freud, the aesthetics of a piece of literature are a way of 'bribing' the reader with 'fore-pleasure' so that the disturbing elements of repressed material can be tolerated. Further pleasure can then be gained by the release of the underlying tension caught up with this repression:

> In my opinion, all the aesthetic pleasure which a creative writer affords us has the character of a fore-pleasure of this kind, and our actual enjoyment of an imaginative work proceeds from a liberation of tensions in our minds. It may even be that not a little of this effect is due to the writer's enabling us thenceforward to enjoy our own day-dreams without self-reproach or shame. (p.140)

Here it is the literary product that is the object of study, but behind it is an examination of patterns of psychological functioning that are seen by Freud as having general currency. They apply to dreams, daydreams, literary production and response, explaining both how creative writing comes about and how it might have an impact on a reader. Psychoanalysis is being used here not so much to interpret the 'meaning' of a piece of literature, but rather to understand the psychological processes that go into its production. As such, this approach is in line

with much work on the psychology of 'creativity' and it can be argued that it lies well within the domain of psychoanalysis' expertise: what mental processes allow a creative writer to work, and what psychological factors are called into play when a reader reads with enjoyment? Freud's answers to these questions might be tendentious and speculative, but the questions themselves are legitimately psychological and both draw on and advance the burgeoning theory of psychoanalysis as it applies itself to the broader, non-clinical arena of psychic life.

The model outlined by Freud in *Creative Writers and Day-Dreaming* is seen by him as possibly applying even to nations, their myths being 'distorted vestiges of the wishful phantasies of whole nations, the *secular dreams* of youthful humanity' (Freud, 1908a, p.140). As noted above, the exploration of myth was an important area of research for the early psychoanalysts because it seemed to offer anthropological support for psychoanalysis' claims, as well as providing a possible route to 'primitive' thoughts that might be seen as foundational for the structure of modern human minds. For Freud, the power of myths as routes to engaging with basic wishes and anxieties also explained the way audiences might respond to works of art that stirred up the same 'primitive' emotions that these myths dealt with so effectively. For example, in *The Theme of the Three Caskets* (1913b), Freud takes the scene from Shakespeare's *The Merchant of Venice* in which Portia's suitors have to choose between a gold, silver and lead casket, and what he convincingly presents as the parallel situation in *King Lear*, in which the true daughter is the third one, Cordelia, and argues that this 'dumb' third is death, now made an object of choice rather than necessity:

> Choice stands in the place of necessity, of destiny. In this way man overcomes death, which he has recognised intellectually. No greater triumph of wish-fulfilment is conceivable. A choice is made where in reality there is obedience to a compulsion; and what is chosen is not a figure of terror, but the fairest and most desirable of women. (p.245)

Literature is being treated as myth (Freud also quotes myths and fairy tales in this short piece), providing insights into basic human psychic mechanisms, in this case the substitution of what is most desired for what is most feared. This also acts as a mode of resignation and had – for the lugubrious, 57-year-old Freud, now at the end of what he had hoped would be a saving relationship with that other great exponent of myth, Jung – much personal resonance:

> We might argue that what is represented here are the three inevitable relations that a man has with a woman – the woman who bears him, the woman who is his mate and the woman who destroys him; or that they are the three

forms taken by the figure of the mother in the course of a man's life – the mother herself, the beloved one who is chosen after her pattern, and lastly the Mother earth who receives him once more. But it is in vain that an old man yearns for the love of woman as he had it first from his mother; the third of the Fates alone, the silent Goddess of Death, will take him into her arms. (ibid., p.247)

Literary analysis is being deployed here, remarkably successfully in many ways, to identify a symptom revealing a general human psychological state. That is, it is being used in the service of psychoanalysis, to advance understanding of psychic mechanisms (wish-fulfilment and reversal, for example) and to gain access to the way that residues from the past of humanity provide motive power for observable regularities in individuals' mental defences.

Occasionally, and less frequently than would be the case with later analysts, Freud applies psychoanalysis in order to enhance the understanding of the work of art itself, with his remarkable if rather unpersuasive analysis of *The Moses of Michelangelo* being a prime example (Freud, 1914). Freud's stance here is ostensibly naïve and rationalistic. Like the person who knows nothing of art but knows only what he likes, Freud has no great feel for the 'formal and technical' – that is, *aesthetic* – qualities of a work of art; but rather, when he finds himself moved, it is by the *content* of the work. For Freud, this indicates that what matters is the extent to which an artwork succeeds in communicating 'the artist's intention', this being understood not merely as an intellectual exercise, but as the capacity 'to awaken in us the same emotional attitude, the same mental constellation as that which in him produced the impetus to create' (Freud, 1914, p.254). It is therefore this element of the art object that needs to be understood, and hence turned into words; yet, until the advent of psychoanalysis, it is precisely this aspect of art that has proved so recalcitrant. If it is the case that the 'meaning' of a work of art, or at least its effect, depends on the mobilisation of emotions in the viewer that reflect the intention of the artist, then one needs a vocabulary of the emotions that is adequate for the articulation of this process in order to make sense of it. This is particularly so if one is, like Freud, so devoutly rationalistic that one always needs to produce an intellectual understanding of what one is going through. Freud writes (p.254): 'It is possible, therefore, that a work of art of this kind needs interpretation, and that until I have accomplished that interpretation I cannot come to know why I have been so powerfully affected.' And it is only with the emergence of psychoanalysis, with its clear and extensive explication of (unconscious) mental life, that such a vocabulary and interpretive scheme are available.

In the specific case of Michelangelo's *Moses*, Freud uses a detailed analysis of the position of the statue's hands, beard and tablets to argue that, contrary to the biblical story, Moses is *refraining* from enacting his anger and smashing the tablets. This reading probably has more to do with Freud's specific biographical circumstances at the time (his response to the final break with Jung and the near-disintegration of the psychoanalytic movement) than with any legitimate rendering of Michelangelo's intentions. That aside, the key point here is that psychoanalysis is being used to make sense of the art object not in order to advance understanding of psychological processes (though this may happen as a consequence), nor of psychoanalytic theory, but rather as a mode of art criticism. Without psychoanalysis, Freud argues, no full understanding of a work of art is possible, because it is only through identifying the emotional intention and impact of the work (awakening 'in us the same emotional attitude, the same mental constellation as that which in [the artist] produced the impetus to create') that its 'meaning and content' can be fully known. And only psychoanalysis, which is the specialist study of such emotional attitudes and mental constellations, can provide the tools required to do this. This is, in some ways, a scandalous claim, displacing specialist art criticism, with its focus on genre, history and aesthetics, in favour of a speculative 'reading into /out of' the art object in terms of the possible psychological intentions of the artist. The intentions in question, of course, are particularly those that are *unconscious* and hence can only be revealed by what Freud (p.265) refers to in passing as psychoanalysis' capacity 'to divine secret and concealed things from despised or unnoticed features, from the rubbish-heap, as it were, of our observations'. Psychoanalysis allows Freud to see the things that the specialists could not see, and to do so not only in order to advance understanding of psychological processes, which could be taken to be the appropriate subject matter of psychoanalysis, but also to provide a fuller and more truthful understanding of what Ehrenzweig (1967) later termed 'the hidden order of art'. It can legitimately be argued that Freud's move here, in *The Moses of Michelangelo*, founds a particularly imperialist strand of applied psychoanalysis. This sets aside disciplinary traditions of criticism in favour of speculative psychologistic readings that shimmer with emotional and intellectual excitement, but are perhaps unbound by respect for, or at times even knowledge of, the specialist tools employed by those who have studied their trade all their lives – something which Freud would never have allowed in relation to critics of psychoanalysis itself.

Biographical psychobabble: Leonardo's sexuality

More characteristically and in principle perhaps more appropriately, given psychoanalysis' concern with individual lives, Freud published studies of creative artists in which he used psychoanalysis to bring to light aspects of their psychology. That is, he practiced psychoanalysis on the artist, on the basis of the traces left in the artist's work and on incidental biographical information. As Freud himself knew, this was an inherently problematic procedure. His notorious paper, on *Leonardo Da Vinci and a Memory of his Childhood* (1910a), is an instance of what can be gained by such an approach, but also shows just how highly risky the strategy could be. The editors of the *Standard Edition of the Complete Psychological Works of Sigmund Freud* note that this was Freud's first full-length application of the methods of clinical psychoanalysis to the life of a historical figure and that it 'seems to have been greeted with more than the usual amount of disapproval' (p.146). The paper itself is a deeply engaged investigation of the sexual issues that might have been at the source of Leonardo's creativity, an investigation which seems to have been sparked off not only by Freud's admiration for the combination of artistic and scientific genius that so marked Leonardo, but also with an identification with him – though the nature of this identification is open to speculation. For some, the emotional intensity of the piece has to do with the employment of mythological elements in the argument: the supposed 'vulture' that swoops down on the infant Leonardo, opens his mouth, and strikes him many times with its tail against his lips, permanently affecting his imagination, is held by Freud to have links with 'hieroglyphics of the ancient Egyptians' (Freud, 1910a, p.178). Once again, it is exactly at this time that Freud is most engaged with the father–son elements in his relationship with Jung (who reacted very enthusiastically to *Leonardo*, despite – or perhaps because of – the hostility it engendered in other quarters), and the terrain of mythology was one on which this relationship was being worked out. But *Leonardo Da Vinci and a Memory of his Childhood* has much more to it than being merely another exercise in mythological speculation. It is very clearly an attempt at psychobiography, using extremely sparse materials and hence totally at variance with the usual psychoanalytic procedure of careful examination of the rich and idiosyncratic details of a person's autobiographical narrative. It also develops an account of creativity which draws out in great detail the sexual components at its root, and in so doing enunciates a theory of homosexuality and also of sublimation, understood as the expression of sexuality in a socially valued form, this being here the work of art. That Freud should have chosen for this a dead, idealised figure rather than a

potentially intractable, but nevertheless responsive, live patient is itself an issue of some interest. Might it be that his pyrotechnics could only be safely achieved with material like this, held at arm's length, *especially* in the light of the ongoing biographical circumstances – the 'homosexual' investment in Jung?

Freud claims that Leonardo's curiosity and creativity were both inhibited and mobilised by his sexual history. The argument about inhibition comes in the form of Freud's objection to the conventional belief that Leonardo was exceptionally speedy in his artistic productions, and that the unfinished nature of so many of them signifies his impatience:

> On the contrary, it is possible to observe a quite extraordinary profundity, a wealth of possibilities between which a decision can only be reached with hesitation, demands which can hardly be satisfied, and an inhibition in the actual execution which is not in fact to be explained even by the artist inevitably falling short of his ideal. The slowness which had all along been conspicuous in Leonardo's work is seen to be a symptom of this inhibition and to be the forerunner of his subsequent withdrawal from painting. (p.156)

Freud uses the early part of his paper to establish that Leonardo's chief psychological characteristic was a search for knowledge, and that the profound and utterly dominating strength of this was directly connected to his 'cool repudiation of sexuality' (p.158). Leonardo's sexuality, he holds, was evident only in an apparently inactive homosexuality expressed mainly by surrounding himself 'with handsome boys and youths'. Using a routine but nevertheless powerfully sexualised metaphor, Freud argues that the energy behind Leonardo's thirst for knowledge was the replacement for sexual activity; that is, the mental mechanism at play here, as in all creativity, is sublimation:

> In reality Leonardo was not devoid of passion ... He had merely converted his passion into a thirst for knowledge; he then applied himself to investigation with the persistence, constancy and penetration which is derived from passion, and at the climax of intellectual labour, when knowledge had been won, he allowed the long restrained affect to break loose and to flow away freely, as a stream of water drawn from a river is allowed to flow away when its work is done. (p.164)

Why should Leonardo have been constituted in this way? Drawing on the memory of the 'vulture' that had so roughed him up in childhood, and on a totally speculative reconstruction, from barely any documentary evidence, of the eroticisation of the young Leonardo by his single mother, Freud constructs a theory of the origins of one form of homosexuality in

an identificatory love for a mother who must not be abandoned or betrayed through loving another woman. Calling upon some of his psychoanalytic cases for corroboration, Freud writes:

> In all our homosexual cases the subjects had had a very intense erotic attachment to a female person, as a rule their mother, during the first period of childhood, which is afterwards forgotten; this attachment was evoked or encouraged by too much tenderness on the part of the mother herself, and further reinforced by the small part played by the father during their childhood ... Indeed it almost seems as though the presence of a strong father would ensure that the son made the correct decision in his choice of object, namely someone of the opposite sex ... The child's love for his mother cannot continue to develop consciously any further; it succumbs to repression. The boy represses his love for his mother; he puts himself in her place, identifies with her, and takes his own person as a model in whose likeness he chooses the new objects of his love. In this way he has become a homosexual. What he has in fact done is slip back into auto-erotism: for the boys who he now loves as he grows up are after all only substitutive figures and revivals of himself in childhood – boys whom he loves in the way in which his mother loved *him* when he was a child. He finds the objects of his love along the path of *narcissism*. (pp.190–1)

By repressing his love for his mother he unconsciously preserves it and from now on remains faithful to her. 'While he seems to pursue boys and to be their lover,' writes Freud (p.192), 'he is in reality running away from the other women, who might cause him to be unfaithful.' The relative absence of a paternal figure is not only made responsible for the lack of a heterosexual object choice (as in the quotation above), but is also drawn on to explain Leonardo's neglect of his finished compositions – he discarded them as his father had discarded him – and his capacity to break with established authority, his relentless curiosity about science and his inventive flourishes. Unlike most people, who remain tied to it, Leonardo had no need for the authority of the father. On the other hand, his 'two mothers' (his actual mother and his stepmother) appear in some of his great works, either separately (*St Anne with Two Others*) or together in the famously ambiguous smile of the *Mona Lisa* ('the contrast between reserve and seduction, and between the most devoted tenderness and a sensuality that is ruthlessly demanding' – p.200). For Freud, what is happening here is that the sexual researches of Leonardo's childhood had been transformed into the search for knowledge (fantasies of flight, for example, being expressions of a desire for sexual potency), and in turn this sublimated energy fuelled the intense creativity of this most profound and productive of artists. This also explains the *effect* of Leonardo's art on others: 'Kindly

nature has given the artist the ability to express his most secret mental impulses, which are hidden even from himself, by means of the works he creates; and these works have a powerful effect on others who are strangers to the artist, and who are themselves unaware of the source of their emotion' (p.199).

There is much in *Leonardo* that is of great contemporary interest, not least the sympathetic account Freud gives of homosexuality, his attempt to construct a convincing sexual history out of biographical materials, and his analysis of Leonardo's 'inhibition'. But here the main issue concerns what it says about the application of psychoanalysis to art. Freud's classical view of 'great art' led him to look for the exemplar of sublimation in a dead (male) artist rather than in one of the struggling real patients of his day, where it is possible that the *complexity* of sublimation as a way of dealing with sexual urges might have been more apparent. In *Leonardo*, however, what we get is a relatively simple account. The boy's sexual history, in this case belaboured with a frustrated mother and an absent father, who then confusingly moves in to take over from the mother and finds a substitute for her, leads to an imperative to make sexual researches. These are theorised as too painful to be integrated into the artist's personality. Instead, he becomes notionally desexualised, and in Leonardo's case this became a 'peaceableness' that seems to have dominated his personality. Yet, in his art he was restless, striving, ambitious, patient whilst at times wilful, and of course immensely original. The sexual energy has not dried up, but rather has been channelled into scientific and artistic curiosity, this being a psychic mechanism which has general significance for art. But how convincing is this? Freud's main worry seems to have been that in analysing Leonardo he would be thought of as somehow denigrating him, which was not in the least his intention or indeed the effect of his work. However, other doubts remain. Apart from the total inadequacy of the historical record on which Freud based his ideas, alongside the clumsiness of some of the detailed aesthetic work in the piece, there is also a problem with his use of mythology to support some of his interpretive claims – the 'vulture' of Leonardo's early memory turns out actually to have been a 'kite', which does not warrant the Egyptian resonances that Freud gives it (Editor's note to Freud, 1910a, p.62). What has been especially criticised, however, is the reductive nature of Freud's reading of the links between creativity and sexuality. Despite his own tolerance and in some ways admirably nuanced account of homosexuality, the mother is at the source of sexual inhibition, the lack of an appropriate father blocks the way to heterosexuality, and the block on sexuality is the source for creativity. Is this *always* so (Freud refers to 'all our homosexual cases' in offering his account)? Does it mean that such blockages are

required for creativity to occur? There seem to be plenty of examples of creative individuals, both heterosexual and homosexual, who have not had problems with expressing their sexuality more directly; indeed there is really no lack of examples of people who seem to be *exceptionally* sexualised and yet still manage to be profoundly creative. If the sexual drive does not need to be sublimated, by what means do they produce their art? And what of Leonardo's artistic *facility*, the traditions upon which he drew and those which he consciously subverted? Are these peripheral issues next to the emotional features of the work, or do they have their own connections with his creativity, independently of anything that might have derived from his sexually fuelled curiosity? This is not to say that Freud had it completely wrong, but he certainly had it incomplete, and while it is unfair to accuse him of pathologising Leonardo, the tradition which this study institutes both in psychobiography and art criticism is deeply problematic for all the plausible, pressing questions that it leaves unaddressed. In some ways it instances the worst excesses of psychoanalytic arrogance – of psychoanalysis when 'applied' non-reflexively in the non-clinical sphere. It takes as incontestable a set of knowledge claims that are in fact dubious (psychoanalysis' *clinical* account of homosexuality is one of its most controversial areas – see Frosh, 2006), asserts them as facts which are established by clinical work (and hence lying within the area of specialist knowledge of psychoanalysis, so unchallengeable by mere art critics) and then imposes them on material that meets none of psychoanalysis' own usual requirements for 'data'. This trail of speculative claims and ungrounded reasoning then hardens into 'reality' and becomes *the* psychoanalytic explanation of a phenomenon that is complex and multifarious, and irreducible to simple, linearly causal psychological factors. In this process, despite the characteristically illuminating and suggestive potency of Freud's text, the artist, the traditions of art criticism and appreciation, and psychoanalysis itself, become devalued.

Using literature to validate psychoanalysis: the example of Jensen's *Gradiva*

So far, a few different uses of psychoanalysis by Freud in the realm of art and literature have been outlined: to explain the creative process; to identify other psychological processes that might be at work generally in people; to elaborate on the impact of an artistic work; and to reveal the biographical sources of a particular artist's activities, thereby also developing a fuller understanding of the relationship between sexuality and sublimation. All these elements have something useful to offer and

have led to further research, but all have problems, particularly in their neglect of the aesthetic domain so central to most artistic and literary criticism – that is, their neglect of the *specificity* of the artistic terrain – as well as their general reductionism and false certainty. These features of this work, particularly the kind of biographical character analysis evident in *Leonardo*, have given a bad name to much psychoanalytic literary and artistic criticism. However, in many other instances Freud was cautious in his approach to art and in particular wary of pronouncing too definitively upon it. Instead, he used literature and art in order to demonstrate the utility of psychoanalytic thinking, whilst remaining highly respectful about the artwork itself. Freud does not always sustain this, for instance slipping into making unsustainable generalisations based on treating fictional characters as real, but he is usually aware when this happens and steps back from the brink. The principle seems to have been that the creative artist (especially the writer) is closer to the mainsprings of phantasy life than most, and has privileged intuition of mental processes that psychoanalysis more laboriously reveals. Creative work consequently can be a source of validation for psychoanalytic ideas. *The Uncanny*, for example (Freud, 1919), with its analysis of Hoffman's *Sandman*, presents a remarkable examination of experiences of doubling, alienness and unsettledness that both increases appreciation of the impact of the literary original and also draws from it some insightful and influential psychological ideas. But is this more than the generation of speculative thought, valuable in itself but still ungrounded, open to a million interpretations?

Freud was a subtle writer and his awareness of the dubiousness of his own claims is never far away, even though he usually both submits to it and wriggles out of it at the same time. The relatively early 'case study' of Jensen's *Gradiva* (Freud, 1907) is perhaps the clearest extended example of this duality. The story, which Freud lovingly describes, or even rewrites, concerns a young archaeologist's pursuit of a girl he believes to be the reincarnation of a young woman portrayed in a Pompeiian sculpture ('Gradiva'), only to find that she is in fact his childhood love. *Gradiva* seems to have appealed to Freud for numerous reasons, including its setting (Pompeii), its imagery (archaeology, the preferred metaphor which Freud used for his own investigative practices), the presence of dreams in it (which he analyses according to the rules used with his patients), and its presentation of a 'treatment by love' (which enabled him to make some useful technical statements about the activities of the psychoanalyst). *Gradiva* may also have been a kind of gift to Jung (although Kerr (1993) states that it was written before Freud and Jung started corresponding in earnest), who introduced Freud to the book and who also proved to be one of the most

receptive readers of Freud's paper: the 'Jungian' realm of the imaginative and mythic is not far off at any time in this piece. The central appeal, however, is that it enabled Freud to indulge in his romantic attitude towards creative writers as the source of intuitive knowledge of the unconscious. This stems, he thought, from their supposed facility with psychological thinking and is a kind of spontaneously generated understanding of the psychological processes that psychoanalysis had inched towards through a more systematic, but also humbler path:

> [C]reative writers are valuable allies and their evidence is to be prized highly, for they are apt to know a whole host of things between heaven and earth of which our philosophy has not yet let us dream. In their knowledge of the mind they are far in advance of us everyday people, for they draw upon sources which we have not yet opened up for science. (p.34)

Freud goes on from this to argue that *Gradiva* can be given the status of a 'psychiatric study', because its representation of psychological processes is so accurate ('all [Jensen's] descriptions are so faithfully copied from reality', p.66), and furthermore that this is a general condition of good writing. Of the creative writer, Freud states: 'The description of the human mind is indeed the domain which is most his own; he has from time immemorial been the precursor of science, and so too of scientific psychology' (p.68).

These claims about the perspicacity and realism of the creative writer allow Freud to do two things in *Gradiva*: first, to interpret the actions, thoughts and dreams of the characters in the story as if they were those of real people; and secondly, to treat the representation of psychological processes in this fiction as if it is true and hence can act as a test of the veracity of psychoanalytic theories. In the former case, for example, Freud provides interpretations of the character Hanold's dreams, discusses his personality and the infantile and sexual sources of his behaviour, and treats the interpretations and actions given by the female protagonist Zoe as if they are genuine interventions that produce a cure. In the course of his commentary, Freud acknowledges the potential difficulties of using fictional characters in this way, showing a sophisticated grasp of the problem of his method:

> My readers will no doubt have been puzzled to notice that so far I have treated Norbert Hanold and Zoe Bertgang, in all their mental manifestations and activities, as though they were real people and not the author's creations, as though the author's mind were an absolutely transparent medium and not a refractive or obscuring one. (p.66)

The neglect of the productive, artistic work carried out by the author is

indeed a major problem here, and on the face of it makes Freud's approach in *Gradiva* even more unruly than that in *Leonardo*, where at least the artist's work was taken as expressing something about the artist himself, not as 'real' in its own right. But Freud dismisses this problem on the grounds of the truthfulness of Jensen's psychological understanding, and then cheerfully moves on to contaminate his material still further by making himself the 'patient' in the case. This happens in a peculiar way. Given the absence of a real person who can be asked to free associate and whose psychic structure can be probed, Freud substitutes himself into the equation and uses his *own* mental processes as the model for what must be happening in the minds of these fictitious characters. There are two moments where this is explicit. The first occurs when Freud quotes 'a doctor's' experience of having mistaken a patient for the ghost of her dead sister: 'The doctor to whom this occurred was, however, none other than myself; so I have a personal reason for not disputing the clinical possibility of Norbert Hanold's temporary delusion that Gradiva had come back to life' (p.95). The second such occasion is when Freud is faced with the impossibility of analysing Hanold's dream because of the unfortunate absence of the dreamer from the couch; so instead of using Hanold's associations, he uses his own:

> We are able to apply to this dream the technique which may be described as the regular procedure for interpreting dreams. It consists in paying no attention to the apparent connections in the manifest dream but in fixing our eyes upon each portion of its content independently, and in looking for its origin in the dreamer's impressions, memories and free associations. Since, however, we cannot question Hanold, we shall have to content ourselves with referring to his impressions, and we may very tentatively put our own associations in place of his. (pp.96–7)

Revealingly, this is rather like Freud's (1905, p.134) approach to the analysis of the second dream of 'Dora': 'I shall present the material produced during the analysis of this dream in the somewhat haphazard order in which it recurs to my mind.' That is, faced with recalcitrant material, Freud is happy enough to use his own mental processes and associations and then present them as evidence, without methodological apology. Treating himself as what one might call a 'normal neurotic', his own psychological imaginings can substitute for those of anyone else. This rather extraordinary slippage from the mind of the other to the mind of the analyst is a methodological strategy used extensively in early psychoanalysis; given that one of the discipline's founding texts, *The Interpretation of Dreams*, is based largely on the analysis of Freud's own dreams, it can perhaps even be cited as *characteristically* Freudian.

This has both positive and negative consequences. On the former, it establishes psychoanalysis as a discipline that from the start takes seriously the relevance of personal issues to supposedly 'scientific' practices, and asserts the importance of reflexivity and of intersubjectivity. On the latter, it allows speculative overgeneralisations derived from personal whims and prejudices a place centre stage in analytic activity.

The treatment of *Gradiva* as providing confirming evidence for psychoanalytic theory in general is equally problematic, but also much more interesting. Again, Freud is aware of the methodological pitfalls, and especially of the charge that could be laid against him that he is simply reading the story in line with psychoanalysis' assumptions – that is, that his method of verification is circular:

> It may be that we have produced a complete caricature of an interpretation by introducing into an innocent work of art purposes of which its creator had no notion, and by so doing have shown once more how easy it is to find what one is looking for and what is occupying one's own mind. (p.114)

But he is quick to dismiss this rather serious problem, both on the grounds of the realism of the author's approach (the 'psychiatric case' argument) and of what is sometimes (Grünbaum, 1984) termed 'consilience' of converging lines of independent evidence. Freud argues that psychoanalysis and creative writing are completely separate activities, so that if they produce the same findings, then this is support for the claims each of them might make about the truthfulness of their representations of life. 'We probably draw from the same source and work upon the same object,' he writes (pp.114–15), 'each of us by another method. And the agreement of our results seems to guarantee that we have both worked correctly.' The psychoanalyst consciously observes mental processes in patients and others so as to be able to state their laws; the author 'directs attention to the unconscious in his own mind, he listens to its possible developments and lends them artistic expression instead of suppressing them by conscious criticism' (ibid.). The psychoanalyst can then get at the laws of the unconscious by analysing the writings of the author, which allows for assessment of the degree to which this intuitive mode of understanding supports findings derived from the scientific approach. The end result is that 'either both of us, the writer and the doctor, have misunderstood the unconscious in the same way, or we have both understood it correctly' (ibid.). It takes no great feat of imagination to work out which of these possible conclusions Freud prefers, and which is preferred by his detractors.

Learning from love

It is surely clear that Freud's analysis of *Gradiva* is so riven with mundane methodological difficulties as to make it untenable as a piece of scientific investigation, and certainly to defuse its prospects of offering 'independent' verification of psychoanalytic claims. As well as the standard difficulty of treating fictional characters as if they were real, ignoring the traditions and structures of literary activity (the relationship of *Gradiva* to the conventions of gothic writing, for example), there is the unabashed way in which Freud uses his own associations and imaginative responses in order to find in the story support for his own theory. This is a process of 'reading in' to the text that is routinely part of a response to literature, perhaps, but is in no way testimony to its evidential value. Noting that others have produced the same ideas independently of psychoanalysis is not in itself a way of assessing its scientific or factual value: all sorts of similar ideas might be produced at roughly the same time in a culture, without any of them being 'true'. After all, religious beliefs are widely shared and deeply held by many, yet Freud would not grant them the status of being scientifically true – a point which will be returned to below. The existence of shared perspectives and 'consilient' ideas is indeed bound to occur, as culture is in large part the process of responding to problematics that appear in specific circumstances, in a range of usually closely related ways. That psychoanalysis and literature can be made to agree with one another, if it says more than that the one is being forced into the image of the other, may simply reflect the fact that both are cultural expressions of a particular set of then-contemporary experiences (in this case, these included the growth of individuality, the production of nostalgia and romantic holism, the conflict between 'surface' and 'depth'). Literature has its own dynamic, its own traditions and modes of response to cultural concerns, and analysing the details of this is a legitimate, indeed important, intellectual activity with which it is possible that psychoanalysis might help. But using the imaginative products of one person's mind to measure the accuracy of the possibly equally imaginative products of another's is not going to establish the veracity of either.

Despite all this, *Gradiva* has some significant gains. One relates to the clarifications that Freud is able to bring into his own theory through his thinking about the parallels with the tale of Hanold and Zoe. The clearest example here concerns the process of analysis itself as a therapeutic endeavour. With the appearance of Zoe, writes Freud (p.93), 'So far we have been present at the development of a delusion; now we are to witness its cure.' Zoe engages in the process of 'giving [Hanold] back from outside the repressed memories which he could not set free from

inside' (p.111), but according to Freud this in itself would not have been enough – what was important was the addition of an affective component, the elicitation or renewal of feelings, in this case of love. This aspect of the story is, according to Freud, in precise and profound agreement with the tenets of psychoanalysis:

> the similarity between Gradiva's procedure and the analytic method of psychotherapy is not restricted to these two points – the making conscious of what has been repressed and the coinciding of explanation with cure. It also extends to what turns out to be the essence of the whole change – to the awakening of feelings ... The process of cure is accomplished in a relapse into love, if we combine all the many components of the sexual instinct under the term 'love'; and such a relapse is indispensable, for the symptoms on account of which the treatment has been undertaken are nothing other than precipitates of earlier struggles connected with repression and the return of the repressed, and they can only be resolved and washed away by a fresh high tide of the same passion. Every psychoanalytic treatment is an attempt at liberating repressed love which has found a meagre outlet in the compromise of a symptom. Indeed, the agreement between such treatments and the process of cure described by the author of Gradiva reaches its climax in the further fact that in analytic psychotherapy too the reawakened passion, whether it is love or hate, invariably chooses as its object the figure of the doctor. (pp.112–13)

At this time in his writing, this was one of the clearest statements made by Freud concerning the nature of the therapeutic process and in particular the effective component of psychoanalysis as therapy. This demands not just identifying the unconscious conflict at the root of the symptom, which is a process of 'explanation' of its logic to the patient, but also 'what turns out to be the essence of the whole change – to the awakening of feelings', specifically, 'a relapse into love'. Psychoanalytic therapy has to reawaken the love that has been repressed, or more broadly (as in the last sentence of the quotation above) the 'passion' that can be love or hate, and it does this through drawing it onto the person of the psychoanalyst. The psychoanalyst as love object is a poor thing, of course, and very much inferior to Gradiva/Zoe, who can 'in reality' give love to the patient Hanold, and this is one of the factors that places a restriction on the efficacy of psychoanalysis itself: 'The doctor has been a stranger, and must endeavour to become a stranger once more after the cure; he is often at a loss what advice to give the patients he has cured as to how in real life they can use their recovered capacity to love' (p.113). What *Gradiva* shows to Freud is how the lover and the analyst are in the same structural position when it comes to knowledge and cure; and also how they differ, how the abstinence practised by the

analyst is problematic – even though later he became clearer that it was itself a necessary part of therapeutic progress.

What has happened here is that the dubious claims to evidencing psychoanalysis through fiction have given away to a reflection on what the nature of the psychoanalytic process might be, and this reflection is both fruitful and well-founded. Without making any truth-claims about what is scientifically necessary, it enables Freud to articulate the way he sees the core effectivity of the analytic process, and to distinguish it from other possible modes – in particular, a 'cure by love' that involves enactment and reciprocation of the patient's desires. This aspect of *Gradiva* is no longer an attempt to use literature to support psychoanalysis, or use psychoanalysis to interpret literature; it is, at its simplest, a trigger for Freud's further examination of how psychoanalysis works. In this lie the seeds of another kind of approach to 'psychoanalysis and literature', in which there is a respectful appreciation of the 'agency' of literature – how it has its effect on the reader, what the imaginative actions of the writer produce – which can be used to reflect back upon psychoanalysis, seeking thereby to clarify its mode of operation and theory. Psychoanalysis is not here as a supplicant, seeking literature's support and guidance. Rather, in investing in an open and intelligent reading of the text, full of curiosity and willing to consider its lessons for his own thinking, Freud shows that it is possible for the engagement between disciplines to be illuminating and respectful, more modest than when in conquistador mode, but also more interesting. Simply by laying bare the comparison – the fictional cure by love, the psychoanalytic transference – Freud manages to address some profound issues about the nature of intersubjectivity, the use of another as a love object, and the avenues through which personal change might occur. There is still plenty of confidence about what psychoanalysis knows in this section of the paper, but there is no particular attempt to impose it on the story, only to meditate on questions raised that might have resonance with, and be clarifying for, psychoanalytic ideas.

Social Freud: the case of religion

The previous sections have argued that whilst there are plenty of occasions on which Freud used psychoanalysis interpretively to make sense of literary or artistic work, so that he was clearly applying psychoanalysis *to* art or literature, he also showed a countervailing tendency which was less colonising and more open to the contribution of creative work to psychoanalysis itself. This was in some instances manifested as an attempt to use art or literature to throw light on psychological processes

or as a way of checking and supporting psychoanalytic claims. More enticingly, there are moments in Freud's work where what is enacted is an openness towards artistic forms that allows them to stir up ideas which can then be taken back into psychoanalysis. This even includes the raising of challenges to psychoanalytic assumptions and developments of theory. Sometimes this too falls into the trap of treating the artwork or literary creation as a 'real' character from whose peregrinations universal truths can be gleaned. However, at other times there is a more humble appreciation that what is going on is a mode of dialogue, in which the text suggests things which allow Freud to associate to new psychoanalytic ideas, or to unblock points of theoretical uncertainty. It is on these occasions that 'applied psychoanalysis' begins to hold promise as a way to articulate something new in the humanities and social sciences, breathing subjectivity into them whilst leaving intact their specific disciplinary contribution. In the case of art and literature, this means respecting the aesthetic and historical conventions that give them cultural weight; in the case of the social sciences, it means drawing on notions of the social that can be reflected back into psychoanalysis' primarily psychological mode of thought, shaking it up and producing fissures that might allow both disciplines to gain. Unfortunately, Freud's personal engagement in social scientific thinking, which was extensive and imaginative and immensely productive in setting an agenda particularly for theorising social conflict, shows few instances of this more open and reflexive approach necessary for a respectful encounter with other disciplines. Nevertheless, it immediately offers a number of psychoanalytic concepts that have proved crucial for later attempts to think in a more 'hybrid' way, even if Freud's actual use of them was to present a one-sidedly psychoanalytic theory of social phenomena.

The capacity to pronounce on social issues from the perspective of a psychological sage seems to have been increasingly expected of Freud as his fame grew. This was the origin, for example, of the exchange with Einstein that became the paper *Why War?* (Freud and Einstein, 1933), in which Einstein pre-empted Freud by evoking an inbuilt human destructiveness that paralleled Freud's notion of the death drive. (Freud commented: 'though you have taken the wind out of my sails I shall be glad to follow in your wake' (p.203).) More generally, the contribution of psychoanalysis to theorising on some characteristic early twentieth-century themes, the origins of civilisation and the 'conflict' between society and the individual, seems to have been seen as an important test of the standing of psychoanalysis. If psychoanalysis is an account of the sources of human trouble, then surely it should be able to comment on how and why these troubles are so often inflicted in the social domain. Especially after the First World War, which clearly revealed people's

extraordinary capacity for self-deception and destructiveness, any psychology that claimed to explain the depths of human nature must also be able to say something novel about what happens to it in what was increasingly ironically called 'civilisation'.

One major premise of Freudian psychoanalysis is indeed that there is a clash between what the individual might wish for and what society might allow. This is implicit in the relations between the pleasure principle and the reality principle and also in Freud's early distinction between 'sexual drives' and 'ego preservative drives'. This version of his drive or 'instinct' theory proposed that the sexual wishes of the individual always have to be moderated, because let loose they would undermine the capacity of the subject to function rationally in a peopled world. As a consequence, Freud had to think about how the conditions of society impinge on the individual, what is necessary by way of constraint and what unnecessary, and what restrictions are both painful and essential. From an early view that the social repression of sexuality produces neurosis, he gradually moved to a more subtle account of the connections between social forces and psychological structure (or, more crudely, between society and unhappiness), culminating in a reappraisal of his drive theory and some great 'social' texts in the wake of the war. The development of his more refined views about the processes through which repression operates, and in particular the emergence of the concept of the superego, described briefly in Chapter 1 (see also Frosh, 1999), led to a variegated understanding of how certain social processes might find their way 'into' the mind of the individual. The key idea here is that the internalisation of authority as a response to the outcome of the Oedipus complex results in there being a kind of 'state' within the mind, with the superego acting as a sort of proxy for the repressive activities of the external social world. Just as unbounded infantile sexuality is channelled through developmental processes into genitality, so aggression is mastered by incorporation into the punitive superego; civilisation advances at the expense of individual happiness. This also means that what is usually seen as 'internal' has external sources and resonance: 'We have also learned how the severity of the super-ego – the demands of conscience – is to be understood', writes Freud (1930, p.127). 'It is simply a continuation of the severity of the external authority, to which it has succeeded and which it has in part replaced.' Freud's narrative focuses on the manner in which impulses or feelings that seem so much part of our 'selves' that one assumes they are basic, inborn consequences of being human, are actually products of our immersion in the social world.

Whilst this might be an important description of how social forces operate at the level of the individual, what is also present in Freud's

thinking is a more sociological urge to make sense of 'civilisation' itself. This is clearest in his accounts of religion (Freud, 1927) and society generally (Freud, 1930), and also in his poignant study of Judaism and anti-Semitism, in one of his last works, *Moses and Monotheism* (Freud, 1939). This raises the question of whether psychoanalysis really is a social theory, or whether it is illegitimate to extend what is actually a psychological, individualistic way of thinking to the social and cultural level. There are various ways into this, but perhaps a useful one is to take up an area in which Freud was always interested yet stood outside of, and which continues to be of importance in contemporary times: that of religion. For Freud, rationalist, committed atheist and 'godless Jew' as he was, religion was an opponent of scientific advancement; but he recognised its significance and devoted a good deal of attention to understanding it, particularly in his later years. One major fruit of this was his 1927 work, *The Future of an Illusion*, part of a series of late texts that all reveal Freud's moralising inclination – not the kind of moralism that preaches 'good' behaviour, but rather the kind that attempts to develop an *ethics*, an approach to human life that focuses on what he clearly regarded as the 'truth'. Put more sparingly, Freud believed strongly in the necessity of seeing through 'illusions', defined in *The Future of an Illusion* as beliefs 'derived from human wishes' (p.30). 'We call a belief an illusion', writes Freud (ibid.), 'when a wish-fulfilment is a prominent factor in its motivation, and in doing so we disregard its relations to reality, just as the illusion itself sets no store by verification.' Exposing the wish at the heart of an illusion was for Freud a way of making humanity own up to the truth, of making people face reality free of the 'consolations' that might indeed buffer them against the worst storms, but only at too high a price – the price of an escalating irrationality that does them no service. Rather disingenuously, in fact, Freud takes up the criticism that in removing the illusion of religion he is damaging civilisation, which of necessity has to allow people to live with defences against anxiety. Maybe so, he allows, but this is not the whole story:

> Religion has clearly performed great services for human civilization. It has contributed much towards the taming of the asocial instincts. But not enough. It has ruled human society for many thousands of years and has had time to show what it can achieve. If it had succeeded in making the majority of mankind happy, in comforting them, in reconciling them to life and in making them into vehicles of civilization, no one would dream of attempting to alter the existing conditions. But what do we see instead? We see that an appallingly large number of people are dissatisfied with civilization and unhappy in it, and feel it as a yoke which must be shaken off; and that these

people either do everything in their power to change that civilization, or else go so far in their hostility to it that they will have nothing to do with civilization or with a restriction of instinct. (Freud, 1927, p.36)

The task of psychoanalysis in exposing the roots of religion is completely parallel to its task when faced with neurotic patients: *of course* their symptoms have developed for good reason, to protect the ego against what might seem to be something worse; but these defences have turned destructive, they cause too much further unhappiness and they need to be outgrown.

Freud sees the analogy between the religious illusions of society and the neurotic illusions of the individual patient as being pretty direct, even though he is careful to maintain the vocabulary of parallelism rather than identity (i.e. he does not explicitly make society a 'patient', even though his argument tends strongly that way). Religions come about because societies need ways to appease their members, who might otherwise panic in the face of the overwhelmingly destructive potential of nature; and also as a way of inculcating moral laws that prevent people from being at each other's throats as they give full vent to the ambitions of their drives. After various discussions of the way in which authority is internalised (through the superego), of the limitations of ordinary people (the 'masses') and their need for leaders, and of how ideals serve as narcissistic gratifications which bind people into the social order, Freud picks up particularly on the theme of the helplessness people experience when confronted with nature, and of how deeply analogous this is to the helplessness of the infant confronted with a world that seems too big, too arbitrary and too dangerous. Under these circumstances, the infant takes refuge in the parent, a figure who is worryingly fierce but who nevertheless presents the infant with the promise of special protection. Maintaining this protection depends on the infant's wishes being constrained and psychic energy being mobilised in the service of the preservation of the relationship itself, much as the gods have to be appeased through prayer or sacrifice. This process starts early, with the mother, but is soon taken over in what Freud calls 'white Christian civilization', by the Oedipal father:

In this function [of protection] the mother is soon replaced by the stronger father, who retains that position for the rest of childhood. But the child's attitude to its father is coloured by a peculiar ambivalence. The father himself constitutes a danger for the child, perhaps because of its earlier relation to its mother. Thus it fears him no less than it longs for him and admires him. The indications of this ambivalence in the attitude to the father are deeply imprinted in every religion, as was shown in *Totem and Taboo*. When the

growing individual finds that he is destined to remain a child for ever, that he can never do without protection against strange superior powers, he lends those powers the features belonging to the figure of his father; he creates for himself the gods whom he dreads, whom he seeks to propitiate, and whom he nevertheless entrusts with his own protection. Thus his longing for a father is a motive identical with his need for protection against the consequences of his human weakness. The defence against childish helplessness is what lends its characteristic features to the adult's reaction to the helplessness which he has to acknowledge – a reaction which is precisely the formation of religion. (p.23)

Religion is thus not just built on the *model* of infantile dependence; it is produced by the *same processes* – the need for protection and the wish that this will be offered by a powerful, superior being who has sought one out. The infantile history of the individual is an exact replica of the infantile history of civilisation: religious ideas, 'which are given out as teachings, are not precipitates of experience or end-results of thinking: they are illusions, fulfilments of the oldest, strongest and most urgent wishes of mankind' (p.29). Moreover, the generalisation of the defensive strategies adopted by each individual into a defence adopted by the whole culture is of great help to all concerned: 'It is an enormous relief to the individual psyche if the conflicts of its childhood arising from the father-complex – conflicts which it has never wholly overcome – are removed from it and brought to a solution which is universally accepted' (ibid.). Thus the generation of religion on the social level supports the well-being of citizens by bolstering the individual's own defensive wish-fulfilments, and the conditions for a neurotic, illusion-preoccupied social world are laid.

There are many issues that could be taken up here, not least the vexed question of the extent to which 'civilisation' can be treated as a person, or as a collection of individuals who all have the same need and consequently project their father-images into the heavens. Freud is not very clear about the specificity of the social in his work, perhaps understandably so: as he states, 'My work is a good example of the strict isolation of the particular contribution which psycho-analytic discussion can make to the solution of the problem of religion' (p.22). In some ways it is fair enough to take the line that Freud's sociopolitical texts are attempts to explore what the psychological insights derived from psychoanalysis might have to add to the sociological perspectives that even in his day were fairly advanced. Marxism, after all, was a well developed theory, instantiated in the Soviet Union, as Freud acknowledges in *The Future of an Illusion;* and Durkheim and Weber had very much established the discipline of sociology on its own feet. Freud shows some awareness of this with his reference to the infantile model

as an 'analogy' (p.41), and he also allows for what might be termed the primacy of the social in arguing that in the life of an individual, society offers religious beliefs ready-made as vehicles for each person's defensive structure. Nevertheless, the explanations given for these social processes are not themselves social: they treat 'civilisation' as a collection of individuals with the same basic psychic structure and existential dilemmas.

A more interesting issue here is the use to which Freud puts his argument, or perhaps the motivation for it. This can best be labelled 'therapeutic'. Just as the individual neurotic needs to shed her or his illusions in order to find a more truthful way of encountering reality, so civilisation as a whole needs to grow up – pretty literally in this case: 'surely infantilism is destined to be surmounted. Men cannot remain children for ever; they must in the end go out into "hostile life". We may call this "education to reality". Need I confess to you that the sole purpose of my book is to point out the necessity for this forward step?' (1927, p.48). Religion does not solve the problem of unhappiness in society, and indeed adds to it by its direct assault on rationality, which is the only hope for humankind. 'Think of the depressing contrast between the radiant intelligence of a healthy child and the feeble intellectual powers of the average adult,' writes Freud (p.46): 'Can we be quite certain that it is not precisely religious education which bears a large share of the blame for this relative atrophy?' In Freud's view, the only reliable instrument that people have with which to deal with the demands of reality is the mind ('we have no other means of controlling our instinctual nature but our intelligence' – p.47), and to use the mind productively requires freedom from ridiculous, irrational constraints that stunt the intellect. Relinquishing illusions may be a painful process, but it is also liberating to encounter this kind of truth – *scientific* truth, drawing on Freud's idealising view of science. In fact it is essential, if humankind is to develop, that the neurotic aberrations and infantile beliefs of the past, such as religion, are set aside.

The contrast between the analysis of religion in *The Future of an Illusion* and the applications of psychoanalysis in the field of art and literature is quite strong. Whereas Freud often seeks to learn from creative artists and writers, in the realm of social issues he is in very strong pedagogic mode, showing what psychoanalysis can teach, and with the exception of anthropology he barely draws on other social scientific work at all. His approach is analytic, but even more noticeably it is strongly *moral* in what it is trying to offer. Through the development of psychoanalysis, he argues, the gains in rationality that derive from the scientific world view have become available to individuals and to social groups – to 'civilisation' as a whole. The self-reflective understanding

that people can now have of their position is radically different from what came before. We can now see the operation of false beliefs in action, how they function as the product of wishes, how they prevent a full engagement with reality, and how this applies to groups as well as individuals, to whole societies and their dominant beliefs. Just as psychoanalysis is evangelical in the field of individual development, interested in setting aside unnecessary sexual inhibitions, for example, and in particular in finding more reality-oriented substitutes for neurotic symptoms; so it operates on the sociopolitical level, able to preach about what is required to make a good society that works. Despite Freud's ironic impulse and his pessimism about what humanity can achieve, this can be described as a kind of utopian project: the insights of psychoanalysis, which themselves are the insights of the rational, scientific world view, can be applied both to make sense of the social order and to offer a programme, however vague it may initially be, for progressive social improvement.

In developing this social analysis, critique and programme, Freud is certainly applying psychoanalysis. Fundamentally, what happens is that his discoveries in relation to patients are being used as templates for understanding what he takes to be the parallel processes that can be observed at work in society as a whole. Additionally, the procedure for reconstructing lost infancy that comes from work on the couch is being extended into a mode of historical reconstruction from the observation of current social behaviour – particularly in religious beliefs and practices, seen as infantilism and neurosis, and in the actions and beliefs of 'savages', taken to be the equivalent of the infant in relation to the adult individual. Along the way, some very powerful observations are made, and some provocative conceptualisations of social processes that integrate understanding of the unconscious with accounts of mass phenomena are provided, a point that will be developed more fully in Chapter 6. But it also exposes a degree of reductive thinking that is untenable in more contemporary times, when the complexity of social processes is – or at least should be – better appreciated. For Freud, whilst there is awareness of how 'society' regulates the wishes of individuals, there is a constant tendency either to theorise society as if it is the same as a person, or to see it as no entity at all, but as simply the accumulation of individual subjects who each express their unconscious wishes in predictable ways. The consequence of this is that the 'application' can only be in one direction: psychoanalysts discover their truths when working with patients; they then observe processes that look like neurosis going on in the social world (e.g. belief in the existence of things that are not there, or ridiculous hopes for protection from imaginary figures, or self-destructive violence); and they account for these with the same explanations that they would use in

the clinic. What is missed here is the *autonomy of the social*, the way features of the social world have causal properties and impact. This is true at the level of the individual, where 'race', gender and class have formative consequences for certain modes of subjecthood. Equally relevantly, it is true at the level of the social itself, which is structured according to its own principles, however much it might also be 'infected' by the unconscious wishes of its subjects. For Freud, there often seems to be no 'social' at all, only the individual writ large; this means that his application of psychoanalysis can only be very limited in its capacity to offer an explanatory account of social events and of what he terms 'culture', 'civilisation' or society. It also misses an opportunity: if the social is entwined with the psychological, then just as psychoanalysis might indeed add something important to the depth of analysis of social events, so appreciation of how the social world operates might fill out psychoanalysis' own thinking. This might refer particularly to how drives come to be articulated or object relations formed, but also to the limits of therapeutic efficacy and the way subjecthood can be disrupted and disturbed by forces that come from outside. It is these mutual encounters that one seeks when advancing 'applied' psychoanalysis, and it is examples of instances in which they take place that will be examined in later chapters.

Conclusion

Freud's forays into art, literature and sociology flag up some of the issues that have recurred throughout the history of applied psychoanalysis, revealing some of its promise and some more of its limitations. Much of his work was in 'conquistador' mode, aiming to colonise areas outside the clinical homeland of psychoanalysis. The motivation for this was partly the appeal of grand theory – psychoanalysis as a kind of 'theory of everything', not dissimilar in this respect from Einsteinian physics. Additionally, applied psychoanalysis was a way of validating psychoanalysis in general, its lines of evidence used to offer supposedly 'independent' support for some of the key claims that had been derived from the consulting room. In the case of applications to social theory, Freud seems also to have been driven by a moralising impulse in which he saw commentary on the disturbances of society as necessary in order to show what might need to be done to protect the well-being of individuals. In this area, psychoanalysis has enough in it of the social to contest other more explicitly sociological theories. Most particularly, its rich account of unconscious processes inserts an appreciation of the 'irrational' into theories that otherwise find the unexpected, self-destructive or fanatical eruptions of social disorder hard to fathom.

The strengths and weaknesses of this work can be summarised briefly in the question of how well it articulates a specific contribution of psychoanalysis to broader intellectual activity that nevertheless respects the non-psychological elements of the fields into which it strays, and indeed learns from them. Freud certainly provokes something important, notably a set of enquiries about how the unconscious seeps into social and cultural events, and what it might mean to recognise this as a fact. He also sets up a one-sided attitude in which psychoanalysis already knows the answers to its questions before it investigates them. How surprised can one be, for instance, that it reveals God as a projection of infantile wishes, given its commitment to Oedipal theory? What kind of analysis or evidence could have produced a different Freudian account of religion? The problem here is of how psychoanalysis can hold onto its capacity for radical deconstruction of the material with which it deals – this being what one might very generally term the 'analytic attitude' (Rieff, 1966) – whilst retaining a reflexive ability to do the same to itself. In the next chapter, which again deals with some historical debates, an attempt will be made to start to describe a way in which this difficult balance might be achieved.

Chapter 3

Psychoanalysis as/of Literature

The previous chapter provided an account of some of the history of 'applied' psychoanalysis in the humanities and social sciences through an examination of Freud's work in this area. At the end, it raised a set of questions about what might be meant by a genuinely open encounter between psychoanalysis and other fields of study, in which a two-way influence is possible. This involves not simply imposing psychoanalytic interpretations on the other discipline, so that psychoanalysis plays the role of an 'expert' system that can force literary criticism or sociology, for example, to take account of unconscious features in their landscape of concern. It also asks for a reciprocal openness of psychoanalysis itself to what might emerge from the movement 'outside the clinic', in particular to anything that might challenge its concepts and assumptions. Additionally, it requires some respect on the part of psychoanalysis for the specific disciplinary terrain in which it is treading, for example in appreciating the aesthetic traditions that might govern the form taken by a work of art, or the political investments reflected in a social event. Put at its strongest, if psychoanalysis is to retain its capacity to disrupt and provoke the research traditions with which it comes into contact, it also has to be ready to face such disruption itself.

Freud provides some hints of such reciprocal openness, particularly in his writings on literature, where his respect for creative authors meant that he was willing to forego some of his authority as the 'master' of the unconscious. In the current chapter, a second historical example is used to try to tease out some more elements required for productive uses of psychoanalysis outside the clinic, focusing especially on some debates around psychoanalysis and literature in the 1980s. This was a particularly interesting moment, as the growing influence of Lacanian theory and the general poststructuralist 'turn' in the arts and social sciences meant that questions of meaning and representation were being avidly reconsidered in academic work. In the field of literary studies, which was rapidly developing many new theoretical perspectives, psychoanalysis came under scrutiny for two opposed reasons. On the one hand, its 'colonial' embrace of literature, in which it claimed to be able to supply to texts the 'real' meaning that would otherwise escape notice, was made problematic by an appreciation of how reading is performed *contingently*. The 'meaning' of a text could no longer be regarded as fixed for all time, with the task of the critic being to identify it accurately. Instead,

it was appreciated that readings are always multiple and partial, linked to very particular perspectives (for example, governed by class or gender). On the other hand, it also came to be understood that literary texts reveal 'traces' of their own history and of the many other texts from which they derive, with which they might be in a kind of 'dialogue'. Sometimes, this is reflected in direct citational practices, but in all cases texts are part of a community of writings that can only be read in conjunction with one another. This recognition of what is termed 'intertextuality' suggests a need for a vocabulary that could track such 'unconscious' traces. As psychoanalysis, mainly but not solely in its Lacanian form, had had its own 'linguistic turn', it could be seen as offering precisely such a vocabulary, so long as one was careful not to assume that the 'unconscious' of a text would be the same as the 'unconscious' of a person. This meant that it could be considered sympathetically even by literary critics who bridled at its actions when in its more colonial mode of action. Finally, some literary scholars were also reading Freud not as a scientist, but as a writer of profound literary works. The attention they paid to the characteristics of these works followed the lines of their usual scholarly activity, meaning that psychoanalysis itself could be treated as a literary endeavour. This offered something back to psychoanalysis: an understanding of its own characteristics, its own textual unconscious, which might otherwise have escaped *psychoanalysis'* notice.

It is such backwards and forwards movements that promote the kinds of open encounters being pursued here. This chapter therefore takes up this debate over psychoanalysis and literature in order to outline a kind of 'model' of what is required to sustain such openness. This will lay some further groundwork for the interventions in subsequent chapters, which explore some exemplary psychoanalytically informed debates in contemporary social and psychosocial studies.

Problems of character and interpretation

Psychoanalysis has always been controversial as a method of literary analysis, particularly amongst writers and critics who regard it as a colonising discipline trying to tell the 'truth' of literature without necessarily appreciating its specificity, including its aesthetic properties. There is certainly much for such critics to get their teeth into, as psychoanalysts have not been coy about applying their clinical insights to literature. Sometimes, as with Freud, this is because they admire creative writing and wish to understand it better; but often they seem simply unable to resist the temptation to speculate freely about literary charac-

ters or their authors, perhaps rejoicing in them as 'patients' who cannot answer back. The most outrageous instances of psychoanalytic 'reading in' to literary productions treat them as somehow transparent indicators of the mental state and psychobiographical attributes of the author. Examples here include Marie Bonaparte's (1933) early study of Edgar Allan Poe, which identified necrophilia as a pathological personality state underpinning Poe's writing, or Ernest Jones' (1910) study of *Hamlet* as Oedipal drama. The limitations of this approach and of the parallel tendency to treat literary characters as real have been well recognised for a long time. As noted in Chapter 2, Freud himself showed anxiety at realising that he was attributing mental processes to the fictional protagonists of Jensen's *Gradiva*. Virginia Woolf firmly opposed psychoanalytic criticism on the grounds of its reduction of characters to 'cases' (Abel, 1989, p.17). Interestingly, however, Woolf also had some sympathy for the idea that literature might be the writer's equivalent of psychoanalytic treatment. Writing about the composition of her novel *To the Lighthouse*, she said, 'I suppose that I did for myself what psycho-analysts do for their patients. I expressed some very long felt and deeply felt emotion. And in expressing it I explained it and then laid it to rest' (Stonebridge, 1998, p.63). Perhaps this relates to the reason Woolf would not countenance psychoanalytic treatment for her own psychological distress; in the version given by Alix Strachey, this was because of the fear (which Strachey endorsed) that psychoanalysis might endanger Woolf's creativity, that is, that unpicking her madness might destroy her work (Appignanesi and Forrester, 1992, p.370; Abel, 1989).

Whatever the 'therapeutic' possibilities of *writing*, many of the classical strategies of *reading* found in psychoanalytic approaches to literature are clearly wrong-headed. As in Bonaparte's and Jones' studies, there is a tradition of treating literary texts as equivalent to dreams, offering a 'royal road' through to the neurosis of their authors. There are numerous problems with this. For one thing, the biographical detail needed to inform psychoanalytic formulations and the opportunity for testing interpretations in the context of clinical transference relationships are not available even if one accepts the premise that a literary work might be akin to a dream. In the case of the dream, each element might open out associations *in the dreamer* that can be subjected to psychoanalytic work; in the literary example, no such associations are available, with the consequence that (as in the example of *Gradiva*) it is commonly the *analyst's* associations that are substituted for the author's. Moreover, whilst an author might well 'inhabit' her or his writing in ways that give rise to biographical curiosity, any interpretive account of a text in terms of the character or psychopathology of the

author is undermined by the *intentional* opacity of textual surfaces employed by writers. Put simply, they *craft* their work in ways that are significantly different from the work of self-presentation and defence that goes on in the psychoanalytic consulting room. This does not belie the existence of some apparent similarities: patients, like writers, use certain cultural conventions in order to express themselves. Suffering and free association both have their genres, and these vary across time and place, as is indicated by the withering away of the once dominant psychoanalytic entities of 'hysteria' and 'neurasthenia' and their replacement by clinical presentations regarded as 'narcissistic' or 'borderline'. The consulting room is a space with its own expectations and traditions, just as the broader self-presentational actions of people in encounters with others have their own traditions and aesthetic properties, and are themselves dramaturgically crafted (Goffman's *The Presentation of Self in Everyday Life* (1969) is the seminal text here). However, this seeming similarity is in fact a difference, and part of the point. The conventions built on to make meaning in the consulting room are not the same as those used by writers to construct their literary pieces. These have their own specificity, lay down their own routines and boundaries, and provoke their own modes of artistic resistance. Writers work with their material in ways that are derived from the history of their profession; even when they challenge and depart from this history (and even, one might say, if they are influenced by psychoanalysis in doing so), it is in relation to the practice of writing that this happens, not the practice of (to use a shorthand) free association. One might be able to read 'through' a literary text to the traditions that inform it, just as one might in principle read 'through' a patient's speech to the unconscious; but these are not the same things.

What happens when such methods are used is that the significance of the text is bypassed in favour of a supposed 'true' meaning that lies behind it in the character of the author – a meaning which is actually unavailable and indeed probably factitious. Lionel Trilling, in his classic mid-twentieth-century book *The Liberal Imagination* (1951), which is by no means unsympathetic to psychoanalysis, notes the key defect of Jones' approach to *Hamlet* along these lines:

> Dr Jones's study of Hamlet search[es] for a 'hidden motive' and a 'deeper working', which implies that there is a reality to which the play stands in the relation that a dream stands to the wish that generates it and from which it is separable; it is this reality, this 'deeper working' which, according to Dr Jones, produced the play. But Hamlet is not merely the product of Shakespeare's thought, it is the very instrument of his thought, and if meaning is intention, Shakespeare did not intend the Oedipus motive or anything less than Hamlet; if meaning is effect then it is Hamlet which affects us, not the Oedipus motive. (p.63)

Whilst the effect of a piece of literature might in part be ascribed to the specific psychological complexes that it calls up in the reader (which is part of Jones' argument as well as Freud's explanation of the continuing hold of the Oedipus story), the idea that that is what the work is *about* is misguided. The literary work exists in its own terms, linked in with its culture and making sense in the context of various modes of intertextuality, including the sophistication of readers in psychoanalytic perspectives. It is produced by the play of textual meanings, from which psychoanalytic narratives might be read out – but not as diagnostic categories, rather as associations. Hence Maud Ellmann's (1994) indictment of traditional psychoanalytic criticism:

> the stories psychoanalyse their own interpreters: the scenes of sexual possession discovered in the texts tell us less about the authors than about the critics, and less about eroticism than about the will to power over literary ambiguity. Only by attending to the rhetoric of texts, to the echoes and recesses of the words themselves, can we recognise the otherness of literature, its recalcitrance as well as its susceptibility to theorisation. Without this vigilance to language, psychoanalysis is doomed to rediscover its own myths grotesquely multiplied throughout the course of literature. (p.3)

This notion of the *otherness* of literature and its link with 'vigilance to language' has become increasingly important in more recent psychoanalytic criticism, which echoes to the footsteps of Lacan, however ambivalently; and it will be returned to below. But it is also worth noting that interpreting the characters in a literary work is just as problematic as reading through the text to the personality of the author or the universal mythological complexes that are seen as the 'truth' of any tale, however entertaining the speculations might be that are thereby produced. The tendency to understand characters as if they were real is a very strong one, even without the psychoanalytic gloss to which Woolf objected, presumably because of the dominance of narrative structures in western culture that pull one towards making a causal story out of even quite fragmentary material. Psychoanalysis' own assumptions (its understanding of how the mind works) are in any case highly influential culturally and are drawn upon strongly by people to make sense of their experiences, giving them enormous purchase and plausibility when mobilised in literary contexts. However, the application of such assumptions to literary characters is illicit for some very obvious reasons. Ellmann, having noted that the tendency to view the character as a 'person' to be analysed is heavily aligned with American ego-psychology's focus on individualism, makes the key point. 'Hamlet', she writes, 'has the disadvantage that he can never contradict his psychoanalyst. Unlike a real analysand, he cannot lie down on the couch and free associate about his

dreams or recapitulate the trauma of his infancy. Amusing as it is to speculate about his early history, Hamlet *never had a childhood*' (p.3). In *Wild Analysis*, Freud (1910b) notes, 'psychoanalytical treatment absolutely presupposes prolonged contact with the patient' (p.7). Even psychoanalytic *interpretation* requires as much – and this is simply not possible with a patient who does not actually exist.

Psychoanalysis 'and' ...

All this is preliminary to an interesting set of issues surrounding the relationship of psychoanalysis with literature, which has some useful implications for the broader question of what it might mean to develop non-clinical applications of psychoanalysis, including in the social sciences. A way in here is presented by Shoshana Felman's (1982a) examination of the 'and' in the phrase 'psychoanalysis *and* literature'. Felman points out that psychoanalysis' approach to literature has been one of attempted mastery, with literature being called on to take a subservient or 'slave' position, in which psychoanalytic interpretation is the key to unlock what literature 'really' has to say. The effect of this approach is to present literature as blind to itself; that is, just like the analyst in relation to the neurotic patient, psychoanalysis knows literature better than literature knows itself.

> Although 'and' is grammatically defined as a 'coordinate conjunction' in the context of the relationship between 'literature and psychoanalysis' it is usually interpreted, paradoxically enough, as implying not so much a relation of coordination as one of *subordination*, a relation in which literature is submitted to the authority, to the prestige of psychoanalysis. While literature is considered as a body of *language* – to *be interpreted* – psychoanalysis is considered as a body of *knowledge*, whose competence is called upon *to interpret*. Psychoanalysis, in other words, occupies the place of a *subject*, literature that of an *object*; the relation of an interpretation is structured as a relation of master to slave, according to the Hegelian definition: the dynamic encounter between the two areas is in effect, in Hegel's terms, a 'fight for recognition,' whose outcome is the sole recognition of the master – of (the truth of) psychoanalytical theory; literature's function, like that of the slave, is to *serve* precisely the *desire* of psychoanalytical theory – its desire for recognition; exercising its authority and *power* over the literary field, holding a discourse of masterly competence, psychoanalysis in literature, thus seems to seek above all its own *satisfaction*. (pp.5–6)

Expressed like this, it is pretty clear why literary critics might object to psychoanalysis, which comes in from the outside as a master discourse

that can sweep everything else away: it *knows*, and in demonstrating its knowledge, it serves the good not of literature, but of psychoanalysis itself. From Freud's appropriation of the Oedipus story, through many of his acolytes as they apply the mighty cudgel of psychoanalytic interpretation, psychoanalysis uses literature in order to demonstrate its own authority, its own capacity to make sense, to be true. This is in some ways simply disrespectful, reducing the long history of literature to that of a patient waiting for the doctor to arrive to pronounce the actual name of the illness; literature takes the position of the hysteric whose lock is picked only by the Freudian key. It is also, as Felman expresses it, a *misrecognition*: 'the psychoanalytical reading of literary texts precisely *misrecognizes* (overlooks, leaves out) their literary specificity; ... literature could perhaps even be defined as that which remains in a text precisely *unaccounted for* by the traditional psychoanalytical approach to literature' (ibid.). This last point marks the beginning of an alternative approach, in which the capacity both of literature and of psychoanalysis to promote openness to what is 'unaccounted for' is given priority. But for the moment the point is merely that in promoting its own interests, psychoanalytic criticism can miss what is specific to its interlocutor – whether this is the patient in the clinic or, as here, the massive and complex body of thought and writing known as literature.

Despite these cautions, criticisms and caveats, the various commentators quoted so far all see psychoanalysis as having something to say to literature, albeit it only once it has escaped from its own masterful tendencies, its own position as what Lacan (1991, p.29) calls the 'discourse of the Master', the subject actually in possession of the truth. Much of the discussion here centres on what might be called style or *process*, in which the issue is to interrogate literature in ways that open out new modes of reading and understanding – not to find a truth, but to produce more effects. Indeed, it is in demonstrating the impossibility of any one true reading that the productivity of an interpretive account can be found, and there are ways in which psychoanalysis can contribute to this by unsettling obvious renderings of a text so long as this is not in order to replace them with what purport to be 'deeper' ones. In addition, there are possibilities produced by the realisation that psychoanalysis is a literary exercise itself, inscribed in writing and publication but also drawing brilliantly on the tropes and conventions of literature – a point again made early on by Lionel Trilling and developed more fully in the wake of Lacan.

The struggle to develop psychoanalysis, usually coded as an attempt to find a scientific basis for this complex depth psychology, is also a development within the broad disciplinary nexus known as the 'humanities'. This recognises it as an attempt to refine consciousness in relation

to human motivation and desire, and to express this refinement in recognisable terms within its own literary genre. In this context, psychoanalysts who recommend the development of literary capacities as a way of mastering technique have something useful to say, not only because of what there is to be learnt from the practice of literature, but also because working *reflexively* in this way leaves psychoanalysis itself open to challenge and change. For example, the leading psychoanalyst Thomas Ogden (1999) describes powerfully (using a Robert Frost poem as an example) how there may be parallels between 'the way he listens to the language of the poem and the way he and his patient speak with and listen to one another' (p.49). For Ogden, the lesson of poetry for the consulting room is not to use language 'poetically' (he describes this as a kind of 'narcissistic countertransference acting in' – p.66), but rather to cultivate a mode of listening and speaking that is attuned to the question of 'what it is "that's going on here" in the intrapsychic and intersubjective life of the analysis, the "music of what happens" in the analytic relationship' (p.50). Ogden argues that both poetry and psychoanalysis make possible forms of 'human aliveness', and the discipline of listening to one can enhance that of listening to the other. In this account the task of the analyst is no longer to unearth the truth of what lies behind the patient's or the poem's words; it is simply to find a way to listen and respond that brings 'feelings and ideas to life in words that will advance the analytic process' (p.66). This moves the discipline towards more of a focus on intersubjectivity, with responsiveness rather than knowingness being a core attribute of the analyst. This too has its direct parallel with the encounter of psychoanalysis with literature. When practised as an expert discipline, interpreting the subservient discipline of literature, psychoanalysis cannot discover anything new. It literally applies its already-existent body of knowledge to make sense of something else, and at best will refine its theories or specific interpretations in the light of problems it might encounter on the way. Its knowledge is demonstrative rather than open and discovering: it knows, and literature must learn. When, however, the encounter is two-way, and psychoanalysis itself is interrogated as a mode of literary discourse, then its doubts and confusions, its unmeant expressions and unresolved conflicts, come into play and can be examined. This produces an aura of uncertainty which might be conducive to change: that is, psychoanalysis can become experimental again, open to feedback. So whilst psychoanalysis becomes rigid when it sets itself up as an expert approach to literature, when understood as literature itself it becomes a more ambiguous and also more productive entity.

The destructive element: Kleinianism and its literary resonances

Before turning more fully to the questions of psychoanalysis *as* litera-ture and of how seeing it this way helps in considering its contribution to literary studies, it is important also to acknowledge that despite all the criticisms of the 'expert' status of psychoanalysis mentioned above, there are ideas that flow from the content of psychoanalytic theory that may add to appreciation of literary works. An example here is the impact of Kleinian theories of destructiveness, particularly in elaborat-ing some of the concerns to be found in interwar British literature. The extraordinary viciousness of the Kleinian world has few counterparts anywhere, except perhaps in twentieth-century external reality. Here, famously, is Joan Riviere (1936), describing the fully Kleinian infant in the mid-1930s:

> Limbs shall trample, kick and hit; lips, fingers and hands shall suck, twist, pinch; teeth shall bite, gnaw, mangle and cut; mouth shall devour, swallow and 'kill' (annihilate), eyes kill by a look, pierce and penetrate; breath and mouth hurt by noise, as the child's own sensitive ears have experienced. One may suppose that before an infant is many months old it will not only *feel* itself performing these actions, but will have some kind of *ideas* of doing so. All these sadistic activities in phantasy are felt not only to expel the danger from the self but to transfer it into the object (projection). (p.286)

Right from the start, Klein's work focused on the conflictual and complex phantasy life of children, uncovering brutalities and hates which fully put paid to any idealised notion of childhood innocence. What Freud had started with the notion of infantile sexuality was devel-oped by Klein to portray infancy as characterised by an inner battle in which good (love) could only precariously triumph over bad (hate), and was always teetering on the edge of destruction. Even though her notions of paranoid-schizoid splitting and envy were not fully worked out until the 1940s and 1950s (e.g. Klein, 1957), from early in her psychoanalytic career, analysing the play of young children in the same way as others analysed adults, Klein emphasised the punitiveness of the infantile psyche and addressed the need for the analyst to pay it due heed. In contrast to Anna Freud, who argued the necessity for a careful nurturing of the treatment alliance and placed value on the 'educative' potential of psychoanalysis, Klein was unstinting in her assertion that analysis is about revelation of the deepest layers of the mind – that only thus could the terrors of unconscious impulses be faced and overcome. 'Analysis is not in itself a gentle method: it cannot spare the patient *any suffering* and this applies equally to children', she wrote (Klein, 1927,

p.344). Riviere (1927) was even clearer: 'analysis ... is not concerned with the real world, nor with the child's or the adult's adaptation to the real world, nor with sickness or health, nor virtue or vice. It is concerned simply and solely with the imaginings of the childish mind, the phantasised pleasures and the dreaded retributions' (p.377). The Oedipus complex and superego formation, dated by Freud to about the fifth year of life, are brought right forward by Klein, so the infantile superego becomes 'pre-Oedipal', present in the obscure pre-history of the human subject, the period which Freud largely forgot. The intensity of this is overwhelming: the biting, needy, hating, desiring infant is an exploding cannon of emotional turmoil.

In the mid-1930s, Klein added a further gloss to this with a major innovation which, according to Segal (1979) amongst others, marked the real beginning of a Kleinian 'school'. This was the introduction of the concept of the depressive position, adumbrated in her 1935 paper, *A Contribution to the Psychogenesis of Manic-Depressive States*. This is a profoundly integrative concept, in which what is stressed is the complexity of the process whereby an infant puts together her or his feelings of love and hate and owns them both. The depressive position is constituted by the movement from feelings of rage to those of loss, carried along by recognition of the reality of ambivalence and the necessity, as well as possibility, of making something reparative out of the impulses towards destruction. Taking hold of hate, recognising its existence, ameliorating it through the containment which a benevolent environment (such as the analyst) can offer, owning one's destructive-ness, creatively repairing the damage one has done to self and other – these are now the tendencies and aspirations of the Kleinian psyche. Abel (1989) comments, thinking of Virginia Woolf, 'For Kleinians, culture, opposed not as (paternal) law to instinct but as creativity to inner chaos, emerges from the impulse to make reparation to the mother' (p.11).

The context for all this in post-First World War culture is self-evident, and in many ways was shared by Freud with his announcement of the death drive in *Beyond the Pleasure Principle* and his acerbic cultural commentary in *Civilisation and its Discontents* (Freud, 1920b, 1930). Schwartz (1999) summarises:

> The psychoanalysts of Europe were responding to the same events as was everyone else. Theory in psychoanalysis, in its own way, had to cope with turmoil, uncertainty and death. Melanie Klein's vision of the child's inner world was as situated in the uncertainties and brutalities of the aftermath of the First World War as was the literature, the movies and the architecture. (p.199)

For writers, too, the concern with tragedy and the fragmentation of the past was overwhelming. By the mid- to late 1920s, the nature of the First World War was very well known and its devastating consequences had been felt across an entire generation. Everything had changed and had to change. T.S. Eliot's *The Waste Land* (1922), despite or perhaps alongside its misogyny and reactionary class bias, grabbed hold of this feeling and represented it with appalling precision, in a manner congruent with Freud's later versions of psychoanalysis and especially with the fascination with destructiveness which was Klein's specific contribution. Ellmann (1990), in a marvellous examination of the poem's 'abjection' (a concept taken from Kristeva, 1983, itself inspired in part by Klein, and referring to what is degraded and cast out), comments on the wiping out of a history which then returns, plaguing the text, like the return of the repressed which in Freud is the prototype of death. 'Whereas Freud discovers the death drive in the compulsion to repeat,' she writes (p.188), '*The Waste Land* stages it in the compulsion to citation.' Biographically,

> written in the aftermath of the First World War, and in the midst of a disastrous marriage, the poem has so much to forget: madness, feminism, sexuality, the slaughtered millions, and the rattle of its own exhausted idioms. Yet ... *The Waste Land* works like an obsessive ceremonial, because it reinscribes the horrors it is trying to repress. For Freud argues that obsessive rituals repeat the very acts that they are thought to neutralize: the ritual, he says, is ostensibly a protection against the prohibited act; 'but *actually* ... a repetition of it'. (pp.179–80)

The 'waste' in *The Waste Land* is what constantly returns, the living dead; the ghosts and fragments, of people and particularly of writing. Obsessed by death, both literature and psychoanalysis have to ask what it is in the modern consciousness that can create such vicious fragmentation, such a violent spell:

> The speaker of *The Waste Land* also stages his own death when he conjures up the writings of the dead, sacrificing voice and face to their ventriloquy. In this sense he resembles the child in *Beyond the Pleasure Principle*, who stages his extinction in the mirror. Freud compares his grandchild to the victims of shell-shock, who relive their terrors in their dreams, repeating death as if it were desire. This is the game *The Waste Land* plays, and the nightmare that it cannot lay to rest, as it stages the ritual of its own destruction. (Ellmann, 1990, p.198)

'Limbs shall trample, kick and hit', writes Riviere (1936), and Klein (1932) describes a vast range of destructive impulses in the young child,

for example, 'an early stage of development which is governed by the child's aggressive trends against its mother's body and in which its predominant wish is to rob her body of its contents and destroy it' (p.128). *The Waste Land*, too, 'stages the ritual of its own destruction', as did, in the First World War, the whole of European society. It is not surprising, then, that Kleinian ideas should have been attractive in Britain and that the growth of fascism and Nazism in the 1930s should simply augment that attraction, as explanations had to be sought for the continued eruption of the bestial tumour out of the body of the modern world.

Kleinianism, in this account, does not simply offer an explanation for, or interpretation of, literature (*The Waste Land* as devouring destructiveness), but rather shares in the culture of destruction which makes sense of its products, whether psychoanalytic or literary. In this regard, the very specific resonance of some Kleinian ideas in the wake of the First World War does not attest to their truth value so much as to their cultural congruence, which again makes them useful in a dialogue with literature. Stonebridge (1998) shows this very powerfully in relation to the notion of reparation, a core Kleinian idea referring to 'the variety of processes by which the ego feels it undoes harm done in phantasy, restores, preserves and revives objects' (Klein, 1955, p.133). Reparation rebuilds the world after destruction; yet, it is only in its cultural context that one can get the full feel of the ambiguities involved. Stonebridge (1998) notes that in the immediate aftermath of the war, 'reparations' not only meant making good the damage done, but – because of the disastrous failure of political imagination accompanying the Versailles Treaty – it also had connotations of being unfair and unduly punitive, hence continuing in the destructive mode. Indexing the literary critic William Empson's (1956) famous book on ambiguity, she explains:

> Like redemption, reparation carries with it both the spiritual sense of salvation and atonement and economic connotations of compensation and dues collected. When in 1919 reparation entered the European vocabulary with a new political charge, it also took on two more meanings: first, as the OED puts it, 'compensation for war damage owed by the aggressor' and second, as a direct result of the former, reparation, in an Empsonian manner, began to haemorrhage into almost the opposite of the rightful justice it was supposed to connote. For vocal if not ultimately influential sections of the European intelligentsia as well as for those suffering under the terms of the treaty, reparation came to mean something exorbitant, excessive and punitive, in short, an invitation to more aggression ... In the period between the wars, reparation, in a Kleinian as well as Empsonian sense, is pregnant with the destructive element. (p.32)

The importance of work like this is that it indicates the problems that both psychoanalysts and literary figures were working on. In this instance, these concerned the ambivalence entailed in 'making good' the destruction of the war in an environment in which nothing had been worked through or resolved, and in which the dynamics of anxiety and hatred released in and by the war had not been owned or understood. It is not that the Kleinian notion of reparation offers the key to understanding the literature of the time, though it does give some useful leverage for exploring its nuances. It is rather that the trope of reparation runs through a range of cultural products, including Kleinian psychoanalysis, giving them resonance and appeal, and filling them with the meaning-effects that make them warrantable at that time and place. Psychoanalysis is in dialogue with literature here because both are infected with the problematics of their period; this is not absolute, masterful 'knowledge', but an encounter that makes meaning more subtle and rich.

Psychoanalysis as literature

Recognition of the way in which psychoanalysis draws on literature, and the possibilities this gives for a creative encounter between the two disciplines, has been spurred on particularly by the Lacanian emphasis on language. However, it has not depended on this development. As noted earlier, Lionel Trilling (1951) very clearly articulated an irony of psychoanalysis: that whilst its direct attempts to 'interpret' literature too often produced crass and patronising interpretations that fail to understand the openness of artistic meanings, when one turns to the decidedly non-literary elements of psychoanalytic theory, useful concepts and parallels immediately stand out. For Trilling, these lie in the way psychoanalysis 'makes poetry indigenous to the very constitution of the mind' (p.64). Indeed, he writes, 'the mind, as Freud sees it, is in the greater part of its tendency exactly a poetry-making organ'. This 'poetry' is not to be found in any romantic notion of, for example, the unfathomable depths of unconscious mental life; rather, it lies in the very specific mechanisms proposed by Freud to explain how the mind works.

> In the eighteenth century Vico spoke of the metaphorical, imagistic language of the early stages of culture; it was left to Freud to discover how, in a scientific age, we still feel and think in figurative formations, and to create, what psychoanalysis is, a science of tropes, of metaphor and its variants, synecdoche and metonymy. (ibid.)

Just as Lacan was led to draw on the work of structural linguistics to explain the functioning of the mind in terms of metaphor and metonymy, so Trilling, writing in a very different tradition, saw the essential literary humanism of Freud as residing in his discovery of mental mechanisms such as displacement and condensation. This was additional to a more general humanistic sympathy that, according to Trilling, Freud had with the great literary traditions, one characterised by openness to suffering and an essentially tragic vision that was without cynicism even when it was characterised by irony. Freud himself is an artist, in this sense, or at least his view of the world has much to offer the artist: 'the poetic qualities of Freud's own principles, which are so clearly in the line of the classic tragic realism, suggest that this is a view which does not narrow and simplify the human world for the artist but on the contrary opens and complicates it' (p.68). There are thus two ways in which Freudian psychoanalysis can contribute to the literary imagination: as a general, tragic vision of human nature out of which a moral system can be welded together; and as a specific, 'scientific' approach that shows how the mind itself obeys literary laws, and is thus open to the reception and expression of poetic modes of being. This approach, it might be noted, to some extent reverses the master–slave dynamic of traditional psychoanalytic criticism. This time, it is literature that is being used to make sense of psychoanalysis. It is literature that has the interpretive and technical facility available to it, and psychoanalysis that draws on literary tropes to theorise its own object of study, the mind. On the other hand, what Trilling is pointing to here is an essential sympathy between psychoanalysis and literature that might be used to the advantage of both, without the struggle for dominance that had thitherto characterised the field.

Two 'classic' accounts of the literary nature of Freudian psychoanalysis are worth noting here. The first is Steven Marcus' (1975) exploration of the 'Dora' case study (Freud, 1905). His title, *Freud and Dora: Story, History, Case History*, captures the way in which his reading proceeds, as a highly sympathetic rendering of it as if it were a novel. Marcus is explicit here, seeing Freud as the master of a new literary form, the case history. As a genre this is directly related to other modernist forms, sharing with them particular attributes such as that of the 'unreliable narrator' who is in many ways at odds with her or his material, and who challenges the reader to make something out of the fragmentary nature of what is presented:

> The general form of what Freud has written bears certain suggestive resemblances to a modern experimental novel. Its narrative and expository course, for example, is neither linear nor rectilinear; instead its organization is plas-

tic, involuted, and heterogeneous and follows spontaneously an inner logic that seems frequently to be at odds with itself; it often loops around itself and is multidimensional in its representation of both its material and itself. Its continuous innovations in formal structure seem unavoidably to be dictated by its substance, by the dangerous, audacious, disreputable, and problematical character of the experiences being represented and dealt with, and by the equally scandalous intentions of the author and the outrageous character of the role he has had the presumption to assume. In content, however, what Freud has written is in parts rather like a play by Ibsen, or more precisely like a series of Ibsen's plays. (p.64)

Marcus tracks the various literary techniques Freud uses, from the framing device in the Prefatory Remarks to the case, which draws the reader's attention to the fragmentary nature of the work and also positions both Freud and Dora as protagonists, through the analysis of Dora's dreams and the way in which the plot line at the end (on transference) calls into question most of what has gone before. Marcus is deeply admiring of Freud's skill even as he speculates that the case history reveals Freud's own blind spots – this too being characteristic of much modernist literature. Freud announces the problematic status of his writing and the 'dubious' character of its achievement, and opens up to the reader the chance of *interpreting him* over and beyond his own work. That is, despite appearances, he is not in command, instructing the reader (and patient) authoritatively in ways that cannot be challenged. Instead, through the very fragmentary nature of the case history and the way in which alternative voices (Freud's own self-doubt being one, but Dora's clearly being another) are allowed to speak, readers can fill in their own narratives, as indeed has been done many times (Bernheimer and Kahane, 1985). Marcus notes:

> the work is also fragmentary or incomplete in the sense of Freud's self-knowledge, both at the time of the actual case and at the time of his writing it. And he communicates in this piece of writing a less than complete understanding of himself, although like any great writer he provides us with the material for understanding some things that have escaped his own understanding, for filling in some gaps, for restoring certain fragments into wholes. (p.67)

By the end, as he shows, Freud has converted everything into writing – transference is *defined* as 'new editions or facsimiles of the impulses and phantasies which are aroused during the progress of the analysis; but they have this peculiarity, which is characteristic of their species, that they replace some earlier person by the person of the physician' (Freud, 1905, pp.157–8). That is, 'The patient does not merely provide the text;

he also *is* the text, the writing to be read, the language to be interpreted' (Marcus, 1975, p.81).

What is happening here, as Marcus explicitly notes, is that psycho-analysis is being forged through the medium of literary expression, and stamps its authority not only (or maybe not at all) through its scientific claims, but also through its capacity to use literary means to articulate the problems facing modern human subjects. The simple bourgeois forms of narrative retained their appeal in Freud's time, but they were also breaking down, and psychoanalysis is a product of a precise moment in western cultural history in which new, often revolutionary forms of expression are coming into view, in politics, art, music and literature. Freud's self-expression is marked by this, his struggle to find a mode of writing that will both persuade and also do justice to the lacunae in his theory that are produced by the real complexities of human psychology. His own multi-layered self-consciousness also comes into play, at times dazzlingly insightful, at others patently defen-sive; and as this happens, so it is transformed into literature. Even the topic of his study and his way of understanding it are deeply literary: the patient may have bodily symptoms, as hysterics such as Dora in partic-ular do, but these are versions of words, written on the body rather than in sound or on paper. For example, Dora's cough is traced eventually by Freud to an unconscious awareness of the oral sex going on between her father and Frau K. Freud (1905) comments: 'But the conclusion was inevitable that with her spasmodic cough, which, as is usual, was referred for its exciting stimulus to a tickling in her throat, she pictured to herself a scene of sexual gratification per os between the two people whose love-affair occupied her mind so incessantly' (p.48). *Naming* it in this way leads to the cough vanishing. The task of psychoanalysis is in large part to restore words that have become lost and embedded in the 'wrong' places to their linguistic and literary origins, to make narratives of them that are more potent than the broken narratives that produce symptoms. Psychoanalysis is not therefore literary only because it has to be expressed in narrative form; it also treats its patients as literary beings, characters in search of stories that make sense; and it struggles with language as a way to achieve this.

If Marcus shows definitively the connection between Freud and modernist literary forms, Peter Brooks' (1982) essay on *Beyond the Pleasure Principle* (Freud, 1920b) looks at Freud's attempt to create a 'masterplot' that will make life itself narratable. *Beyond the Pleasure Principle* is the moment in Freud's writing when the whole of his drive theory is recast in the light of the work he had previously done on narcissism and, especially, of the encounter with trauma and destruc-tiveness in the First World War. This was a war which he had at first

welcomed, like so many who saw it as an opportunity for the listless stagnation of pre-war society to be overcome; but gradually, again like so many others, he understood it as a devastating assault on the assumption of inevitable human progress. Where previously the drive model had proposed an opposition between sexual and ego-preservative drives, with an appropriate compromise between 'pleasure' and 'reality' being the key to individual and social mental health, *Beyond the Pleasure Principle* invents a new metapsychology, in which what governs human activity is a more fundamental opposition between 'life' and 'death'. A postulate of psychoanalysis had been that the aim of the drives was satisfaction experienced in the form of pleasure. Yet, in neurotic behaviour and dreams and even in the childhood play of Freud's own grandson (the famous game in which the mother's disappearance is symbolised by throwing away a cotton reel), the apparently willed re-emergence of disturbing material could be observed again and again. This was not just temporary pain caused to the ego in the service of later drive satisfaction (for instance, the pleasure of the mother's return); it represented a 'remarkable fact', namely, that the compulsion to repeat often brings up material which can never have been pleasurable, and which 'can never, even long ago, have brought satisfaction even to instinctual impulses which have since been repressed' (Freud, 1920b, p.20). Traumatic dreams, of the kind characteristic of war neuroses, are an example of this phenomenon and apparently contradict the well-known formulation that dreams are wish-fulfilments, making it necessary to consider whether there may be another force at work other than the achievement of happiness. Instead, there must be something in human psychology more basic than pleasurable satisfaction, that is, something 'beyond' the pleasure principle. For Freud, oppressed by the legacy of death all around, perhaps by his own emerging cancer and the tired irascibility of what was already becoming his 'late style' (Said, 2007), this 'beyond' would not contradict the idea of a drive achieving satisfaction by restoring the organism to rest, but would exaggerate it, or follow it through to its logical conclusion. Observation of the sexual life of humans had revealed that there exists a drive which aims at preserving living substances and joining them together into larger units. Now it was also clear that there must be 'another, contrary instinct seeking to dissolve those units and to bring them back to their primaeval, inorganic state' (Freud, 1930, p.118). And what could this be, but a state of perfect rest and nothingness, a relief from all tension and unwanted stimulation? 'The aim of all life is death', wrote Freud (1920b, p.38).

Laplanche and Pontalis (1967) suggest that the death drive is not simply a balancing force opposing the life drive, but is better understood

as a basic postulate grounding Freud's motivational theory. 'What is designated here,' they write (p.102), 'is more than any particular *type* of instinct – it is rather that factor which determines the actual *principle* of all instincts', this principle being that of movement away (life) and then return. For Brooks (1982), reading *Beyond the Pleasure Principle* with a literary eye, Freud's reconfiguration of his drive theory was more than just a scientific one; it also constitutes what he calls Freud's 'masterplot', 'the text in which he most fully lays out a total scheme of how life proceeds from beginning to end, and how each individual life in its own way repeats the masterplot' (p.285). Moreover, embedded deeply in this masterplot, in Brooks' rewriting of it, is *narrative structure*, and this is what gives it its literary feel and relevance. There are two main elements to this. The first lies in the idea of the 'compulsion to repeat' itself: repetition has always been core to psychoanalysis, for example in the way neuroses are forged out of 'memories', and how transference is a repetition, in the presence of the analyst, of earlier relationships. In *Beyond the Pleasure Principle*, repetition becomes the defining motif of life itself, both in the sense of the death drive's 'desire' to return to an earlier state of inorganic inactivity, and in the way traumatic moments plague the mind and drive it to actions aimed at mastery or self-defence. For Brooks, repetition is also a defining feature of narrative: 'Narrative must ever present itself as a repetition of events that have already happened, and within this postulate of a generalized repetition it must make use of specific, perceptible repetitions in order to create plot, that is, to show us a significant interconnection of events' (p.288). More than just interconnection is at work here: repetition in psychoanalysis and in literature is a matter of the 'baseline of plot, its basic "pulsation", sensible or audible through the repetitions which take us back to the text' (p.291). The parallel between Freud's account of the psychic centrality of the compulsion to repeat and the way narratives are built out of replicable materials to be found scattered around the plots of literature is hardened by Brooks in the further rendering he gives of the way Freud's postulation of the 'journey' of life away from and back to death is itself a model of how narrative works. This holds the implication that this is in some way intrinsic to (perhaps 'hard-wired into', as might be said in the wake of the neuroscientific revolution) human consciousness. For the Freud of *Beyond the Pleasure Principle*, life is a deviation from death, what Brooks calls an 'arabesque' the aim of which is not to avoid death, but to allow each organism to return to death *in its own way*. 'What we are left with is the fact that the organism wishes to die only in its own fashion', writes Freud (1920b, p.39) – to find the death that is fitting for it. In narrative, tension is similarly produced by a process of 'detour', a middle that embellishes and delays the progress from

beginning to end, a kind of arc that deliberately takes up more space and time than would the straight line that is the shortest connection between these two points. In life, too, according to Freud, the arc of activity has precisely the same function. It defends against death, but it also brings the subject back to death, albeit in its own way: the right death, the appropriate end or dénouement; this is what is required. Brooks comments: 'The complication of the *detour* is related to the danger of short-circuit: the danger of reaching the end too quickly, of achieving the im-proper death' (p.292). Both narrative development and Eros work to counteract this threat. Brooks continues:

> We emerge from reading *Beyond the Pleasure Principle* with a dynamic model which effectively structures ends (death, quiescence, non-narratability) against beginnings (Eros, stimulation into tension, the desire of narrative) in a manner that necessitates the middle as *detour*, as struggle toward the end under the compulsion of imposed delay, as arabesque in the dilatory space of the text. (p.295)

Much of Brooks' argument involves drawing parallels between the death drive and narrative, which offers some intriguing insights into how narrative works and also suggests that in inventing his model of life and death drives, Freud might have been drawing implicitly, perhaps unconsciously, on familiar and cogent western thought structures and cultural repertoires. Perhaps this is more specific than Brooks suggests: rather than being a universal characteristic of human plot lines, the particular cultural assumptions of modernism are organised around the idea of narrative as 'beginning, middle, end' in ways which may not be true of all cultures, nor even (totally) of postmodern western times. Indeed, Brooks wants to go further here, using Freud's 'masterplot' to make sense of all literary endeavour, arguing that in identifying the basic structure of psychic life, Freud is also offering an interpretive account that can be applied to all texts. In contrast to the traditional psychoanalytic strategy of imposing readings of the author's, reader's or character's 'unconscious' on the text, Brooks argues that

> It is rather the superimposition of the model of the mental apparatus on the functioning of the text that offers the possibility of a psychoanalytic criticism. And here the superimposition of Freud's psychic masterplot on the plots of fiction seems a valid and useful maneuver. Plot mediates meanings with the contradictory human world of the eternal and the mortal. Freud's masterplot speaks of the temporality of desire, and speaks to our very desire for fictional plots. (pp.299–300)

Freud's account of the tension between life and death drives is used here

as an explanation of the psychic appeal of fiction, not just as a parallel account – the 'temporality of desire' *explains* the pull of narrative. Yet despite Brooks' assertion that this avoids the reductionism of traditional psychoanalytic criticism 'applied to' literature, it is hard to see how exactly this can be the case. Clearly, literary understanding may be enriched by the parallel with the 'detour' postulated by Freud, but we are still faced with an idea that originates in psychoanalysis and is then applied to literature to explain why narrative has such a profound appeal, why western readers constantly push for satisfaction, for completion, for the 'right' end, and feel frustrated and challenged – sometimes still outraged – when this is not provided. This is 'because' the mind is built that way, as a detour between death and a satisfactory return to death; what else can 'the superimposition of the model of the mental apparatus on the functioning of the text' signify? To that extent, it is difficult to see this kind of analysis moving things forward.

On the other hand, returning to the parallelism between narrative and Freudian theory has its own productivity. What it suggests is that in developing his theory of drives, Freud was not (or not just) building on careful observation and clinical and scientific knowledge, but was ordering those in terms of culturally given narrative structures. The pattern of origin, tension, resolution that is so embedded in 'beginning, middle, end' in literature, as in everyday personal accounts of events, was one that underpinned his model from the start. For Freud, the idea of tension pushing for relief was built on a sexual analogy, and maybe this is one source of the power of the narrative model anyway: that it recapitulates or brings to mind a basic psycho-physiological experience. But more significantly, this reading produces psychoanalysis once again as a literary activity with something to say to other literary activities. It is a *narrative*, for the very good reason that narrative of this kind structures psychology under the conditions of western modernity.

Signs and signifiers

Much contemporary engagement of psychoanalysis with literature has taken place under the sign, one might say, of Lacanianism. This is not a simple procedure, not only because of the famous opacity of Lacanian theory, but also because Lacan himself did not really mark out an approach to literature that solves the problems of psychoanalytic 'mastery' discussed above. Even his most famous literary diversion, the seminar on Edgar Allan Poe's story *The Purloined Letter* (Lacan, 1954–55), 'cannot possibly constitute a model for [psychoanalytic liter-

ary] criticism, since on the contrary the literary work is in it a mere pretext for a dazzling illustration of a non-literary thesis', as Jameson (1982, p.375) notes. Indeed, Lacan follows in one strand of Freud's tradition by using literature to show a certain kind of 'truth' of psychoanalysis, specifically to indicate ways in which meaning is produced through the flow of signifiers rather than being the product of 'character', a reading which also articulates the mode of operation of sexual difference in the discursive field (Frosh, 2006). What this does not do, however, is offer any *literary* analysis of Poe's text. Rather, it uses the text to make a point about psychic structure, not about literature itself. Despite this, Lacan's general approach has given leverage on textual analysis, for two related reasons. The first is simply the Lacanian focus on language: whereas the literary and linguistic origins of Freudian psychoanalysis have had to be uncovered philosophically and historically, Lacan was always explicit about language as the core phenomenon of psychoanalysis. His rather misleading slogan, 'the unconscious is structured like a language', is the most famous illustration of this, but more broadly the Lacanian understanding of psychoanalysis as a linguistic endeavour focuses attention on the movement of textual elements as they work across the speech of patient and analyst. This has the important result of shifting analytic attention away from a 'depth' reading of what lies hidden beneath the surface of the text, and more towards an examination and provocation of the 'disruptive' elements of textual play – towards the *effects* of language as they appear in the analytic situation. In comparison with traditional psychoanalytic attempts to find the 'real' meaning of a symptom or text in terms of the unconscious impulses and conflicts that lie behind it, the Lacanian push is on the whole towards tracking the effect of signifiers as they work in speech itself. This gives rise to some promising parallels between the analysis of the discourse of patients and the analysis of other kinds of text, including literary ones. In particular, Lacanian psychoanalysis refutes what it regards as the 'imaginary' task of producing full readings or explanations of unconscious meaning. Meaning for Lacan is a 'retroactive' phenomenon, produced after the event as a way of closing it down; for example, the meaning of a sentence is determined only at its end. In psychoanalytic practice, Lacan (1954–55) gives the following rule for literature, dreams and analysis:

You must start from the text, start by treating it, as Freud does and as he recommends, as Holy Writ. The author, the scribe, is only a pen-pusher, and he comes second ... Similarly, when it comes to our patients, please give more attention to the text than to the psychology of the author – the entire orientation of my teaching is that. (p.153)

Meaning has to emerge from the play of the text – the movement of signifiers, in the linguistic terms preferred by Lacan; it is not something fixed and definite. Lacan (1973) is insistent that this does not result in arbitrary interpretations, but that interpretation 'has the effect of bringing out irreducible, *non-sensical* – composed of non-meanings – signifying elements' (p.250), with the aim ('what is essential') being that the subject should 'see, beyond this signification, to what signifier – to what irreducible, traumatic, non-meaning – he is as a subject, subjected' (ibid., p.251). Although this is a confusing and difficult idea, implying that there might indeed be a 'meta-meaning' (the 'irreducible' one) lurking 'beyond' the text, the literary attraction of Lacanian psychoanalysis is that it is not devoted to the exercise of interpretation, as are most other psychoanalytic schools, nor to a meaningful intersubjective encounter. Rather, it holds what is in some ways a more modest aim, that of surprising the patient – and, if possible, the analyst – with the appearance of unexpected links or associations that open out new signifying chains, but which do not in themselves present a particular truth or final knowledge. Nobus and Quinn (2005) lay down their version of this right at the beginning of their book on *Knowing Nothing, Staying Stupid*:

> Rather than reintegrating the analysand's stupidities within a consistent body of knowledge, or replacing them with a more adequate, adapted and competent knowledge whose market value is recognised by the authoritative discursive ideologies, the analyst fully exposes the formations of the unconscious as headless pieces of knowledge, disruptive eruptions of meaninglessness against the comfortable backdrop of established reason. (p.4)

The notion that literature might engage in an encounter with psychoanalysis that offers such 'surprises' to each is quite close to the position adopted by some post-Lacanian literary critics. The most influential example here is Shoshana Felman, whose contribution to her own edited collection *Literature and Psychoanalysis* (1982b) is a study of Henry James' story *The Turn of the Screw* prefaced by a penetrating account of what an open dialogue between psychoanalysis and literature might do. Felman's search is for a way in which psychoanalysis and literature can genuinely invest in each other as equals – not one mastering the other, either as psychoanalysis speaking the truth of literature or literature exposing the narrative assumptions of psychoanalysis, even though both disciplines do have something to say to the other from these 'expert' positions. For Felman, the important thing is to expose the fictional nature of psychoanalytic authority (hence exposing the unconscious underside of psychoanalysis) and the dubious authority to

be claimed by fiction (hence exposing the unconscious traces within literature itself). Each is deeply entwined in the other, and through this intense face-off, something unexpected can be called on that keeps open the possibility of surprise, refuting the claims of either literary studies or psychoanalysis to have an answer to the question of meaning. Felman (1982b) writes:

> In view of this shift of emphasis, the traditional method of *application* of psychoanalysis to literature would here be in principle ruled out. The notion of *application* would be replaced by the radically different notion of *implication*: bringing analytical questions to bear upon literary questions, *involving* psychoanalysis in the scene of literary analysis, the interpreter's role would here be, not to *apply* to the text an acquired science, a preconceived knowledge, but to act as a go-between, to *generate implications* between literature and psychoanalysis – to explore, bring to light and articulate the various (indirect) ways in which the two domains do indeed *implicate each other*, each one finding itself enlightened, informed, but also affected, displaced by the other. (pp.8–9)

As already noted, literature is deeply embedded in the origins and structure of psychoanalysis, and the congruence between literary and psychoanalytic thinking was one source of 'evidence' used by Freud to support his developing ideas. Equally, as shown in Brooks' (1982) examination of how psychoanalysis throws light on the appeal of, and desire for, narrative, it is almost impossible to undertake literary studies in the post-Freudian world, without also engaging with psychoanalysis, for better or worse. What Felman pushes for in this quotation is recognition of this mutual implication and the teasing out of its effects – what each does to the other, how the strategies of reading involved in textual and clinical work draw on one another and produce new ideas. And it is this question of *reading* that is perhaps central. This concerns not just the masterful analyst reading the patient's discourse for its unconscious significance or the sophisticated literary critic reading the text for its nuances and resonances, but the awareness present in both disciplines that reading is a process of involvement that draws the reader in. Reading is a productive process that changes the reader/analyst as much as it explores any text. Ellmann (1994) comments:

> For Lacan, this complicity between the subject reading and the object read represents the crux of Freud's discoveries ... In other words, it is impossible to understand analysands or literary texts without participating in their dreams or their delusions. The critic necessarily conspires in the text's imaginings; the act of reading is a process of mutual seduction, whereby the reader and the read arouse each other's fantasies, expose each other's

dreams. It is when we think we penetrate the text's disguises that we are usually most deluded and most ignorant, for what we see is nothing but our unknown selves. (p.10)

The question structuring Felman's (1982b) account of *The Turn of the Screw* is '*What* is Freudian in a Freudian reading, and in what way can it be defined and measured?' (p.103). She rapidly deals with the 'classic' psychoanalytic reading of this text, that of Edmund Wilson (1934), arguing that its rendering of James' ghost story as a product of the governess' fevered sexual imagination is a way of doing Freud that takes sexuality as the pre-given answer to all questions, and then unfailingly finds it in the text. The problem here is not only the importation of a preconceived psychological motivation from the clinical arena, where it might be established as part of the specific, hidden story of an individual, to the fictional one in which this is impossible. It is also that this is what Felman, echoing James himself, calls a 'vulgar' reading of the text, one that 'blocks and interrupts the endless process of metaphorical substitution':

> The vulgar, therefore, is anything which misses, or falls short of, the dimension of the symbolic, anything which rules out, or excludes, meaning as a loss and as a flight – anything which strives, in other words, to eliminate from language its inherent silence, anything which misses the specific way in which a text *actively* 'won't tell'. (p.107)

The problem with 'vulgar' Freudian readings is precisely their *lack* of ambiguity, their capacity to tie the text up too neatly, so nothing new can occur. Felman opposes this through a reading very different from that offered by Wilson, even though she also takes sexuality as the core psychoanalytic concern. In her case, sexuality is understood as that which always problematises meaning, as that which will not let things alone. Sexuality, in the general Lacanian view, always fails, because it can never be fully satisfied except in the 'imaginary'. Felman explains: 'If, far from implying the simplicity of a self-present literal meaning, sexuality points rather to a multiplicity of conflicting forces, to the complexity of its own divisiveness and contradiction, its meaning can by no means be univocal or unified, but must necessarily be *ambiguous*' (p.112; original emphasis). This produces an opposite mode of reading to the one which makes sexuality the source of a text's 'real' meaning. Instead, sexuality (and, one might add, the whole notion of an unconscious) constantly undermines any chance of fixing a single meaning to any text, whether that of a patient or an author, because it signifies something that always fails, a gap that can never be fully overcome,

'that through which meaning in the text *does not come off*, that which in the text, and through which the text, *fails to mean*, that which can engender but a *conflict of interpretations*' (p.112; original emphasis). A Freudian reading is consequently not one that gives Freudian 'answers', but rather one that opens out a text for questioning. It recognises that every text has areas of ambiguity and silence that can only produce more questioning; it demands a reading strategy, therefore, that is shuttered off from interpretive certainty. When psychoanalysis misses this, when readings are presented that 'master' the text, what is at work is not the creative use of Freudian interpretive tactics, but rather a mode of repression in which the 'desire' of the text – its potential for subversion, or for the proliferation of meanings that makes literature rich – is denied. Felman addresses this as precisely a repression of the unconscious:

> To *master*, then (to become the Master) is, here as elsewhere, to *refuse to read* the letters; here as elsewhere, to 'see it all' is in effect to 'shut one's eyes as tight as possible to the truth'; once more, 'to see it all' is in reality to *exclude*; and to exclude, specifically, the unconscious. (pp.193–4)

Samuel Beckett's (1984) famous line comes to mind: 'Ever tried. Ever failed. No matter. Try again. Fail again. Fail better.'

One can see a further example of the potential fertility of an 'open' psychoanalytic engagement with literature in Barbara Johnson's (1996) exploration of the triangular encounter between Poe, Lacan and Derrida over the *Purloined Letter*. Poe's tale is told by a narrator who is foil to the investigator/analyst Dupin and who extracts from him his philosophical musings and his account of how he outwitted the Minister who had stolen a potentially compromising letter from the Queen. The police fail to find the stolen letter because their ludicrously exact investigation is couched at the wrong level: they can only act according to their own beliefs about how a thief might behave. Dupin, on the other hand, imagines himself inside the mind of the Minister, identifies with him, and thus comprehends what his course of action is likely to have been. He understands that the thief's actions will have been determined not by reason alone, but by something more imaginative and compelling – something constituting *enjoyment* in the sense of an excessive and unnecessary involvement – which Dupin suggests is made possible by the Minister being not just a mathematician, but also a poet. Dupin himself also writes verse, giving him a capacity to transcend the simple logic of those who just follow the rules and to enter into the mind of the other, to understand his rational irrationalities, eventually to trick him and recover the lost object.

One of the key components of Poe's tale as recognised by Lacan is that the *content* of the letter, its exact conventional 'meaning', is never revealed. Instead, it is the *lack* of meaning that is suggestive, and the way that the letter acts in a chain of signifiers that produces the story's effect. For Lacan, the letter represents the 'pure state' of the symbol, the 'original, radical subject'. 'One can say that, when the characters get a hold of this letter, something gets a hold of them and carries them along and this something clearly has dominion over their individual idiosyncrasies' (Lacan, 1954–55, p.196). This lack is itself interpretable as a mode of castration; lack becomes the core of the story, as the empty signifier is passed around, positioning the subjects as it moves. It is the position of the letter that is crucial – who has it and to what use it might be put. For Derrida (1975), however, there is a problem with Lacan's reading of the story in terms of castration: rather than appreciating the continual slipperiness of language and text, so that meanings are only ever provisional and partial, Derrida sees Lacan as having alighted on castration as the 'truth' of the tale. Thus, although the Lacanian reading appears to promote the abstract movement of symbols as the mode of operation of textuality, in the certainty and mastery with which this happens a 'truth' of the text – that of castration – is established, which in a sense makes lack 'full', gives it a positive meaning from which all else follows. 'The displacement of the signifier is analysed as a signified, as the recounted object in a short story' (Derrida, 1975, p.48). Derrida's case here is that in operating within a certain psychoanalytic frame, Lacan finds in the text what already exists in the theory, which positions castration and lack as the core of meaning. Lacan, that is, does not analyse the analytic frame itself, does not, for example, see himself in the analytic process – any more than does the Minister in the story. He takes what he knows as a psychoanalyst to be the baseline for his rendering of the truth. Once again, it seems, psychoanalysis finds itself in what it reads, is unable to enter into a truly open dialogue with its texts.

Johnson (1996), however, problematises this once more. She queries the looseness with which Derrida reads *Lacan's* text, for example his readiness to find castration at the heart of the account, when it is not actually mentioned by Lacan (though it is hard not to see its implicit functioning, as described above). For Johnson, Derrida is not actually engaged in the kind of close reading here for which he was famous; rather, it is something about the authority or 'effect' of Lacan with which he is taking issue:

> Derrida's consistent forcing of Lacan's statements into systems and patterns from which they are actually trying to escape must correspond to some

strategic necessity different from the attentiveness to the letter that charac-
terizes Derrida's way of reading Poe. And in fact, the more one works with
Derrida's analysis, the more convinced one becomes that although the
critique of what Derrida calls psychoanalysis is entirely justified, it does not
quite apply to what Lacan's text is actually saying. What Derrida is in fact
arguing against is therefore not Lacan's text but Lacan's power, or rather,
'Lacan' as the apparent cause of certain effects of power in French discourse
today. Whatever Lacan's text may say, it functions, according to Derrida, as
if it says what he says it says. The statement [by Lacan in the Seminar] that
a letter always reaches its destination may be totally undecipherable, but its
assertive force is taken all the more seriously as a sign that Lacan himself has
everything all figured out. (p.91)

There are many complexities in Johnson's (and of course Derrida's and
Lacan's) accounts of the reading of the Poe story, but a couple of issues
stand out here as summations of this chapter's argument. First,
Derrida's critique of psychoanalysis and indeed of all interpretive
approaches that do not interrogate their own interpretive frames as they
work, points firmly both to a major difficulty with 'psychoanalysis and
literature' and to a way through it. The difficulty is that without self-
interrogation or reflection any interpretive method becomes an expert
one, which can do no more than display its mastery by revealing
precisely but solely what its concepts make it possible to reveal. Whilst
clever puzzle-solving might well result, surprise does not; and in the
course of this a kind of mis-recognition of the otherness of the text (for
instance, its specifically literary qualities) occurs. The potential way
through this is to reveal the workings of the frame itself. One contribution made by the *Purloined Letter* debate is that it does this by showing
how on top of each interpretation of the story, another one can be made
– Lacan can be read by Derrida, whose reading has its own lacunae and
polemical cause. The second point builds on this: as each reading
displaces the apparent truth of the previous one, raising doubts and
elaborating associations, so the richness of both literature and psychoanalysis can increase. Meanings proliferate, not exactly randomly, but
provocatively, shading each other as different features of the cultural
environment come into play. Feminism, for example, has radically
changed the terms of the 'Dora' debate; it is doubtful whether many
people read *The Purloined Letter* at all now except as a way of reading
Lacan. This proliferation of meanings allows the 'unconscious' traces
that can be found in any kind of text to bubble up for acknowledgement
and enjoyment, for instance in the way in which repetition occurs –
including, perhaps especially, repetition of a fantasy. Psychoanalysis
contributes to this not as an exercise in mastery, but as a particularly
well-attuned literary endeavour itself. When its questions are not

pitched as a way of producing unassailable truth, they can be the kinds of intervention that make new links, or enrich the associative power of what one might find on the page. Conversely, literature challenges psychoanalysis to examine its own tropes and narrative assumptions, its own cultural indices and modes of expression, and in doing so it can at times produce an enriched psychoanalysis, more able to listen analytically to what it might itself be saying.

Conclusion

This rendering of the 'implication' of psychoanalysis in literature, as Felman (1982a) has it, has its own implications for the 'application' of psychoanalysis in the social as well as the literary sphere. As noted in the previous chapter, Freud's tendency was to use psychoanalysis to 'explain' social phenomena, not just observing how unconscious factors feature in the behaviour of social groups, but also theorising them either as if the social itself has 'an unconscious', or simply in terms of the unconscious impulses of the individuals that make up any society. Ironically, rather than construct psychoanalysis as an effective new master discipline, which is the aim of such an application, this *reduces* its significance to one of many competing social psychological theories, with some useful and provocative concepts but limited theoretical and empirical reach. This is also the situation when psychoanalysis is applied in a heavy-handed way to literature. However, as this chapter has shown, the alternative trend amongst cultural critics to counterpose psychoanalysis and literature more equally grants new opportunities for an open engagement that provokes each discipline and subverts their assumptive worlds. Much of this can be drawn together under the general heading of enhancing 'reflexivity', as each discipline reflects on itself in the light of the impact of the other. So, literature is opened up by psychoanalytic querying of the way linguistic and affective traces appear and repeat; and questions such as why narrative should be such a 'draw' are exposed to psychological as well as literary examination. Conversely, psychoanalysis becomes situated as a specific cultural project which is built on literary as well as scientific tropes, having its own rhetorical investments in certain modes of intellectual mastery. The effect of this is, at best, to catalyse practices of renewal in which disciplinary assumptions become unsettled and new thoughts generated, producing new insights – however fragmentary these might be.

Generalising this 'method' outside that of literature, one might now ask whether such an openness of encounter, such an 'inmixing of subjects' (Lacan, 1954–55, p.193), or 'implication' of one with another,

provides a basis for a creative involvement of psychoanalysis with those disciplines that try actively to theorise the social world. There are of course highly significant differences between social theory and literature, for example in relation to evidence, the space given to imagination, and the way language is used. Literary studies often seek to 'expand' readings of texts, exploring associations and creating multiple narratives in order to suggest new meanings, an approach congruent with the kind of psychoanalytic strategies advocated here. Social theory, and particularly social scientific research, tends by contrast to try to 'compress' meanings, seeking out carefully grounded, minimal, clear and specific explanations. This is more compatible with ways of approaching knowledge that value linear, causal accounts and hence are susceptible to 'expert' claims. On the other hand, one legacy of the post-structuralist turn in the social sciences and humanities is to broaden the notion of 'text' away from simply literary products to include social actions and cultural and political materials – anything, that is, that can be treated as a symbolic form. This has allowed interpretive ('hermeneutic') strategies to be adopted throughout the social sciences, resulting in a growth in the use of qualitative research methods. Many of these, such as ethnography, are taken from anthropology, but others draw on clinical interviewing techniques derived indirectly from psychoanalysis (e.g. Hollway and Jefferson, 2000; Frosh and Saville Young, 2008). The textual move has also allowed social theory more generally to benefit from the 'expansive' reading strategies previously associated with literature. One consequence of this is to make the debates outlined here – debates about how to hold meaning open rather than close it down – relevant throughout the field of social research.

The rest of this book takes up this argument through a series of examples from, or interventions in, the social field. These examples concern spaces of encounter between psychoanalysis and social research: social psychology, ethics, political philosophy and psychosocial studies. In each instance, the focus is on how psychoanalysis has and can be used not as a 'master narrative' to trump the claims of the 'host' discipline, but rather as a provocative interlocutor that can shake things up, and also be stirred itself.

Chapter 4

Psychoanalysis as Social Psychology: The Case of Identity

The interventions of psychoanalysis in social theory and research described in the next three chapters are characterised by a kind of open interdisciplinarity in which the influences are two-way. In each case, what is being presented is an area of debate in which an existing discipline (social psychology, social theory and political theory) is augmented by psychoanalysis, but also offers a reciprocal challenge *to* psychoanalysis. This challenge is not only to provide grounds for its claims, though this is in each case part of what happens. It also addresses the need for psychoanalysis to reflect on its own theoretical assumptions and to combat its 'regressive' tendencies, in the sense of those that pull thinking back into a conformist, moralising mode. The fourth chapter in this sequence, on psychosocial studies, is slightly different in that the area concerned is not yet a well-established discipline, but is seeking to establish its vocabulary, methodology and focus and is looking to psychoanalysis as an aid in doing so. However, the issues are similar: how psychoanalysis can contribute to the emergence of psychosocial studies in ways which advance rather than close down its innovations, and which also promote the critical capacity of psychoanalysis itself.

In this chapter, the focus is on an area of social psychological research that has spread across the social sciences to be a rather amorphous and all-embracing concern, that of identity. As will become apparent, this is a key notion for much social theory and research, and it recurs in the topics to be presented in the rest of this book. Identity is obviously not a new topic of research, but interest in it has grown remarkably since the late 1990s. Margaret Wetherell (2010), who led a major British research initiative into 'social identities', comments that it has become 'one of the most widely used terms in the social sciences and humanities, appearing in the titles of many thousands, if not hundreds of thousands, of books and articles. Very few concepts can have been as generative' (p.3). The source of this interest is perhaps a convergence of social studies on the location of the human subject in culture. This can be partly understood as one of the legacies of poststructuralism and also of postmodernism, and includes a move within social and political theory towards identity studies as a development of a previous concern

with *ideology*. In brief, this means that whereas earlier generations of critical theorists were impressed by the way certain social beliefs came to govern the consciousness of subjects, becoming 'internalised' by them in a manner that always tended to be seen as *passive* (Frosh, 1999, ch. 6), the more recent trajectory has been to examine how each subject is actively constructed in and through culture, and comes to locate her or himself in certain specific identity positions. These identity positions may be quite fluid and even mutually contradictory, but they have the power to draw subjects into social locations or 'positions' in which they become heavily invested.

One of the interesting points about this 'identity turn' in the social sciences is that it brings together a range of sociological, political and psychological considerations and therefore demands a high level of interdisciplinarity. Is identity a primarily psychological phenomenon, referencing the feelings and actively chosen self-definitions of individuals? Is it more sociological, relating to the patterns of group membership and divisions between 'insiders and 'outsiders' that operate in a society? Does it refer to the 'internal' state of subjects or to their observable social positions? It seems obvious that these dichotomising questions simply reveal the complexity of identity issues and the need for approaches that stretch across the conventional distinction between psychological and social, between 'inside' and 'out'. It is perhaps equally obvious that this involves considerations of *affect*, exploring the emotional investment subjects might have in particular identities, and *power*, allowing one to discuss how people accept or resist identity ascriptions placed on them through their social positions. These multiple concerns suggest the likely insufficiency of any one disciplinary approach to identity. They also carve out a specific invitation to psychoanalysis, as a conceptual system that might be particularly well honed to address the kinds of 'intersections' that identity studies demand.

Identity politics

Wetherell (2010) tracks the development of identity studies, noting especially that there has been a historical bifurcation between those that approach identity as referring to a 'subjective individual achievement' (p.3) and those that examine it as a matter of group membership, translating it 'into investigations of social divisions and social solidarities and the practices of marginalization, exclusion, inclusion, resistance, segregation, denigration, etc., linked to belonging' (p.4). In the former case, that of 'personal identity', the focus is on how people construct their sense of themselves, the basis being an assumption of the normativeness

and stability of individuality as a developmental achievement. A central task of life is to find an identity within which one can live, which organises one's experiences and allows one to become a 'person'. Identity is *agentic* when thought of this way: it is centred on the human subject as an individual and enables that subject to integrate experience in what Wetherell terms a 'personal project'. It is empowering in its presence and disturbing in its absence, and whilst being an achievement rather than a given, is nevertheless a normative psychological state. This means that the failure to achieve a satisfactory identity is a sign – and maybe a cause – of psychological disturbance. Put this way, it is relatively easy to see how the 'invention' of identity as a social issue corresponds with the emergence of individualism within modernity; that is, it is intimately linked with the idea of separate selves as the core unit of psychosocial analysis. If, for example, one lives in a society in which people are defined totally in terms of their social position (for example, as serfs or slaves), their identity does not have to be sought psychologically – it is given as an aspect of the roles made available by society. If, on the other hand, subjects are seen as individual persons, possessing the capacity for self-actualisation and the potential to change their social position as a consequence of their own actions, then identity is something *achieved*, and it makes sense to ask about the 'fit' between psychological and social identity.

This connects with the second approach to identity, strongly advanced in social psychology and sociology, which sees it as 'social belonging'. Here, group membership is taken to define personhood, and the question of identity becomes that of what determines the group one belongs to, and then of what are the characteristics of that group. On the whole, the effect of adopting this particular lens is to remove agency from the subject and instead grant it to the social group: it is as a consequence of one's class, 'race' or gender position, for example, that one has certain identity attributes. Personal identity then becomes a more or less determined, perhaps even passive, outcome of the social order. A racist society, for example, produces differentiated ethnic divisions and contracts identity positions accordingly; similarly, in a sexually differentiated society gender identity is given from the outside as a condition of the dominant social assumptions about masculinity and femininity. Identity thus becomes a primarily social concept that is to be understood sociologically and politically, rather than as the life project of individuals. Since the 1960s, the more deterministic aspects of this version of identity have been contested by social movements which have reclaimed derogated social identities and given them positive content. This has involved a turn to 'identity politics' in which, for example, the feminist, gay and lesbian and anti-racist movements have enabled their

members to adopt newly assertive public positions, buoyed up by social solidarities and coherent political critiques of traditional social norms. This reveals one way in which the 'social belonging' version of identity might be progressive, even though one tends to think of having one's identity fixed by an outside force as somehow constraining and politically reactionary. The idea that it is in social solidarities rather than personal development that people's hopes for freedom might lie is a crucial legacy of this understanding of identity, which one would be loath to abandon.

The notion of *fixed* identities, whether given as personal projects or group membership, has become unsustainable under the weight of evidence that people not only shift their identities over time, but also adopt different identities in different settings. People are heavily influenced in their identity formations by the social situations they are in, yet they can also struggle against these and develop ideas of what might be 'true' for them that are at odds with their social positions. Alongside this, there is equally compelling evidence that identities are often multiple and fragmentary (Phoenix and Rattansi, 2005), plus a corresponding awareness that even apparently fixed social categories breed divergent and sometimes contradictory identities ('masculinity', for example, is much more than one thing, as is 'whiteness'). 'Intersectionality' (Brah, 1996) has become the default position in identity studies; it emphasises the way different identity positions have to be read in conjunction with one another. For example, 'masculinity' is a concept that is heavily racialised, which means that it intersects with categories such as 'blackness' and 'whiteness' and cannot be understood fully without reference to them (Frosh, Phoenix and Pattman, 2002). The idea that identities might be fluid rather than fully achieved is also routine even amongst those who still regard identity as an important psychosocial category and a developmental as well as social achievement. Identity is thus seen more as a *process* than a state. One consequence of this is that *identification*, referring to the active way in which certain identity positions are adopted or invested in, becomes the key social psychological – and in some places sociological (Hall, 1996) – concern.

It is not difficult to argue that psychoanalysis should be a major disciplinary site through which these alternative notions of identities can be explored. The psychoanalytic concept of a dynamic unconscious gives leverage on a number of central issues in the study of identities. These include the tension between an understanding of identity as something fixed (developmental histories producing stable ways of being that are resistant to change) and of identities as fluid and multiple (unconscious ideas are variable, contradictory and partial). Both these positions are

visible in the psychoanalytic literature itself. For instance, there is a strong though now dated tradition of understanding identity as a process of social adaptation. This sees it as a developmental requirement that unconscious wishes should be brought into line with cultural expectations and possibilities under the guise of 'ego identity' – perhaps understandable as the capacity to know who one is in the context in which one finds oneself. More recently, the vision of a general, overarching personal identity has been displaced by awareness of specific types of identity, particularly sexual, gender, ethnic and racial identities. Nevertheless, the sense of coming to know the 'reality' of oneself in these more circumscribed situations still prevails. Whilst this approach addresses some important phenomenological questions, for example about why people are so often strongly invested in what appear to be self-limiting identity positions, it is arguable that it relies on ideas about character and selfhood that are no longer sustainable in identity studies. On the other hand, there are alternative modes of psychoanalysis that question the stability of identities, preferring to track them as forms of 'masquerade', or as fragile and momentary assemblages of contradictory forces. Lacanian psychoanalysis is particularly cogent here, but relational psychoanalysis offers its own routes to conceptualise how human subjects become invested in particular identities, for example through allegiances or emotional connections with specific groups or social fractions. Its key postulate is perhaps that whilst the original source of identity is based on a relation to body parts, identification with parents and others subsequently leads to more complex and elaborate experiences of identity in a variety of contexts. Identities are constructed through such processes of identification and recognition, and emotional investment by subjects in these processes gives identities their significance, explaining why they can be experienced as constituting psychosocial reality. Because both the constructive processes (such as identification) and the investment are largely or wholly unconscious, identities are lived as if they were 'given' rather than chosen. That is, they are often felt to be fundamental to the subject, as if they have been received whole and constitute the subject's essence. The implication of this is that identities may be lived as real, but are in fact constituted in the flux of contradictory impulses, putting psychoanalysis in line with the generally deconstructive tendency in modern thought.

In summary, if any of the different psychoanalytic approaches are to contribute to identity studies, they have to take account of a contemporary context of fluidity. This is produced by the awareness that the construction of the modern 'self' is a fragile and contingent process, and that the normative assumption that a stable identity is an expectable developmental achievement is hard to sustain. To be compelling, iden-

tity theories need not only to show how it is that subjects become located in particular social positions, nor solely how certain ways of being and representing the self become invested in as patterns of belonging and exclusion, though both these things might be necessary. Identity theories also need to convey the shifts that occur as subjects encounter one another and the social formation, including in this the broader context of globalisation in which there is greater awareness than ever before of the multiplicity of identities available to people across the world. That is, they need to engage with the blending of 'identity' with 'subjectivity', understood along with Wetherell (2008) not as opposed categories in which the former refers to group membership and the latter to the 'substantive acting, thinking and feeling being' (Venn, 2006, p.79), but as a site for psycho-discursive practices in which both these things are constantly being negotiated. This brings together questions of agency and ethics as well as of social power, making identity studies an important area for theoretical contestation. The question here is whether psychoanalysis can contribute productively to this contestation, or whether it simply reinforces old 'inside–outside' bipolarities. In what follows, this question will be addressed partly historically, through an account of classical psychoanalytic ideas on identity, and partly through examining how psychoanalytic concepts have infiltrated non-analytic theory.

Classical psychoanalytic formulations of identity

Identity as a term is used only once by Freud in his writings, in a way described by some commentators as 'incidental ... with a psychosocial connotation' (Grinberg and Grinberg, 1974, p.499). In fact, this reference is a very interesting personal one. It is found in a letter by Freud written on the occasion of his seventieth birthday in response to greetings from the Vienna Bnai Brith, the Jewish organisation with which he was deeply involved in the late 1890s, at the time when he was formulating the new psychoanalytic science (Frosh, 2005). Reflecting on the reasons that drew him to the Bnai Brith, Freud (1926/1961) comments on how he had neither religious nor nationalistic (i.e. Zionist) beliefs, but nevertheless, 'there remained enough to make the attraction of Judaism and the Jews irresistible, many dark emotional powers all the stronger the less they could be expressed in words, as well as the clear consciousness of an inner identity, the familiarity of the same psychological structure' (p.368).

Erik Erikson, whose work on identity is the foundation stone for most psychoanalytic – and many other – accounts of the topic, reads

this quotation as evidence that identity is necessarily tied up with the social environment. 'It is the identity of something in the individual's core with an essential aspect of a group's inner coherence which is under consideration here', he writes (Erikson, 1956, p.57). Moreover, 'The term identity expresses such a mutual relation in that it connotes both a persistent sameness with oneself (self-sameness) and a persistent sharing of some kind of essential character with others' (ibid.). Certainly, Freud's reference to 'the familiarity of the same psychological structure' that linked him with his Jewish peers supports the idea that he is using identity in this psychosocial sense. However, it should be noted that whilst 'the clear consciousness of an inner identity' is offered by Freud as one element making 'the attraction of Judaism and the Jews irresistible', it is not the one that exercises his *psychoanalytic* interest; that place is given over to the 'many dark emotional powers' to which he refers, but of which he can give no straightforward explanation. The attraction of a shared 'psychological structure' is not mysterious; it is straightforwardly observable and comes largely under the heading of what Freud calls in the same place 'ethical' demands ('I was always an unbeliever, have been brought up without religion, but not without respect for the so-called "ethical" demands of human civilisation.'). The other thing, however, the thing that he calls 'dark', is described elsewhere as the 'essence' of his link with the Jewish people and its culture, and yet as currently inaccessible to science (Freud, 1913a/1930, p.xv). It requires more than simple reflection, more even than the psychoanalytic tools then available, to account for it. This announces a debate that has surrounded the question of identity itself, and Erikson's reading of it in particular: is it really a psychoanalytic concept, or a psychosocial one that goes no further than describing predominantly conscious material? That is, what is it that psychoanalysis adds here to what might be known from more straightforward accounts?

According to Grinberg and Grinberg (1974), the term 'identity' was introduced formally into psychoanalytic literature by Victor Tausk in his classic paper, *On the Origin of the 'Influencing Machine'* (1933), which dealt with the disintegration of selfhood and identity and the manifestation of that identity-loss in paranoia. In the passage in which the term appears (p.543), Tausk discusses early infantile development and specifically differentiates between a stage of identity that is congenital, designated as 'the innate narcissistic one', and a later stage that is 'actively established', which seems to mean that it arises as a consequence of interchanges between the infant and the mother. Tausk's assumption is that the individual 'comes into the world as an organic unity in which libido and ego are not yet separated, and all available libido is related to that organic unity, which does not deserve the name

"ego" (i.e., a psychical self-protective organization) any more than does the cell' (p.542). That is, the 'identification' which is the source of narcissistic identity is congenital and relates to oneness with the infant's body. Tausk goes on, discussing innate narcissism:

> In this situation the libido is directed outward, first cathects the subject's own body by the indirect way of projection, and returns by way of self-discovery to the ego. In the meantime, the ego has undergone a decided alteration under the influence of these first psychic stirrings, which one may call experience, and is now again cathected by libido. Let us call this stage, acquired narcissism. (p.543)

The difference between the two types of identity is therefore that one originates with the body and the other with 'experience', but in both cases the notion of 'identity' is being called on to mean narcissistic unity, a mode of psychological functioning *defined* as 'absolute self-satisfaction, no outer world, no objects'. Interestingly, although this formulation of narcissism bears only very indirectly on identity as understood in the broader psychological and sociological literature, it is a reminder of the way in which identity signifies wholeness and singularity, a mode of self-sufficiency that tends to exclude the ongoing functioning of the social world.

It is in the work of Erikson, however, that the most influential psychoanalytic account of identity can be found. Erikson understood identity to be concerned with ego functioning and to connote something like 'social character', the relatively stable sense of oneself in a culture. This approach was consistent with the ego-psychological dominance of the American psychoanalysis of his time. For Erikson, ego analysis was laced with a commitment to a culturally or socially aware psychoanalysis, one that viewed the great task of life as bringing the individual into a constructive relationship with society. However, as was the case within the broader ego-psychological movement, the social aspects of Eriksonian theory seemed to lose their potentially critical bite and drift towards a vision of the task of development as *adapting* the individual so as to ease the potential tension with her or his social environment (Frosh, 1999). This adaptation is required particularly at those developmental points involving transitions between one cultural setting (for instance, the family) and another (society), most notably during adolescence. Erikson (1956) describes his use of the term 'identity' as 'to suggest a social function of the ego which results, in adolescence, in a relative psychosocial equilibrium essential to the tasks of young adulthood' (p.104). Identity is here understood as a long-lasting sense of self as continuous, combined with a feeling of belonging in a community. He

comments, 'At one time … it will appear to refer to a conscious *sense of individual identity*; at another to an unconscious striving for a *continuity of personal character*; and, finally, as a maintenance of an inner *solidarity* with a group's ideals and identity' (p.57; original emphasis). One side point is that this formulation shows awareness of the differing kinds of identity discussed in the literature, specifically identity as personal journey and as social categorisation, with the link between them given by a form of emotional investment, here termed 'solidarity'.

Identity is, crucially and centrally, a developmental achievement of the ego, and one that is necessary for the well-being of each subject. 'I have been using the term *ego identity*', writes Erikson (1956), 'to denote certain comprehensive gains which the individual, at the end of adolescence, must have derived from all of his pre-adult experiences in order to be ready for the tasks of adulthood' (p.56). For Erikson, in language that resonates strongly with Winnicott's roughly contemporaneous writings, the roots of identity 'go back all the way to the first self-recognition: in the baby's earliest exchange of smiles there is something of a *self-realization coupled with a mutual recognition*' (p.69). This experience of having one's reality reflected back to one produces 'tentative crystallizations' that make the child feel known to the other and hence to the self. These crystallisations are disrupted from time to time by the actual 'discontinuities of psychosocial development', but a reasonably reliable family and a supportive community will lead to more integrated development to the degree to which they permit the child 'to orient himself toward a complete *"life plan"* with a hierarchical order of roles as represented by individuals of different age grades' (p.70). 'From a genetic point of view,' states Erikson, 'the process of identity formation emerges as an *evolving configuration* – a configuration which is gradually established by successive ego syntheses and resyntheses throughout childhood; it is a configuration gradually integrating *constitutional givens, idiosyncratic libidinal needs, favored capacities, significant identifications, effective defences, successful sublimations, and consistent roles*' (p.71). It has conscious, preconscious and unconscious components, is never fully finalised (albeit largely focused on the period up to the end of adolescence, with its characteristic 'identity crisis'), but is part of a lifelong developmental unfolding, and is a mixture of dynamic and psychosocial components.

In some ways, Erikson's account of identity formation, and in particular his very detailed description of the 'tasks' of adolescence, have been more influential in social psychology (particularly through their partial parroting in numerous undergraduate textbooks) than in psychoanalysis itself. This may be because of its interactionist flavour, with both sides of what that means. It is relational and links with much contem-

porary theory (the language of 'recognition' is striking here), but also has problematic psychoanalytic, as opposed to social-psychological, standing. Early on, Edith Jacobson (1964) labelled Erikson's work as not truly psychoanalytic, a description that has often been applied to potentially productive concepts that might disturb psychoanalytic orthodoxies. In Erikson's case, the disturbance may have come from the emphasis he placed on the surrounding social world, although looked at through the lens of critical social theory this does not seem particularly subversive – the community is imagined as essentially benevolent, able to lend its support to the process of identity formation, allowing the individual's life plans to develop and integration to occur. Wallerstein (1998), in a paper that reconsiders Erikson's legacy, suggests that his work is ever more relevant, but that this has been obscured by the language of the new theories of the 'self', which has largely replaced the ego psychological vocabulary of Erikson's time. That is, the ego psychologists rejected him because his concepts were too social, and the self psychologists and relational psychoanalysts have neglected him because they regarded him as too focused on ego structures. Wallerstein comments: 'though the concept of identity, so central to Erikson's conceptualizations over a lifetime, has come in the past two decades to the forefront of psychoanalytic attention, it has done so under the rubric of the self, thereby obscuring the obvious relation of Erikson's earlier theorizing to these new emphases' (p.239). Whilst the ego identity theory of Erikson became peripheral to psychoanalysis, many of the concepts deployed in contemporary intersubjectivist and self theory have connections with it. In particular, the transactional nature of Erikson's approach, in which individual and social components of development support one another, can be traced in the sometimes anodyne psychosocial elements of a fair amount of later work.

Bodies, objects and identifications

In their post-Eriksonian account, Grinberg and Grinberg (1974) emphasise the significance of the integrative function of the sense of identity, the way it registers 'the idea of a self which bears essentially upon the continuity and likeness of unconscious fantasies referring to bodily sensations and emotions experienced by the ego' (p.500) and hence has 'spatial, temporal and social' aspects. These relate to 'self- non-self differentiation', continuity of self-representations over time, and 'the relationship between aspects of the self and aspects of objects by means of the mechanisms of identification' (p.502). This formulation captures a good proportion of the shared ideas of psychoanalysts on this topic.

Identity is a developmental notion and is formed in response to internal and external forces. It has a bodily source that grounds it in a sense of unity or unification. Grinberg and Grinberg claim that

> The idea of the body is essential to the consolidation of the individual's iden-
> tity ... When Freud pointed out that the 'ego is first and foremost a bodily
> ego, it is not merely a surface but is itself a projection of a surface' (1923),
> he was underlining one of the most important factors that form the basis of
> identity. (p.502)

Revealingly, this claim has the effect of blurring the distinction between identity, self and ego, because as the quotation from Freud reveals, it is not *identity* that is classically thought of in this way, but the *ego itself*. It is the ego that is built up out of perceptions of the body and its functions, from relationships with others that are mediated through the skin and the mouth (Greenacre, 1958), or from the kind of introjective processes based on bodily functions that are so beloved of the Kleinians, a point which will be developed below. Given that the ego is both the site of consciousness and imbued with unconscious features (the defence mechanisms are found within it), and that identity is usually thought of as a 'sense' of being and belonging, this conflation of the two concepts begs a large number of questions. In particular, identity seems to be compressed into 'ego-identity', in the Eriksonian tradition, with attendant assumptions of integration of the ego and its absorption into notions of the 'self'. It seems to suggest a normal outcome for identity formation as fully at one with the subject's self-conceptualisation, understood as reflected in an ego that is not subject to splits or discontinuities in its self-perception. This sets it at odds with many contemporary formulations of the fragmentary and contingent nature of identity as a set of not necessarily reflected-upon lived experiences. Within psychoanalysis, too, the assumption of ego-integrity is contentious. Lacanians, for instance, famously criticise it as a normalising assumption mistaking apparent bodily unity for psychic integrity; for them, recognition of the split nature of the subject is absolutely central to psychoanalytic thought (Frosh, 1999).

Co-option of the notion of identity into that of the ego opens up another strand of psychoanalytic developmental thinking, the idea that the ego is formed through the internalisation of lost objects. Faced with reality, the growing child has to give up desired sexual objects, but doing so leaves it feeling depleted and suffused with loss. To deal with this, the ego takes the objects in (in fantasy), internalising them and in the process altering itself. These forsaken desires and lost objects are absorbed into the ego, along with the psychic energy invested in them,

making it possible 'to suppose that the character of the ego is a precipitate of abandoned object cathexes and that it contains the history of
those object choices' (Freud, 1923, p.29). This is one Freudian basis for
object relations theory and also encompasses a social account of identity formation as something founded on the fantasised relationship with
real objects in the interpersonal or intersubjective world. That is, as the
ego itself is formed from the internalisation of objects first experienced
externally – the mother's breast predominant amongst them – so the
formation of identity can be understood to derive from processes of
internalisation and identification. In these, what is 'found' externally
and related to affectively becomes taken in to provide the model,
schema or template for representations of the 'inner world'. Moore and
Fine (1990), for example, draw on the concept of identification in their
statement of what produces sexual identity:

> Identification with both parents gives a bisexual quality to the self-represen-
> tations and schemas, and self-concepts of children of both sexes. Eventually,
> however, an integrated self-organization is created out of the multiple former
> identifications contributing to its character traits. ...The sense of identity
> achieves relative stability when bisexual identifications are resolved and
> adolescence completed. (p.93)

What can be seen in this is both the assumption of a normative heterosexual developmental sequence leading to stable and integrated identity,
and the understanding that this might result from a process whereby
'multiple former identifications' based on relationships with parents, are
in some way worked on to produce this integrated self.

This type of theory reflects a widely shared perception amongst
psychoanalysts that identity, selfhood and even the ego are built up,
defensively or not, on the basis of taking in experiences with external
'objects' and combining them with 'internal' factors such as bodily
experience or primitive phantasies to create conscious and unconscious
representations. This raises the question of how 'external' things –
ideas, representations of self and others – get 'into' the subject's 'inner
world'. The mind is in constant dialogue with the world, putting into it
some of its own contents (through projection, for example) and finding
ways of producing internal representations of what it finds there.
Without such engagement, it would consist only of what was produced
from within; it would be a 'closed system', generating meanings on the
basis perhaps of drives or in response to external stimuli, but unable to
absorb features of the outside world into itself. What psychoanalysis
claims is not only that external stimuli are processed by the perceptual
system, but more radically that they are somehow 'internalised', taken

in to become part of the mind, infecting its structure and its unconscious contents. That is, psychoanalysis models an 'open system' in which external experiences – encounters with 'objects', relationships, ideas – can become part of the person in a deep way. At its most sophisticated, what this produces is a theory in which 'self' and 'other' are always entwined, so that there is no way of considering any mind in isolation from any other. Thought of that way, identification is a *constructive* process, in that the internalised attributes are not destroyed but are employed in the service of some kind of development (hence, it remains distinct from *incorporation* in the psychoanalytic sense, which devours what it takes in), and it is likely that it is one of the most powerful methods whereby personal change occurs.

Freud (1923) seemed to recognise this with his notion of the ego as the 'precipitate of abandoned object cathexes', even though his theory implies that the first 'thoughts' are representations of the drives, coming from within rather than without. As his work progressed, so identification became seen as more central. This is particularly the case in relation to the Oedipus complex, the outcome of which is theorised as a set of powerful identifications laying the foundations of all later personality development and specifically of sexual and gender identity. As the boy, threatened with the castrating power of the father, represses his desire for the mother, so what emerges for him is a saving identification with the father which creates gender security as well as the promise of later recovery. For the girl too, even though the processes described by Freud are more confused and less potent, there is identification with the mother's position in relation to the father that leads to the gendered construction of identity alongside the channelling of desire. In addition, the construction of the superego as a response to castration anxiety is one big internalising process: what is taken in here is the fantasy of the paternal prohibition, with all its associated aggression. Hinshelwood (1991), writing out of the Kleinian tradition in which there is an emphasis on processes of projection and introjection operating from birth, phrases this about as strongly as could ever be:

> The internal objects are phantasies, but at first phantasies are omnipotent, so through these primitive phantasies involved in identification the object is the self ... Phantasy 'is' reality, and phantasy constructs the reality of the internal world on the basis of these primitive forms of introjective and projective identification. (p.320)

Because the infant is always engaged in a process of 'putting out and taking in', of projecting feelings into the external 'object' and then seeking to absorb properties of these objects, the emerging psyche is filled

with representations, however crude, of the object, and it is around these object representations that it becomes structured. Hence, there is no firm division between inside and out, but rather a fluid interchange in which each penetrates the other.

A subtle recent rendering of identifications in the context of gender has been given by Jessica Benjamin (1998). She holds on to the distinction between identification and incorporation, the latter being a kind of cannibalistic taking in of the other until it becomes part of the self and is no longer psychically distinct. She argues that what is precious about identification is that it allows the other to *survive* as a living and appreciated aspect of the self. Identification is consequently built out of an already-existing awareness of the other's existence *as a subject*; that is, it is a loving 'intersubjective' relationship in which aspects of otherness are accepted and used by the self, without destroying the other in the process. It is 'not merely a matter of incorporating the other as ideal, but of loving and having a relationship with the person who embodies the ideal' (p.61). Identification can thus be seen as a form of *relationship*, not just a way in which one person acts upon another. Developmentally, for example, it can be a way in which a boy aspires to be linked to his father rather than to be rivalrous with him. Indeed, in the context of gender development, Benjamin claims that boys and girls both identify with the loving father just as they do with the powerful and loving mother, making multiple identifications along the way. The effect of these multiple identifications is to produce in the child a greater range of possible gender positions, particularly enhancing 'complementarity' rather than the kind of exclusivity which results in the triumph of one gender position over another. On the basis of such complex patterns of identification in which the child incorporates aspects of all her or his loved objects into the self, it is possible to recast development as a process of making increasingly fine internal differentiations which does not necessarily take place at the expense of the valuing of difference, though this depends on the quality of actual object relationships. That is, the classic view of identification, particularly in the Oedipus complex, is that it involves taking in one thing and repudiating another. Benjamin, however, outlines a more mature, post-Oedipal complementarity which brings back together the various 'elements of identification, so that they become less threatening, less diametrically opposite, no longer cancelling out one's identity' (1998, pp.69–70). Multiple identifications forge the basis for identities (including gender identities) which themselves are multiple and fluid, less defensive and hence less caricatured and stereotyped. *Connectedness* is emphasised here, recognising difference but not discounting the other because of it.

This rendering of identification with others as a way of taking in

multiple possibilities for development is one important strand in contemporary work. However, the Lacanian critique of the ego and hence of identity applies here, with identification being understood as an 'imaginary' process of taking on an image and 'appropriating' it *as if* it represents the self. That is, identification is primarily a way of losing oneself in the other. More precisely, the fact that identification is at the root of the formation of the ego reveals that the ego is itself 'specious', a false acceptance of an image as real. Identification, psychoanalysis attests, is that process whereby the ego takes the object and makes it *subject*, incorporating each object as part of itself. According to Lacan, this is indeed a formative process, but its effect is specifically to create a kind of radical *misperception*, in which the ego is taken to be the 'truth' of the person when it is actually just 'bric-à-brac' (Lacan, 1954–55, p.155), made up of bits and pieces latched onto from outside. Hence there is a sense in which identification *falsifies*, with the subject 'using' the object to sustain a fantasy of integrity of the self. This is why Lacan was opposed to the idea that psychoanalytic psychotherapy should aim at enabling the patient to identify with the analyst; rather, he suggested, analysis should aim to show the patient how identifications are all impossibly fantastic. No one can become the model for another; instead, suggests Lacan, the 'real' of the subject lies outside what can be organised and known. Identification, therefore, may well be a major mechanism through which what is outside comes to be registered within, but this also makes it a mode of alienation, whereby the human subject is made a stranger to itself. Needless to say, 'identity' as a term does not appear in dictionaries of Lacanian psychoanalysis (e.g. Evans, 1996).

To summarise so far, psychoanalysis has a number of not necessarily compatible ways of understanding the formation of identities. Some of these, following the lead set by Erikson, see identity as a developmental process of the ego through which the subject deals with a set of social experiences and demands (including necessary losses) by adapting her or his internal structures. The end result is, ideally, an ego that is attuned to reality, with positive integration both within the ego itself and of the subject with her or his environment. Sources of identity integration are given as the body and the internalisation of objects that have been emotionally invested in; these become part of the 'self'. Such internalising processes, conceptualised as forms of identification, are central both to Kleinian and relational theory. The latter is also interested in ways in which multiple, non-exclusive identifications can occur (Benjamin's 'post-Oedipal', 'over-inclusive' model), allowing for appreciation of the layered and complex nature of identity formations. Amongst the many attractions of these positions is the way they offer an account of the mechanisms that might be at work in connecting the social version of

identity as belonging with the personal version of it as an internal, self-actualising state. On the other hand, this raises questions over whether what is being described is an elaborate form of *alienation*, in which the structures of sociality (for instance, the 'message' given to the subject concerning the kind of person she or he could be) are taken to be the 'truth'. This issue will be returned to below, in the context of a slightly fuller account of Lacanian thinking in this area.

Post-integrative identities

The view of identities as potentially integrated, if multifarious, constructed entities formed through internalising relationships with external objects, connects with broader notions of selfhood to be found in British and more recently American psychoanalytic schools. These posit the self as arising in the crucible of caring (usually maternal) relationships that give rise both to a set of capacities and attributes and a reflexive function that itself constitutes the 'sense of identity'. Winnicott's (1960) description of false and true selves, and in particular his ideas on the formation of secure selfhood in the context of maternal responsiveness, have been very influential in this. Without rehearsing the details of Winnicott's account unnecessarily, it is worth recalling that the 'true self' is understood to be a *potential* for growth that will naturally unfold under the right circumstances, and that can be damaged or hidden in a hostile environment. The mother is supposed to provide her infant with the conditions under which her or his potential for selfhood can be realised. Interference with this function, for instance because of the mother's depression, is experienced by the infant as an 'impingement' on the natural organisation of experience, and leads to anxiety about total disintegration. This results in a defensive hiding away of the child's spontaneous desires in the form of a secret true self, which avoids expression because of the danger that it will be destroyed by the inadequate environment. To enable transactions with reality, a conformist 'false self' is formed, split off from the true self and protecting its integrity. The false self is inauthentic because it is built up on the pattern of the mother's desire, not the child's, hence its conformity. The child is formed in someone else's image of her or him, acting in line with the mother's expectations and wishes so as to win her love. In Phillips' gloss (1988),

> It is part of Winnicott's demand on the mother that she be robust; if she is in any way rejecting, the infant has to comply with her response. It is the strategies of compliance that Winnicott calls the False Self Organization.

Because of this primary and enforced attentiveness to the needs of the mother, the False Self, he writes, always 'lacks something, and that something is the *essential element of creative originality.*' (p.133)

The true self is the essential creativity of the human subject in action, consisting of a variety of capacities such as the ability to be alone, to be in states of 'disunity' out of which new modes of experience can emerge, to live with risk, and so on. The false self, on the other hand, is something close to what other psychoanalytic authors would call 'narcissistic' – a defensive shutting-down, organised around close scrutiny of the other and an inability to feel real.

The impact of Winnicott's thinking on selfhood has been immense, especially when combined with his seminal notions of transitional objects and transitional spaces – those intermediate, half-imagined, half-material entities used by subjects to establish their relationship with the world, and to manifest their creativity. At its core is, however, a set of assumptions that may be deeply evocative – as much of Winnicott's writing is – but also problematic for a poststructuralist context that refuses to take as given the idea of an easy fit between subjecthood and society. For Winnicott, everything depends on what Phillips calls 'robustness', or perhaps is better coded as 'maternal resilience'. The capacity of the mother (and in therapy, the analyst) to *survive* in the face of her infant's psychic attacks on her allows the child to absorb an experience of her- or himself as real and legitimate, and of loved objects as actually existing, not just as a figment of the child's imagination. This gives the child a firm sense of location in her or his own needs, which are now experienced as legitimate and acceptable, and of a setting that is not going to collapse. From this, the true self can emerge as an integrated, spontaneous, creative entity that can deal with the world on its own terms. Without such early maternal resilience, the self remains fragmentary and takes refuge behind the conforming false self striving desperately to appease a persecutory environment or – in cases where the mother is depressed and unresponsive – to bring it to life. It should be noted that this is a theory of self as an experiencing core, not of identity as a 'sense' of self, but that the latter is implicit in the former: the foundations for a clear sense of continuity, integrity and belonging lie in these early experiences of maternal holding.

In theorising clinical phenomena, many psychoanalysts operate with a loosely similar set of perceptions, understanding psychopathology as a breakdown in selfhood subsequent to failures of maternal holding and psychological recognition. This is roughly true not just of Winnicott and object relations theories, but also of followers of Klein and Bion in the British School and self-theorists and relational psychoanalysts in the

United States. However, there is something troubling about the assumption that there is a normative progression from adequate ('good-enough') recognition of the infant's needs to a secure selfhood and an integrated self-reflexive capacity that can be called a 'sense of identity'. From outside psychoanalysis, postmodernism and poststructuralism emphasise the 'normality' of fragmentary experience; there is also a strong strand within psychoanalysis that questions the idea that psychic integration should be either a developmental or a mental health norm. This leads to a much greater interest in identity as a formation-in-process than as fixed, and also asks about the degree to which the focus on self-representation and egoic knowledge of the self (for example as represented in integrated self-narratives) is an actively defensive process. That is, given that psychoanalysis is in many ways *deconstructive* in that it pursues the analytic decomposition of all the phenomena with which it is faced, is the search for integration, reflected in the views of self and identity to be found in much of the psychoanalytic literature, a way of avoiding psychoanalysis' own most radical insights? Does it represent an abandonment of what Laplanche (2003) refers to as 'the properly "analytic" vector, that of de-translation and the questioning of narrative structures and the ideas connected to them?' (p.29). In other words, the 'analytic attitude' is always suspicious of entities that appear integrated, because it senses that this appearance is likely to be covering over states of contradiction and conflict. That is, after all, the nature of a symptom. Consequently, when psychoanalysis itself advocates integration, one is always liable to wonder whether this too is symptomatic of an unanalysed conflict; it suggests something that is not fully thought through, or perhaps even a motivated state in which the disturbing realities of contradiction are being denied.

In this respect, the Lacanian deconstruction of the ego, mentioned above, is fundamental to much contemporary thought. In Lacanian terms, identity acts in the register of the Imaginary, which is always over-inflated in terms of its claims to mastery and completeness. Identity is thus a narcissistic entity, yet one with great power and significance. In contrast to the way much classical and object relational thinking on identity references a stable ego as the necessary underpinning of a secure sense of self, Lacan's work has as one theme the exposure of the ego as something fabricated *as a defensive structure*, hence embedding an alienation of the subject within its own psychic life. This is famously explicated in Lacan's (1949) notion of the 'mirror phase', which continues to act as a source for theorising the paradoxical fragility and rigidity of selfhood, despite the fact that there are many difficulties with the concept and with his paper on it (Billig, 2006). In contrast to Winnicott (1967), who uses the idea of mirroring to convey the importance of a

developmental process in which the child sees her- or himself accurately and thoughtfully reflected back by a concerned mother (that is, who enters into her or his true self/identity through this interpersonal process), Lacan emphasises the impossibility of identity as related to a 'true' self. In his view, the ego is used to create an armour or shell supporting the psyche, which is otherwise experienced as in fragments. The subject thus takes refuge in seeming-security (rigidity) as a bulwark against actual-insecurity (fragility). In a move that is intimately connected with a strand of theorising that makes otherness primary in the formation of subjecthood, Lacan (1949) emphasises the *exteriority* of this process. That which appears to us as our 'self' is in fact given from the outside as a refuge, an ideal ego, a narcissistically invested image that is simplistically thought of as a mode of alienation:

> The fact is that the total form of the body by which the subject anticipates in a mirage the maturation of his power is given to him only as a *Gestalt*, that is to say, in an exteriority in which this form is certainly more constituent than constituted, but in which it appears to him above all in a contrasting size that fixes it and in a symmetry that inverts it, in contrast with the turbulent movements that the subject feels are animating him. (p.2)

Here, Lacan is portraying the subject as gaining relief from the intensity of fragmenting internal impulses through the imposition of boundaries and the apparent stability of the mirror image – something external but connected to the subject, holding a promise of future 'power'. Whereas Winnicott portrays the mirroring function as one which, when accurate, allows the child actually to grow into her or his self – to genuinely find the 'maturation of his power' – for Lacan this is a process in which the subject is hoodwinked into taking on the image as if it were real. The subject becomes a dupe of the external world, lured into the belief that its spectral image reflects an actual psychological integrity; this belies the absence of integrity that really operates in the subject's formation. This can also be read as a statement about the nature of the specific social world into which this mirror-phase subject is being ordained as a 'self'. The message that the ego has integrity and wholeness is a socially constructed one, legible in the reflecting surfaces and faces of an order stressing the autonomy and psychological independence of individuals; that is, it is a social order premised on *individualism*. The society that works in this way hides its power by holding out the promise of individual autonomy to subjects; but behind this lurks an uncanny sensation that something is being denied. The consequence of this is the haunting of the satisfying image of the integrated self by the spectre or memory of something else: despite appearances, each subject knows that it is not

really whole, that this seeming-self of 'identity' is a cover for a disturbing dis-integrative pulsation. This produces a paranoid sensation, which it might be argued is one of the characteristics of the triumph of capitalism under late modernity, arising from the sense of being promised something that is always about to be taken away. The mirror is thus a source both of reassurance and of threat, its seemingly smooth surface containing unexpected ripples caused by that which can be seen yet not quite named. Bodily unity is no guarantee of psychic unity, which in fact is disrupted continually by the play of drives.

The mirror stage reflects the impossibility of becoming a self without taking on the meanings of the other – without becoming *identified* with another's gaze, with the pre-existing desire of the other that one should be some one thing and not anything else. The social order is lurking behind the mirror phase as that which offers to the subject the pacifying image of self-integration. In the move to the Symbolic order, which is the next stage of the Lacanian progression and which is built on the classical Freudian understanding of the Oedipus complex, society becomes an explicit figure for the subject. The structures of language interfere with the image-making process, revealing that it is already organised by a law indifferent to the emotions and desires of the individual subject. The importance of this in terms of the existence of an Other that regulates the intersubjective encounters of people will become more evident in the discussion of ethical violence in Chapter 5. In relation to identity, the theory of the Symbolic emphasises that the positioning of the subject with respect to language requires an encounter with otherness in a way that fractures the omnipotence of the mirrored 'I' in the Imaginary, just as the father blocks the incestuous relation of mother and son in classical theory. If the Imaginary celebrates the fictitious identity of subject and ego, it is the tearing of this identity that moves the subject into the Symbolic order and at the same time constructs the unconscious: what is 'left out' becomes repressed. This is the relevance of the familiar statement that Lacan invokes an empty subject, constituted through lack and marked by the impossibility of fulfilment or of recognition of the actuality of the other. The Symbolic order positions the subject in relation to other subjects, marking each as incomplete, only present through its relationship with what lies outside. Claims that identity is fixed and legitimating become understood as defensive manoeuvres protecting the psyche against its own inherent splits. This account, it might be noted, is radically different not only from normative versions of identity that celebrate it as a way of integrating the self, but also from 'social belonging' versions that see it as a consequence of specific features of the social. The Lacanian version of things has the subject always mis-located in a phantasmatic framework that constructs and undermines it at the same time.

Disruption of notions of secure identity is not confined to Lacanian theory, but is engaged in by many who try to weave a poststructuralist and postmodern sensibility into psychoanalysis. Jane Flax (1996), for instance, also sees the defensive structures of stability and integrity at work, in her example when there are claims to stable gender identity. 'A "stable" gender identity', she writes, 'may be partially constituted by, and may serve, multiple defensive purposes, including warding off unwanted aspects of subjectivity or affects, such as aggression' (p.585). The idea that identities form through identifications and introjections that may be multiple and partial is widespread. In addition, the division between external objects and inner worlds is undermined by the way inside and out mutually construct each other. This is an area of general agreement between relational and Lacanian psychoanalysts, theorised for example by Kleinians through the interchanges of projection and introjection, or evoked in Lacan's (1973) use of the image of the Moebius strip to convey subtle processes of interpenetration. The point here is that there is no clear distinction between 'internal' and 'external', but rather there is a pattern of forces that runs through the subject so that wherever one looks, 'inner' and 'outer' are both present. Tracing the path of the apparently internal and individual leads to the social, and vice versa. This needs to be seen as a worm of dissent at the heart of anything that might be thought of as a fixed, stable identity: we always consist of something alien at our core. 'Identity' is consequently not only always fabricated and provisional, but also it *is* the 'social' just as it *is* also the 'personal' or individual – it is not the adaptation of one to the other, but another emanation of the indissolubility of the two. This raises a set of issues that have at their core a certain kind of ethics, questions of what it might mean to live a 'good life' psychoanalytically, that might radically enlarge our current conceptualisation of 'identity politics'.

Relational and diasporic identities

Despite its congruence with poststructuralism, there is an elusiveness to this kind of psychosocial formulation which may not be necessary and which makes it hard to bring it to bear on the practical study of identities (or anything else). It is worth tracking back to see what is being evoked and what responded to in this attempt to wriggle out of too much knowledge and fixedness and instead to focus on the constant disruption that is seen both as a necessary state of knowledge (epistemology) and a paradigm for subjective encounters (ethics). In part, this is a derivative of contemporary events in the 'real' world of

technological change, war and terrorism, in the rising consciousness (but neglect of action) over ecological disaster, in the spread of AIDS and the promises of biomedicine and the genome. One might expect that these developments will impact on people's psychological states and their sense of identity and selfhood, now perhaps more panicked than before, but also more technologically mediated through, amongst other things, the explosive growth of the internet. Indeed, the argument that we are biotechnical subjects is well established in certain branches of academia. Examples here include Donna Haraway's (1991) theorisation of 'cyborgs' and Rosi Braidotti's (2006) exuberant evocation of the nomadic subject, fluidly repositioning across a multifarious terrain of non-human life, with any notion of identity well and truly dismembered as a consequence. Social and cultural theory has responded to this by seeking out models of biosociality that emphasise multifariousness and networked connections, displacing the human subject and introducing in its place a sense of productive activity that gives rise to sensations and identities. In Haraway's (2006/2007) work on 'companion species', for instance, the emphasis is on 'knots' of entanglement, a process of 'knott[ing] companion and species together in encounter, in regard and respect' (Haraway, 2006, p.102). This relates to Judith Butler's recent (2008) writing on 'precacity', and on which lives are recognised as 'grievable' – and hence to which people the status of 'human' is granted, whose life is treasured, whose death is named, who therefore has conferred upon them an 'identity'. The point is that in being 'knotted' together, certain subjects (and not others) are made recognisable. Wetherell (2010) notes that this move is in line with the general development of identity studies 'from the already formulated and established individual and the group to the relational constitutive process', the issue being 'how in any particular site nature, culture, subjectivity and matter coalesce along with the divergent histories pulled together in these new figurations' (p.22).

Much of this is relevant to theorising identity, including a resurgence of interest in the work of Gilles Deleuze and the adoption of his metaphor of 'rhizomes' as a model of spreading networks of articulated forces (Deleuze and Guattari, 1988). This lays the foundations for a return to affect as that which gives rise to subjectivity, rather than following on from it. As well as being a political philosophy, this perspective addresses psychological experiences in a way that is antagonistic to the depth perspective of traditional psychoanalysis, emphasising relationality and 'assemblage' (Latour, 2007). Within psychoanalysis, it also has resonances with the Lacanian interest in the de-narrativising encounter between a subject who desires and one who is 'supposed to know', an encounter that is always waiting to be punc-

tured, for example by the famously sudden ending of a 'short' psycho-analytic session or more soberly by the emergence into speech of something completely unexpected. These ideas give priority to disruption over meaning making, to paradox over order, and most importantly to the crisscrossing of bodily and symbolic networks as they create points of coherence that fade away and re-form. In relation to 'identity', they argue for a restless coming-and-going of the subject. Overall, what is celebrated here is not only fluidity, but also a kind of non-human impersonality that runs as a force through subjects, activating them whilst also conferring agency upon them, in networked yet unpredictable ways. All this is at odds with traditional notions of identity formation, though it can be aligned in part with intersectionality, if that is understood broadly as the procedure whereby one category of sociality or experience is disrupted by its exposure to another. At its simplest, what is being described here is the production of the subject as a kind of 'nodal point' in which different lines of force meet. In relation to identity studies, these include the common categories of race, gender and the like – that is, points of difference that fix the subject in certain positions, albeit not as a stable entity, but as one that is constantly on the move.

If one is to root this turn to a theory of intersectional identities in something that can also draw on contemporary psychoanalysis, one way to do it is through the notion of 'diaspora', as a set of material displacements that provoke multifarious, unstable identities that are nevertheless experienced as lived realities. Wetherell (2010) comments that amongst the social changes which have decisively altered identity studies 'are those associated with post colonialism, trans-nationalism, the emergence of new diasporic communities, new complexities in cultural relationships, new mobilities and migratory flows' (p.20). The theoretical stance towards these that has made most difference has been postcolonialism, with its orientation towards 'subaltern studies' as a way of examining the impact of colonial histories on social subjects (e.g. Spivak, 1988). 'Diaspora' itself relates both to the historic uses of the term to refer to Jewish, Greek and Armenian diasporas and also more recently particularly to African and Caribbean ones, but also to those of the Chinese, the South Asian, the Irish, the Italian and others (Quayson, 2007). From the point of view of identity studies, however, what is important is the expansion of diaspora studies away from simply mapping the routes of connection between and within communities, to a comprehensive examination of the way in which these distributed relationships construct subjects. Laying out an agenda for diaspora studies, Quayson (2007) comments:

The arts of memory, the dialectics of place, the ethnographies of nostalgia, the intersubjectivities of social identity, and the citational practices that ground senses of cultural particularity outside the homeland (names, family photographs, memorializations of the homeland, special community journals, etc.) along with the categories derived from a social typology (village of provenance, race, class, gender, generational differentiations, and degrees of capacity and opportunities or lack thereof for integration into the host land) are all crucial for understanding diasporas (p.589).

Couze Venn (2009) offers a description of the impact of diaspora when he presents it as the defining state of contemporary life, and also as fundamentally disruptive of classical identity claims and politics.

[T]he analysis of global diasporas has demonstrated the suspect character of the assumption that identities or cultures are basically unchanging, homogenous entities, rather than heterogenous, polyglot, plural, relational, existential and in-process. If subjectivity is relational and metastable by reference to the material, discursive and psychological conditions that constitute it, it would follow that dislocations provoked by displacement occasion mutations in subjectivity and identity. (p.4)

Diasporic identities are *essentially* fluid, produced as unstable by the displacements of massive social forces (colonialism and capitalism, to be brief). They are also, however, concrete and heavily invested in, not thrown on and off as mere fashion statements. In this way, they can be seen as iconic for all contemporary identities and subjectivities. Venn claims that the artworks that explore diasporic identities are 'canonical for interrogating identities today' (p.6). The same could be said for such identities themselves: they define the state of identity as something which can be laid claim to and deployed (so diasporic identities have their political and emotional uses), but can never be reified as secure, permanent or real. 'Deracination', one might say, is the natural state of affairs for human subjects and the topic of core narratives from the Bible and the Odyssey through to today. With this realisation comes the demise of a mode of identity that reflects the classical psychoanalytic idea of a naturally developing path.

Stuart Hall (1990) retains some space for historically rooted notions of identity when he argues that

There are at least two different ways of thinking about 'cultural identity'. The first position defines 'cultural identity' in terms of one, shared culture, a sort of collective 'one true self', hiding inside the many other, more superficial or artificially imposed 'selves', which people with a shared history and ancestry hold in common. (p.223)

Hall notes the importance of this kind of shared identity for mobilising postcolonial struggles, particularly in bringing to light 'hidden histories' that played a critical role in emancipatory political activity. But, in line with the emphasis on the disruptions produced by diaspora described above, a second, more fluid conceptualisation of diasporic cultural identity also makes itself felt:

> Cultural identity, in this second sense, is a matter of 'becoming' as well as of 'being'. It belongs to the future as much as to the past. It is not something which already exists, transcending place, time, history and culture. Cultural identities come from somewhere, have histories. But, like everything which is historical, they undergo constant transformation. Far from being eternally fixed in some essentialised past, they are subject to the continuous 'play' of history, culture and power. Far from being grounded in a mere 'recovery' of the past, which is waiting to be found, and which, when found, will secure our sense of ourselves into eternity, identities are the names we give to the different ways we are positioned by, and position ourselves within, the narratives of the past. (p.225)

A central trope here is 'becoming'. Cultural identity is something inhabited in a precarious way, what Hall calls 'the unstable points of identification or suture' (p.226); they exist as a reinvention of a past that is real, but which is neither determining nor unequivocal in its effects. In terms of identity studies, what this produces is an interest in specific histories out of which the impact of colonialism and diaspora emerges, as well as a theoretical thrust towards an understanding of identities as unstable registers in which these histories of subjectification and oppression materialise but also are transformed.

For Hall and Venn, as for others, much of the analytic thrust of diaspora studies is given by explorations of art works of various kinds, including music, writing, performance and installations as well as visual arts. The reason for this is that for many such writers, the 'voice' of diaspora has often struggled to be heard in academic work, and instead is expressed through modes of representation that trigger affective rather than 'intellectual' responses. Venn (2009) claims that art is particularly effective here because 'It is in the gap between representation and the un(re)presentable that something dwells which ushers in the question of the "there is" which is the signifier of the "thrownness" as well as the ex-centredness of the subject' (p.11). Despite his own doubts about the place of psychoanalysis, there is already visible in this quotation an inkling of where it might be introduced back in as an explicatory tool. The 'something' that dwells 'between representation and the un(re)presentable' is a common formulation both for the Lacanian Real (that which drops out of the Symbolic) and for the unconscious itself.

Venn goes on to speak more fully of the relationship between this mode of psychoanalytic thinking and the social discourses more characteristic of diaspora studies, as follows:

> [E]xpressive or creative media such as novels, painting, film and so on are themselves the means or vehicles whereby what cannot be presented in the form of critiques or sociological data can be intimated or presented at the affective and emotional levels. The importance from the point of view of transformation in subjectivity and identity is in emphasising the aesthetic-affective labour which is necessary for this to happen, in the form of an anamnesis, that is, a process of working through that produces a rememori-sation ... and in the form of self-reflection working at the thresholds between unconscious psychic economy and conscious activity, individual identity and collective identity, the process of individualisation and the trans-subjective domain. (p.15)

What might be meant by this kind of 'aesthetic-affective labour', and how can psychoanalysis contribute to its promotion as well as its comprehension? Venn himself draws on the work of a psychoanalyst who is also an artist, Bracha Ettinger, whose theory of the 'matrixial' as a kind of intrauterine-originated connective network offers a way of thinking about subjectivity and identity that immerses them in a pattern of connectivity and encounter. The passage Venn draws on here comes from Ettinger (2006, p.63) and refers to a conceptual space defined in terms of 'the matrixial stratum of subjectivization proposing a matrix-ial *subjectivity-as-encounter* as a beyond-the-phallus feminine field related (in both men and women) to plural, partial, and *shared* uncon-scious, trauma, phantasy, and desire having imaginary and symbolic impact'. The emphasis here on what is *shared*, what links across subjects, will be returned to in the next chapter, but it is characteristic of a mode of psychoanalytic reasoning that has moved away from the classical 'closed' system of mainstream Freudianism and also from its focus on 'depth', and towards issues of relationality and intersubjectivity. What is additionally specific to psychoanalysis is the constitution of affectivity as that which 'fuels' subjectivity, that is, in this context, as a mode of *invest-ment* which promotes the materialisation of identity as linked to specific practices of belonging and becoming. 'Affective labour' does not have to be theorised psychoanalytically: the Deleuzian turn is a major example of an alternative tendency in the social sciences. However, the psychoan-alytic apparatus allows it to be conceptualised as a process in which the different specific forces acting in and on the subject – drives, bodily expe-riences, social positions, ideologies, practices of oppression and emanci-pation, phantasies and fears – can be brought into contact with one another as the framework for an understanding that is genuinely

'dynamic', in the sense of being 'on the move'. Venn refers to 'a process of working through that produces a rememorisation'; these terms ('working through', 'rememorisation') are saturated with psychoanalytic resonances. Indeed, one might argue that psychoanalysis makes such ideas thinkable.

In relation to the impact of this work on psychoanalysis itself, it is clear that the emergence of theories stressing migrancy, unsettledness, fluidity and networks shifts attention away from drive models and towards relational approaches. However, there is nothing cosy in this. If psychoanalysis allows space for such moves, through its object relations and more recent intersubjectivist traditions, it also maintains an investment in what was earlier called 'pulsations': fields of force that interrogate and disrupt, that puncture even the most carefully maintained relational networks. Many contemporary theorists emphasise the reimagining of identity that is constantly demanded in the light of diasporic movements. In so doing they advance a critique of theories – including psychoanalysis – that seem to neglect the social and historical forces operating on the subject, and also to focus only on loss and lack rather than on the transformative fullness of subjecthood. Psychoanalysis has to respond to this if it is to continue to contribute to identity studies, but it also has something additional in its armoury. This is linked to its understanding of what Lacan (1959–60, p.139) calls 'extimacy', which refers to the problematisation of the distinction between 'inside' and 'out' and the way the 'centre of the subject is outside; the subject is ex-centric' (Evans, 1996, p.59). But more than this, it also resides in psychoanalysis' fascination with what is disruptive and uncertain, so that disturbance in the stability of what is taken to be identity is at the core of its concerns. Psychoanalysis certainly must develop its awareness of how the positioning of the subject in historical and contingent networks of relations produces identities of various kinds, fluid and partial in their nature. If it can do this, it can then offer back to the field its own peculiar expertise, that of a discipline that knows about unsettledness, that has marginality and diaspora as part of its own source (in the historical development of psychoanalysis out of certain Jewish diasporic experiences – see Frosh, 2005); and that is always reminding its acolytes that nothing can be taken for granted, that no self-definition or affective state is ever quite what it seems.

Conclusion

Identity has become a major concern of social studies in recent years, as a result of the interest in culture and in how the human subject is

constructed both as subject *to* power and as an agentic subject making sense of itself and of the world. Understood in the various ways outlined in this chapter, identity is a summary term referring to subjects' investments in certain ways of experiencing themselves, and in their affiliations with particular groups and social roles. It stands at a meeting point of processes of self-construction that arise from what are usually seen as 'internal' psychological states and 'external' social forces. Despite the convention of thinking about identity as if it is a fixed and stable developmental achievement, this conceptualisation of it as a nodal point at which various forces meet shows how transitory and elusive it is. Added to now routine observations about the multiplicity and fluidity of contemporary identities, and the input from diaspora studies, this emphasises the need for concepts which can appreciate the general 'intersectionality' of identities. This does not refer so much to places at which apparently fixed social categories such as race and class can meet, but more, echoing Hall's (1990) terminology, to moments of 'becoming'. What this emphasises is the illusory nature of identities as stable entities; they are, rather, momentary snapshots, gathering together a variety of influences and investments before these slip away again and become something else.

Utilisation of psychoanalytic ideas in identity studies has been widespread, if ambivalent. It has often been used as an interpretive categorisation procedure with perhaps too firm a diagnostic subtext. That is, psychoanalysis is called on in its traditional role of making sense of apparently irrational material, or of explaining the investment that subjects might have in discursive positions that in some respects might seem to go against their own rational 'interests' (Frosh et al., 2003; Hollway and Jefferson, 2005). Whilst this role is important in drawing discussions of the unconscious back into the social psychological domain, it also neglects a more recent contribution of psychoanalysis to 'making interpretation stupid' (Nobus and Quinn, 2005, p.186). What this refers to is a mode of reading against the grain in order to track the idea of a subject in process, with no fixed identity however strong the identifications might be. 'Making stupid' involves holding to the provocations of psychoanalysis as an approach that continually deconstructs, without looking out towards eventual fullness of knowledge. Using psychoanalysis to 'explain' identities may miss the point: taken that way, psychoanalysis is just one of many vocabularies for naming the momentary stabilities of subjectivity and trying to pin them down. Instead, the specific contribution of psychoanalysis could be to draw on its understanding of unconscious processes and of the endless cycles of emotional investment, defensive psychic manoeuvre, identification and encounter to keep open awareness of how identity functions as a kind

of sticking-plaster over disruption and uncertainty. That is, through its understanding of defence and of imaginary processes, psychoanalysis is well placed to remind the social sciences that there is no integrative psychic system that can draw together all the forces acting upon it to create a stable, fully formed human subject. Once again, however, psychoanalysis itself needs to reflect on this. In its classical forms, it actually buys into the idea of a possibly stable, mature kind of identity. Identity studies themselves, however, talk back to psychoanalysis about this: where ego-identity was, there something fluid, partial and ambiguous must come to be.

Chapter 5

Recognising Others: Towards a Relational Ethics

This chapter traces an engagement between psychoanalysis and 'ethics' pursued by some social theorists who are either psychoanalysts themselves or who draw on psychoanalysis in conjunction with philosophical works. The area is one that is particularly well attuned to the involvement of psychoanalysis because it deals with intersubjective encounters of a kind that, on the face of things, might have links with what goes on in the psychoanalytic consulting room. Psychoanalysis in the clinic trades on the quality of the contact between analyst and patient, and on the subtlety with which the dynamics of this contact can be formulated. In its contemporary forms, psychoanalysis is particularly interested in the transference, which means that it focuses on how fantasy enters into human relations, how one subject can become a loved or hated other for another, on what it means (or feels like) for people to be in close yet troubled connection with each other, and on ways of articulating and ameliorating discontent through the construction of relationships that are open and in important senses truthful. It is therefore always advancing a very practical type of ethics, because it is concerned with the 'right way' to treat people and, specifically, with how to enhance their standing as human subjects. If one can use this loosely as a definition of ethics itself, one can perhaps see immediately how central it is to the interests of much contemporary social theory.

The question of how one relates to others is of special importance in late modernity, perhaps particularly in the wake of the immense destructiveness of the twentieth century and, in the West at least, the 'post-9/11' situation of the construction of an 'other' that is hostile and somehow incomprehensible. It is not that this is a totally new concern, but the *centrality* of questions about how to conceptualise, and forge human relations with, the apparently alien other might be seen as a specifically post-Holocaust phenomenon, fuelled additionally by postcolonial interest in racism and the impingement of global networks of communication. One could possibly argue that the contemporary moral panic over ways in which apparently sovereign boundaries and walls are transgressed by strangers, some of whom constitute 'barbarians' (the kinds of populations that walls are meant to keep out), reveal that the threat of the other is being felt as more immediate. Some theorists (e.g.

127

Reinhard, 2005) have used this to reconstitute the other as a *neighbour*, drawing attention to the way the issues are no longer just those of how to manage a stranger who is separate from oneself, but rather how to deal with what is experienced as an intruder, as someone who is living right up close. This retains the connotations of promise and intimate exoticism present in the concept of the other, but adds to its already-existing threat a sense of coupling, of dependence on the other/neighbour of whom one is also fearful. But the central question is shared across these different nomenclatures: how does one craft relationships with others that are not colonising (reducing the other to the same, failing to appreciate difference), yet also not premised on the positioning of the other as an alien, with its connotations of hostile threat? And how does one deal with the real threat of the other, which derives both from the other's aggression and from the way in which one's dependence on her or him makes one vulnerable?

Much of the debate here has been in the realm of political philosophy, bordering on a philosophy of ethics. However, key terms drawn on in the debate, such as 'intersubjectivity' and 'recognition', are also staples in the vocabulary of contemporary psychoanalysis, often presented to evoke intense encounters between one person and another. This has resulted in a situation in which, whilst psychoanalysis is not always referenced by philosophers, it is always present at least at the margins of debates on relationality; and in places it is particularly central. In this chapter, the concern is with some psychoanalytic thinking on what it means to 'recognise' others; and beyond that with some ways in which psychoanalysis is being deployed as a critical tool in developing an 'ethics' of otherness. More broadly, this involves identifying the components of a stance towards knowing, singling out, or being in a relationship with an other who in her or his impact on the subject can be a disturbing yet longed-for neighbour. In the course of this, psychoanalysis is being looked to both for 'technical' backing for philosophical ideas (for example, the provision of a developmental account that will support or refute particular philosophical claims about the ontology of otherness) and as generative of new ethical possibilities. This chapter takes up some elements of these debates to ask whether and in what ways psychoanalysis is genuinely such a resource.

Recognising others: lessons from relational psychoanalysis

For Freud, the primary entity of study was the individual, driven by internal forces to seek out others in order to accomplish wishful impulses. Relationality was a kind of secondary phenomenon, in which

the individual subject had to negotiate her or his way as a consequence of needing an object to satisfy the drive, especially the sexual drive. That is, sexuality was seen as motivating the formation of relationships with others, rather than being an expression of enjoyment within those relationships. Essentially, biological drives were theorised as the motor of human action. Whilst there was always an 'object-relational' element to Freud's thought, specifically in the formulation of the Oedipus complex as a moment in which the 'cultural' prohibition imposed by the father put paid to the biological possibility of incest, the main thrust of the theory was from inside to out. The problematic, if one can call it that, was the regulation of inner wishes to make it possible to live safely in a peopled environment; relationality was needed, but only for protection or to service one's impulses (Frosh, 1999). This position has changed radically in post-Freudian psychoanalysis, as witnessed particularly in object relations theory but also in post-Kleinian and even contemporary Freudian thought, as well as in much American work. In fact, as noted in my *For and Against Psychoanalysis* (Frosh, 2006), 'To a considerable degree, all the mainstream psychoanalytic schools, including those in the U.S.A., have turned their attention to what is best termed "intersubjectivity" – the ways in which mental representations of relationships are formed and the effects these have on the development and actual social relationships of individuals' (p.18). The language of objects, of representations, of 'inner worlds' in which relational constructs dominate, and of 'intersubjectivity' to reference particularly the interweaving of the 'subjective worlds of child and caregiver or of patient and analyst' (Stolorow, 2006, p.250), is now central to the vocabulary of psychoanalysts of all persuasions. Stolorow comments: 'Recognition of intersubjectivity does not entail adherence to or rejection of any specific psychodynamic theory. In fact, acceptance of the foundational significance of intersubjectivity enables therapists to employ the various psychodynamic concepts with greater discrimination and effectiveness' (ibid.). This might not actually be completely true, with the Lacanians (to whom this chapter will return), as ever, coming in as an exception to this generalisation. Nevertheless, outside Lacanian thought, it is fairly hard to find any contemporary psychoanalyst who does not accord central significance to object relationships, even if they differ on many other aspects of theory (such as the place of drives or the order of developmental accomplishments) or practice (such as the way interpretations should be phrased, or the use of the negative transference). Included in this is the notion that 'bridging' difference is key; that is, that the task is to find ways to link with others, to translate their needs and one's own into something that can form the basis for relationships that can be mutually fulfilling. This is a model both of therapeutic activity and

'ordinary life'; the question of the other thus becomes one of how to draw people together rather than just how to survive.

In much contemporary psychoanalysis, the stance that otherness is something to be bridged is reflected in a relational position which takes the self–other link as constitutive of human subjectivity. From this position relationality does not need to be explained, but is rather the starting point out of which all analysis flows. Jessica Benjamin's take on intersubjectivity, which is rooted in feminist scholarship and critical theory and hence oriented towards emancipatory practice, is an especially significant variant of this general approach. For Benjamin, the intersubjective stance is a specific move within the general domain of relational theorising, one which holds on to a position in which the other is related *to* but is not *appropriated*. It is a stance that understands the appeal of omnipotence (in knowing the other we come to colonise her or him), but works against it. The manner in which omnipotence is contested is through a process that Benjamin calls 'recognition', which acknowledges the other as a source of subjectivity and gives rise to what Benjamin (1998) calls a 'subject–subject' psychology. This stance echoes the 'I–thou' relationship described by Martin Buber (1959), a mode of reciprocity in which there is engagement with the other as a full being, in contrast to the more instrumental 'I–it' relationship in which the other is a means to an end. Similarly, 'subject–subject' recognition is built out of an understanding of the other's continuing otherness, maintaining the subjecthood of both participants in the exchange who are thus autonomous and yet also exist in relation to one another. In 'the intersubjective conception of recognition,' writes Benjamin (1998), 'two active subjects may exchange, may alternate in expressing and receiving, cocreating a mutuality that allows for and presumes separateness' (p.29).

Benjamin's approach seeks a balance between theories that emphasise difference and those visions of subjectivity that implicitly require disappearance in or of the other, either through self-effacement (as in many theories of mothering), or through instrumental use of the other (the main thrust of rationality). Recognition staves off the absorption of self into the other just as it prevents the other being colonised by the self; rather, the possibility is raised of allowing difference yet also appreciating similarity. Benjamin (2000) herself makes explicit the distinction between omnipotence and recognition:

> The tension between recognizing the other and wanting the self to be absolute (omnipotence) is, to my mind, an internal conflict inherent in the psyche; it exists independent of any given interaction – even in the most favourable conditions. It is not interpersonally generated but is, rather, a

psychic structure that conditions the interpersonal. The problem of whether or not we are able to recognize the other person as outside, not the sum of, our projections or the mere object of need, and still feel recognized by her or him, is defining for intersubjectivity. (p.294)

Recognition of this kind is not a merely cognitive event, nor is it a passive reflection or mirroring of what is already somehow 'in' the other. It is, rather, something actively reaching out that makes what it finds, yet also lets the other be. It is, in this sense, a process of *sanctification*, in which what is found in the other is also cherished specifically for its capacity to be different, and its otherness.

Building on the work of Winnicott, to whom Benjamin (2000) states herself to be deeply indebted, the argument can be restated as privileging the role of respect for the other *as other*, with whom one has connections, but whose inner space cannot be fully known. This is a surprisingly difficult aspiration to realise, even in theory. In many psychoanalytic accounts, for example, the highest point of an intimate relationship is a process of identification or even incorporation, rather than recognition of the otherness of the other. More generally, there is a small space between the liberal urge to understand the other and the wish to remove the other's otherness – as can be seen in recent debates about the limits of 'multiculturalism', in which as soon as the other claims a right to maintain its difference, it is regarded as hostile. Clearly, just seeing the other as different is not the solution: that can be a defence against recognising relatedness where it exists, of noting and experiencing the similarity of human experience. There is plenty of circumstantial evidence, indeed, that this kind of 'othering' can be a source of social hatred, especially when 'different' is cast as 'alien', for example, in ethnic and racist hate (Frosh, 2002). Instead, the idea of recognition embraces the acknowledgement of existence of the other as other in the context of relatedness: there is a real difference, yet this difference is not necessarily marked by preference, it is 'just' difference. There is an other who or which cannot be made 'same', but that does not mean that there is a lack of connection, only that this connection is for the sake of bridging rather than for invasion or incorporation. Benjamin's idea, read this way, suggests that becoming 'real' is premised on the situation in which one's otherness is noted and valued for what it is.

In her analysis of the implications of Benjamin's theory for mothering, Lisa Baraitser (2009) describes how Benjamin's account draws on Winnicott's (1969) ideas about a developmental phase that involves 'object use'. Winnicott's argument is that what he calls the use of an object is made possible through seeing that the (paradigmatically,

maternal) object survives unconscious destruction. Assuming that the infant, through frustration and also the expression of 'natural' aggression, attacks the object, Winnicott claims that the infant's perception of the existence of a real external other is enhanced so long as the mother survives and is non-retaliatory in her response. That is, what the infant is supposed to discover is that the mother is not subject to the infant's 'internal' experience of having destroyed her, and hence is an object with more than merely imaginary existence. Benjamin builds on this idea by suggesting that recognition depends on processes of destruction in the form of 'negation' which test the reality of the other by establishing the degree to which it is resilient and hence has a subjective trajectory of its own. Baraitser comments: 'In Benjamin's view there is an ongoing and endless cycle of the establishment of mutual recognition followed by its negation, constituting a never-ending tension between complementarity and mutuality, between relating to the other as object or like subject' (p.30). Further:

> In Benjamin's work, we are not fundamentally constituted through loss, but through processes of separation that are tempered by the pleasures of mutual recognition and the possibilities of shared understanding made possible through surviving destruction. And if we follow this through, difference can then be experienced as something that can be identified with, not just repudiated, negated or controlled. The infant can enjoy the fact that the mother has a life of her own to get on with, as it means that she is like me, with desires of her own. (ibid.)

The idea of 'enjoyment' here is a potentially important one as it conveys the sense of erotic charge existing when the subject confronts the other in its *difference* from the self. Indeed, the threat of the other, which produces the impulse towards omnipotence in the subject, always has erotic components – something reflected in much of the discourse of racism as well as in the attractions of the 'exotic' (Frosh, 2006). Baraitser's use of the term 'enjoy', however, has a less sexual connotation and points to the domination of the relational stance by concepts such as 'holding' and 'containing'; it seems to mean something more akin to 'feeling secure and satisfied' than to feeling excited. This might mark up one of the deficiencies of relational theory in the context of the revelations of psychoanalysis about the passionate feelings so often associated with destructive urges. It sometimes seems as if the humanistic component of relational work trumps its analytic rigour; even the notion of 'destruction' lacks the passion of, for example, the Kleinian concept of envy, with its connotations of greed and murderous violence. Judith Butler (2000) comments on this:

Although Benjamin clearly makes the point that recognition risks falling into destruction, it seems to me that she still holds out for an ideal of recognition in which destruction is an occasional and lamentable occurrence, one that is reversed and overcome in the therapeutic situation and that does not turn out to constitute recognition essentially. (p.273)

This translation of destruction as a fall from grace that can be overcome by a reparative relationship is perhaps part of the legacy of an object-relations position which assumes the existence of an integrated psyche at birth that then becomes split because of frustration and loss (Frosh, 1999). In contrast, the Kleinian view is that destructiveness is a basic force that always has to be contended with and can never be fully resolved. Without being a Kleinian, Butler (2000) picks up this issue to wonder about the authenticity of an approach that assumes destructiveness can be overcome. Addressing Benjamin's use of negation, she asks:

And if negation is destruction that is survived, of what does survival consist? Certainly, the formulation implies that destruction is somehow overcome, even overcome once and for all. But is this ever really possible — for humans, that is? And would we trust those who claim to have overcome destructiveness for the harmonious dyad once and for all? I, for one, would be wary. (p.285)

The bridging-across-differences element in Benjamin's work reflects both the strengths and perhaps the dangers of her stance, and can be seen too in her more recent and highly productive concern with 'thirdness'. This is a concept that has a considerable history in psychoanalysis, and in the guise of Oedipal thinking has been the main element in its approach to social theory, from Freud (1930) onwards (see Frosh, 1999). Whilst acknowledging the utility of Oedipal scenarios for understanding aspects of development, however, Benjamin (in line with other relational theorists such as Guntrip, 1968) has long been critical of the Oedipal framework as the overriding element in analytic theory. She sees it as fixing a bipolarity (father *versus* mother; reality *versus* narcissism) that is not only misogynist in its assumptions, but also misses the true 'overdeterminism' of psychic life. Benjamin's critique of Oedipal theory in *The Bonds of Love* (1988), as well as in later texts, has established a line of thought in which the dichotomy of pre-Oedipal (seen as referring to narcissistic relationships) *versus* Oedipal functioning (relationships based on reality) is seen as insinuating itself into a denigration–idealisation dynamic. This dynamic is both heavily gendered (the mother's intimacy versus the father's separateness; the mother's narcissism versus the father's symbolic power) and individualistic. With this kind of approach, she argues, it is inevitable that difference will be

marked by repudiation rather than acceptance or linkage; otherwise selfhood cannot be sustained. What Benjamin argues for in its place is recognition built on the subject–subject dynamic, in which new modes of identification are central. The infant is involved in 'over-inclusive identifications' that facilitate absorption of difference and the experience of the other as a separate subject of consciousness (Benjamin, 1998). The question then becomes not that of how to survive the pull to narcissistic disappearance of the self in the other, nor of the acceptance of castration, but rather how to connect in a 'post-Oedipal' way across difference, experiencing the other as one amongst many possible and actual objects for identification and love.

The idea of the 'third' developed here moves psychoanalytic theory away from Oedipal structures. Benjamin formalises her interest in connectedness and relationality through postulating a 'space' in which contact occurs. This space is a dynamic space, 'a principle, relationship or function which is constantly collapsing and needing to be repaired' (Baraitser, 2006). It has two elements, the 'third in the one' and the 'one in the third' (Benjamin, 2004). The 'third in the one' is the capacity of the mother or the analyst to hold in mind what subject and other can create together, a kind of reparative ability to believe that it is possible to comprehend the other even when the other is destructive and alien. The 'one in the third' is a pattern of being that links subject and other and produces something new, a space (for example the projected space of the analytic encounter) for meeting, reflection and creativity, owned by neither party but an aspect of them both. For Benjamin, this links further with the idea of the analyst being actively present in the therapeutic encounter, ready, for example, to acknowledge errors, and hence very much engaged in the process of negotiating the relational dynamics of the session. Thus, building on intersubjectivity as an active nexus of relatedness, Benjamin (2004) rejects the Kleinian tendency to speak from the countertransference but not to become relationally involved with it, to insist 'that the patient is ultimately helped only by understanding rather than by being understood' (p.35). For Benjamin, it is necessary for the analyst who is 'caught in enactment' (ibid.) to find a way to acknowledge it to the patient, a stance or position that Benjamin (2009) refers to as the 'moral third', referring to 'those values, rules, and principles of interaction that we rely upon in our efforts to create and restore the space for each partner in the dyad to engage in thinking, feeling, acting or responding rather than merely reacting' (p.444). It is this that differentiates the relational from the Kleinian perspective. Benjamin (2004) comments: 'The analyst says, in effect, "I'll go first." In orienting to the moral third of responsibility, the analyst is also demonstrating the route out of helplessness' (p.33).

'I'll go first' or 'after you'? Benjamin and Levinas on ethical responsibility

Benjamin's emphasis on responsibility has direct implications for working with others, and indeed governs her thinking on reconciliation work in Israel–Palestine (Altman, Benjamin, Jacobs and Wachtel, 2006). Political involvement in this specific instance is coded as the need for engagement with Palestinian suffering from the perspective of accepting responsibility as a Jew. Benjamin links this with the analyst's realisation that whilst she or he might be the 'activator of old traumas, old pain' rather than their instigator, 'you acknowledge that you have, you know, bumped into the person's bruise, and you acknowledge that there is hurt and pain and that you may have responsibility for that, and in doing this, you alleviate a whole level of tension that makes it possible, then, to talk about, to explore' (p.170). In both the political and the therapeutic context, recognition and responsibility go hand in hand, with each entailing the other. Taking responsibility for others arises from recognition of their existence as genuine centres of subjectivity, not just possessing rights but also having the capacity to be hurt. The analyst 'bruises' the patient merely by being there, though her or his infelicities might make this bruising greater; hence, in the tradition of Winnicott, Benjamin (2009) advocates acknowledging mistakes rather than simply interpreting their effects. For her, this is not a matter of making the patient in some way responsible for the analyst's actions, nor of requiring from the patient forgiveness of the analyst. 'On the contrary,' she writes: 'it should serve to reveal how the analyst takes on the responsibility for forgiving herself and thus being able to transcend the shame of her difficulties enough to talk about and analyze them (without excessive or impulsive self-disclosure)' (p.449–50). Through this means the patient may be helped to contribute reciprocally to the analytic relationship, becoming 'an interpreter of the analyst and a co-creator of dialogue, and so develop her own sense of agency and responsibility' (p.450). The emphasis on mutuality here is strong, but it still relies on the analyst's capacity to start it off. 'Bumping into the person's bruise' is bound to occur; it is a necessary part of therapy, because if one is to look truthfully at what exists, then pain is bound to be felt. But this does not mean it can all be put back onto the other; the subject/analyst has responsibility, even if the damage is unavoidable.

Despite the analytic 'I'll go first', Benjamin is cautious about always making the other's needs primary, always taking responsibility in this way, because she wants to warn against a kind of self-abasement in which the subject gives up her or his agency and indeed her or his rights. That is, taking responsibility is not the same thing as always giving way;

and indeed the analytic situation (characterised by 'analytic abstinence') is precisely one in which not giving way (by avoiding becoming involved in the patient's life or by refusing to allow even small shifts in the time boundaries of the session) is seen as crucial both for the containment of a patient's anxiety and for the exploration of deep trauma. The analyst does not say, 'Tell me what you want and I will meet your need.' A kind of robustness is required, again to match Winnicott's idea that the existence of the other is realised through her or his capacity to survive the subject's destructive attacks. This means that the analyst has to hold firm not only to maintain her or his sanity, but in order to become 'real' for the patient; this must be tempered with acknowledgement of errors and readiness to participate in the intersubjective exchange, but not at the price of obliterating one's own subjectivity.

A comparison can be made here with Emmanuel Levinas' approach to 'ethics as first philosophy', which is one of the most influential areas of work in which the 'face-to-face' encounter has become central to comprehension of human subjectivity. The intensity of his argument for the prior recognition of the other as the foundation of ethics is immense and extraordinarily demanding, taking, if one can think of it this way, the notion of *hospitality* to an extreme. However, many therapeutic and social encounters deal with extreme situations, extreme states of mind and extreme politics. In that context, there is something to be said for starkly presenting the impossible ideal, that towards which one needs continually to gesture:

> In my analysis, ... the relation to the Face is the relation to the absolutely weak ... and there is, consequently, in the Face of the Other always the death of the Other and thus, in some way, an incitement to murder, the temptation to go to the extreme, to completely neglect the other – and at the same time (and this is the paradoxical thing) the Face is also the 'Thou Shalt not Kill'. A Thou-Shalt-not-Kill that can also be explicated much further: it is the fact that I cannot let the other die alone, it is like a calling out to me ... at the outset I hardly care what the other is with respect to me, that is his own business; for me, he is above all the one I am responsible for. (Levinas, 1991, pp.104–5)

The Levinasian primacy of the other has given rise to a great deal of philosophical debate, and it is not clear that all its implications stand up to scrutiny. However, there is something powerful here: nothing contingent is assumed in relation to how the other will treat the self, there is no expectation of there being any pay-off from 'love of one's neighbour', no reciprocity such as is demanded by Buber's I–thou relationship. Being responsible for the other does not mean that a positive response will come back to the subject; it exists simply as an ethical imperative, as that which makes one human.

Levinas (1985) makes it clear that this relationship of responsibility – this ethical relation – is in his view *primary*, rather than following on from something pre-existent. It is not the case that the human subject exists and then engages in ethical relations; rather, ethics is the defining feature of subjectivity itself: 'I understand responsibility as responsibility for the Other, thus as responsibility for what is not my deed, or for what does not even matter to me; or which precisely does matter to me, is met by me as face' (p.95). Levinas insists that responsibility for the other comes before the subject can even know what the other is; it is, consequently, an absolute given, and the recognition which is part of it is as non-contingent as can be. Indeed, the term 'recognition' is inappropriate within the Levinasian domain, because of its implication that somehow, through the act of recognition, the other becomes known. Realising that one 'does not know and has never seen' the other, yet that the other exists, is not the same as recognition in the conventional sense. Rather, it is an absolute refusal of the impulse to believe that the other can ever be brought within the realm of the self. Even more so, Levinas states, 'at the outset I hardly care what the other is with respect to me'. Knowledge of what the other might be, what use or reciprocity might derive from it, is irrelevant; the other is not any *specific* 'person', but that which is outside what can be claimed by the self. Knowing the other would be part of the colonising act of reducing it to the same; in the Levinasian scheme, the otherness of the other is always maintained.

Levinas' ontology here is distinct from Benjamin's in a number of ways that have a bearing on the limitations of an account that assumes the bridgeability of difference. In focusing on the 'third', Benjamin is extending her analysis of complementarity in intersubjective relations into an attempt to think about how recognition and reconciliation go together. The point about the third is that it offers a space in which intersubjective recognition can take place; in demonstrating a capacity to think beyond the dyad, the subject creates a third space in which the other can also move. If the analyst abjures the responsibility to move 'first' into this third, then the *analyst's* fear of losing the safety of distance is blocking the possibility of an encounter of this kind. This is best thought of as a mode of 'practical ethics' in which the route to taking responsibility is to move both participants in the intersubjective exchange into a new domain, making thought and mutual recognition possible.

For Levinas, there is no intersubjective meeting; there is rather the construction of the subject *as an ethical subject* through responsibility for the other, whatever that might be constituted by, whatever strangeness it might imply. Baraitser (2009) glosses this as follows:

> Levinas' argument is in a different register from that of sameness and differ-
> ence, recognition and reciprocity. Recognition ... is not identical with
> responsibility. Self-recognition that relies on recognition by another subject
> will perhaps always run into difficulties with how to prevent an infolding of
> alterity due to the colonizing impulse that is inherent, not only in 'knowing'
> another but in recognizing too. In contrast, describing the relationship with
> the Other as an ethical relationship prior to self, a relationship that estab-
> lishes the subject as a responsible subject prior to 'being' a subject at all,
> Levinas redefines both the notion of the subject and the Other, as well as the
> nature of their relationship and that of recognition itself. (p.37)

In Levinas, this is an assertion of the irrevocable otherness of the other
as something that stands over and above us and is best coded as the infinite. It makes demands on the subject which are not necessarily recipro-
cated; 'responsibility' as an approach to the other institutes the subject
as an ethical subject rather than simply an intersubjective one. It raises
a question that is central to issues of non-violence and care, which can
be phrased as, *'how do we take responsibility for the other through
exposure to the other prior to the possibility of recognition by that
other?'* (Baraitser, 2009, p.39). In relation to other subjects, this means
seeing the infinite in the face of the other, in all its inapproachability.
Acknowledgement of this primary mode of being, this 'you go first',
irrespective of desire, understanding or contact, makes the subject ethical and – definitionally, it seems, at least for Levinas – in so doing
constructs the human being.

Language, murmuring and silence

The vocabulary of recognition and responsibility raises a set of issues
about the 'mediation' of subject–other contact through language.
Questions such as the degree to which language is expressive or determining of thoughts, and also of the structural characteristics of language,
have been central to social science for decades, and to psychoanalysis –
the 'talking cure' – since its inception. For Freud (1915), the difference
between an unconscious and conscious idea was that the former was
restricted to the 'thing-presentation' whilst the latter had the 'word-pres-
entation' attached to it (p.200); for Lacan, the unconscious was structured
'like a language'. The question here, however, is what role language might
have in the *relationship* of subject to other, and what psychoanalysis
might contribute to elucidating this relationship. It should be noted first
that whilst psychoanalysis recognises the potency of words, it is also interested in their underside, the continuing murmur of the non-linguistic, of
that which falls out of symbolisation (the Real, in Lacanian terms), those

experiences that seem to slip away just when we are about to speak (of) them. Language needs to be differentiated from the non-linguistic to make it language, but this also has structural implications for what can be symbolised and what cannot. That which is silenced underpins speech but is also excluded by it. It is also the *impersonality* of speech that is important here, by which is meant the way language works as a system that is not simply at the disposal of individual speakers, but has its own rules, its own way of doing things. As social theory has long recognised, language is both the product of human speakers and is abstracted from them – there are strict limits on the novelty with which it can be used if communication and meaningfulness are to be retained, despite the fact that completely novel utterances are being made all the time. Language has its own life, independent of its speakers; once the genie of words has been let out of the bottle, it cannot be controlled by any human will. This double-facedness of language contributes to the complex way in which it underpins subject–other relations: it both *enables* them (through communication and symbolisation), and subjects them to a system that stands outside them (the linguistic or symbolic 'order'), hence making direct, unmediated contact impossible.

Whilst concern with language is by no means confined to theorists with psychoanalytic interests, psychoanalysis is often close at hand in these discussions, offering reflections on how language and desire operate in tension and in tandem with one another. In particular, psychoanalysis contributes to conceptualisations of how language both links people and alienates them from each other. It offers a vocabulary to writers whose concern is with the emotional or 'affective' connections between people, and how these are constructed, mediated or 'distorted' by words. Denise Riley (2005), for example, notes how 'the deepest intimacy joins the supposedly linguistic to the supposedly psychic' (p.11), making it clear how these realms are 'scarcely separable'. Instead of opposing the psychic and linguistic, she suggests that we maintain an idea of 'affective words as they indwell', pushing forward an appreciation of how language insinuates itself within people and enforces the impersonality at the heart of each human subject. Riley offers a modest form of this impersonal core, arguing that what she calls 'linguistic will' – fundamentally, a person's ability to choose what to articulate – is restricted to moderating the inward impulse that would otherwise tear things apart. Speech wells up and we can only do what we can to rein it in, a process that demonstrates time and again quite how fragile is our control over our own being. In the light of this, Riley suggests, the most that can be made of a human subject is as something recognising its own contingency, its own status as being-produced rather than producing. For her, this is the project of a lifetime:

> It's only through my meanders and slow detours, perhaps across many
> decades, towards recognizing language's powerful impersonality – which is
> always operating despite and within its air of a communicative 'intersubjec-
> tivity' – that I can 'become myself.' Yet I become myself only by way of fully
> accepting my own impersonality, too – as someone who is herself acciden-
> tally spoken, not only by violent language, but by any language whatsoever
> – and who, by means of her own relieved recognition of this very contin-
> gency, is in significant part released from the powers of the secretive and
> unspeakable workings of linguistic harm. (p.27)

This impersonality of language working as the enigmatic other within
the subject is a familiar image in contemporary writings, owing much to
deconstructionism and to Lacanian psychoanalysis. Riley, like many
authors deeply in love with words but troubled by their power to go
wrong, points to the paradox of language as something impersonal yet
apparently the instrument of human agency. Her solution to the paradox seems to be *insight*, possibly of the psychoanalytic kind, the
'relieved recognition of this very contingency' that then somehow
releases the subject from 'the powers of the secretive and unspeakable
workings of linguistic harm'. Yet the impulse that she identifies as
welling up in the subject is that of words that speak without being
willed, that speak, often destructively, through an impersonal force –
language itself, autonomously drawing on its own structures to deliver
its blows. If what we have to do is accept our own 'impersonality', then
maybe this is a source of the feeling of distance in human relationships.
How can one feel connected to others if one is merely a language
machine, and one full of *bad* words at that?

The more the focus is on language, the more significant seems to be
the 'left over', that which remains unsymbolisable and inarticulate. If
language forces being into shape, the question of what it is that lies
'beneath' or outside it keeps recurring. On the whole, this thing outside
language is presented as a threat. However, there is also a rendering of
the non-linguistic 'murmur of the world' that can be cast broadly as
'humanistic', albeit couched in the shadow of an understanding of the
human as a being constituted in the flux of affective forces, and hence
as a product of something outside it, rather than as the source of meaning. This mode of humanism evokes the possibility of recognition which
is not dependent on language, precisely because it acknowledges the
existence of this shared experience of an unspoken background 'real'
out of which all subjects arise, and the workings of which we can
observe, and draw on, in one another. As such, this approach opposes
the stance towards communication that sees it as the transfer of information lucidly from a speaker to a hearer. Alphonso Lingis (1994)
expresses a variant of this idea most compellingly in his appositely enti-

tled book, *The Community of Those Who Have Nothing in Common*. Writing about the experience of being in the presence of someone who is dying, he shows how some kinds of communion rest not on the belief that it is possible to exchange 'meaning' through the transmission of messages in which each is the recipient of the other's sense, but rather on an acknowledgement that we are all rooted in something elemental. This kind of encounter depends not on reaching agreement between subjects who are similar to each other but of drawing on the other's existence in all its *alien* form, so that one has marked out the vista of a world that is not the same as one's own:

> We do not relate to the light, the earth, the air, and the warmth only with our individual sensibility and sensuality. We communicate to one another the light our eyes know, the ground that sustains our postures, and the air and the warmth with which we speak. We face one another as condensations of earth, light, air, and warmth, and orient one another in the elemental in a primary communication. We appeal to the others to help us be at home in the alien elements into which we stray: in the drifting and nameless light and warmth of infancy, in the nocturnal depths of the erotic, and in the domain of dying where rational discourse has no longer anything to say. (p.122)

The appeal of the other here is less harsh than as represented in Levinas, but it is just as unbridgeable. We are linked in the elemental, not through some mediated communication, but as a response to an appeal. The 'third' is transformed into the light of each other's face, its recognition of the mutual being and enlivening power of subjects who are nevertheless not just distinct, but alien from one another.

We have here, in its austerity, a different model from one that assumes the potential linkage of subjects through shared perspectives, drawing-together of narratives or meta-level transformation of points of view. Lingis (1994) characterises traditional models of communication as a search for rational clarity based on rescuing the specificity of the message from the constant interferences that threaten to submerge it. Rationality needs quiet as an unambiguous and transparent medium; it is opposed to 'interference and confusion' (p.70). Yet, he asks, 'is there not also a communication in the hearing of the noise in one another's voices – the noise of one another's life that accompanies the harkening to the message? What kind of communication would that be?' (p.88). To which he gives the partial answer:

> The one who understands is not extracting the abstract form out of the tone, the rhythm, and the cadences – the noise internal to the utterance, the cacophony internal to the emission of the message. He or she is also listening to that internal noise – the rasping or smouldering breath, the hyperventilating or

somnolent lungs, the rumblings and internal echoes – in which the message is particularized and materialized and in which the empirical reality of something indefinitely discernible, encountered in the path of one's own life, is referred to and communicated. With this internal noise it is the other, in his or her materiality, that stands forth and stands apart making appeals and demands. The other is not simply the recurrent function of appealing to and contesting me; he or she is an empirically discernible vulnerability and intrusion. (p.91)

The 'noise', when listened to, becomes what marks out the other as *human*, as a being excessive to itself, as more than a 'function' because she or he is a significant presence, marking a 'vulnerability and intrusion'. It is the 'internal noise' that makes the other so; deleting this and holding only on to the abstract form of the message also misses what is peculiar about it, hence what makes it real. This notion links with Slavoj Žižek's (2006b) comment that 'The ultimate lesson of psychoanalysis is that human life is never "just life": humans are not simply alive, they are possessed by the strange drive to enjoy life in excess, passionately attached to a surplus which sticks out and derails the ordinary run of things' (p.62). Human life is just too much; that is its nature and its definition, and losing the background noise, screening out the seemingly desolate murmur that lurks behind spoken language, loses life itself. What links us to one another is *access to the excess*: something is being hinted at here that has to do with a mutual core that does not satisfy our usual notions of human essence at all.

Žižek (2006b) similarly emphasises the intractability of the mystery of the other as what is essential; indeed, he argues that *not* knowing the other is crucial to intersubjectivity itself. He writes:

If I were to 'really know' the mind of my interlocutor, intersubjectivity proper would disappear; he would lose his subjective status and turn – for me – into a transparent machine. In other words, not-being-knowable to others is a crucial feature of subjectivity, of what we mean when we impute to our interlocutors a 'mind': you 'truly have a mind' only insofar as it is opaque to me. (p.178)

The *solidity* of the other comes over in this, its absolute otherness that links both with Winnicott's (1969) ideas on how the other becomes real to the subject by surviving attack, and with the contrary Lacanian emphasis on how all psychoanalytic knowledge is constituted through language, and hence is characterised by 'mistranslation'. However, whilst this parallels Levinas' ideas in suggesting the unknowability of the other and, alongside this, the importance of that unknowability in resisting acts of colonisation and reduction of the other to the same,

Žižek also differs from Levinas in his reading of what is 'human' in this formulation. For Levinas, the ethical turn is crucial: we give the other primacy ('after you'), and that is the excessive act that defines human subjectivity as such. For Žižek, this omits a key element of the encounter of each subject with the other; precisely, its *inhuman* form. 'What Levinas fails to include in the scope of the "human"', he claims, is 'the *inhuman* itself, a dimension which eludes the face-to-face relationship between humans' (p.111). Here Žižek (2006b) draws on Giorgio Agamben's (2002) use of the figure of the *Muselmann*, the most extreme figure of regressed human suffering in the concentration camps, depicted with unremitting clarity by Primo Levi (1960):

> In a properly dialectical paradox, what Levinas, with all his celebration of Otherness, fails to take into account is not some underlying Sameness of all humans, but the radically 'inhuman' Otherness itself: the Otherness of a human being reduced to inhumanity, the Otherness exemplified by the terrifying figure of the *Muselmann*, the 'living dead' in the concentration camps. (p.112)

The point here is that *Muselmänner* do not respond, which is why, according to Agamben, they are both the true witnesses of the horror of the camps and impossible witnesses, who registered nothing. As such, they manifest the reduction of the human to 'just life', as Žižek terms it, or in Agamben's (1995) famous phrase, the 'bare life' of *homo sacer*.

For Žižek, this lifelessness reveals the limitation of Levinas, whose system depends on there being a 'call' from the other to which the subject has the duty to react. 'When we are confronted with a *Muselmann*,' he writes, 'we precisely cannot discern in his face the trace of the abyss of the Other in his or her vulnerability, addressing us with the infinite call of our responsibility – what we get is a kind of blank wall, a lack of depth' (p.113). However, this raises the next challenge:

> What if, facing a *Muselmann*, we are made aware of our responsibility toward the Other at its most traumatic? In short, what about bringing together Levinas' face and the topic of the 'neighbour' in its strict Freudo-Lacanian sense, as the monstrous, impenetrable Thing that is the *Nebenmensch*, the Thing that hystericizes and provokes me? (p.113)

As will be described more fully below, the *Nebenmensch*, the neighbour, which includes within itself the Freudian 'Thing' as understood by Lacan, embodies essential alienness. Žižek emphasises the challenge of this 'monstrous, impenetrable Thing' as the most traumatic extreme of ethics, because the 'facelessness' of the *Muselmann* still calls on the subject precisely because it asks for nothing. That is, the ultimate chal-

lenge is to deal with this inhuman thing, which provokes and hystericises by virtue of its deathliness. What makes it inhuman? Is it perhaps not just because of the loss of agency, the unresponsiveness and impenetrability of the *Muselmann*, but also because this terrifying neighbour invokes precisely the deracinated other who is cut off from the 'elemental', the murmuring deep, its capacity to draw on life – even if only to register horror – drained out of it? Levinas assumes the existence of a question, a demand in the other, to which the subject responds; hence, the other is immersed in the same elemental as the subject. Žižek's example pushes the limit case here, suggesting that the ultimate inhuman thing is the one who cannot draw on the elemental at all; the murmuring deep has been silenced.

There is something slightly distasteful about Žižek's critique of Levinas, embedded as it is in the ground of the Holocaust, and perhaps inaccurate in this portrayal of Levinas as reliant on the activity of the other in 'asking' a question – there is plenty of evidence that the mere being of the other is enough in the Levinasian scheme. For Agamben, too, this does not appear to be the whole point. In the context of his meditation on witnessing, Agamben (2002) examines how the *impossibility* of witnessing by the *Muselmann* is matched by the *insufficiency* of witnessing by the survivor – the one who cannot be the end product of the extermination camp, the absolute bare life. Agamben draws this together through an examination of what it might mean to explore the 'inhuman' core of the human: 'this means that the one who truly bears witness in the human is the inhuman; it means that the human is nothing other than the agent of the inhuman, the one who lends the inhuman a voice' (p.120). This rendering of witnessing, which can perhaps be thought of as a way of maintaining contact with the being of the other, produces an alternative to what Agamben describes as the humanist discourse, 'all human beings are human', and the anti-humanist discourse, 'only some human beings are human'. 'What testimony says', writes Agamben, 'is something completely different, which can be formulated in the following theses: "human beings are human insofar as they are not human" or, more precisely, "human beings are human insofar as they bear witness to the inhuman"' (p.121). This suggests that at the core of the tension around language and silence is a space of potential recognition that is impersonal and in that sense 'inhuman' (its origins are not in the subject); but, paradoxically, access to it sustains the 'inhuman' aspect of human aliveness that makes contact with others, and change, feasible. Without access to this elemental, the inhuman becomes deathly; with it, connection is possible. Being 'in' a relationship with another is also a matter of being outside it, sharing in the impersonality that comes from being lived *through* by the forces that

constitute the human subject – perhaps affective elements, acceptance of what Riley (2005) terms 'contingency', or of the 'void', as Badiou (2004) has it, referring to the disappearance of the subject which is always threatening to collapse into 'pure, indistinct being' (p.99). This connects back to the Levinasian possibility that what unites people is not something 'intersubjective' at all, but rather that there is an *inhuman* feature that runs through all things as backdrop and elemental, the ground and deep of human activity and therefore of what is experienced in and of the other. We come close to this at those times when we manage to cease seeking out the 'abstract form' in what the other says, as Lingis puts it, and in which we acknowledge the excess of the other – the other's intrusiveness, perhaps – as what is essential. This is perhaps one of the more subtle yet central discoveries of psychoanalysis: it is not what is *in* the message that is important, but what is *transmitted* by it, however untranslatable that may turn out to be. Seeking this out is what gives rise to intersubjective thought, including those projects of 'thirdness' (such as Benjamin's, 2004, discussed above) that convey the attempt to understand what it might mean to be in some kind of full therapeutic contact with another. But these approaches seem to be hampered by a kind of therapeutic zeal, which translates eventually into an extracting, colonising process. A certain kind of withdrawal is necessary, an acknowledgement that the place in which subjects meet may not be one of human encounter at all, but rather of an apparent emptiness, in which subjectivity is evacuated. This place is fought against but drawn upon, feared and exulted in. It is neither silence nor speech, but the source of both. Indeed, one might call it the void, but one that is full of murmuring.

On ethical violence

The question of what it might mean to single out the other as a human subject is also key to discussions of the nature of 'ethical violence' that have materialised particularly between Judith Butler and Slavoj Žižek. The terminology here is somewhat idiosyncratic, but what is being debated is how the other should be acknowledged as connected to the subject, yet also existing in a terrain of its own subjecthood. Put crudely, this means asking how one can avoid the 'violence' implicit in forcing another subject into a frame not of its own choosing whilst holding on to a concern with relationality and social justice. Butler (2005), staking out the ground in relation to Levinas and the psychoanalyst Jean Laplanche, focuses on the question of recognition, which for her is not a humanistic acceptance of the other, but a rigorous and in some ways

impossible process of self- and other-scrutiny built on the impossibility of full knowledge. Her account draws both on the philosophy of ethics and on psychoanalysis, using each to interrogate the other, but particularly employing a psychoanalytic understanding of the 'opacity' of the human subject, its organisation around a point of *unknowability* (the unconscious), to develop an approach to engaging with the other without appropriation. Key here is the idea that acknowledging the opacity of the self is a necessary foundation for ethical appreciation of the other, who must also be opaque to the subject in her or his intrinsic formation. Just as one cannot fully know oneself, so one cannot fully know the other; consequently, the other stands in the same relation to the subject as the subject does to her or himself. Butler (2005) comments: 'we might consider a certain post-Hegelian reading of the scene of recognition in which precisely my own opacity to myself occasions my capacity to confer a certain kind of recognition on others. It would be, perhaps, an ethics based on our shared, invariable, and partial blindness about ourselves' (p.41). For her, this is a possible counter to what she terms 'ethical violence', which seems to be best understood as the promulgation of a version of the other that forces the other to become something it should not be. At the source of this is a demand for a certain mode of narrative integrity that is simply not possible without doing violence to the actuality of the fragmented psyche, itself a fundamental discovery of psychoanalysis.

For Butler (2005), the realisation that one is an opaque subject acts against the demand that the other should be transparent:

> Suspending the demand for self-identity or, more particularly, for complete coherence seems to me to counter a certain ethical violence, which demands that we manifest and maintain self-identity at all times and require that others do the same ... one can give and take recognition only on the condition that one becomes disoriented from oneself by something which is not oneself, that one undergoes a de-centring and 'fails' to achieve self-identity. (p.42)

The ethics of this is a kind of tolerance of the other that recognises it as not fully knowable, and hence resists the temptation to appropriate the other through an act of colonisation. Expressing herself with slight echoes of Žižek's emphasis on the 'excess' of human life, Butler sees the interrupted nature of subjectivity as crucial, the way it cannot ever be fully expressed as a whole:

> By not pursuing satisfaction and by letting the question remain open, even enduring, we let the other live, since life might be understood as precisely that which exceeds any account we may try to give of it. If letting the other

live is part of any ethical definition of recognition, then this version of recognition will be based less on knowledge than on an apprehension of epistemic limits. (ibid.)

Recognising the other means being aware of the limits of recognition, and this is an ethical act because it 'lets the other live' without forcing her or him to be whole and knowable, without imposing a kind of narrative integrity that 'may be preferring the seamlessness of the story to something we might tentatively call the truth of the person, a truth that, to a certain degree ... might well become more clear in moments of interruption, stoppage, open-endedness – in enigmatic articulations that cannot easily be translated into narrative form' (p.64). This 'tentative truth' is something that can only be glimpsed, never known; it revolves around an interruption that is always present, from well before the subject exists. The subject is grounded in interruption, in opacity, in the unknowability that stems from being at odds with itself. Recognition therefore has to tolerate the otherness of the other and not try to make it 'same'. Butler writes: 'If the other is always there, from the start, in the place of where the ego will be, then a life is constituted through a fundamental interruption, is even *interrupted prior to the possibility of any continuity*' (p.52).

This notion that 'the other is always there, from the start' is an important one in Butler's thought, and it partly explains the use she makes of psychoanalysis to fill out what could otherwise be a purely philosophical argument founded in Levinas. The choice here seems to be between a *static* approach that hypostatises the other and makes it a universal call on the subject, and an ethics that is grounded in actual human practices, particularly the relational practices of infancy out of which the subject is formed. To this end, Butler draws in detail on the psychoanalytic account of the other given by Jean Laplanche, whose focus is on the way the other is *inserted into* the subject, constructing the subject by virtue of a 'message' which is in important ways indecipherable not only because it is beyond the ken of the subject, but because the other – the originator of the message – also does not have control over its unconscious resonance. As John Fletcher (2007) explains, one of the key elements in Laplanche's rereading of Freud is to make the origins of the subject 'extrinsic', a matter of partial translation, failed translation or mistranslation of 'messages' from the adult other to whom the subject is exposed, which are 'implanted' in the subject. Whilst some elements of the parental message are successfully translated by the infant, and hence are 'bound into' the ego and its internal objects so that they can be used (Laplanche's version of sublimation), other elements are untranslatable. They are a 'remainder' that

cannot be integrated into the subject but rather inhabit the subject as something alien yet constitutive. Fletcher (2007) describes this untranslatable remainder as

> a *psychical thing* that has become the source of the exciting, traumatizing drives pressing toward absolute discharge, drives that attack the homeostatic body-ego from within ... In particular, the drive is the byproduct of the psychical *work* of the infant, both opening up to and defending against the seductive ministrations of the adult. (pp.1257–8)

This means that there is no paradise of integrity from which the subject falls as a consequence of a failed environment, which is the implication of the Winnicottian and often broader object-relational scheme of things. Using Butler's phrase, the subject is rather '*interrupted prior to the possibility of any continuity*', always inhabited by something from outside that prevents integrity, continuity, wholeness or individuality from proceeding. In contrast to the position that claims each one of us as separate from each other, having to reach out to the other from across an abyss and to negotiate difference as a way of surviving – having to modify our aims and drives, our desires and expectations – we have here an increasing focus on the already-present nature of the supposed other. The immediacy of the other is therefore both an ethical demand and an ontological claim: there is no subject without the other. The subject exists in the space of the other, inhabited by the other, disrupted and interrupted; our life stories are fragmented by the presence of the other 'where the ego will be', our boundaries are always crossed.

Butler (2005) emphasises both the disruptive effect of this primacy of the other and the way it instigates sociality as the first cause, with the ethical implications that follow from that. These two elements – disruption and sociality – are closely linked. On the former, she notes that the impact of finding the other's message at the heart of subjectivity is to realise that the demand for narrative coherence does violence to the subject: there is always something 'too much' at play, and denying this is a way of failing to live with the unconscious:

> To understand the unconscious, however, is to understand what *cannot* belong, properly speaking, to me, precisely because it defies the rhetoric of belonging, is a way of being dispossessed through the address of the other from the start. For Laplanche, I am animated by this call or demand, and I am at first overwhelmed by it. The other is, from the start, too much for me, enigmatic, inscrutable. The 'too-much-ness' must be handled and contained for something called an 'I' to emerge in its separateness. (p.54)

Moreover:

To hold a person accountable for his or her life in narrative form may even be to require a falsification of that life in order to satisfy the criterion of a certain kind of ethics, one that tends to break with relationality ... To say, as some do, that the self *must* be narrated, that only the narrated self can be intelligible and survive, is to say that we cannot survive with an unconscious. (pp.63, 65)

Because the unconscious is the domain of uninterpretability, founded in response to the untranslated messages of the other, it operates as a site of continued incoherence within the subject, yet also as a site of truth; this truth being that the subject is always open to otherness, always formed in its image. This is the core of the second element of this psychoanalytic ethics, as tuned by Butler. The constitutive presence of the other means that sociality is primary in the formation of the subject, that identity is not 'owned' but is shared, and hence that ethics is always forged in relationality. This is a stance that is closely aligned with that of Levinas, even whilst differing from it on the basis of its tighter understanding both of the disruptive presence of 'infantile' otherness within the adult subject, and of the social. In particular, whilst Levinas gives an account of the 'passivity' of the subject in relation to the impact of the other, he has little to say about the developmental emergence of the subject. He consequently underestimates the impact of the other's message, the way in which it is felt as an impingement producing a range of affective impacts, from anxiety to desire. The psychoanalytic supplement to his philosophy fills out the internal space of the subject as a cauldron of activity which is stirred by the social other; that is, the agency of the subject is itself generated by the other's enigmatic embrace. What Butler calls the 'sociality at the basis of the "I"' (p.75) is an obvious foundation for an ethical relationship with the other: 'I find that my very formation implicates the other in me, that my own foreignness to myself is, paradoxically, the source of my ethical connection with others' (p.84). Insisting on one's own integral identity is a way of doing violence to the self; obliterating the opacity of the other through knowing too well, through, for example, a thirst for absolutely transparent 'communication', also amounts to a mode of violence in which the disturbingly interrupted nature of social subjectivity is overlooked.

As well as utilising Laplanchian psychoanalysis for her model of the formative intrusion of sociality in the subject, Butler also draws on psychoanalysis for an understanding of the significance of the other in an ethical reconstitution of a troubled self. For her, this revolves around psychoanalytic listening, which has the characteristic not of offering a holistic narrative where none should be found, but of giving back a kind

of subject in fragments. Psychoanalysis, in this vision, is a mode of necessarily disrupted narrative and failed listening, a kind of witnessing that leaves the subject alone precisely at the moment that it acknowledges relational sociality. It is also, as Butler explicitly notes, a model encounter because it is constructed around the transference.

> The other represents the prospect that the story might be given back in new form, that fragments might be linked in some way, that some part of opacity might be brought to light. The other witnesses and registers what cannot be narrated, functioning as one who might discern a narrative thread, though mainly as one whose practice of listening enacts a receptive relation to the self that the self, in its dire straits of self-beratement, cannot offer itself. And it seems crucial to recognize, not only that the anguish and opacity of the 'I' is witnessed by the other, but that the other can become the name of one's anguish and opacity: '*You* are my anguish, surely. *You* are opaque: who are you? Who is this you that resides in me, from whom I cannot extricate myself?' (p.80)

Transference operates here as a way of breaking into the tendency to narrativise experience. The phantasmatic presence of the other, embodied in the listening analyst but not coincident with the *person* of the analyst, disrupts the sense that one is in communication with an other who can fully understand. Butler draws attention to the way the receptivity of the analyst to 'what cannot be narrated' draws in the subject's 'anguish and opacity'. That is, the opacity of the subject is named, but not resolved: transference dramatises the necessity to be in relation to one who cannot be known, as an outcrop of the impossibility of knowing oneself. This argument has links with the Lacanian idea that the transference operates in the Imaginary as a kind of impossible promise that the analyst will have the remedy for all the patient's suffering; the end of analysis occurs when the subject takes back her or his projections, acknowledging the necessary failure of the analyst to offer a 'solution' to the questions of psychic existence. The *ethical* claim here thus depends on a psychoanalytic rendering of the unknown within – the unconscious – alongside a developmental account of the insertion of this 'unknown' from the outside other. It is coupled with a claim that recognition, as that which gives value to the other, selects the other out, is built on an appreciation of alterity as something which all subjects share.

The use of psychoanalysis here is a powerful one, rooting recognition theory in a concrete developmental account that provides an ontogeny for the subject as something 'always-already' social. In a way, it offers a 'new norm' for ethical relationality, based on developmental considerations (the subject is constituted through its others), which has radically

critical effects when counterposed to the traditional developmental sequence of increasing 'maturity' and independence. In terms of social theory, it offers a revised 'master discourse' in which the primacy of relationality is forged as a necessary consequence of the existence of an unconscious populated by otherness, the denial of which is therefore an act of ethical violence. Žižek's response to this is characteristically provocative, from the title of his chapter on the topic ('Neighbours and Other Monsters: A Plea for Ethical Violence' – Žižek, 2005) to its content. There are a number of significant dimensions to his argument. For Žižek, drawing on Lacan rather than Laplanche, psychoanalysis offers no new norm, however radical it might be. Rather, it is used disruptively to accentuate the impossibility of a norm, or at least its undesirability, and the necessary maintenance of a place of emptiness where that norm might be ('The question, however, remains: how, *structurally*, does this new Master differ from the previous, overthrown one ...?' – Žižek, 2006a, p.307). His first move involves conflating the 'monstrosity of the Thing' and the presentation of the neighbour as the embodiment of threat and also of unknowability. He comments (2006b):

> What Levinas obfuscates is the monstrosity of the neighbour, a monstrosity on account of which Lacan applies to the neighbour the term Thing (*das Ding*) ... One should hear in this term all the connotations of horror fiction: the neighbour is the (Evil) Thing that potentially lurks beneath every homely human face' (p.43)

Reinhard (2005) clarifies the nature of this supposedly 'evil' thingness in the neighbour in the context of a careful elaboration of Lacanian claims. Lacan, he writes,

> defines *das Ding* as the encounter with something in the other that is completely alien – an intrusive foreignness that goes beyond the compositions of self and other, and their politicizations as 'friend' and 'enemy'. The Thing materializes the constitutive ambiguity of the primal object, the trauma of its uncertain disposition between excessive presence and radical absence ... the Thing is that part of the other that is 'mute', but the neighbour speaks and thus forms a template for the subject's emergence. (pp.30–1)

The neighbour contains the Thing – it is not the neighbour itself, but rather an area of unassimilable alienness within the other, that both intrudes on the subject and allows it to gather something in, to refine itself, make distinctions, and form. Žižek (2005) captures the mediating role of the neighbour and yet the essential nature of the Thing here,

arguing that 'if there is no neighbour to whom I can relate as a human partner, the symbolic Order itself turns into the monstrous Thing which directly parasitizes upon me'; on the other hand, without the Thing, 'we find ourselves in a Habermasian "flat", aseptic universe in which subjects are deprived of their hubris of excessive passion, reduced to lifeless pawns in the regulated game of communication' (p.144). Liveliness, that is, depends on the Thing, however disturbing it is and however much mediation by human presence is required to make it tolerable. What is captured here is the sense of dependence on the neighbour in the process of social subjectification out of which the subject emerges, and the accompanying inbuilt feeling that there is always something else at play, a little piece of the real that cannot be accommodated but still has its effect. Laplanche's (1999) 'enigmatic signifier' again comes to mind, despite the significant differences between his developmental approach and the stance taken by the Lacanians.

The negativity of the other – its horror-inducing, Thing-like status – counterbalances the vulnerability of the other that is emphasised in Butler's account, with her concern for the precariousness of contemporary life and her valorisation of the areas of opacity in both subject and other. Žižek acknowledges Butler's move, but disputes what he calls the 'solidarity of the vulnerable' (p.139) opened up by Butler's insistence on human 'weakness'. In contrast, Žižek proposes two things. The first stresses a kind of radical capacity to take responsibility, a 'negativity of freedom' inherent in the agentic ability of the subject to refuse the blandishments and coercions of the symbolic order. This is no liberal fantasy: Žižek is well aware of the power of the social order, but he holds out for a space in which the subject can nevertheless stage a refusal, find a way to say 'No!':

> This negativity of freedom provides the zero-level from which every positive content can be questioned. Lacan's position is thus that being exposed/overwhelmed, caught in a cobweb of preexisting conditions, is *not* incompatible with radical autonomy. Of course, I cannot undo the substantial weight of the context into which I am thrown; of course, I cannot penetrate the opaque background of my being; but what I can do is, in an act of negativity, 'cleanse the plate,' draw a line, exempt myself, step out of the symbolic in a 'suicidal' gesture of a radical act – what Freud called 'death drive' and what German Idealism called 'radical negativity'. (p.140)

This negativity should not be mistaken for passivity, even though one criticism of Žižek's position is that it promotes a political indifference that does not, as is claimed, have radical effects, but is simply a way of disengaging from struggle. However, here Žižek is proposing that the subject does have access to a way of being that steps out of the

constraints of the symbolic – a position perhaps akin to that articulated many years ago in Deleuze and Guattari's (1977) *Anti-Oedipus*, where the 'deterritorialisation' embodied in schizophrenia is taken as a model for revolutionary action. But Žižek offers what might be thought of as an ironic twist here. Foregrounding the Thing in the neighbour, Žižek argues that an ethical act – 'ethical violence' – *breaks up* the encounter with the other by introducing the realm of the third, the very structure of the symbolic order, of sociality:

> In order to render our coexistence with the Thing minimally bearable, the symbolic order qua Third, the pacifying mediator, has to intervene: the 'gentrification' of the Other-Thing into a 'normal human fellow' cannot occur through our direct interaction, but presupposes the third agency to which we both submit ourselves – there is no intersubjectivity (no symmetrical, shared relation between humans) without the impersonal symbolic Order. (pp.143–4)

The opacity of the neighbour, in Žižek's view, is not something to be 'gentrified' and romanticised; it is the arena of threat and horror, and the point of a social ethics is lost if one engages in the 'reduction of the radically ambiguous monstrosity of the Neighbor-Thing into an Other as the abyssal point from which the call of ethical responsibility emanates' (p.163). Recognising the other through the Levinasian dynamic adopted by Butler consequently ameliorates something that has to be kept alive in its forceful destructiveness. A true ethics will be one that breaks into this and usurps it with a commitment to an objective – hence genuinely 'ethical' – justice.

Žižek is here making a crucial distinction between love and justice. The former does indeed separate out the one from the mass: love is an act of choosing, of preferring, of specifying an other who the subject will recognise. Levinas, whose theory is based on this kind of recognition, consequently has problems with the 'Third': what does one do when a third appears on the scene, how does one distribute one's attention, one's recognition and singling-out? For Žižek, the Third is always there, not as a kind of space of encounter as in Benjamin's model, but as an impersonal, inhuman force that acts against preference and is consequently the bearer of justice. The Third is primary (even developmentally so, for Žižek, in that 'the first relationship to an Other is that to a faceless Third' – p.184) and regulates the encounter of subject and other. It is 'a positive condition of ethics' precisely because it does not reduce to understanding, but rather insists on the always-present otherness that provides the backdrop to any loving selectiveness that might occur, that in being selective and preferential is always *un*just. 'In

contrast to love,' writes Žižek, 'justice begins when I remember the face-less many left in shadow in this privileging of the One. Justice and love are thus structurally incompatible: justice, not love, has to be blind; it must disregard the privileged One whom I "really understand"' (p.182). If ethics is about truth, then this kind of understanding has to be relinquished, an act which is always a mode of violence.

> This brings us to the radical anti-Levinasian conclusion: the true ethical step is the one *beyond* the face of the other, the one of *suspending* the hold of the face, the one of choosing *against* the face, for the *third*. This coldness is justice at its most elementary... Every preempting of the Other in the guise of his or her face relegates the Third to the faceless background. And the elementary gesture of justice is not to show respect for the face in front of me, to be open to its depth, but to abstract from it and refocus onto the face-less Thirds in the background. (p.183)

This, finally, constitutes a kind of psychoanalytic critique of intersubjectivity, and hence a disputation with those who also talk of the Third, but make it a space for recognition and understanding. For Žižek, the lesson of the Third is precisely that there is no space in which such understanding or communication occurs; rather, the ethical stance is to resist understanding but nevertheless stay alongside the other in so doing. Psychoanalysis here is used in an 'anti-humanist' way to puncture the argument that relationality is primary and that ethics should be based on countering the violence of subject-formation with the non-violence of recognition of the subjectivity of the other. In Žižek's formulation, what psychoanalysis shows is rather the way in which something outside subjectivity and intersubjectivity is always primary: a faceless Third that must of necessity be given priority if justice is to prevail.

But can psychoanalysis, which has its origin in an intersubjective, personal encounter in the clinic, sustain itself in a vision of 'coldness', of ethical violence? There is perhaps a lesson here in what happens when Žižek turns to an image of the consulting room to bolster his thinking about how psychoanalysis might model this anti-humanist turn. Warning against the reduction of psychoanalysis to therapy and human relatedness, he nevertheless gets drawn into a way of speaking that emphasises linkage and a kind of alternative mode of human warmth. The starting point is the Levinasian 'face', which, Žižek argues, is definitely not the subject of psychoanalytic intervention:

> We can clearly see, now, how far psychoanalysis is from any defence of the dignity of the human face. Is the psychoanalytic treatment not the experience of rendering public (to the analyst, who stands for the big Other) one's most intimate fantasies and thus the experience of losing one's face in the most

radical sense of the term? This is already the lesson of the very material dispositif of the psychoanalytic treatment: no face-to-face between the subject-patient and the analyst; instead, the subject lying and the analyst sitting behind him, both staring into the same void in front of them. There is no 'intersubjectivity' here, only the two without face-to-face, the First and the Third. (p.148)

Ironically, perhaps, this image of the analyst and the analysand 'staring into the same void' does not seem so different from Butler's idea about the ethical significance of shared opacity, nor indeed of the Levinasian 'elemental' evoked by Lingis (1994) as 'the alien elements into which we stray' (p.122). There always seems to be some wish for a kind of shelter in the presence of the other, even amongst those most opposed to the humanistic emphasis on the meaning-producing individual subject. Perhaps the ethical pull here will always be compromised when psychoanalysis is brought into play: the contract between analyst and subject may well be to 'analyse', not cure, but something happens between them, something that locates itself in a relationship which always feels 'personal' and specific and consequently caring and 'unjust'; and revealing its unjustness and ethical ambiguity does not always succeed in wishing it away.

Conclusion

This chapter has explored the way some theorists of what is here called 'relational ethics' have drawn on psychoanalysis to secure and advance their claims. A good deal of the debate revolves around the question of recognition. Derived separately from psychoanalytic theory and from philosophy, recognition gives voice to the aspiration for ways of acknowledging others as subjects with whom one might be able to forge reciprocal relationships. For some writers, this form of full recognition is possible, at least in theory. For others, it is a misleading aspiration, caught up in an imaginary fantasy of completeness that is belied by the existence of the unconscious. Psychoanalysis has also been used to supply a grounded, developmental dimension for some more abstract philosophies of otherness, and to offer a critical understanding of 'thirdness' as that which stands outside the subject–other couple. The more 'optimistic', relational theories read this thirdness as offering an opportunity for meeting and reconciliation; the more structural, Lacanian approaches use it as a way of promoting the concerns of 'justice' over those of 'love'. In each case, the thrust is to deploy psychoanalysis in ways that will clarify thinking on ethical relationality, using its familiarity with intersubjective

encounters as a legitimation for believing it has something to say about all subject–other relations.

The quality of much of the work described here is very impressive, and shows the potential for deepening philosophical enquiry in this area by drawing on psychoanalytic concepts and experiences. It also provisionally opens up psychoanalysis itself, for instance by placing questions of thirdness in the context of their ethical implications. In this regard, it is interesting to note how there always seems to be some kind of pull back into relationality whenever one draws on the psychoanalytic clinic as a model, however hard one might struggle against this. Whether this is 'good' or 'bad' seems hardly to be the point; rather, it reveals how psychoanalysis' own ethical grounding is crucial. It functions as a kind of anchor for social debate in which the complex layering of subjectivity is highlighted and revolved. This has a certain kind of austerity embedded in it, as psychoanalysis at its best insists on never looking away from what it confronts; but it also continually reinserts an investment in the significance of subjects into what could otherwise become a more abstract theorisation of social processes. It is a kind of high waterline for contemporary scholarship, insisting that the complex affective and fantasy dimensions of subjectivity should always be included, offsetting the abstractly philosophical tendencies of much social theory.

Chapter 6

The Radical Politics of Psychoanalysis

It will be clear from the previous chapter that applied psychoanalysis is often implicated in politics. To some extent this follows automatically from its adoption of an ethical stance on the conditions necessary for people to lead a good life, something which many writers see as essential to the psychoanalytic outlook (e.g. Lear, 2005). If one is to pronounce on this – if, for example, one is to do as Freud did and criticise standards of sexual morality (e.g. Freud, 1908b) – then this is bound to represent an intervention in a political field, even if one is suspicious of politics, as Freud himself was. A clear separation of psychoanalysis and politics is thus never easy to sustain; psychoanalysis is a 'moral' discipline and this always involves making some kind of commentary on social life.

This indirect involvement of psychoanalysis with politics is complemented by a tradition of direct application that has many sources. There is a rather rich seam of work on the politics *of* psychoanalysis, which includes infighting between its various schools as well as investigations of the sometimes dark history of psychoanalysis' collusion with oppressive regimes (e.g. Frosh, 2005). As noted in Chapter 1, this reveals the difficulty psychoanalysis, like other critical disciplines, has had in maintaining itself as a socially progressive practice. However, there are also many examples of ways in which psychoanalysis has been used as an instrument to advance progressive politics by supplying a theory of the social subject that is compatible with radical critique. This theory has various attributes, depending on how it is drawn upon. Some writers have been interested in what psychoanalysis has to say about 'mass psychology', understood as a form of social psychology that reveals patterns of irrationality and desire that fuel many societal occurrences. Others have focused on the apparent mismatch between 'objective' social conditions and the feelings and beliefs of subjects, which is really to say that psychoanalysis is being looked to in order to flesh out a theory of ideology. Still others have drawn on psychoanalysis as a contributor to a grand theory of the social and political sphere, seeing in some of its ideas (for example, envy, phantasy, narcissism, the lacking subject) concepts that offer leverage for accounts of contemporary society. In each case, psychoanalysis' understanding of subjectivity,

fuelled by its clinical work, is being extended to provide material for broad political analysis. In each case again, this extension sometimes seems legitimate, and sometimes seems to push logic almost to breaking point. This chapter takes up some of these claims and considerations, asking about the status of these applications of psychoanalysis, both in terms of their contribution to political theory and their impact on psychoanalysis itself.

Psychic colonialism and political parallels

Psychoanalysis has been engaged with what might be broadly thought of as 'the political' from early on in its formation as a discipline. Freud's paper, *'Civilized' Sexual Morality and Modern Nervous Illness* (1908b), can be understood as an intervention in the social and political mores of his time, with its argument that neurosis is in large part caused by the hypocritical relations governing sexuality in the Europe of the early twentieth century. The memoirs of writers such as Stefan Zweig (1943) attest both to this hypocrisy and to the impact of Freudian thought in freeing sexuality, though perhaps it could be equally well argued that Freudianism itself was a *symptom* rather than cause of the rebellion against this particular mode of repression. Zweig (1943), looking back on the European 'world of yesterday' at the end of the 1930s, notes about the period 40 years earlier: 'It is quite possible that there is no sphere of public life in which a series of factors – the emancipation of women, Freudian psycho-analysis, physical culture, the independence of youth – have brought about so complete a change within one generation as in the relation between the sexes' (p.61). It may actually have been the First World War rather than psychoanalysis that exposed the deathliness of the morality of deference in so compelling a way that these previously repressive norms were bound to be swept away, as they were – temporarily at least. Freud's own political position was at best liberal (he was suspicious of socialism, despite having sympathy for the argument that economic and political equality should be sought) and in many ways conservative, with a liking for order. In line with many other social thinkers, he assumed that the drives and desires of the individual always need constraining by society. As has been described elsewhere (Frosh, 1999), this theory that society is ineluctably opposed to individuality is one of the most pessimistic strands of thought associated with the bourgeois era. For Freud, knowledge of the unconscious did not lead to a celebration of its disruptive actions. The aims of psychoanalysis as a therapy would always be to channel what was formless and dangerous into social usefulness, converting 'id' into 'ego' in the famous words

of his 1933 *New Introductory Lectures*, as 'a work of culture – not unlike the draining of the Zuider Zee' (p.79). The point here is that culture consists in making the unconscious passions of the individual into works of social value, and this involves 'draining' them, channelling them into good use; in this way, sublimation is made into the organising principle of sociality. That this is a conservative view is clear: social organisation is not only essential but is also inherently constraining; human society could not survive if the terrors of unconscious life were let loose unregulated, and there is consequently no hope for a perfectly utopian future world in which everyone will be libidinally satisfied. Such politically revolutionary ideas, for Freud (1930), were 'consolations' (p.145), similar in function to the illusions and wish-fulfilments that underlie religion.

However, as with much else in Freudian thought, the social theory explicitly promulgated by Freud in works such as *Totem and Taboo* and *Civilization and its Discontents* may be less productive and interesting than his apparently more technical, 'psychological' model of the mind. This is not to overlook the fecundity of the social texts: in each case, Freud's grand and provocative 'sociological' readings have given rise to an extensive literature, much of it critical but also deeply engaged with the question of the relationship between individual desire and human sociality. Yet the most compelling of these engagements are those which address Freud's conceptualisations not so much on the level of his discussions of how society works, but rather through the lens of his account of 'metapsychology'. This refers to his theory of mental structures and mechanisms and the way they construct subjecthood in the warp and weft of drives and relationality. To give just one recent example, Jacqueline Rose's (2007) introduction to Freud's writing on the 'mass' is a meditation on what can be learnt from 'social' texts such as *Moses and Monotheism* and *Mass Psychology and Analysis of the 'I'* (the version of the title used in the translation to which Rose's piece is an introduction), and involves a subtle illumination of how 'mass formations' operate in relation to its subjects. Rose deploys Freud's understanding of society as a kind of necessary evil, marking out the function of mass formation as 'one of the most effective systems a culture creates to keep its subjects sane', and arguing that particularly in the case of religion, this is done by 'deluding them with the false consolations of belief' (p.69). She points out, again with Freud, that the psychology of the mass reveals what humans might be like in the absence of social constraint. This both underlines the need for the protection that society offers, and also shows up the crudeness with which it fulfils its task, producing unnecessary suffering along the way.

> Ugly, the mass lifts the veil of the night, releasing humans from cultural constraint – in the mass, man is allowed to do what no individual would dare. At moments, it is as if the mass *becomes* the unconscious – without logic, knowing 'neither doubt nor uncertainty', living a type of collective dream. Freud may be repelled, he may be frightened … but he has also made man in the mass the repository of a universal truth: that human subjects suffer under the weight of repressive cultural imperatives that force them against their nature. (p.65)

This is, exactly, the Freudian mode of social analysis, yet what has to be observed here is that apart from explaining that society or 'culture' is repressive, little is said about the structure of society itself. That is, as a 'psychosocial' approach, Freudian theory remains very much on the 'psycho' rather than the 'social' level. There is nothing, for example, stated directly about class, race or gender, to use (in some ways anachronistically) some of the major axes around which sociological and political analysis is constructed. Nor is there anything about 'interests' in the way familiar from much political theory. However, what we do get is a means of understanding the *irrationality* of the social in a form that owes a great deal to the general psychoanalytic understanding of unconscious irrationality, and which is novel in relation to most political approaches. As Rose notes, 'it is as if the mass *becomes* the unconscious', as if, that is, the processes well understood by psychoanalysis as operating in the mind can also be observed – metaphorically or actually – in the workings of the social world. At the heart of this is Freud's insistence on *conflict*: not just the evident one between the individual and society, but the internal conflict that becomes the driver of irrationality in the public sphere. Rose (2007) articulates this in relation to the construction of the individual subject through its encounters with alterity, which is a modern rendering of Freud's understanding of the formation of the ego and the superego through the internalisation of objects and their values. The context for this is given by Freud's post-First World War examination of the sources of destruction, an examination which led to the reformulation of drive theory to include a 'death drive', and which is at one and the same time an account of what drives people to war with others and of what leaves them at war with themselves:

> From *Mass Psychology* to *Moses the Man*, all Freud's writings on collective life share a question. What drives people to hatred? … As if Freud had made two utterly interdependent discoveries, that also threaten to cancel or wipe each other out, taking the whole world with them. No man is an island: you are the others who you are. But the mind is also its own worst enemy; and there is no link between individuals, no collective identity, which does not lead to war. (p.63)

'Ambivalence' is one way of conceptualising this, 'the cruel ambivalence lurking within our most cherished forms of allegiance' (p.68), but as will be seen there are other ways too, including those that focus more on 'lack' than on conflict, and those that use psychoanalytic formulations to elaborate a vision of social life in which modes of excess and 'enjoyment' are of central significance.

Amongst the various lines of division here, one that stands out is a comparison between those approaches – loosely speaking, Lacanian and post-Lacanian – that focus on the drive or drive-like components of unconscious life, and those that are object-relational in their primary orientation. Despite her unusually strong grasp of Lacanian thought, Rose emphasises the *relationality* inherent in Freud's work, stressing how certain readings of Freud produce a model that makes others the foundation of what is experienced as the 'self', 'ego' or 'identity'. This means that the personae of each subject's social world are always 'in here' as much as they are 'out there'. Society itself is therefore foundational for what is taken to be individual, removing any meaningful distinction between these two classically opposed categories:

> We only exist through the others who make up the storehouse of the mind: models in our first tentative steps towards identity, objects of our desires, helpers and foes. The mind is a palimpsest in which the traces of these figures will jostle and rearrange themselves for evermore. From the earliest moment of our lives – since without the rudiments of contact, the infant will not survive – we are 'peopled' by others. Our 'psyche' is a social space. (p.62)

Identification is a key mechanism here – at its most active, a process of 'devouring' the other in order to become them, to appropriate them for use by the self. The subject is thus built up as a kind of colonialist project, taking in the others upon which its identity and personal economy is to be based, and then denying or repressing the original source of these riches. This denial is always of necessity specious, because it hides the interdependency upon which all psychic life, not just its overtly social formation, is based. Interestingly, this colonial model can also be read the other way around: not so much the subject as coloniser, but as colonised, as the unknowing, subjugated recipient of the intrusions or 'messages' (as Laplanche [1999] names them) of the other. By a further turn of the screw, the subject believes itself to be an active conqueror of the domain of otherness, consuming its gifts in order to strengthen itself; but it is also at the mercy of the other, dependent on it, unconsciously infiltrated and knocked off course by it, tied to it by processes of desire and need, yet always fighting against this awareness. As mentioned in the previous chapter, Butler (2005) describes this as follows: 'If the other

is always there, from the start, in the place of where the ego will be, then a life is constituted through a fundamental interruption, is even *interrupted prior to the possibility of any continuity*' (p.52). Perhaps as a metaphor of colonial and now postcolonial states (of mind as well as of politics), this is as precise as it can be.

Rose (2003, 2005, 2007) uses this understanding of the politics implicit in the psyche as a way into discussing significant issues surrounding oppression and ideology, most notably through explorations of South African literature and examination of what might be termed 'counter-currents' within Zionism. In the latter case in particular, she is interested in ways in which Zionism acts as a fragile container for social identities, and how as an 'excessive' set of beliefs and practices – originally seen as a form of insanity by many of its Jewish critics – it both mobilises aspirations and enthusiasms and creates pressures that have potentially damaging consequences. Rose (2005) notes the contemporaneity of the rise of modern Zionism and the foundation of psychoanalysis, and comments:

> Precisely because Zionism had to make itself out of nothing – create a unity, a language, a homeland where there was none before – it knows itself as a child of the psyche, a dream, a figment of the brain ... he who enters here plumbs the depths of the political mind. This makes Zionism, for better or worse, the most wonderful exemplar of the work of the psyche in the constitution of the modern nation-state. (pp.67–8)

Zionism is a political force built out of dreams, and hence out of the elements of the unconscious that have evaded censorship, but that reflect conflictual, disturbing and dangerous wishes. This idea, that Zionism as a political force is expressive of, and inhabited by, unconscious desires that are parallel to, or *the same as*, those to be found in the psyche of the individual subject, allows Rose to explore different resonances of Zionism for some of its opposed progenitors. In particular she invokes those whose voices might be construed as resisting the development of Zionism as a narrowly nationalistic creed and political practice. These writers include Hannah Arendt, Martin Buber and Ahad Ha'am, all working from within Zionist thought but in a way that was countervailing to what became the dominant, aggressive form of Zionism characteristic of the Israeli state. What is rehearsed here, in Rose's reading, is an opposition between different forms of psychoanalysis. The mainstream is paralleled to ego psychology, that classical approach which dominated particularly in America from the 1950s onwards and is centred on promoting conscious control over unconscious urges and adaptation of the subject to the demands of the

social world. This notion is one towards which most radical critics have been hostile (see Frosh, 1999), and here too it is the derogated position, despite being recognisably the way in which much of the world works. Politics, read through this lens, is a process of management whereby what is slippery, subversive and counter-intuitive is converted into something solid, orderly and normative. As in the example of Zionism, priority is given to the security and sovereignty of the nation-state as a homogenous element that stands firm against the internal and external forces threatening to fragment it. As a model of psychic life, this kind of psychoanalysis has a strong affiliation to an image of mental health as rationality, in which managing the unconscious – turning id into ego in the most concrete reading of that formula – is the primary aim. As politics, this is an account of identity as forged through the repudiation of doubts and visions, through the loss of dreams, and, most importantly, through the sloughing-off of alternatives. Rose (2005) identifies Weizmann as a proponent of 'normality' for the Jews in this way, and Buber as one of its critics: 'The ego, like the normal nation, carves out its identity. Buber quite explicitly makes the link: "The typical individual for our times," he wrote in his 1939 lecture "The Spirit of Israel and the World of Today," "holds fast to *his expanded ego, his nation*." ... The nation should not be normal' (p.74).

The opposed strand to ego psychology within psychoanalysis has taken a number of forms, including most voraciously Lacanianism with its antagonism towards the idea of the 'norm' and of the integrated ego as the measure of mental health. The end point of Lacanian analysis is, amongst other things, a moment of stepping aside from the place of knowledge, in which fantasies of perfect integrity and wholeness give way to an awareness and enjoyment of the fissures of non-knowledge, of 'lack' – a point which will be discussed in more detail below. But it is not only Lacanianism that promotes this kind of 'openness' against the 'closures' of the hermetic system of ego dominance. Relational psychoanalysis, with its interest in how the 'other' is embedded in the 'self', also challenges the idea that any subject can be truly 'individual'. The presence of otherness within the subject creates an experience of contingency, of uncertainty and untranslatability (to use a notion from Laplanche) that contradicts claims for homogeneity and rational self-government. The political analogy is taken up by Rose (2005) in several ways, first using material from Hans Kohn:

> For a brief moment, Zionism had the chance of molding a nation that would be not an 'expanded ego' but something else. At the opening of his essay 'Nationalism', Kohn describes how 'shifts of consciousness' are always

accompanied by 'deep shocks,' creating a time of 'disquiet, tension, isolation, dissociation'; such processes are 'obscure,' 'ambivalent,' 'uncertain.' He
could be describing glimpses of the unconscious, those moments – dreams,
slips, symptoms – when the unconscious is allowed to steal past the wires,
past the defences of the conscious mind, and makes its presence felt. Precisely
because of the tragic peculiarity of Jewish history, because Jews have indeed
in some sense been lost to the world ... Zionism, as a unique national movement, had the opportunity to forge a model of nationhood, neither belliger-
ently nor preemptively, but ambivalent, uncertain, obscure, something closer
to this disquieting and transformative space. But did not take it. (p.86)

The parallel between psychodynamic processes and the political, nation-
alist movement of Zionism in this is very striking – indeed, is part of
Rose's point when she calls this chapter of her book 'Zionism as
Psychoanalysis'. Towards the end of the passage above, Rose precisely
compares the two modes of management of the unconscious: 'belliger-
ent and pre-emptive' versus 'ambivalent, uncertain, obscure' – but she
does so as modes of understanding Zionism rather than as ways of
formulating mental processes. Similarly, she goes on to examine Ahad
Ha'Am's writing on 'hypnotic agency', whereby the internalised voices
of the past (specifically, biblical voices) ventriloquise the present, so that
personal and national identity are understood as always part of someone and something else. 'I like to think', she writes (p.100), 'that Ahad
Ha'Am is calling on his forebears to soften or modulate their voice
(rather like psychoanalysis aiming to reduce the ferocity of the superego
in the mind of the child).' Once again, the paralleling between psychoanalytic and political instances is direct and concrete – in this mode of
thought, they are the same thing.

Resistance

There are a set of issues here about the legitimacy with which psychoanalytic categories can be made into political ones. Can a movement
like Zionism be understood as the expression of a people's unspoken
desires in the way that a person's speech and actions can be understood
as an expression of unconscious wishes and conflicts? Is it intellectually
viable to bring these together, or should we simply understand the use
of psychoanalytic categories here as metaphoric? When a writer as
subtle as Rose uses psychoanalysis like this, is she seeking to deploy
psychoanalytic ideas in an explanatory way, or as a kind of literary
device to open out thinking? Is it a mode of speculative, even poetic,
elaboration that is itself a 'disquieting and transformative space' rather

than a way of fixing our political understanding? It is obvious that there is a risk here of reading Zionism as a kind of psychic activity close to madness, and neglecting its historical, political, economic and military levels of specific operation; but the gain of introducing the 'irrational' and also the fragmentary, alternative wishes of those involved in the movement might still be worth the candle. Some of this comes into the light still further in relation to another component of political thought in psychoanalysis, of great interest to Rose as well as to others, that of *resistance*. This term has the striking characteristic of referring to a political activity and a psychodynamic one that have the same name, yet in important respects describe opposed practices.

Resistance is a prime category of political thought, and of common political parlance. As 'resistance movements' it has a basically good press, though tainted and made more complex by the label of 'terrorism'. Its key resonance is as a force opposed to a greater force, a liberatory activity set against an oppressive structure – resistance stands firm, as power assaults it. In this sense, resistance is what the *healthy* subject does, refusing to be cowed. Of course, the imagery has to be more complex here: governments resist the will of the people, and so on; but it seems fair to argue that the main thrust of the representation of political resistance is that it comes *from* the people against those who would take away their liberties. As referenced in the immensely influential writings of Michel Foucault, however, the picture is more complicated, and makes of resistance not a single oppositional force to the implementation of unwanted power, but rather as power's symbiotic twin. Each goes along with the other, and as the one (power) is always present in all interactions, so the other (resistance) is equally ubiquitous. Resistance here can be read as a *plurality*, in which power operates in and through subjects, so resistance also occurs as an essential element in the field of force. Foucault (1976) famously presents it as follows, in his *History of Sexuality* – itself a key text for critical (oppositional/resistive) appraisals of psychoanalysis. Asserting the 'strictly relational character of power relationships,' he writes:

> Their existence depends on a multiplicity of points of resistance: these play the role of adversary, target, support, or handle in power relations. These points of resistance are present everywhere in the power network ... Are there no great radical ruptures, massive binary divisions, then? Occasionally, yes. But more often one is dealing with mobile and transitory points of resistance, producing cleavages in a society that shift about, fracturing unities and effecting regroupings, furrowing across individuals themselves, cutting them up and remolding them, marking off irreducible regions in them, in their bodies and minds. (pp.95–6)

Despite the radical difference between this model and that familiar from psychoanalysis, which deals with resistance as a mode of psychic activity, the fluidity and omnipresence of resistance is starting to feel familiar. In some ways it sounds like the model of ordinary developmental attunement that can be derived from Winnicott's (1969) idea that what establishes the reality of the world is its capacity to resist – to survive, that is – the attacks of the subject upon it. As noted in the previous chapter, Winnicott's notion here is that the reality and 'usefulness' of the object is established when the object resists the infant's destructive impulses, when, that is, it shows it has a life and solidity of its own, outside the infant's fantasies. The infant may, in fantasy, destroy the mother, but in fact she survives. In the current context, the resistive power of the other is what makes the subject's existence possible, marking out a space which is 'real' in the sense of being beyond the subject's control. This continuous process of assertion and resistance is what constitutes the possibility of a stable kind of life.

There is more to it than this, of course: the Foucauldian reading of the power-resistance nexus has revolutionised understanding of these forces as they play out across the social and political terrain. Still, the psychoanalytic idea is lurking not far behind, itself functioning as a mode of 'resistance', or at least as a shadowy presence. Rose (2007), this time in the context of the relationship between Freud and Arnold Zweig as it responded to the rise of fascism, brings out some of the complexity of the intertwining of political and psychic resistance. Despite awareness of the contrast between these two forms of resistance, she sees them as in fruitful dialogue with each other, with the psychoanalytic reading trumping the political:

> If in political vocabularies, resistance is the passage to freedom, for psychoanalysis, it is repetition, blockage, blind obeisance to crushing internal constraint. For Zweig, only the overcoming of resistance in this psychoanalytic sense will allow the world to be saved. ... In this vocabulary, then, resistance is not the action of the freedom fighter, the struggle against tyranny, the first stirring of the oppressed; it is the mind at war with itself, blocking the path to its own freedom and, with it, its ability to make the world a better, less tyrannical, place. (p.21)

Resistance here is something to be overcome. Echoing Adorno et al.'s (1950) account in *The Authoritarian Personality*, Rose presents the fascist mind as full of resistance to freedom, to the terror produced by deep and truthful thought which does not back away from reality. Fascism is 'a carapace against what the mind should, ideally, be able to do with itself. Something shuts down, closes cruelly into its allotted and

unmovable place' (ibid.). The task of psychoanalysis, therefore, is to break down such resistance, which is precisely *not* fluid; rather, it is specifically, rigidly *defensive*, closing off possibilities. It lacks the sense of mobility and cunning to be found in Foucault's evocation of political resistance, it creates walls, not tunnels.

Nevertheless, as with all political as well as psychological barriers, the construction of defences shows where something valuable is being kept; so resistance is both an obstacle to change and an indication of where change is most needed. Rose notes how for Freud, resistance became the key to analytic progress: spot the area of resistance and one knows what is most defended against, and hence not only what is most threatening, but also what is most significant in a person's psychic life. The hiding place of repressed material is given away by what happens in analysis, by how the patient goes quiet at certain points, denies the significance of things she or he does, refuses to accept the analyst's inter- pretations, or messes around with the analytic boundaries (for example by missing or appearing late to sessions). In particular, resistance denotes the patient's ambivalence, whereby she or he might be genuinely seeking therapeutic help, yet might also be undermining attempts to achieve insight into the unconscious source or meaning of the symptoms which have been causing trouble – hence subverting the therapeutic process. Sometimes even the act of apparently seeking help is a way of resisting it. Going to therapy means one has tried one's best to change, even if nothing actually happens. Resistance, therefore, has general significance as a way of indicating how a person might want something but not want it at the same time.

The politics of this psychoanalytic understanding of resistance are consequently complex and uncertain. On the one hand, resistance is what opposes life – it is the way in which subjects and 'masses' avoid having to come to terms with what they really want, that which they seek and at the same time fear. On the other hand, resistance reveals the existence of an unconscious wish that gives glimpses of a subject's desire, of that element of 'enjoyment' which the subject is defending against. Hence the continuing attraction of the most 'resisted' and loathed objects, for example, the racialised other, commonly both eroticised and despised (Frosh, 2006). Resistance here does begin to look Foucauldian in its protean nature, but also ambiguous in its multiple meanings: both necessary signal of conflict and force to be overcome, both resistance 'to' and resistance 'of', both impulse towards death and towards life. This grafting of the psychoanalytic understanding of the dynamics of resistance onto theorising of *politi- cal* resistance certainly deepens both concepts, but at the same time it calls for careful distinctions to be made, between types of resistance

and also between the different functions that resistance might have. In particular, whilst the psychoanalytic notion well conveys the dynamic tension in resistance, the way in which it is always soaked in ambivalence and hence can never be taken at face value (so resisting something might also imply desiring it), it nevertheless is more restricted than the political model. It does not really encompass the idea of resistance as a positive liberatory force – as something seeking political freedom and emancipation from oppression. In the end, in psychoanalysis resistance is always something to be overcome if the subject is to be freer than before, more able to express and live with her or his wishes; in politics, one might hope, at least from time to time, that resistance might triumph.

This limitation on the efficacy of psychoanalytic notions of resistance for politics does not, however, mean that there is no gain from engaging with the subtleties of understanding of ambivalence and conflict that these notions contain. Perhaps this reveals itself most powerfully when it comes to questions of 'resistance to change', which act both at the level of the individual subject and of masses and even nations. If one desires the thing one resists, it may be hard to overthrow it completely. In relation to this, Freud himself, as his thinking developed, was led to differentiate between a number of different types, or at least sources, of resistance – a differentiation which has remained influential amongst analysts (see Sandler, Dare and Holder, 1973). These different types include resistances of the ego and of the id, and also those due to 'secondary gain', but the most interesting for political purposes is perhaps that arising from the operation of the superego, the 'part' of the mind in which guilt is held, and which is constantly appealing for punishment. This is a source of one weird reality of psychoanalytic progress: patients can come seeking help, but then reject it when it is offered, because they do not feel they deserve it. For Rose (2007), this type of resistance is the most important one for political analysis, the most 'deadly, because it arises out of the pleasure the mind takes in thwarting itself ... Freud is talking about the superego – the exacting, ruthless and punishing instance of the mind through which the law exerts its pressure on the psyche' (p.31). That is, this kind of resistance is the one which is most embedded in the subject, the one which arises not only out of a fear of change, but also out of the sheer *pleasure* of resistance itself, the enjoyment that comes out of the investment of psychic energy – '*jouissance*' – in destroying the opportunities for progress. Increasingly, this idea has been imported into political thinking to explain why it is that so much, so consistently, goes wrong.

Subjective politics and social repression

The terrorising of the psyche by the superego is an issue that has long concentrated the minds of political thinkers drawing on psychoanalysis, as it offers some kind of an account of the widespread resistance to change and of people's investment in staying in 'punishing' situations – those it might seem obvious that they should escape from. From the emergence of political psychoanalysis after the First World War, when the conditions for revolution in Europe were apparently ripe and when steps were indeed taken towards this – in Germany, most of all – yet when reaction set in quickly and fascism rather than revolutionary socialism emerged, the question of why people are 'chained to their chains' has been thought of as a potentially psychopolitical question. Simply, it seems that people somehow embrace conditions under which they are oppressed, or at least fail to take up opportunities to resist them, and this inertia has always puzzled revolutionaries. This need not mean reducing it to a purely psychological phenomenon, a kind of neurotic fear of change to be addressed through psychiatric treatment, though there are elements of that view to be found in some writers. Rather, the question is how and why the repressive features of the existing bourgeois society come to be 'internalised' to such an extent that the subject believes in them, is emotionally invested in them, unconsciously committed to them, and hence self-sabotaging when it comes to the opportunity for release. This question forces an engagement with the political concept of ideology as something more than a superstructural consequence of economic processes.

There was a small pantheon of early Freudo-Marxists who took this question on, for example the members of the 'Children's Seminar' run in the Berlin Psychoanalytic Institute by Otto Fenichel for the purpose of studying relations between psychoanalysis and politics (Jacoby, 1983). Amongst these, the excessive figure of Wilhelm Reich has come down to later generations as the embodiment of a politically daring thinker, part revolutionary icon, part tragic figure of persecution, part madman. As has been rehearsed in many places, Reich's (literally) energetic account of psychopolitics holds tremendous attractions as an early riposte to linear reductionist thinking in which all psychic trials are understood as the straightforward, unmediated consequence of economic woes, to wither away once the economic structure of society is set aright. For Reich, there is an important intervening process in which the 'character' of the subject is installed as 'armour' through patterns of authoritarianism, operating particularly through the family, and this character holds in check and distorts the natural sexual ebullience of the free subject. *Sexual* revolution is thus as necessary as political revolution if anything is to

significantly change. Reich thus articulates the modern notion that political structures enter into the core of individuality, constructing each person's consciousness and creating personality around ideological axes. In so doing, he delineates a broad concept of ideology as something that determines not just a person's perceptions, but her or his character. Thus, he moves rather close to the contemporary notion of ideology as a force that positions, or 'hails' (Althusser, 1971) subjects so that they experience themselves in the world in certain ways which are given by society but upon which they also have some capacity to act. Even though Reich still treats ideology as an error or distortion of reality, denying the individual expression of her or his basic and 'natural' desires, the manner in which he describes the insertion of ideology into this natural core is actually both subtle and helpful, particularly his account of the tendencies central to the patriarchal–authoritarian family.

As argued elsewhere (Frosh, 1999), it is the assertion that there is a fundamentally 'true' and healthy core within the human personality, which is only waiting to recover from the assaults of ideological distortion in order to find its proper expression, that is the major drawback to Reich's theories, at least to contemporary eyes. This idea is always problematic, not only because it implies an unchanging, biological 'human nature', but also because it reduces society's role to inhibiting or facilitating the expression of this natural impulse, rather than giving social forces a role in *constructing* 'human nature' in the first place. In Reich's case, it is sexual energy that is seen as the physically measurable natural driving force of the individual, to be liberated as part of a socialist revolution, thence to achieve satisfaction in ways that are no longer restricted or distorted by repressive authoritarianism. Such sexual essentialism (the irreducible core of humanity is biological sexuality) is always problematic for the attempt to create a genuinely 'Freudo-Marxist' theory that understands 'psychosocially' the merging of apparently individual and social forces. One can argue that even in his early works, where Reich avoids the simple reduction of politics to sexual liberation, it is clear that it is the latter which fascinates him, and which also prevents him from uncovering a path towards a genuinely socialist future. For whereas socialism is concerned with the possibilities of enriched relationships between people that are more egalitarian and less oppressive and limited than those available under capitalism, Reich has virtually nothing to say about relationships as such. His utopia is not concerned with a more developed network of social relationships; rather, it is libertarian in the individualistic sense, a system under which each individual's biological urges are to be played out in complete freedom. This form of politics returns to the individual rather than to the

transformation of social structures. Consequently, and whatever the intent, politics is reduced to biology just as mental life is reduced to attempts to achieve orgasm, and society and sex are opposed to one another rather than theorised in their complex interrelations.

Reich's provocative yet problematic theory has acted as a partial springboard for many discussions of psychoanalytic politics. These tend to go on to debate the contribution of Marcuse (1955) and the Frankfurt School in elaborating a more sophisticated model that develops further the idea that society enters the psyche as sedimented orthodoxy, as a mode of 'second nature' that represents itself as truth in order to manage or repress the actual desires of the subject. Key elements in Marcuse's argument (see Frosh, 1999, for a detailed account) include his deployment of a distinction between 'basic' and 'surplus' repression, in which the former is what is required for any social polity to exist – and hence is really an alternative conceptualisation of sublimation, of how basic human drives get converted into usable social energy – and the latter is the intensification of repression by the hierarchical distribution of scarcity and labour. The addition of the concept of surplus repression makes repression a specifically historical notion and one which depends on the organisation of any particular society. The necessity of repression varies with the maturity of civilisation, at least in terms of the extent of achieved mastery over nature through technology; given a constant level of repression, more will be 'surplus' in a culture of plenty than in one of scarcity. Under the conditions of late modernity, the potential for release given by technological advances is counteracted by the creation of an 'administered society' in which repression is sustained through the management of pleasure itself. Repression is therefore not a one-off phenomenon but rather (in a move reminiscent of Foucault's rethinking of the operations of power) creates its own modes of subjectivity. That is, the administered society *manages* pleasure rather than simply places restrictions upon it – it creates certain ways of enjoying, leading its subjects to believe that their needs are being met.

The notion that society is in some way 'administered' to *provide* enjoyment as a way to contain it, is important for some contemporary thinking on how pleasure and lack go together, and on what this has to do with political processes. In both Reich and Marcuse, there is an image of a kind of fullness or 'too-muchness' of the drives that has to be managed in order for society to maintain itself. In the case of Marcuse (as in Freud), there is a level at which this is necessary for society to survive at all, whereas with Reich the issue is one of revolutionary transformation – a society purely of the drives is envisionable as the outcome of genuine sexual revolution. Commenting on Theodor Adorno's version of this, which also employs the idea of 'naturalised'

drives to which the subject becomes submitted, Žižek (1994) identifies the paradox that arises. In this, repression is made both essential and oppressive, feeding into a kind of paralysis of psychoanalysis when faced with the question of political liberation:

> According to Adorno, this 'naturalistic' notion introduces into the Freudian edifice an irresolvable contradiction: on the one hand, the entire development of civilization is condemned, at least implicitly, for repressing drive-potentials in the service of social relations of domination and exploitation; on the other hand, repression as the renunciation of the satisfaction of drives is conceived as the necessary and insurmountable condition of the emergence of 'higher' human activities – that is to say, of culture. ... There is thus a radical and constitutive *indecision* which pertains to the fundamental intention of psychoanalytic theory and practice: it is split between the 'liberating' gesture of setting free repressed libidinal potential and the 'resigned conservatism' of accepting repression as the necessary price for the progress of civilization. (p.12)

The 'indecision' to which Žižek refers has indeed characterised the history of psychoanalysis' involvement with radical politics, revolving around the question of whether there is an ineradicable core of anti-social impulse within the individual which has to be managed – 'administered' – for society to survive. The distinction between repression and sublimation, which Žižek describes as being obscured in much theory, including that of the Frankfurt School, becomes important in making it possible to theorise a difference between a society that works solely to keep its subjects' urges in check by instituting an internal, repressive process, and one which allows expression of these urges in socially recognisable ways. The latter is more aligned with social reformist situations, and does two related but politically distinct things. On the one hand, it allows one to conceptualise rebellion as 'resistance' in the political sense, as a non-pathological articulation of wishes that has an impact on the social environment. With no distinction between repression and sublimation, every political act can be written off as motivated by unconscious wishes – after all, the main differentiation between a neurotic symptom and a supposedly healthy sublimation then lies only in the difference of response to, say, public masturbation and artistic expression or political grandstanding. If, however, there is a legitimate distinction between repression as a process that drives wishes 'underground', and a life-enhancing way of expressing these wishes, there is a way of conceptualising political resistance as something more than another form of pathogenic defence, and also a way of thinking about the prospects for change that does not have to adopt the attitude of 'resigned conservatism' described by Žižek above. On the other hand,

resistance turned into sublimation is also a good description of much that occurs in the administered society. As this society becomes more complex, so it allows expressions of dissent which then get picked up and used in the service of the social order itself, thus averting radical change. The remarkable ability of late capitalism to deal with its critics by co-opting them is an excellent example of the workings of this kind of sublimation. For instance, the originally anarchic wildness and demo-cratic ebullience of the world-wide web is now enjoyed more as a vehi-cle for entertainment and online shopping than as political critique.

Relationality and social conflict

The relational turn in psychoanalysis, drawn on previously for the discussion of ethics, has seeded some other useful developments in psychopolitical theorising. The British social context has seen some important thinking on social issues in the work of writers influenced by Kleinian psychoanalysis (e.g. Rustin, 1991), as well as some influential interventions by object relations and Jungian analysts promoting new models of emotional integrity in political contexts (e.g. Samuels, 1993). Internationally, the rise of intersubjectivist and relational psychoanaly-sis has been very important in the development of a politically commit-ted psychoanalysis, both through the feminist-originated work of Jessica Benjamin, discussed in Chapter 5, and in the writings of a group of American psychoanalysts inspired by both the object-relations and the American relational tradition. The core idea worked on in rather differ-ent ways in these approaches is that psychological and political well-being both depend on relational conditions that promote rather than stunt growth. These conditions are seen as entwined with processes of recognition and affirmation that are crucial for the developing human subject, but that are systematically stymied by social inequalities and oppression. Lynne Layton (2008), for example, writing about the 'subject versus object' division argues, like Benjamin (1998), for the importance of being recognised as a subject rather than treated 'like an object'. The latter, she claims, is a description of what it is like to be embedded in social processes of exclusion and derogation.

> Each of us, if we are lucky, grows up with some predictable experiences of mutuality in relating. But each of us as well is vulnerable to the shaming assaults that arise from being treated as objects. One major source of these shaming assaults is cultural hierarchies of classism, racism, sexism, and heterosexism – the power structures that establish norms of recognition. Such hierarchies tend not only to idealize certain subject positions and

devalue others, but also to do so by splitting human capacities and attributes and giving them class or race or sex or gender assignations. The culturally desirable attributes go to the dominant group; the ones the culture least rewards to the subordinate. Thus, social processes such as gendering, racing, classing, and sexing are at the very heart of subjectivity and subjective trauma, not accidental add-ons (as they are conceived to be in most psychoanalytic theories). (pp.66–7)

These social processes determine attitudes to dependency which in turn explain 'how cultural demands to split off capacities such as vulnerability, assertion, connection, dependence are lived both intrapsychically and interpersonally' (ibid.). That is, social processes produce certain kinds of subjects in particular through their openness or otherwise to dependency, something tied up intimately with the class–gender–race nexus into which subjects are socialised.

For Layton, relationality is forged in a psychic space divided between tendencies to maintain the splits induced by cultural hierarchies, and hence shaped by 'relational trauma' that 'divide the subject against itself', and 'those parts of self that have known and are able to seek out relationships based in mutual recognition of self and other as separate but interdependent subjects' (p.67). This kind of theorising, as Rustin (1995) has persuasively argued, is based on a 'positive' view of psychoanalysis in which the emphasis is on finding alternatives to, or ways out from, the constraints on human capacities wrought by oppressive social processes alongside (for the Kleinians at least) psychic impulses that are themselves destructive in form. Conflict and destructiveness are recognised as real and are not wished away, but the psychological and political momentum is towards identifying means to overcome them and to produce a more settled society, characterised by more fulfilling ('based in mutual recognition') relationships. Along the way, this involves identification of requirements for healthy psychic development and the kinds of social arrangements that might promote this. So, for example, Winnicott's (1960) ideas about the conditions under which 'false', conformist selves arise have been influential amongst relational psychoanalysts in adumbrating the conditions of early parenting that result in secure subjects attuned to the possibility of trust and relational interdependence. In the hands of some sociologists, this account of the necessary conditions for secure development also provides one basis for opposition to alienating and oppressive political systems.

Many of these ideas have been taken up credibly in social theory, for instance in the work of Axel Honneth, to produce a reformist account of social change. Honneth (e.g. Fraser and Honneth, 2003) examines social and political conflict as derived from a 'fundamental struggle for

recognition that itself is the key to understanding the long-term development of social interaction in capitalist societies' (McNay, 2008, p.271). Drawing directly on object-relational and intersubjectivist psychoanalysis, Honneth suggests that healthy development is dependent on an accurate and sustaining experience of recognition from the parent, and that this developmental necessity can be writ large as a simple fact of human experience. The argument here is that 'the desire for recognition is so fundamental to individual self-realization that it is the motivating force behind social development' (McNay, 2008, p.273). 'Affective recognition', grounded in childhood experiences in the family, is thus the source for the kind of emotional stability and security of selfhood that is necessary for sustaining social life. It gives rise to 'legal' and 'status' recognition in a triad that, as it develops, produces new forms of human opportunity, but if blocked evidences distortions and constraints on freedom. In particular, claims for legal and status recognition can become the fuel for social struggle and collective resistance; that is, an essentially affective condition (the demand for recognition rather than, for example, for resources) leads to political activity.

Honneth's model of social conflict has stirred up a great deal of interest and debate, with the positioning of affect at the heart of sociality being one of its attractive elements (because it counters the hyper-rationalism of much social theory), as well as a source of contention. What is of interest here is the use it makes of psychoanalytic theory as an account of recognition that is then extended into a description of the foundations of the human subject and thence as a prescription for social progress. Winnicott and Benjamin in particular are drawn on to provide a theory of the subject based on the idea of mutual recognition, with the resilience of the object in the face of the subject's demands being one key trope upon which personality and consequently social stability are based. As previously noted, this has much face-value plausibility, and in particular it evidences the possibility of linking the intimacies of the supposedly personal sphere (the parent–child encounter, for instance) with the rationalities and irrationalities of social action. This link might explain the passion with which people struggle for fairness and equality, for recognition of themselves and for all the other elements that go into an 'identity politics'. However, there is also a considerable amount of criticism of Honneth's reliance on this psychoanalytic model, which says something about the problems of importing psychoanalytic developmental thinking into political and sociological theory. Some of this relates to the familiar danger of reducing the political to the psychological. For instance, in her critique of Honneth's model of recognition, Fraser (in Fraser and Honneth, 2003) argues that its psychological focus 'displaces' and 'reifies' economic and social concerns to make all politics a matter

of identity struggle. Not only is this unhelpfully reductionist in neglecting the specificity of the political domain, but it also tends towards conservatism (despite Honneth's attention to a wide range of modes of resistance) because of the adaptational tinge to it in which survival and acknowledgement in a particular social environment become central to healthy citizenship. McNay (2008) summarises the strengths and limitations of Honneth's reliance on a psychoanalytic formulation of social identity most comprehensively in the following passage:

> There is no doubt that Honneth's phenomenology of social suffering emphasizes a crucial realm of catalyzing emotional experience that remains hidden in the rational and instrumental orientation of other sociological perspectives. The difficulty is that the unidirectional causal dynamic of his ontology of recognition, where social relations are seen as extrapolations of social dynamics, reifies these emotions and the realm of experience in general. The prepolitical realm of social suffering is seen as some unmediated realm of experience characterized by spontaneous and authentic feelings with inherent moral status. It is not evident, however, that all suffering leads to any kind of political insight or can be accorded such moral significance in the politics of experience and this is partly because all experience is mediated through a web of potentially distorting symbolic relations. (p.218)

Amongst the issues raised by McNay here is the differentiation implicit in Honneth's writing between a realm of politics and a 'prepolitical' realm of feelings, which in essence involves relational immediacy and a mode of genuineness that lays down markers for later authenticity. In many respects, this derives from his specific choice of psychoanalytic model. Winnicottian developmental thinking, built upon by later relational and intersubjectivist work, assumes the possibility of a kind of ideal state in which the mirroring of the child's needs by the mother is accurate. Within this theory, the child's aggressive, even destructive, assaults on the maternal object are survived with an appropriate amount of loving resilience to enable the child both to feel recognised for what she or he is, and to recognise the other/mother as a separate being with whom a relationship can be forged, and on whom the child can reliably draw. As described in Chapter 5, in the work of Jessica Benjamin this model is extended into a subtle interrogation of the necessary conditions for recognition both in the psychotherapeutic and the political sphere, in both of which it also meets the issue of reconciliation as an approach to the resolution of conflict. For Honneth, the stakes are equally high: the conditions of recognition, based in fundamental psychological needs, are what govern social striving and antagonism. The power of this account is that it facilitates a focus on emotion in social life and so allows one to gain theoretical leverage on the intensity

of people's investments in politics. The problem, as McNay points out, is that it makes the political and social sphere subsidiary to the psychological. As with the very different theory of Reich, this means that the needs of the subject come first; the social is restricted to either blocking or meeting these needs. Ontologically, this means that there is a psychic space which is non-political, or prior to politics, which then occupies an idealised position within the theory as a whole. Put more broadly, the relational model of psychoanalysis deployed in this way becomes one in which the subject loses its sociality through being postulated as an entity that is self-constituted prior to the operations of social forces. Relationality may be originary (as it is in Winnicott's thought), but it tends to be reduced to promoting or thwarting the growth of the subject rather than *structuring* the subject from the start. It is not that this necessarily leads to a neglect of economic and political factors in social life – in principle, there is no reason why it should do this – but it makes their function and significance that of servicing the needs of individuals, who themselves are described only in terms of necessary psychic and intersubjective processes, but not as formed in and of the social itself.

Lack and enjoyment in political thought

As noted in Chapter 5 in connection with Judith Butler's work, the psychoanalytic theorising of Jean Laplanche is currently being posited as an alternative basis for an understanding of identity politics that conceptualises the subject as split and socially riven from the start. The extrinsic formulation of the subject is expressed in the theory of enigmatic signifiers, those untranslatable messages from the adult which become the foundation for the infant's unconscious life and which are the residue of the process of unconscious seduction passed on through generations from parent to child. This adds a strand of 'alienness' at the core of subjecthood: central to each subject is an unconscious dimension, as we know, but this unconscious does not 'belong' to the 'person', but rather arises from an act of mis-communication, a mode of unwitting seduction, in which the parental desire excites the child, without being understood. 'So we have the reality of the message and the irreducibility of the fact of communication. What psychoanalysis adds is a fact of its experience, namely that this message is frequently compromised, that it both fails and succeeds at one and the same time. It is opaque to its recipient and its transmitter alike' (Laplanche, 1999, p.169). It is no longer a matter of intention; what comes from the other to the subject is something unknown to both, yet intense in its effect (and affect). The infant is invaded by an unconscious message, its

private spaces inflicted with the sense of 'something else', something excessive and too strong, always hinting at its presence without ever letting itself be fully known. The adult, too, holds an alien message inside: there is something no one can ever properly know. If this model has force, it is very difficult to imagine what a personal, authentic pre-social space can be; however 'deep' we go, we find the other already there. In contrast to the object-relational stance, the split human subject 'hidden' behind the ego (which is really a Lacanian formulation, but has influenced a generation of French analysts) is brought into being by the other. It is not excisable from the other and hence is 'always-already' social. Identity struggle is consequently never going to be a matter of striving for recognition of what one authentically 'is'; it is rather a matter of *producing* a subject in line with certain aspired-for values, creating a subject with force in the world. Specifically, recognition of the subject as a being with rights, for instance as 'black' or 'gay', is not a matter of putting a name to a mode of authenticity that is pre-given, but rather of creating the conditions under which discursively constructed possibilities are given shape and allotted agentic power. Psychoanalysis of this kind would not by any means preclude identity struggle; but it also places under scrutiny the notion of 'identity' itself as something constructed rather than basic, something importantly flawed rather than assumed to be ideally whole.

This brings us back to the perspective offered by Lacanian psychoanalysis, the exponents of which have framed the issues somewhat differently. In the context of this discussion, a symptomatic element is the apparently arcane debate about 'lack' and 'fullness' in psychoanalytic thought. This refers specifically to whether the subject is driven by lack in seeking its desire, or whether there is a kind of overflowing of psychic activity out of which things happen as an expression of the essentially *sui generis* imaginative life of the human subject. In classic Lacanian theory, there is little doubt that it is lack, concretised in castration, which is the key element. The division between the registers of Imaginary, Symbolic and Real classifies a discrepancy between what is imagined to be true (the holistic fantasy of an ego that can function autonomously and with integrity, of a subject that can fully know the truth); what can be symbolised and consequently manipulated, investigated and analysed (so psychoanalysis itself operates in the domain of the Symbolic); and what can never be known, or can be known only at the edges or by its sudden appearance in moments of breakthrough, never fully symbolisable, always at work but never quite there. These elements of the Lacanian scheme frame a set of 'lacks' contributing in different ways to the subject as a social and political entity. One is the theorisation of the subject as riven with splits; a second portrays the

subject as intrinsically lacking in the sense of being cut off from the source of power, which always lies outside it as an Other that gives form and force to the subject's being. Both these types of lack are central to the Lacanian account of how the human subject is constituted. Indeed, the second type, which is essentially a description of how the Symbolic works, is vital to Lacanian ideas on sexual difference and on the construction of the subject in language. It stresses that the subject is not *a centre to itself*, but rather, in line with Freudian theory, is displaced and inhabited by something outside it. The subject is always constructed according to the desire of the Other, always answerable to a 'big Other' that is over and beyond itself and can perhaps be thought of as 'society' (amongst other things).

What is of great importance here in distinguishing the Symbolic from the Imaginary relationship to the Other is the postulation of the Other itself as *lacking*, not as a fully formed answer to the subject's desire. That is, the subject is lacking because it is placed in a web of symbolic positioning which cuts it off from the source of its desire; but the Other is also lacking, because it makes demands on the subject, facing the subject with the question, 'What does the Other want?'

> A lack is encountered by the subject in the Other, in the very intimation that the Other makes to him by his discourse. In the intervals of the discourse of the Other, there emerges in the experience of the child something ... namely, *He is saying this to me, but what does he want?* The desire of the Other is apprehended by the subject ... in the lacks of the discourse of the Other, and all the child's *whys* reveal not so much an avidity for the reason of things, as a testing of the adult, a *Why are you telling me this?* ever-resuscitated from its base, which is the enigma of the adult's desire. (Lacan, 1973, p.214)

Hook (2008a) draws out the political implications of this position, commenting:

> Once we realize that the linked questions of desire (*'What do I want?'*) and social location (*'What makes sense of the position I occupy in society?'*) are really unanswerable – because they always rebound in the form of another question – then we start to understand the futility of such recourse to the Other, at least within the realm of the signifier, and the alienation of the subject that inevitably results. (p.279)

The interesting point here is that the Other is conceptualised not as a solid structure of power that acts over and against the subject, but as lacking, as having a desire of its own, which the subject is also immersed in. Out of this overlapping of lacks, if one can enunciate the Lacanian theory of desire in this way (desire as always being built on a lack),

comes a nodal point for the investment of the subject in the social. If the Other is lacking (if 'it needs me'), then the subject is faced with the question of what it is in the subject that is desired, and hence of what kind of lack in the Other can be filled by the (also lacking) subject. This is linked to the Lacanian notion of the *objet a* as the object cause of desire – the thing in the other that provokes the desire of the subject, that moves it into action. In this complex array of interlinked abstractions surrounding lack, one can just about glimpse a political theory, one which has been taken up by an array of commentators (e.g. Bosteels, 2006): the mutual construction of lacking subjectivities produces a play of investments that circulate between subject and Other and operate in the social field.

There is a third type of lack here, however, produced by the impossibility of symbolisation of the Real. Stavrakakis (2007) frames it like this:

> In fact it is this constitutive and unbridgeable gap between the symbolic/imaginary nexus (the field of social construction and institution) and the always escaping real which also makes history possible: if it was feasible for a particular social construction to symbolise fully the real, then history would come to an end, together with the permanent play between human creativity (desire) and social dislocation (lack). (p.40)

The Real is constitutively unsymbolisable, and as such always features as a lack at the centre of the human subject: there is an impossibility always in play, and this has effects in generating a gap into which subjecthood must fall. Out of this come some possible political readings linked to the Lacanian endeavour. One is to conceptualise lack as promoting human creativity but also as always setting limits to it: there is never any closure in the political field, because there is always something left out. Whilst this is anti-utopian in its implications, it also creates a constant pressure for newness, for seeking something else. This has some implications resonant of Castoriadis' (e.g. 1995) divergence from Lacanian orthodoxy, in which he focuses on the constant creativity of the human subject *in the imaginary* as a kind of generator of a stream of signifiers that gets broken into and constrained by the institutions of society, but which nevertheless is the source for constant radical imagination. However, this approach suffers from dividing the originary, essential psychic 'monad' off from the social, returning them to an oppositional relationship akin to that fallen into by object relations theory. In contrast, the 'orthodox' Lacanian position maintains a stance that the Other (and hence the institutions of society) and the subject are never separable, that desire and creativity are produced by

the Real. As Žižek (1994) states, in a different domain (in this case about the limitations of Habermas' theory):

> Here we confront the incommensurability between hermeneutics ('deep' as it may be) and psychoanalytic interpretation: Habermas can assert that distortions have meaning as such – what remains unthinkable for him is that *meaning as such results from a certain distortion* – that the emergence of meaning is based on a disavowal of some 'primordially repressed' traumatic kernel. (p.27)

That is, meaning – creativity and imagination included – is not something pulsing away which is shaped or distorted by social pressures; there is no pure, transparent communication between subjects, for example. Instead, the openness of the Lacanian field is given by the fact that there are always gaps in the functioning of the Symbolic. It can never quite hold together because of the presence of something unsymbolisable at its core – which does not mean that the effort is never to be made to symbolise it, but rather that it can never be mastered. Stavrakakis (2007) comments:

> From a Lacanian point of view, the fact that the imposition of the symbolic is never total can only mean that the real, being ultimately incommensurable with the symbolic, resists symbolisation and persists alongside our sociosymbolic identifications. ... First of all ... it persists through the continuous resurfacing of negativity, through the dislocation of subjective and social identities. By encircling these encounters with the real, Lacan seems to register the importance of a moment that, in social and political theory, could only be described as the moment of the political *par excellence*. (p.53)

The 'political' here is the response to the constitutive lack within the subject and the Other. It

> refers to the moment of failure of a given identity or social construction; a failure which not only dislocates the identity in question but also creates a lack, stimulating the desire for a rearticulation of the dislocated structure, stimulating, in other words, human creativity, becoming the condition of possibility for human freedom. (p.54)

That is, the fact of lack creates the desire for change – an idea which drives Stavrakakis' belief in and commitment to radical democracy.

The emphasis on lack in Lacanian political thought has been much criticised for its tendency to posit irrevocable exclusions to the social order and also for its abstractness (no doubt more than adequately represented in the description above), which to some has meant that it

is more an account of ontology than of politics. It is also attacked for its negativism, even nihilism, which ironically can result in a conformism that reduces the prospects for change to that of coming to accept its impossibility. Robinson (2004), for instance, in a review of books by Žižek, Badiou, Laclau and Mouffe and Stavrakakis, complains:

> For Lacanians, the return of the Real is always a disruptive, almost revolutionary event which shatters the entire social totality constructed around its exclusion. Every social order, therefore, has a single touchy 'nodal point' which it must maintain, or else it will collapse. Since the exclusion of a Real element is supposed to be necessary, Lacanians urge that one reconcile oneself to the inevitability of lack. Lacanian politics is therefore about coming to terms with violence, exclusion and antagonism, not about resolving or removing these. The acceptance of lack takes the form of an Act or Event, in which the myth of subjective completeness is rejected and the incompleteness of the self is embraced. The primary ethical imperative in Lacanian politics is to 'accept' the primacy of antagonism, i.e. the central ontological claim of the Lacanian edifice itself. (p.260)

Whilst this is probably an extreme formulation, lumping together a variety of authors who have significant differences with one another, there is a genuine critical point arising here, which has to do with the extent to which social change can occur if one assumes that lack is constitutive and unavoidable. As is suggested by the query posed by Žižek to Adorno's work, quoted earlier, there is a difficulty about whether psychoanalysis is ever to be in a position to advocate change, or whether it will always retain a 'diagnostic' edge which means it can never commit to anything. In some of Žižek's writing, the result of this is a foregrounding of 'terror' and also a writing style that is often apparently wilfully contrary, working through a systematic process of unsettling expectations by reversals and provocations. 'Today's "mad dance"', he writes, '... awaits its resolution in a new form of Terror' (Butler, Laclau and Žižek, 2000, p.326); elsewhere he emphasises the difference between a false resistance and a radical act that basically smashes apart the symbolic order through the insurgence of the Real. Stavrakakis (2007) argues that this idea radically revises and is incompatible with the Lacanian emphasis on lack. It is a kind of impatience with it, which also relies on a belief in a 'divine miracle' that will dispense with negativity and create a new order. Faced with the Lacanian argument that the 'constitutive division' of the subject can never be displaced,

> Žižek's response is to reverse the argument and argue that the true source of evil is assuming finitude, mortality, and lack as such, ignoring the dimension

of 'divine miracles': '[acts] occur, on the contrary, as a totally unpredictable *tuche*, a miraculous event which shatters our lives. To put it in somewhat pathetic terms, this is how the "divine" dimension is present in our lives' (p.120)

Even Žižek's use of the Lacanian trope of *jouissance* buys into this, despite its efficacy in instigating a penetrating analysis of apparently 'irrational' investments in political turmoil. At its broadest, *jouissance* references the 'enjoyment' that comes with immersion in the Real – how the subject gets taken up in unsymbolisable, irrational activity that makes it feel alive, yet is also bizarre, overstated, excessive to the apparently realistic demands of the situation. The individual subject does this in relation to the symptom, which can be a nodal point holding the psyche together. Enjoyment also operates at the core of the political, as excessive phenomena (war, terror, nationalism) overwhelm the social order and subjects find themselves caught up in them. This is, as noted, an important idea that gives leverage on the extensive questions brought up by apparently irrational political and social acts – internecine conflicts, self-destructive political claims, obvious 'cost-benefit losers' that are clung onto until the bitter end. The idea that subjects might find these enlivening precisely because they draw on the unsymbolisable, excluded core of subjecthood is one that Lacanian theorists, and Žižek in particular, have contributed to political thought. But whether the Žižekian use of the concept is really 'Lacanian' and is not rather an appeal to a kind of vitalist life energy that fuels action, is a moot point. That is, if *jouissance* is the answer, then perhaps the Lacanian/Freudian emphasis on avoiding pretence that there is a cure – that the analyst actually knows the truth of the subject – has been forgotten.

That said, Žižek often shows an exemplary allegiance to the Lacanian lesson that psychoanalysis is not a programme or policy for action, but rather a critical discourse that is committed to returning subjects to what they can and cannot know. In *The Parallax View*, for example (2006b), he presents an extended examination of psychoanalysis' response to contemporary cultural shifts that are not only marginalising it institutionally, but also seem to reflect a move away from the Oedipal structures with which psychoanalysis is most familiar. Žižek identifies three conventional psychoanalytic responses to this:

1. In a disavowal similar to that of the few remaining 'orthodox' Marxists, it continues to act as if nothing has really changed: the fundamental structure of the Unconscious and its formations as formulated by Freud still reigns supreme, the changes are merely superficial, so one should resist the temptation of the fashionable calls for a 'new paradigm.'

2. While recognizing the shift, the move toward a 'post-Oedipal society,' it perceives this as a dangerous development, as a loss of our very fundamental ethico-symbolic coordinates; as a result it advocates some kind of return to the symbolic authority of the paternal Law as the only way to halt our slide toward the global chaos of autistic closure and violence.

3. It regularly tries to 'keep up with the times,' and thus acquire a new legitimacy: either by searching for proofs that the new neurosciences confirm its hypotheses, or by redefining its therapeutic role against the 'new anxieties' of our 'postmodern' epoch (for instance, focusing on 'pathological Narcissism'). (p.298)

Žižek asks which of these three ways is the right one, and gives a characteristic answer: 'The *fourth* one, of course: that of asserting that, on the contrary, it is only today that we encounter in our daily lives the basic libidinal deadlock around which psychoanalysis circulates' (ibid.). He then goes on to deliberately set up a straw-person argument that Lacanian psychoanalysis differentiates between two failed responses to the 'crisis of authority' (the crisis of the discourse of the Master, in more Lacanian terms): first, what Lacan calls the discourse of the University (total administration and bureaucratisation of knowledge) and, secondly, the discourse of the Hysteric ('the excess of doubt, of permanent questioning' [ibid.]). In contrast to these, the discourse of the Analyst stands for

> the emergence of revolutionary-emancipatory subjectivity that resolves the split into university and hysteria: in it, the revolutionary agent (*a*) addresses the subject from the position of knowledge which occupies the place of truth (that is, which intervenes at the 'symptomal torsion' of the subject's constellation), and the goal is to isolate, get rid of, the Master-Signifier which structured the subject's (ideologico-political) unconscious'. (ibid.)

This seems to make the analyst into the one who speaks the revolutionary truth, but as Žižek is quick to point out, this in itself is at odds with the Lacanian doctrine that no one knows the truth. Where, for example, many contemporary social theorists see the reflexivity of contemporary society as a move towards emancipation, Žižek argues that it is now precisely this reflexivity that operates to preserve things as they are, for example by making the interpretations that could be offered by a psychoanalyst into something already known to the subject, who thinks about her or himself in this way in the first place. That is, one comes to psychoanalysis to have confirmed the narrative of oneself as a psychological subject. The result is that the Symbolic is unable to provide effective interpretations, because interpretation is itself part of the 'symptom' of the contemporary world; hence, according to Žižek, the taste for

violence which breaks through the Symbolic itself, which is, in important respects, a taste of the Real. 'What if', he asks (p.303), 'the gap between the Symbolic and the raw Real epitomized by the figure of the skinhead is a false one, since this Real of the outbursts of "irrational" violence is generated by the globalization of the Symbolic?'

Žižek's argument here is relatively subtle and is pursued into a consideration of superego violence and the changing role of the *objet a*, but for current purposes it is interesting mostly for its understanding of the efficacy of psychoanalysis as a model for activity in the current political culture. 'Reflexive modernity' of the kind that would be promoted for example by Giddens (1991), is seen by Žižek as an instance of the absorption of analytic discourse into the administered society. It is an example of what Ian Parker (1997) describes as 'psychoanalytic culture', the saturation of contemporary consciousness by psychoanalytic concepts. Rather than giving leverage for revolutionary activity, this tendency removes the sting from psychoanalysis; that is, it becomes another instance in a long history (as long as the history of psychoanalysis itself – see Jacoby, 1975; Frosh, 1999) of the blunting of the subversive edge of psychoanalysis, so that it becomes an agent, rather than a critic, of the status quo. If everyone is adept at using psychoanalytic ideas reflexively – if everyone already knows what their dreams mean in Freudian language – then psychoanalysis cannot surprise anyone, cannot any more speak from the margins in a way that will produce a radical shock. The question asked right at the beginning of this book, of how psychoanalysis can be rescued from its collapse into conformity, is therefore, *one shouldn't start from there*. In Žižek's account, psychoanalysis always has to stay one step ahead, doing the unexpected – just as he does, perhaps playing the fool:

> Traditionally, psychoanalysis was expected to allow the patient to overcome the obstacles which denied him or her access to 'normal' sexual enjoyment; today, however, when we are bombarded from all sides by different versions of the superego injunction 'Enjoy!', from direct enjoyment of sexual performance to enjoyment of professional achievement or spiritual awakening, we should move to a more radical level: today, psychoanalysis is the only discourse in which you are allowed *not* to enjoy (as opposed to 'not allowed to enjoy') ... The desire that no longer needs to be sustained by the superego injunction is what Lacan calls the 'desire of the analyst'. (2006b, p.304)

Much feeds into this idea of the desire of the analyst, including a set of images that more than border on antisemitism, in which Žižek claims that the correct model of the analyst is the 'Jewish moneylender, a shadowy figure to whom all the big figures of society come to borrow money, pleading with him and telling him all their dirty secrets and

passions' (p.305). But at the end of it there is an important question about the outcome of Lacanian politics. Žižek writes:

> Lacan's claim is that the discourse of the Analyst prepares the way for a new Master ... The question, however, remains: how, *structurally*, does this new Master differ from the previous, overthrown one ...? If there is no structural difference, then we are back with the resigned conservative wisdom about (a political) revolution as a revolution in the astronomic sense of the circular movement which brings us back to the starting point (p.307)

Žižek's own aspiration seems to be to construct new 'Master-signifiers' based on the disappearance of the Freudian unconscious (collapsing under the weight of self-reflexivity) and its replacement with a revolutionary break. He acknowledges, however, that what this means is there could be a very narrow dividing line between the analyst and the totalitarian leader: 'both are objet petit a objects of transferential love; the difference between them is the difference between the perverse social link (in which the pervert knows what the other really wants) and the discourse of the analyst who, while occupying the place of supposed knowledge, keeps it empty' (p.380). Can one trust the analyst to do this? Can one trust any revolutionary leader to provoke a break without reverting to the authoritarian mastery that she or he supposedly seeks to replace? The Lacanian answer to this would seem to be that it is unlikely that one can. Perhaps once again we are back to the ambivalence found in the psychoanalytic concept of resistance: everything we intensely oppose, we also desire; every position we seek to overcome, we also wish to occupy. Žižek seems to try to avoid this by wriggling out of all expected positions, by remaining unsettled and continuously provocative, but it may be fair to say that in the course of doing this he becomes 'predictably unpredictable', his celebrity status generated not just by the extraordinary vivacity and depth of his discourse, but also by a search by his readers and audiences for a kind of entertainment that comes from being once more surprised. Without the surprise, without the fireworks, it would not be Žižek. Similarly, Lacan's apparently disruptive opacity became predictable, his anti-eloquence, which may initially have been produced by a genuine concern not to rush to simple conclusions, itself turning into Lacanian orthodoxy. The predictability and eventual mundanity of these recurring events possibly contributes to the appeal of the call to 'revolutionary terror' as a way of breaking through repetitions by sweeping them all away; until, that is, one thinks of the consequences. Psychoanalysis offers a great deal of leverage here, in outlining the patterns of desire in which subjects become stuck – whether due to lack or fullness, it does not really matter. But there is still

little evidence that psychoanalysis can point a way through it to something 'more real than the Real', which will put a stop to the cycles of power that continually impose themselves and create subject positions of predictable kinds, whichever individuals end up occupying them.

Conclusion

This chapter has been concerned with how psychoanalysis is drawn on in political theory as a resource for radical critique. Moving from Freud's ideas on the psychology of the 'mass' to the parallel worlds of psychoanalytic and political resistance, it argued for the fertility of some basic psychoanalytic notions in generating ideas about the complex and ambivalent ways in which political investments occur. Classical 'Freudo-Marxist' theory such as that of the Frankfurt School trace the psychic operations of ideology, whilst contemporary relational theory provides insights into the intersubjective conditions that might be necessary for the production of a more equal society. Finally, the powerful and voguish application of Lacanian ideas in the political sphere was debated. Here, the emphasis on lack and on constant critique from a position of 'emptiness' offers a rallying point for those who regard radical politics as requiring suspicion of all fixed positions, including those advocated by radicals themselves. As such it is probably true to some basic Freudian premises, for instance that everything can and should be analysed, and that utopias are always imaginary consolations. One wonders, however, whether this position of continual criticism can ever form the basis for a political programme that might actually improve the conditions of people's lives.

The work described here is so disparate as to make it difficult to come to any straightforward conclusion about the contribution of psychoanalysis to this particular space outside the clinic. Nevertheless, there seems little doubt that this contribution is significant, supplying a vocabulary and a set of substantive ideas for exploring the investments of subjects in the political sphere. This is not just a matter of ideology, identity or affect. Psychoanalysis allows one to speak of the reasons people become deeply involved in politics, as well as of how the social order 'infects' them so that particular political arrangements come to feel necessary and absolute. But it also offers a broader set of concepts around resistance, desire, recognition and lack that might usefully feed into general political thought. At the very least, this would oppose the rationalism present in much conventional political theory, and offer leverage on the irruptions of violent and intense emotion that seem endemic to the lives of social groups, including whole nations. This

might reflect back on psychoanalysis itself, not only as a motivation to examine the political stance taken by psychoanalysts (which has only been mentioned here but has been worked on quite extensively in the literature), but also as a set of questions about how social and political processes mediate the construction of individual subjects. As such, the questions raised are psychosocial in their import and orientation. That is, they question the convention of distinguishing between subject and society and suggest instead the need to look for what runs through both.

Psychoanalysis and the 'Psychosocial'

Throughout this book, I have been claiming a general 'psychosocial' perspective that addresses ways in which what are conventionally taken to be the separate spheres of the 'personal' or 'individual' and the 'social' are actually bound up together. In each example of the application of psychoanalysis in social research, I have been interested in how psychoanalysis might help bridge this particular gap. This has partly been through appreciation of the structuring power of the social order (the 'big Other' of Lacanian thought), and of dynamic mechanisms such as identification that offer a model of how the subject might experience the 'external' world as 'internal'. In particular, the constitutive function of otherness, as theorised especially by Laplanche (1999), is an idea that has taken hold across a wide range of approaches, including relational and Lacanian psychoanalysis. Taking this seriously involves accepting that there is no subject without the other; that is, that the subject is permeated from the start by the 'interruption' represented by other subjects and by society.

Whilst the perspective adopted here is 'psychosocial' in this sense, the specific disciplinary locus of *psychosocial studies* is only just emerging in the social sciences. As this chapter will show, psychoanalysis plays a considerable part in this emergence, lending psychosocial studies some authority and providing it with one of its distinctive perspectives. Conversely, psychosocial studies is fast becoming an arena in which psychoanalysis can recover some of its ground within the academy. It is also a space for contestation between different forms and understandings of psychoanalysis, partly because as a new discipline it is as yet unclear about what it wants from it. Should psychosocial studies buy in completely to a world view in which its focus is on the affective and unconscious components of social being, with psychoanalysis offering the language and concepts that make this viable? In that case, psychoanalysis would be drawn on as an expert discipline that has the knowledge base available to it to make psychosocial studies possible. Alternatively, is psychoanalysis just one of a range of tools that can be used to make sense of psychological and social material? This too makes psychoanalysis an expert system, though a more circumscribed one, jostling with other approaches (for example, phenomenology) and being

189

seen more as a technology than an ideology. Or is there something to be developed from the version of psychoanalysis that sees it as a universal methodology of 'undoing', provoking and questioning rather than supplying solutions to research questions? This would use it to prise open psychosocial studies, challenging it to produce understandings of the social human subject that are uncertain and equivocal, allowing breathing space for critical visions. This is, of course, the rather idealistic aspiration of much of what has been presented in this book to date; but it has its own difficulties. Not least, it might make one wonder whether this kind of critical instability is a sufficient basis on which an academic discipline can be founded.

This chapter debates some of these issues. It begins with a brief genealogy of psychosocial studies and a discussion about the kind of psychosocial studies with which a critical psychoanalysis could engage. It then looks at how two forms of psychoanalysis – loosely, Kleinian and Lacanian – have been advanced in British psychosocial studies, and examines some of the implications of this. It finishes with an account of some of the difficulties of 'applying' psychoanalysis in this field, an account which also draws together some of the broader challenges of the book as a whole.

Critical psychology and psychosocial studies

In the study of mind, behaviour and now brain, the discipline of academic psychology is a powerful force. Originating at roughly the same time as psychoanalysis, in the latter half of the nineteenth century, and partly in response to the same individualising tendencies in the surrounding culture, psychology has developed to become a field of astonishing virtuosity and extensive application, with vast cultural currency as well as research and vocational appeal. It is bought into by media and government; it is perhaps the predominant 'psy' discipline (Rose, 1998) in relation to the regulation or administration of the contemporary subject; and it has significant productive power in the organisation of health and education services, in management practices in organisations, and in judicial work. Its primary self-narrative is as a 'scientific' discipline, based on rigorous observation and experimentation and as far as possible following the traditions of the natural sciences in the grounding of its claims ('psychological science' and 'scientific psychology' being terms of approbation in the community of researchers). As such, it presents itself as an 'expert' discipline, a kind of advanced technology of knowledge, capable of offering independent information about people's psychology and not amenable – at least ideally – to subjective beliefs that distort the nature of its facts.

Psychology thus diverges from psychoanalysis particularly around the issue of subjectivity. Where psychoanalysis attends to the 'subjective' as its core project and also in its methodology (for instance in the transference but more broadly in its use of affective responses to guide interpretations), psychology has traditionally avoided anything that might interfere with the 'objectivity' of its observations. This also means that it has claimed independence as a scientific profession and presented itself as separate from political pressures and processes. However, as Nikolas Rose (1998) indicates, despite its apparently individualistic focus (the mind and behaviour of the individual subject, thought about as a mechanical and/or biological entity, is its proper topic of study), psychology operates in a *social* field. It is not just a body of knowledge, but a branch of activity that has its own ideological and hence political investments – rather a different point of view from the one adopted by those who claim for it some kind of scientific 'neutrality'. It is part of the state apparatus for selection, categorisation and treatment, as witnessed in its applications in education and health as well as in management, policing and the military (e.g. Burman, 2007). Psychologists have also not infrequently been co-opted by governments as participants in repressive policies. This has occurred in relation to psychiatric treatment of dissidents, for example in the Soviet Union (Bloch and Reddaway, 1984), but is not confined to countries where professional bodies lack strong ethical codes. A recent example is the involvement of US psychologists in military interrogations in Guantánamo Bay, a practice eventually repudiated by the American Psychological Association in August 2008, but only after an acrimonious debate within its ranks (Summers, 2007). Additionally, the emphasis on the individual as the object of knowledge makes specific ideological claims, which can be seen most clearly in assumptions about the separation between what is individual (seen as 'personal') and what is social. The sub-discipline of social psychology, for example, has rarely had much to say about the nature of the social itself, but has largely been restricted to investigations of cognitions in social settings (attitudes, prejudice, social judgements, etc.) and of people's behaviour in groups and other social situations. It thus studies the individual in social contexts but without deconstructing the notion of individuality itself. Instead, the separate status of the individual is assumed as a 'given' (and not as a historical construct), however much it might be acknowledged that the practices of individuals vary from one sociocultural setting to another. The individualising tendency of psychology can thus be seen as a particular kind of intervention in social science, paralleling the separation of 'private' from 'public' and 'personal' from 'political'. Within it, the links between what are separated out as 'social' and 'individual'

are reduced or even removed absolutely, ostensibly either because they are indeed distinct elements, or because they consequently become easier to study; but perhaps actually as a further contribution to the smooth running of the administered society.

The development of psychology in this way can also be seen partly as a product of an intellectual division of labour with the contemporaneous development of an empirical discipline of sociology, which took on the study of the social (social structures, class and race, and so on), whilst psychology inhabited the domain of the individual. Whilst the demarcation could clearly never be absolute, it has been quite strong, and has limited the possibilities for exploration of the *intersection* of supposedly social and individual from within these two disciplines. In addition, the strict division between individual and social risks reducing one to the other (so that, for example, the social is seen as no more than the free interactions of individuals, or the individual is seen as fully constituted by her or his social class, or gender or 'race' position), or of essentialising each element so that the social is 'bracketed off' in discussions of the individual, or vice versa. The conceptualisation of the individual/social divide is itself the problem here. Whilst one might make tactical decisions in any research project to investigate at the level of the 'person' or the 'social', in fact these are not distinct entities, but simply ways of carving up the research field to make it manageable, with the effect of reproducing ideological assumptions about the nature of the social world. Both psychology and sociology have treated these distinctions as real, with repetitive and mostly fruitless debates about 'individual *versus* society' and 'nature *versus* nurture' being the consequence.

As happens within hegemonic disciplines, psychology has produced its own internal critics who have drawn on broader political and social theories to contextualise and analyse the discipline itself so that its conditions of emergence and modes of operation become more visible (e.g. Parker, 2007). Many of these critics have worked against oppressive psychological practices operating in the specific areas of 'race' and intelligence, mental health and evolutionary psychology (e.g. Gould, 1996; Banton et al., 1985; Rose and Rose, 2000). Others have sought a broader development in forming a 'critical psychology' that has two main tendencies: offering a political critique of psychology; and using psychology for 'emancipatory' ends, involving empowerment of oppressed groups and theoretical and practical critique of social forces. This latter tendency has been entwined with liberation movements of various kinds, including anti-psychiatry and patients' rights, and predominantly offers a 'social justice' perspective (e.g. Fox, Prilleltensky and Austin, 2009). Although psychoanalysis has occasionally been drawn on by exponents of this approach, on the whole the emancipa-

tory agenda has been opposed to what is seen as psychoanalysis' own conformism, expressed in what are regarded as normative practices particularly in relation to sexism and ethnocentrism. This type of critical psychology is primarily activist in orientation and has had a powerful impact on community psychology in general.

The other perspective, which offers a critical account of psychology itself, is closer to the concerns of this chapter. It seeks to find a way to move beyond the complacent individualism of psychology not only to understand how the discipline itself collaborates in the apparatus of administration (e.g. Hook, 2007), but also to develop a set of theoretical tools that will make it possible to overcome the individual–social split and instead think through ways to bring together or 'suture' these supposedly opposed entities. Amongst other things, this type of critical psychology has fed into a set of approaches loosely grouped together as 'psychosocial studies'. These have their other origins in social work and sociology, but also in an applied psychoanalytic tradition associated with the Tavistock Institute from the 1950s onwards, committed to radical shifts in public and institutional practices (Frosh, 2003; Walkerdine, 2008). In addition to this basically psychoanalytically driven type of psychosocial thinking, social psychology has also spawned a set of new research perspectives that partake very actively of the 'turn to language' evident in all the social sciences since the 1970s. In this 'discursive' tradition, the human subject is understood as an entity produced in and by language – an understanding that has been implicit in much that has already been addressed in this book, albeit not necessarily arising from the same epistemological stable. As will be discussed, this discursive turn, whilst engaged in the same critical endeavour as much psychosocial studies research, has some significantly different views of the utility of psychoanalytic concepts for advancing this work.

Psychosocial studies is a fragile entity, perhaps reflecting the difficulty of maintaining the thinking-together of social and individual that are constantly pushed apart by the fundamental ideological impulses of liberalism and late capitalism. As noted elsewhere (Frosh, 2003), its characteristics include looking out from psychology and sociology towards interdisciplinary theories and methodologies that allow it critical leverage; and in doing this psychoanalysis has seemed to have much to offer. In many ways this seems obvious. Psychoanalysis, as evidenced throughout this book, has always ranged across conventional disciplines, never quite having a home in any of them, and at its best has managed to sustain a vision of the human subject as born in and of both bodily, internal drives and social relationships. More importantly, the central notion of psychoanalysis, that of the unconscious, has an

evidently 'trans-individual' aspect to it (Hook, 2008b), in the sense that unconscious ideas are both 'in' and 'outside of' the subject, neither owned by the 'person' nor completely separate. This means that psychoanalysis has clear potential for offering theoretical models that traverse divides – neither inside nor out, neither one discipline nor another, going its own way, speaking from the margins (as it always has done), with a strong critical tradition behind it. It also offers the most developed vocabulary for theorising 'subjectivity' that is currently available, answering a significant need amongst researchers interested in exploring the construction of the subject in the social field. Additionally, as will be discussed further below, two of the dominant versions of psychoanalysis available in the 'academy' draw on and contribute to intellectual frameworks that are of considerable significance in the broader field of the social sciences: the Kleinian and relational psychoanalysts to 'intersubjectivity', and the Lacanians to the poststructuralist tradition of discursive constructionism. This all means that psychosocial researchers using psychoanalytic perspectives of this kind are also plugged into contemporary social theory and can draw on sophisticated developments in those areas, as well as (feeling that they are) contributing to a larger intellectual mission.

The gradual emergence of psychosocial studies has thus created a fresh opportunity for the reinsertion of psychoanalysis into academic social research. This has not been uncontroversial. For example, many psychosocial researchers share the traditional sociological suspicion of psychoanalysis because of its strongly individualising tendencies. Those who have been most influenced by poststructuralist and/or discursive perspectives resist the 'top-down', expert-knowledge epistemological claims of many psychoanalysts, with their apparent certainties about the 'true' nature of human subjectivity and their interpretive practice that seems to know best, or at least to know subjects better than they know themselves (e.g. Billig, 1997; Wetherell, 2003). The conservative or regressive tendencies in psychoanalysis are evident at times, here as in all fields. This includes the powerful sense that once one has developed a psychoanalytic perspective one has been transformed through a procedure that has often been compared with mystical conversion (Gellner, 1985), after which it becomes impossible to see things in any other way but through a psychoanalytic lens. This has understandably raised some hackles amongst psychosocial researchers struggling to develop more fluid and open ways of thinking. On the other hand, the concern of psychosocial studies with the interplay between what are conventionally thought of as 'external' social and 'internal' psychic formations has resulted in a turn to psychoanalysis as the discipline that might offer convincing explanations of how the 'out-there' gets 'in-here' and vice

versa, especially through concepts such as projection, internalisation and identification. As with the other topics addressed in this book, the appeal of psychoanalysis as a critical approach 'from the margins' that can be deployed against common-sense readings of the surface of things, which are seen not only as superficial but also as ideologically constrained, is considerable. It reflects those elements of psychoanalysis that are open, disruptive and challenging to received ideas, without dogmatically asserting that there is some alternative 'truth' that only psychoanalysts know.

There is also a tussle visible about the kind of psychoanalysis that might be appropriate in psychosocial studies. In the British academic context in which much of this debate has been developed, this has produced a lively debate between thinkers influenced by Kleinian and Lacanian ideas, with the former being associated more strongly with an empirical outlook, and the latter with a more critical but also more abstract stance on the limits on what can and cannot be known. Amongst the issues that this throws up is a question about whether what some regard as the possible critical edge of psychoanalysis is being blunted by a humanistic rendering that appropriates psychosocial studies to what is effectively object relational thinking; or whether the influence of psychoanalysis can grant to this relatively new field a capacity to maintain an open, querying stance towards the objects of its study. As with the other areas discussed in this book, much depends on avoiding adoption of psychoanalytic certainty – of the type of reading of psychoanalysis that sees it as harbouring the deep truths of human nature – and developing a psychoanalytic stance that is both tentative and creatively disruptive.

Defining the psychosocial

It should be made clear first that the kind of psychosocial studies being discussed here is different from the common use of the term to describe normative work dealing with social adjustment or interpersonal relations. As Wendy Hollway (2006) comments: 'In the largely positivist tradition of health sciences, for example, it is often found hyphenated, along with biology ('bio-psycho-social'), to refer to the additive treatment of different levels of analysis in the same research framework' (p.467). Whilst such work addresses important issues, it is not distinctive or theoretically innovative – each of its components is left more or less untouched. In contrast, the tradition with which this chapter is concerned understands psychosocial studies as a critical approach interested in articulating a place of suture between elements whose contribution to the production

of the human subject is normally theorised separately. Rustin (2008) describes the appeal of this trajectory as follows:

> The attractions of psychosocial studies, to students and researchers alike, arise from reaction to the continuing scientism, biologism, and individualism of much mainstream academic psychology, as well as to the limitations of academic sociology's understanding of individual subjects and subjectivity. Furthermore, the study of the emotions, central to psychosocial studies, has long been a marginal concern for both psychology and sociology. It has, therefore, been possible to create an educational and academic space in which the psychological and the sociological can be brought together, outside the control of either of the two main parent disciplines. (p.407)

The origins of this mode of psychosocial studies lie in psychoanalysis, sociology, applied social studies and social work, critical social psychology, poststructuralist theory, social constructionism, queer theory and feminist social research. Though deeply influenced by both Marx and Freud, its concerns have moved on considerably from those theoreticians whose primary interest was in how social repression operates to constrain the libidinal individual. Rather, contemporary psychosocial studies of this kind focuses on conceptualising and researching a type of subject which is both social and psychological, which is constituted in and through its social formations, yet is still granted agency and internality.

The main dilemma that this genealogy produces is one familiar from the previous chapters, that of finding ways of staying committed to an agenda that gives value to personal experience, interconnectedness, intersubjectivity, affect, embodiment, agency and most importantly the impulse to articulate a kind of ethical subject; whilst at the same time acknowledging and drawing on the complete disruption of this agenda through the force of the revelation that there is no such human subject. What we take to be the realm of the personal, including the famous 'inner world' of psychoanalysis, is either wavering and fragmentary, or a thoroughly fictional entity, produced and sustained by various manifestations of the 'big Other' (Hook, 2008a). Amongst the many problems this gives rise to is the repeated difficulty of uncovering a space for bringing together the psychological and the social without postulating these two spheres as distinct from one another. Their assumptions are so divergent, that often it seems that separating them completely for analytic purposes is all that can be done. In this respect, the apparently obsessional question about whether to have a hyphen between 'psycho' and 'social' has some meaning. Representing a mainly humanist, object relational and socialist tradition, Paul Hoggett (2008) argues that 'preserving the hyphen' is an important indicator of analytic clarity, in

that it acknowledges that 'critique' demands the making of distinctions, the maintaining of a clear eye about the different components out of which an apparent whole is made. Blurring distinctions, he argues, including the distinction between 'inside' and 'out' and hence 'psycho' and 'social', is a way of losing touch with this important critical mode of thought, has ethical consequences in relation to ways of approaching otherness, and may even be an indication of a loss of mental health:

> Respect for difference necessitates a constant effort to resist the temptation to blur, assimilate, and merge. That is why I believe that the preservation of the difference between the psycho- and the social is crucial, a task I believe is best accomplished by preserving the hyphen, as in 'psycho-social', and by preserving the kinds of distinctions that we have between inner and outer, private and public, and so on. As a clinician, if I am working with a patient who constantly confuses inner and outer, I know I am in the presence of someone in serious difficulty. (pp.382–3)

Against this forceful idea, one might suggest that 'preserving the hyphen' results in taking as given precisely what needs to be analysed: how it is that social and psychological become separated from one another both as modes of 'reality' and also as structures of disciplinary knowledge. To a considerable degree, it might also be argued that holding on to the social–individual divide is a kind of political move, sometimes drawn on in order to oppose totalitarianism (the individual is precious; everyone has a right to exist), but more often used to obscure the mechanics of subjectification. It suggests that individual and society are irreducibly distinct, so whilst one might talk about their interaction, one never needs to examine how they are constructed, and hence how they necessitate analytic deconstruction and critique. The division is thus a way of doing politics, and the psychosocial becomes a contrary way of doing politics, a rebellion that asserts that one cannot be had without the other, that they are warp and weft and signifier and signified, and so on through the different ways of saying that they are two sides of the same thing.

In theorising what is meant by the 'unhyphenated' psychosocial, a potent image, with or without its Lacanian gloss (Lacan, 1973), is the Moebius strip: underside and topside, inside and outside flow together as one, and the choice of how to see them is purely tactical, just like the decision as to whether to look at the subject from a 'social' or 'psychological' perspective. Thinking through the implications of the psychosocial as a Moebius strip, however, rather than falling back into the relatively familiar opposition of psychological and social, is a difficult task, and as the quotation from Hoggett above indicates, this is complicated by the way in which psychoanalysis is drawn on in much of this

work. Rather than following the agenda of offering a kind of critical deconstruction that develops from the history of psychoanalysis as a mode of radical critique, the more relational aspects of psychoanalysis often have ascendancy in psychosocial studies, fuelled by the politically reformist and emancipatory aims of certain modes of critical psychology and mental health practice. This means that the dominant impulse is a kind of humanistic, therapeutic one (particularly reflected in a concern with 'emotion' in the public sphere, as in the quote from Rustin, above, and in Perri 6 et al., 2006), a mode of personalising or humanising opposition to the industrial-military complex as it rolls over the vestiges of human feeling. This is a reason not only for the influence of relational psychoanalysis, valued for its rigorous attention to the quality of subjectivity as forged and understood in relational contexts, but also for the widespread use of qualitative research methods as the preferred empirical approach within psychosocial studies. As argued elsewhere,

> Qualitative psychology enters here as part of a turn in the so-called human sciences towards the rolling-up of experience into narrative form: without discounting the reality of events, the key research question becomes not what happens to a person, but how this is accounted for, how it is put into a frame that makes sense. This *humanizes* reality, placing the emphasis on the agentic, meaning-making activity of the research (and human) subject. (Frosh, 2007, pp.635–6)

Both the therapeutic agenda and the narrative one are responses to the acute awareness of the alienating structures of mainstream, normalising social practices (including those of research and of much that passes for mental health treatment), and so fall clearly within the traditions of community and emancipatory activism that have fuelled interest in the psychosocial in the first place. However, the main thrust of work that rescues agency and emotion in the name of the psychosocial is to reconstitute a holistic individual who still has to be theorised in relation to an often persecutory 'outside'.

The psychosocial as a 'sutured' unit consequently remains an ill-defined entity. This might actually be part of its productivity, allowing flexibility in the methods and foci of its research. Nevertheless, without a clear vision of its own object of study, or at least a detailed rendition of the ongoing difficulties with articulating such a vision, psychosocial studies is at risk of being reappropriated by its more conventional, 'foundational' disciplines. Philosophically and practically, this suggests that psychosocial studies is at a stage of development in which the priority is *reflexivity*, understood as an interactively critical practice that is constantly feeding back on itself and is always suspicious of the productions of its own knowledge. This stance also argues the necessity for the

psychosocial and the critical to go together to develop a resistive practice based on what Marcuse (1965) and others have called 'negation'.
Fundamentally, this is rooted in a constant probing of assertions and
apparent knowledge in the light of the entities that constitute them; or
in psychoanalytic terms, a refusal ever to abandon the 'analytic attitude'
(Rieff, 1966). What are sought are ways of resisting the tendency to
invest events and objects with too much familiarity, for instance dividing them into inner and outer or same and different; to oppose this,
ways of 'making-strange' are needed, leading to encounters with the
oddness and newness of these objects, their resistance to appropriation
(Latour, 2007). In the same way, as psychosocial studies seeks to be a
trans- (as opposed to inter-) disciplinary practice that negates the easy
assumption of 'in here, out there', subject and object, psychic and social,
it needs to constitute itself in such a way as to constantly unsettle its
own activities and assumptions. This means testing itself through negation, querying its own premises, and always seeking to renew its engagement with a space that is neither 'psycho' nor 'social', and is definitely
not both, but is something else again. The question here is whether and
in what ways psychoanalysis can contribute to this agenda, given that
many of the same issues apply to psychoanalysis itself. It too needs to
rescue itself from its own claims to mastery, and in particular to a kind
of universalised knowledge that pays insufficient attention to the conditions under which it arises. As discussed particularly in Chapter 1 and
evident in the other applications of psychoanalysis that have been
debated in this book, this especially concerns the question of what
Hook (2008b, p.398) refers to as 'the epistemological and ethical
disjunction that accompanies attempts to apply psychoanalysis' clinical
forms beyond the confines of the clinic'.

Psychoanalysis and discourse

The engagement of psychosocial studies with psychoanalysis centres on
questions about the nature of subjectivity and subjecthood, and also on
ways in which psychoanalytic ideas can be employed in the collection
and analysis of research data. For example, for those researchers seeking to use psychoanalysis as a methodological approach that can add
something to empirical psychosocial studies, a likely contribution from
psychoanalysis derives from the sophistication of its ideas about
emotional investment and fantasy. These can offer a 'thickening' or
enrichment of interpretive understanding brought to bear on personal
narratives, especially those arising out of interview situations.
Psychoanalytic interpretive strategies may be able to throw light on the

psychological processes, or perhaps the conscious and unconscious 'reasons', behind a specific individual's investment in any rhetorical or discursive position. This may offer a more complete (because more individualised as well as emotion-inflected) interpretive re-description of interview material, with helpful links to clinical perceptions and practices.

There are many examples of this kind of work now available in the literature (e.g. Frosh et al., 2003), most of it from Britain and often formulated in the context of a debate with discursive psychology, which also uses qualitative research procedures to try to map identity and subjectivity, and to understand the construction of the social subject. The different approaches here generally follow from different theoretical principles. Psychoanalytically inclined researchers start from the position that unconscious processes infiltrate the narrative accounts given by research participants, so that interpretive strategies aimed at uncovering these unconscious processes will be needed. Discursive researchers, on the other hand, assume that these same accounts are produced through social activity and the linguistic transactions between subjects, and are not ghosted by any underlying unconscious presence. As an example of the former tendency, Wendy Hollway, delineating her use of the term 'psycho-social', assumes immediately the existence of a certain kind of psychoanalytic subject. Her usage, she writes,

> derives from a commitment to understand subjectivity and agency in a way that transcends individual–social dualism and draws on psychoanalysis for this purpose. In this perspective, we are *psycho*-social because we are products of a unique life history of anxiety- and desire-provoking life events and the manner in which they have been transformed in internal reality. We are psycho-*social* because such defensive activities affect and are affected by material conditions and discourses (systems of meaning which pre-exist any given individual), because unconscious defences are intersubjective processes (i.e. they affect and are affected by others with whom we are in communication), and because of the real events in the external, social world which are discursively, desirously and defensively appropriated. (Hollway, 2006, pp.467–8)

It is noticeable here that Hollway incorporates the psychoanalytic subject into both the 'psycho' and 'social' sections of her hyphenated term, but actually makes both of them psychological in the process. The former, as one might expect, is made up of the transformation of material conditions into 'internal reality'. This renders psychoanalysis as usefully explaining the way in which external events become incorporated 'into' the psyche or self, notably through concepts such as introjection and identification. But the social is also psychoanalytically

invested. The social as intersubjective is inhabited by psychic defences; and the individual 'appropriates' aspects of the external world which thereby become saturated with psychological significance. This certainly seems like a legitimate attempt at using psychoanalysis psychosocially: in this model, it would be very difficult to separate out one sphere (the personal, say) from the other. However, there is also an imbalance produced by the psychoanalytic orientation. Although there is a space marked out for the 'social', it is given significance in the 'psycho-social' terrain primarily as the source of internalising strategies undertaken by the individual. That is, social practices act as a kind of fodder for the psychodynamic processes of the subject. In some ways this makes it hard to see the difference between the 'psycho' and 'social' elements of Hollway's formulation: both are described in terms of how events in the 'external' world have an impact on the subject's 'internal reality'. What seems to happen is that the external world is colonised by the internal, and in so doing the dichotomy between the two is obscured but not erased.

As Hollway herself notes, a variety of what she calls 'constructionist' approaches reject this view because of the assumption about 'innerness' that it involves. They also object to the presentation of psychoanalysis as an expert system that has access to this inner world and knows what it is like, and posits it as something that exists in and of itself, however linked it might be with a social order which is also permeated by unconscious processes. This is a key element in the dispute amongst often good psychosocial colleagues (e.g. Hollway and Jefferson, 2005; Wetherell, 2005) about 'top-down' and 'bottom-up' interpretive approaches; it is also part of the debate about the functioning of the 'discursive' and whether anything stands outside language (Frosh, 2002; see also Chapter 5). Many psychosocial researchers recognise differences between discursive social psychology and psychoanalysis, yet also argue that there is a degree of congruence between them deriving from a shared interest in subjective meaning and in the constructive role of language. In essence these relate to a concern with language or communication as the medium through which people compose themselves. However, the differences that exist between psychoanalysis and discursive psychology are significant. Michael Billig describes them like this:

> Discursive psychology ... argues that phenomena which traditional psychological theories have treated as 'inner processes' are, in fact, constituted through social, discursive activity. Accordingly, discursive psychologists argue that psychology should be based on the study of this outward activity rather than upon hypothetical, and essentially unobservable, inner states. In this respect, discursive psychology is inimical with psychoanalytic theory,

which presumes that hidden unconscious motive-forces lie behind the surface of social life. Psychoanalytic theorists often treat outward social activity as a cipher for unobservable, inner motivational processes. (Billig, 1997, pp.139–40)

For most psychoanalysts, talk is primarily determined by relational dynamics and unconscious processes; while, for discursive psychology, talk is mediated by the availability of discourses in the social and political realm. While discursive psychology explores the cultural resources that people draw on when giving accounts of their experiences, the relational tradition is more interested in talk as suggestive of underlying psychic positions that organise individuals' internal worlds in particular ways. This psychic realm is seen as being informed by actual events and therefore social structures, but as being located 'in' and primarily constituted through unconscious processes. Individuals are 'unconsciously impelled' to express themselves in particular ways in discourse, resulting in discernible patterns that will differ from individual to individual. A relational psychoanalytic reading therefore goes 'behind' the text as the positions that individuals construct through their talk are taken to be indicative of anxieties, defences and particular ways of relating that develop in infancy and recur throughout their lives. By contrast, discursive psychology reads the text for the identity positions that are constructed for the person talking and the audience listening, and for the broader cultural discourses and subject positions it draws on in these constructions. This relates to Wetherell's (2003) criticisms of psychoanalysis as predicated on a problematic psychological–social dualism. She argues that the deep psychological properties or structures that psychoanalysis is interested in are separated from social relations and therefore presented as static, confined to early development, without any exploration of their possible transformation through subsequent and ongoing social relations and practices.

Whilst psychoanalytically oriented psychosocial researchers can justifiably claim that their acknowledgement of each person's 'unique life history of anxiety- and desire-provoking life events' (Hollway, 2006, p.467) introduces more developmental fluidity than Wetherell allows for, the deeply rooted infant-centredness of psychoanalysis, perhaps especially in its object-relational form, often produces rather predictable motivational accounts and interpretive strategies. Acceptance of a developmental account leads strongly to viewing adult relationships as structured by these developmental processes, with the task of analysis being largely to understand this structuring. By its very nature, it is difficult to escape a determinist viewpoint here, and this is what often makes discursive social psychologists, and hence some exponents of psycho-

social studies, uneasy about psychoanalytic claims. This also links with a continuing prioritising of the 'inner' over the 'outer'. Despite the reference to material conditions in Hollway's description of the 'psychosocial', both elements are theorised as infiltrated by 'the' unconscious, which in turn is understood as residing in the 'inner world'. Hollway positions herself against what she calls the 'post-structuralist' anti-psychoanalytic position by arguing that it is 'insufficiently cognizant of the psychological processes whereby the recursive formation of selves within their life settings is not only mediated by complex material, discursive and relational influences but also by dynamic, intersubjective, unconscious processes' (2006, p.466). This seems to assume the thing it posits (the existence of 'dynamic, intersubjective, unconscious processes'), a problem aggravated by the further claim that what is lacking both from Foucauldian poststructuralism and from discursive psychology is 'that neither adopts a developmental account of subjectivity. In contrast, I want to ask, … how subjectivity (or "self") is formed within primary relations, and for this I draw on the tradition of object relations psychoanalysis, even while critiquing certain individualized notions of the self' (2006, p.467). Object relations theory is thus made foundational for the psychosocial position, which is assumed to need a developmental account and also to require ways of specifying mechanisms which will link the 'out-there' with the 'in-here'. This is not to suggest that such an approach is illegitimate – quite the contrary, as questions of relationality and of ways in which notions of 'unconscious' and sociality can be brought together must be central to any discussion of critical uses of psychoanalysis. But it does not solve the problem of whether appealing to an inner mode of subjectivity, a 'depth' layer, is a way of achieving this – it simply restates that it is.

The terminology of 'internal reality' widely used by object-relational and Kleinian theorists can be interestingly contrasted with a more classic psychoanalytic notion of 'psychic reality'. Despite its reference to the 'psychic', this may actually be more psychosocial in the sense that it figures something that is never totally 'internal'. Psychic reality is what the subject *lives in*; this replaces an abstracted opposition of the 'outer' as against the 'inner' with a conceptualisation of the 'psychic' as that which stands in for both. Laplanche and Pontalis (1967, p.363) note: 'This notion is bound up with the Freudian hypothesis about unconscious processes: not only do these processes take no account of external reality, they also replace it with a psychical one.' This means that the subject is always immersed in a flux that is neither inside nor out, but something else – a folding of space that is perhaps closer to the Moebius ideal. Psychic reality is already hybrid, and deterministic renderings of psychoanalysis that differentiate between its elements by claiming that

'defensive activities affect and are affected by material conditions and discourses' and by postulating 'real events in the external, social world' may miss the psychoanalytic point. This links to an argument put forward by Hook (2008b) that what should be focused on in psychosocial studies of this kind is not the 'inner world' or unconscious of any individual subject, but rather 'analysis of the libidinal economy underlying specific discursive formations' (p.399). He goes on to say that this 'proposes a non-reductive analytical strategy, asserting that discourses themselves maintain the coherence, the repetitiveness – indeed, the cycles of jouissance – that mark certain well-established patterns of libidinal functioning, a strategy which does not attempt to fix such discursive patterns as merely the outcome of intra-psychic processes, of individual psychopathology' (ibid.). Examples that he draws on include nationalism, colonialism and apartheid. The key point is that instead of focusing on individuals and their separate anxieties and defensive structures, it is the swirling around of repetitive *discourses* or perhaps patterns of enjoyment ('cycles of jouissance') that can be observed on a social level, and which link the functioning of unconscious structures and libidinal economies with social formations. Hook (p.400) argues that certain beliefs or ideological elements garner 'a je ne sais quoi quality, something "in them more than themselves," and hence take on a disproportionate libidinal status by virtue of the degree of investment of a given community'. Examining the processes whereby this comes about, and the functions of these nodal objects in the social world, draws on psychoanalytic insights about the unconscious fixing of desire, without necessarily appealing to the separation of individual from social, or inner from outer. Instead, it is the flows and blockages of desire that become the focus of analysis, not an individual's anxieties. This kind of argument can be seen at work in the discussions on the application of psychoanalysis to political thought in the previous chapter; but it may be that it also has something to say to the more psychological orientation of psychosocial studies.

Types of psychoanalysis

This raises the broader issue of whether the deployment of psychoanalysis in much psychosocial studies works from the point of view of psychoanalysis itself – if it can be said to have a 'point of view' – or whether it is a way of sanitising psychoanalysis so that it loses its specificity, and becomes just a kind of verbal bridge that makes it seem like something new is known. This relates to the question of what kind of psychoanalysis one might draw on. In Britain, the two main approaches

adopted in this kind of work have been Kleinian and Lacanian. Whilst there are many points of convergence and divergence between these (see Frosh, 1999), and whilst the broader contrast between relational (such as Kleinian) and structural (such as Lacanian) psychoanalytic models has been returned to several times in this book, the central point at issue in relation to psychosocial studies is about their different attitudes to the uncovering – or perhaps making – of 'meaning'. Loosely, Kleinian interpretive approaches, as they are used in psychosocial research, seek to make narrative sense of material, telling a story of a subject's unconscious life, for example, or her or his investments in certain problematic positions (Hollway and Jefferson, 2005). This connects with the way in which Kleinian theory retains a 'redemptive' element in it (Stonebridge, 1998), both explicitly in the notion of reparation and implicitly through its therapeutic trajectory. It recognises the split nature of the subject – hence is genuinely psychoanalytic – but pursues a sense-making agenda that makes everything come together in the end. For instance, the integrative capacity of the 'depressive position' is taken as the norm of mental health, even though there is usually an acknowledgment that people continue to oscillate throughout their whole lives between this and a more fragmentary 'paranoid-schizoid' mode of functioning, and that this is a necessary and creative process. The productive consequences of this 'positive' view of the psychoanalytic task have been very marked in British psychoanalysis and its applications (e.g. Rustin, 1995), as it presses a key question about social relations: how, given the prevalence of destructiveness in the social world, can it nevertheless be possible to produce a society in which violence can be kept at bay, envy ameliorated and community created? The application of this approach in studies of institutional dynamics has been a major area of real-world impact for psychoanalysis, and as noted in Chapter 6, its importance is considerable in political theory. It is particularly well attuned to investigations of destructiveness and envy as they manifest between people, both in therapy and in social and organisational life. Ironically, however, it is Kleinianism's unexpected *optimism* – its claim that paranoid-schizoid functioning can be topped by a depressive scenario in which reconciliation of ambivalent extremes can be managed and destruction made good – that defines what on the surface looks like a despondent and fateful theory. This can also lead an analyst (of texts as well as patients) to be propelled towards a 'curative' focus, one of reparation, of putting things together so that they will make narrative (or therapeutic) sense. The question is, what does this do to the subject understood as a fragmentary being made up of multiple, conflicting 'identities' and standing at the focal point of numerous forces? Or put more simply, what if the subject's experience does *not*, in fact, make sense?

Amongst the assumptions of Kleinian thinking, as taken up in psychosocial studies, that are at odds with a deconstructive approach, is the notion of the presence of a permanent, real unconscious – something inhabited by the truth of the subject, and sought for by the analyst whose task it is to comprehend apparently meaningless activity. This is part of its affiliation to 'depth', for it is below the 'surface' of observable phenomena that the truth of the subject lies. Rustin (2008) comments: 'The recognition or disclosure of such "depth" (of beliefs, desires, meanings, and intentions) is what psychoanalysis has always been about, both in its clinical and broader social applications' (pp.411–12). For Lacanians, however, as described particularly in Chapter 3, it is precisely the constant *deferral* of meaning that is at issue. The role of psychoanalysis is not to make narrative sense in which the depth unconscious is drawn on as an 'explanation', but rather to *disrupt* sense, to examine the building blocks out of which sense is being produced as a kind of epiphenomenon. The argument here is that narrative sense is always made post hoc. In relation to research it is always a process of the researcher rereading the subject's discourse in order to even it out, to find anchor points for it and consequently to make it safe and orderly, however complexly and aesthetically this may be done. It is in principle a *defensive* process. Just as a psychoanalytic patient might organise disturbing material into a satisfying narrative, so taking refuge in an attractive interpretation can be a way for a researcher to defend against the disturbance produced by the material that gave rise to the interpretation in the first place. Parker notes here: 'There is an important twist that Lacan adds to our understanding of the process of fixing meaning through repetition of certain signifiers or metaphorical substitutes in their function as quilting points or master signifiers, which is that the process of anchoring occurs *retroactively*' (Parker, 2005a, p.170). The *analytic* as opposed to interpretive process is geared to refusing this retroactive fixing of meaning, and instead to bringing out the 'non-meaning' (Lacan, 1973, p.250) of each component of the subject's discourse. The task is thus to avoid making something whole and integrative but instead to concentrate on the *productivity* of speech – on what it leads to and by what it is constrained.

This emphasis on what might be seen as the productivity of discourse is taken up in the Lacanian recasting of interpretation as *interruption*: something brought in to produce a new motion, a movement of signifiers freed by the analyst's response, but not thereby made meaningful. 'Rather than revealing a hidden unconscious that is already there,' writes Juan-David Nasio (1992, p.46) about the act that surprises and exceeds the intention of the analysand, 'this act produces the unconscious and causes it to exist.' The patient finds her- or himself speaking

in an unexpected way, perhaps with more affect than intended, or possibly about a memory that she or he never realised was present, and – as in all psychoanalysis – this becomes the source of analytic attention. However, instead of seeing it as a product of an unconscious state that has always been there, secretly carried around by the patient wherever she or he goes, the Lacanian view is that it is a product of a very specific situation, the analytic encounter itself. 'When the "word" erupts in the analysand,' writes Nasio (p.24), 'we call it, among other things a symptom, a lapse, or a witticism, and when it erupts in the psychoanalyst, we call it an interpretation.' The unconscious comes into being only in the relationship between analysand and analyst. It is a specific product of that relationship, of, for example, the transference, which itself appears only in the special situation of the consulting room 'as the particular moment of the analytic relation when the analyst becomes a part of the patient's symptom' (p.17). Nasio describes the interpretive act of the analyst with great caution, in a way that links it with the desire to make sense of narrative. Both of them threaten to become a kind of over-enthusiastic therapeutic consciousness that tries to do too much: 'It is indeed the demand that engenders the blind passion to heal, a passion that is akin to another passion, that of wanting to understand' (p.74). Nasio encourages the analyst to withstand this temptation to understand and instead allow her or himself to be 'open to surprise' (p.75). Parker (2005a) relates this specifically to the psychosocial practices of discourse analysis, which he subjects to Lacanian interrogation:

> The reflexive position of the discourse analyst is an issue here, for when one approaches a text in hermeneutic mode as something we can 'understand' because it is like our own framework (or even because we recognize it as being the mirror opposite of what is familiar to us), this, for Lacanians, would betray the stance we are taking as lying on 'the line of the Imaginary' (imagining that we interpret from outside the text). The task of an analyst is to work on 'the line of the Symbolic' (working within the domain of the text), and to open up the text by disrupting and disorganizing it so that its functions become clearer, including its functions for us. (p.177)

There is no analytic knowledge that stands outside the symbolic, hence no true interpretation that can tie the fragments together to create an integrative meaning; only a constant probing and search, and where possible a set of unexpected moments in which both analyst and patient are thrown off balance.

There is something of a risk of apparent frivolity in some of these comments, when faced with the *clinical* reality of the distress brought to psychoanalysis by clients. 'Disruptive eruptions of meaninglessness against the comfortable backdrop of established reason', as Nobus and

Quinn (2005, p.4) name the psychoanalytic process, or 'disrupting and disorganizing', as Parker portrays the Lacanian imperative, do not seem quite adequate to the experience of suffering. There is a reasonable claim to be made that the stance of relational psychoanalysis, with its valorisation of the narrative worth of the subject's speech in the context of a listening, 'recognising' other, might have more to offer in a political context in which reducing people to meaninglessness is one of the *problems*. This is a point made in slightly different ways by Lynne Layton (2008) in her examination of psychoanalysis' response to neoliberalism (which pushes people into the position of being commodities) and by Rustin (2008) in his comment that 'The distinctiveness of this tradition is that it has upheld a commitment to analytic truth as the best way of enhancing the mental well-being of patients and refused to separate the pursuit of understanding and achievement of therapeutic benefit' (p.413). In terms of both therapeutic need and emancipatory practice it would be indefensible to criticise clinicians who engage with patients' feelings, who focus carefully on transference and countertransference in the consulting room, and who try to act ethically to give their patients an experience of being recognised and understood. Clearly, the theoretical apparatus of psychoanalysis facilitates this necessary work.

The situation of psychosocial studies, however, is different from that of clinical work, both as a mode of research (e.g. in the utility of its concepts in empirical investigations) and theoretically, as it lays out the nature of the 'psychosocial subject'. The 'non-sensical' stance of Lacanian psychoanalysis reflects a distinction to be made between the 'therapeutic' and 'analytic' elements of psychoanalysis, a distinction which has long been familiar from discussions of the 'analytic attitude' (e.g. Rieff, 1966), and has also resurfaced in critiques of narrative in psychoanalysis (Laplanche, 2003). The central idea promoted in this work is to oppose the normativeness present in assumptions around individualism and the priority of reparation and care. This produces a more analytic, so clearly a more 'austere' attitude, but also one that opens out possibilities for thought and action that might be closed down by too definite an interpretive stance. Parker's contention that we should not approach a text as something we can understand, but rather as something waiting to be opened up, derives in part from his reading of the end of a Lacanian analysis as 'bringing the subject to the point where they are a perfect Saussurean, such that they recognize that the language that bears them is made up only of differences without any positive terms' (Parker, 2005a, p.168). For him, this motif of 'absolute difference' sets up the task of the Lacanian as 'searching for patterns and connections between signifiers, but as connections that differentiate them from each other and hold them in tension rather than divining

connections that reveal an underlying order' (ibid.). Not down and deep, that is, but out and wide – that is the motion whereby something started off in the subject, something unexpected and surprising, gives rise to something else, that might be a kind of tag or answer, or perhaps a new version of the unconscious. 'The unconscious', writes Nasio (1992), 'is a constantly active process that exteriorizes itself incessantly through acts, events or speech that meet the conditions that define a signifier, namely, to be an involuntary expression, opportune, devoid of meaning, and identifiable as an event in connection with other absent or virtual events' (p.3). If this is the reading we have of the unconscious, there is no pre-existing grid that can be drawn on to find the defended subject and trace her or his manoeuvres when faced with the anxiety that undoubtedly pervades everything. Such a grid would reflect an imaginary stance, in which the existence of an 'answer' to the subject's 'problem' (for instance, her or his confusion of narrative) is postulated. Rather, the unconscious emerges only in what happens when expectation is exceeded and some kind of response is drawn out of the other with whom the subject is in contact; this response might or might not be containing or interpretive, but most of all it will be a surprise.

Reflexivity, countertransference and psychosocial research

Both the productivity and restrictiveness of psychoanalysis applied in this area can be examined finally through reference to the issue of reflexivity. The familiar idea within psychosocial studies and more broadly in the critical social sciences is that the existence of an objective 'out there' that can be studied from a position of neutrality is not tenable, at least not in the social arena, because of the responsiveness of people to the ideas that surround them. People *use* ideas in order to create themselves; they are, in this specific sense, meaning-making machines. Reflexivity is thus part of a movement against objectivism in the social sciences (Bourdieu, 1999), and hence is an approach which challenges the claim that there can ever be a 'truth' that is separate from the practices that give rise to it. In this way, reflexivity points to a potentially subversive procedure in which the conditions of emergence of knowledge are analysed as well as the apparent objects of knowledge themselves. In research terms, this means that when faced with human subjects the researcher is not able to assume a naïve or external other to be investigated, but rather must think about the way in which the subject is a source of meaning-making agency, using the props of the research situation actively to reconstruct her or his consciousness in the flow of social experiences. An example here is the transformation of

understanding of the research interview when one shifts from a classical view of language as representation to one of language as performative. The act of speaking about something changes the speaker; what the subject 'knows' shifts as a result of the interview, as it is co-constructed in and through the interchange with the researcher. So, for example, it would be reasonable for a respondent to answer an interview question with the phrase, 'I've never thought about it like that', and then go on to construct a response that is as new to her or him as it is to the interviewer. This poses considerable problems for traditional notions of reliability and validity in research, and makes awkward any assumption of knowledge about a subject, as all knowledge becomes temporally and interpersonally positioned. It does not, of course, make such knowledge *impossible*; rather, it makes it contingent, strategic and provisional, best construed as the closure of theory around an arbitrary fixed point or full stop, as Stuart Hall (1996) terms it, or perhaps linked with Lacan's (1956) idea of 'points de capiton' ('quilting points') knotting signifier and signified together. Nevertheless, reflexive theory emphasises how people construct themselves through positions taken on cultural axes, including that offered by psychoanalysis. That is, the 'truth' of psychoanalysis lies in its power as a social, sense-making discourse. Research is not a process of uncovering (even relative) 'truths' about people, but rather exposes the ways in which subjects are positioned by the theoretical structures used (by them as well as by researchers) to understand them.

Under these circumstances, researcher and research activity have to be theorised as contributing to the production of knowledge. For Bourdieu, reflexivity involves a type of objectification of the researcher, in which the researcher (and her or his discipline) is explored for the effect that she or he may be having on the subject, but also

> to objectify the act of objectification: to consider the position of the researcher within his or her own milieu alongside the field position of the object of research, and comparatively to reflect upon how positions within the field, both of the researcher and of the researched, might exert determinative influence upon the end product of social analysis. (Stepney, 2003, p.131)

Consistent with this is the vision of research as a mode of knowledge production that directly implicates the subjective presence of the researcher within the account of the object of study. In other words, social research operates in and through a particular relationship between researcher and subject, which, in Bourdieu's account, is not completely arbitrary but is determined by the social structure itself.

Doing social research requires knowledge of this structuring process and the way in which it positions the research that is generated. Such knowledge is achieved through reflection on how 'research' is constituted, how its power structures are realised, what is regarded as useful and meaningful, what expectations are generated, and so on. More prosaically, this kind of reflexivity requires the researcher to keep an honest gaze on what she or he brings to the research process: how it is set up, what is communicated to the subject, what differences of race, class, gender, etc., might prevail and what impact they might have, and how her or his actions might influence the subject's own active meaning-making activities. This is commonly addressed through transcription procedures that allow close scrutiny of the researcher's words (in interview research), diaries recording everything that strikes the researcher, feedback from and to the research subjects, and attempts to talk rigorously with supervisors and others about the nature and impact of the work.

These practices are important and indeed necessary in relation to the complexities of the research process (e.g. Potter and Hepburn, 2005). However, a major difficulty with them concerns what account can in fact be given of the investments of the researcher in the knowledge-making process. Hook (2008b) comments:

> inasmuch as reflexivity involves a type of ego-judgement on its own productions, it cannot but be part of the problem, a means of insulating the méconnaissance of ego-misrecognition within a closed circuit. Neither the perspective I have on my own perspective, nor my coresearcher's input on my own input entails an adequate degree of otherness; for reflexivity to work, a far more radical break, a more forceful discontinuity needs to be introduced. (p.410)

Here, psychoanalysis has considerably more sophisticated concepts available to it than can be found in much social science, but this very sophistication makes the issues more problematic. For example, some social researchers seem to imply that describing researchers' investments in their work might be a relatively simple, technical matter, perhaps an issue of confession or self-revelation. But what is to be revealed? The researcher's gender, class and 'race' positions may well be relevant and it may be important to declare them as a way to increase the transparency and richness of the data produced. This is, indeed, the strategy employed by some of the best practitioners of the new social science. For instance, Margaret Wetherell acknowledges that her work on racism in New Zealand is influenced by her own history as a white New Zealander (Wetherell and Potter, 1992). However, even where

researchers have been scrupulous in laying out the ways in which they might have promoted certain 'responses' or narratives from their research participants, the most they are able to do is declare their conscious intentions and include material such as full transcripts to enable a reader to form an impression of the researcher's own contribution. Psychoanalysis would regard this kind of reflexivity as both too restricted and too general, in that it recognises social structures and can track interpersonal interactions, but has a deeply impoverished vocabulary for describing the intersubjectivity of the research process – the ways in which each person 'uses' the other, unacknowledged and unconsciously. Declarations of relatively explicit aspects of the researcher's persona will therefore never be complete enough to understand what her or his contribution to the research might be, let alone to comprehend the nuances of the interpretive strategy employed in data analysis. There are likely, for example, to be complex unconscious processes interacting with the research work, encouraging some ways of going about things, inhibiting others. Psychoanalysis draws attention to this and also shows how complicated it is. How does one attend to the moment-by-moment flows between, for instance, interviewer and interviewee, and what can be learnt from these that might pass muster under the heading of 'research'?

The reflexivity argument has a number of implications in relation to the employment of psychoanalysis in qualitative psychosocial research. For Parker (2005b) it focuses and limits the possibilities of psychoanalysis itself, understood as a compelling narrative that is culturally specific and even functional:

> What psychoanalytic research can do, then, is to turn psychoanalytic knowledge around against itself so we understand better the way that psychoanalytic ideas have themselves encouraged us to look for things deep inside us as the causes of social problems. Psychoanalytic subjectivity – our sense of ourselves as having hidden childhood desires and destructive wishes – is the perfect complement to economic exploitation in capitalist society, for both succeed in making the victims blame themselves. (p.105)

This takes to its logical conclusion the constructionist argument that subjects are produced discursively, though exactly how psychoanalysis will reveal the conditions of its own operation as an exploitative system is left open to speculation, and the claim in the quotation that psychoanalysis promotes self-blame misses an important distinction between blame and responsibility. More conventionally, Parker draws attention to the impact of psychoanalysis' emphasis on the ways knowledge (specifically of the analysand) is mediated through the person – the

subjectivity – of the knower (the analyst). That is, knowing the other involves knowing the impact of the other on (or 'in') the self, and requires a capacity to reflect on this in a way that openly recognises both the pre-existing investment of the knower/researcher in the material, and what is added to this by the specific concerns of the other. Parker (2005b) comments on how this produces a reassessment of conventional research ideas on subjectivity as a problem:

> Subjectivity is viewed by psychoanalysis, as with much qualitative research, not as a problem but as a resource (and topic). To draw upon one's own subjectivity in the research process does not mean that one is not being 'objective', but that one actually comes closer to a truer account. In psycho-analytic terms, the 'investment' the researcher has in the material they are studying plays a major role in the interest that will eventually accrue from the research. (p.117)

This is a familiar point in relation to psychoanalytic infant observation, where it is held that knowledge of the child can *only* be obtained through registering the observer's emotional response to what she or he sees (Waddell, 1988). Coded more broadly as 'countertransference', it is also a feature of most contemporary psychoanalytic practice, especially that influenced by Kleinian and British School thinking. Hence Hollway and Jefferson's (2005) assertion that in their psychoanalytically-inflected qualitative work they can ground their interpretive claims through what they describe as an analysis of the 'countertransference'. Referring to their case study of 'Vince' from their research into anxiety and fear of crime, they claim that information is generated through comparing the different responses the two researchers had to the participant himself:

> We used these and the triangulation of them between the two of us. For example, while WH [Wendy Hollway] wanted to describe Vince as quiet-spoken and unassertive, TJ [Tony Jefferson] was more inclined to describe him as timid. We used this information to reflect on how we were differently positioned in relation to Vince through these different countertransference responses. Wendy, who conducted both interviews, found herself feeling suspiciously protective of him, while Tony, having met him briefly, listened to the audiotapes and read the transcripts, felt critical of his timidity. This observation is an example of how to use the psychoanalytic principle of unconscious intersubjectivity to theorize the effect of research relationship(s) on the production and analysis of data. (p.151)

The value of this procedure is that it provides a space for checking out the researchers' responses to the research participant and thinking

through what these responses might signify. It also draws attention to the position of the researcher in qualitative work, where the end point of research might be various constructed versions of experience rather than full knowledge of an objective and fixed external reality. The task of the interviewer, therefore, shifts from one of eliciting the interviewee's 'real' views to creating the conditions under which a thoughtful conversation can take place. In doing work of this kind, the person of the researcher is deeply implicated. If it is the case that psychological knowledge is constructed in the context of an interchange between 'researcher' and 'researched', then understanding the determining characteristics of that interaction – including what the researcher brings to it – is crucial for evaluating the significance of any research 'findings'.

However, the practice Hollway and Jefferson describe is in some important respects significantly different from the kind of exploration of unconscious material characteristic of psychoanalytic reflection on the countertransference in the *clinical* situation. What the researchers do is notice how a participant made them feel (protective, critical) without the necessary limitations of the analytic session and contract which would allow one to understand the validity of this response. Vince does not come to them for help – does not announce that he feels something to be wrong, or that the researcher can offer him anything. Indeed, he does not set up that particular transference on which the whole analytic encounter is based. On the contrary, Hollway (who conducted this interview) goes to Vince, wants to interview him, wants to find out something about him, wants to 'make sense of him', so the interaction is primarily driven by *her* desire. In this context, her feelings and responses are better thought about as *her transference*, not her countertransference; they are rather like Freud's (1907) insertion of his own associations to the dreams in *Gradiva*, described in Chapter 2. Clearly, both Hollway and Jefferson have thoughts and feelings about their interviewees, but what might be termed the 'conditions of emergence' of these are so far removed from the analytic situation as to make their affiliation with psychoanalytic terminology strained and potentially misleading. Hook (2008b) summarises the more general version of this argument:

> We might admit that psychoanalytic interpretation remains always poised on the verge of wild analysis. This, it would seem, is the inherent epistemic risk posed by a discipline that hopes to trace the unconscious in its most unlikely and absurd manifestations. If this is indeed the case, then the factors of supervision, clinical technique, the provision of an appropriate ethical code, and the contextualization of a detailed and ongoing (week-by-week, year-by-year) life history – that is, precisely those factors that in part define the clinic

– are all of absolute necessity. It is thus difficult to see how one can justifiably extend clinical psychoanalytic warrants (such as diagnosis and interpretation of individuals) beyond the parameters of the clinic. (p.399)

The grounding of psychoanalytic interpretive practices so that they do not wander away into complete speculative freedom requires numerous factors that have evolved over time to regulate the conduct of clinical encounters. As Hook suggests, these hedge the tendency of analysis to become 'wild' and make it into a more ordered process. This can of course always be challenged (it is part of the argument here that no interpretation can come near the 'truth'), but at least has the traditions of the clinic to bolster it and make it into a predictable framework in which the significance of events can be evaluated and judgements can be made about the reasonableness of what is claimed and said. Research has its own such traditions, but they are different, and this difference needs to be marked up rather than obscured by using the vocabulary of psychoanalysis as if the things referred to (for example, transference and countertransference) mean the same in whatever social context they appear.

A number of other psychoanalytically informed psychosocial researchers have tried out ways of incorporating this kind of sensitivity to subjectivity into their work. This has been done perhaps most notably through the use of group procedures to check and examine researchers' systematic responses to their material (e.g. Marks and Mönnich-Marks, 2003, who used this approach to identify possible unconscious motivational mechanisms at work in their sample of Nazi sympathisers) – a way of working congruent with the standard infant observation training methods mentioned above. Nevertheless, significant problems remain. Many of these are methodological and refer to the difficulty of knowing what to do with the richly subjective, suggestive texts that derive from free and evocative interviewing procedures and personal modes of interpretation (Frosh and Saville Young, 2008). More generally, however, there is the tendency already noted to adopt psychoanalytic ideas of countertransference as if they are the same as social-science notions of reflexivity. The difficulties with this are due to deployment in one context of psychoanalytic interpretive strategies and grounding procedures that have arisen most convincingly in another context with strikingly different characteristics – that of the clinical situation of the 'consulting room'. This returns us to some of the most intractable and general issues about psychoanalysis in psychosocial studies. Where psychoanalysis is mined for its *technology*, as for instance where notions of countertransference are applied to discussions of how researchers feel, there is a danger that it will be used as an

ungrounded expert system of knowledge in precisely the way objected to by its critics. Even the more cautious approach of Marks and Mönnich-Marks (2003) relies on a pre-given idea that the emotional reactions of the researchers (all of whom will be socialised into a certain kind of consciousness and are likely to become more similar to one another through their repeated discussions and shared stories of their research) are meaningful as indicators of the actual *unconscious* state of mind of the participants. This is a direct result of the application of a Kleinian style of psychoanalysis in which the truth of the subject can be known through mediation by (or through the unconscious of) an interlocutor who has more knowledge and understanding than does the subject. In Lacanian terms, we are in the domain of the imaginary here, expecting there to be a real totality that can be understood from outside it, instead of appreciating the fictive nature of all totalities, and the way that necessarily means that all subjects – analysts as well as analysands, clever and reflective researchers as well as recalcitrant participants – relate *partially*. Psychoanalysis is normative (or in Lacanian terms, untruthful) when its reflexivity is seen as a way of knowing the subject 'better'. In that mode it has relatively little to contribute to psychosocial studies other than a set of rather mechanistic ideas that explain processes of internalisation but risk separating and reifying the 'inner' and 'outer' in a manner that goes against the psychosocial ambition to theorise them together. Psychoanalysis has more to offer when its disruptive and performative elements are placed in the foreground; that is, when the kind of reflexivity it advances is one that acknowledges the way the phenomena of the psychosocial are produced *through the actions of* analyst and analysand, researcher and researched as a way of 'throw[ing] us off the psychoanalytic subject' (Baraitser, 2008, p.426). This means that cherished psychoanalytic ideas have to be rethought for the different context of investigation and expression: transference and countertransference, for example, are simply not the same in and out of the consulting room. But it also holds onto an important psychoanalytic insight that helps significantly with the task of thinking 'psychosocially'. This is the claim that psychological and social, inner and outer, are only artificially separated, and are constituted by something else that runs through them, sometimes emerging in surprising ways that psychoanalysts code as the 'unconscious' in its signifying, 'non-sensical' materialisation.

Conclusion

Psychoanalysis has an important part to play in the establishment of psychosocial studies as a disciplinary practice in which the social and

the psychological are 'thought together'. In contrast to the other areas discussed in this book, which have their own substantial traditions with which psychoanalysis has to contend if it is to intervene in their fields, psychosocial studies is relatively new, and is still seeking to fully define its methodological approach and its object of analytic interest. Indeed, in most respects psychoanalysis is the senior partner in the encounter between them. Rustin (2008) comments: 'Psychoanalysis is more securely rooted and institutionalized as a field of practice and (clinical) research than is psychosocial studies, not less' (p.409), and this is undoubtedly true, with the consequence that psychosocial studies often looks to psychoanalysis for intellectual bolstering of its own still nascent conceptual armoury. This seems to have resulted in a kind of three-way split amongst researchers in this area. On one side, there is a debate about whether psychoanalysis is the best place to look for an underpinning for psychosocial studies, with the major alternative being discursive psychology, but with others such as phenomenology and Deleuzian philosophy certainly being fully in the ring. Amongst those who do draw predominantly on psychoanalysis, there is a division between those adopting a relational, particularly Kleinian, perspective and those more enamoured of Lacanian ideas. Members of the former group have adopted a more empirical basis for their work, seeking ways of filling out narrative and discursive qualitative research with psychoanalytic methods and interpretive procedures. The latter group, as tends to be their wont, has more commonly taken the high ground of theoretical critique, although there are now a few examples of psychosocial research that employ Lacanian ideas when carrying out analysis of empirical data (e.g. Saville Young and Frosh, 2009).

In this chapter, some of these issues have been revolved from the point of view of considerations of what happens to psychoanalysis under these promising yet somewhat fraught conditions. There certainly seems to be a considerable space available for psychoanalysis to impact upon psychosocial studies, and considerable benefit in it doing so. This is not to say that it should automatically be hegemonic here. The debate with discursive psychology, for example, is potentially a very productive one and has already led to important clarifications about how to theorise people's investments in particular discursive positions, about the emotional and even 'therapeutic' significance of narrative, and about different meanings of the term 'interpretation', some of them deeply challenging to psychoanalysis. Divergence about the kind of psychoanalysis best deployed in psychosocial studies also has its productive side, though there is a risk that it will reduce to a contest over the 'purity' of the position taken by different protagonists. In this chapter, it has been argued that the critical practice of psychoanalysis requires

considerable caution over the use of its concepts in research, without recognition of how far this means they must travel from the clinical situation which gives them meaning. This has been coupled with an attempt to hold onto a position in which psychoanalysis is used to query and disrupt attitudes towards psychosocial data, or indeed to psychosocial studies itself, that are too immediately 'knowing' and authoritative. This has meant that the primary advocacy has been of a Lacanian perspective that might stand back from offering interpretive expertise and instead concentrate on observing the kinds of traces of unconscious impulses that were met with much earlier in this book, in the chapter on psychoanalysis and literature. The reciprocally destabilising effect of texts on psychoanalysis and psychoanalysis on texts that was tracked there is still the requirement for maintaining an open psychoanalysis that can be reflexively located as *analytic* rather than as the source of institutional expertise. Nevertheless, the alternative psychoanalytic position taken up by more empirically minded psychosocial researchers offers some important correctives to this somewhat abstract and possibly idealised high-mindedness. For example, it raises very practical questions about the reading of interview texts, the role of the researcher in constructing psychosocial data and the place of emotions in interpretation. As noted here, the difficulty is that these questions cannot be answered by assuming straightforward translation of psychoanalytic concepts and principles from the clinic to the 'outside': the distance is too great.

Many of these issues relate to the general concerns of this book, as well as being salient in the particular domain of psychosocial studies. *Why* psychoanalysis and *which* psychoanalysis are questions that apply in all the areas in which psychoanalysis intrudes; and *how* this intrusion then feeds back into psychoanalysis itself is crucial for determining whether it can remain an open intellectual discipline. In psychosocial studies, the ground is still sufficiently unmarked for these various contestations to be visible and lively, perhaps creating some of the best opportunities for psychoanalytic 'implication' in another discipline that have been available for some time.

Conclusion: Reflexivity Outside the Clinic

Re-view

There is much that is unstated in this book, or at least hinted at but not completely articulated. My assumption is that this is true of all books, as it is of all texts, narratives and discourses. At least, that is what both psychoanalysis and contemporary cultural theory would suggest, and what the new 'discipline' of psychosocial studies has taken in from both these traditions. The question is really whether what is stated is enough to convey my argument, and also to unsettle it sufficiently to prevent it from drifting into becoming another 'master discourse' of the kind that I have been criticising. I have plenty of doubts about this and so want to use the small space of this conclusion to reflect back on the claims made here, to consider what perspective they reveal, and to ask what can be done to query this without losing whatever force it might have.

The broad argument itself can, I hope, be fairly baldly stated. Psychoanalysis grew up in, and derives its authority from, the clinic. It is essentially a practice rooted in a live encounter between analyst and patient, with theory abstracted from this. The 'clinic' can be defined as any space that promotes this kind of live encounter. Psychoanalysis *outside* the clinic consequently refers to the intervention of psychoanalytic ideas and practices of interpretation drawn from psychoanalysis into environments not characterised by such live encounters. This includes empirical settings in which there is contact between a researcher and a research participant (for example, interviews or ethnographic studies), but where these have neither duration nor intensity comparable to that which allows psychoanalysts to ground their claimed knowledge of their patients. This book has considered a range of such interventions, focusing on social theory and psychosocial studies, but acknowledging that many others could have been chosen. Of particular interest has been the extent to which psychoanalysis can hold on to an ambition which is in some ways modest, when faced with the temptation to pronounce as an 'expert system' in these interventions. This means holding back from explaining the 'truth' of social phenomena to the host disciplines concerned, and instead limiting itself to asking some provocative questions, ensuring that emotion and irrationality are included in the relevant discussions of subjectivity. That is,

219

the task of psychoanalysis is to direct attention towards the unconscious, without asserting a privileged position in doing so.

Drawing on some historical encounters (Freud's writings on literature and religion; the reconsideration of psychoanalysis and literature that took place in the 1980s), I have preferred Shoshana Felman's (1982a) notion of *implication* to that of application as a framework for describing and evaluating this work. This signifies an approach dealing not only with what psychoanalysis offers *to* the fields in which it operates, but also with what is reflected back into psychoanalysis *from* these applications. I have been particularly anxious to present a critique of the 'normalising' tendencies in psychoanalysis that construct it as what one might loosely call a 'bourgeois science', in order to advance its claim that it might retain a critical edge that can contribute to some kind of progressive move in social research. What is suggested here obviously has some political connotations, but at its most general it simply means using psychoanalysis to gain increased leverage on how social forces act to construct the human subject, rather than assuming that any particular version of the subject is the *necessary* norm. Because psychoanalysis is concerned with subjectivity, this means drawing together perspectives usually thought of as separate. That is, where the subjects of sociological or psychological analysis currently reside, the psychosocial subject is sought.

Despite its limitations, this book has been quite wide-ranging. One aim has been to achieve something genuinely transdisciplinary that reflects the history of the use of psychoanalysis, but also retains a critical stance towards it. In this regard, some of the material covered looks carefully grounded and fits the bill relatively well. Some, however, retains a speculative dimension that is attractive in many ways (without flights of fancy, it is difficult to think new thoughts), but might lead us back into the seductions of mastery. This applies to both the psychoanalytic traditions focused on in this book: relational psychoanalysis (broadly described, to include Kleinian approaches) and Lacanian psychoanalysis. In the former case, the move from the clinic to social and psychosocial studies is sometimes made too easily, without proper consideration of what this radical shift of setting means for the psychoanalytic concepts being used. This problem was flagged up particularly in the final chapter, on psychosocial studies, where Kleinian ideas have been imposed rather uncritically in some empirical work. It can also be seen in some of the ways both classical and emerging clinical ideas such as 'resistance' and 'recognition' have been extended to the political field and to a general philosophy of ethics. The *suggestive* power of these translations from the clinic is great and means that they are worth taking very seriously; but the requirement is to retain awareness of how

they function as metaphors rather than as identities. Lacanianism, on the other hand, has largely infiltrated the academy through its cultural, philosophical and political applications. As such, it is in some ways better attuned to the task of 'implication', because it functions more like the other theories in these domains. However, this very compatibility risks the loss of the specific contribution that psychoanalysis can make. If this form of Lacanianism has already moved out of the clinic, then what is it that it can offer that is distinct from, for example, poststructuralist theories of the subject? How can the unconscious be kept in mind if it is not grounded in the actuality of the clinical encounter? Perhaps here the issue is to ensure that the continuing clinical fertility of Lacanian psychoanalysis is held in contact with its theoretical work in the academy in ways that are more common amongst adherents of the relational and Kleinian schools.

The previous chapters have made claims for a number of contributions by psychoanalysis to the social sciences. Psychoanalysis has genuine insights to offer about the formations of subjectivity and the place of the social (for example, through the 'other') in the emergence of the human subject. It opposes rationalism and positivism as philosophical stances because it demonstrates the strength of the 'irrational' in human conduct and the need to think through the impact of the unconscious when considering social as well as personal events. It has a subtle understanding of trauma, language and memory, of fears and desires. It can be used productively to trace the way discourses operate in 'texts' of various kinds, understood to include social and cultural materials as well as speech and writing. At its best, at least within the framework adopted in this book, it can be seen as making excursions into the social sciences which disrupt their taken-for-granted positions and augment or even overturn them by insisting that knowledge of the human subject can never be as they believed. Instead, it is always partial, always potentially undercut by some other way of being. More broadly, I have been making claims for the development of a new mode of academic practice, *psychosocial studies*, which attempts exactly the 'transdisciplinarity' mentioned above. Psychoanalysis intervenes to disrupt this emerging field as well, even as it provides it with some of its vocabulary and methodological procedures. In being taken up both as a substantive contributor to psychosocial studies and as a point of tension within it, psychoanalysis may have found a new space for the kind of implication in social research that gives it value outside the clinic. But, as with all the areas discussed in this book, this requires a continuing folding back on itself, a practice of reflexivity which is not always easy to achieve.

Reflexive practice

The demands of reflexivity do not only apply to the doing of psycho-analysis or social science, but also to the writing of books. Without being on the couch, it is difficult to trace all the sources of the choices made here, but it is perhaps possible to track some of their implications. As noted in Chapter 1, I have been rather under-inclusive in my selection of psychoanalytic theories for consideration, notably in paying what many (especially those in psychosocial studies) might regard as insufficient attention to what is known as British School psychoanalysis. This refers primarily to the tradition of Klein and Bion, but also to much object relations theory. These have instead been incorporated in a broader category of relational psychoanalysis, but it has to be acknowledged that whilst relational psychoanalysis draws heavily on Winnicott, it is much less connected with Kleinian thought. Indeed, in some of its manifestations – including the 'intersubjectivist' work of Jessica Benjamin, which has been used extensively in this book – it is *opposed* to Kleinianism. As my previous work attests (Frosh, 1999, 2006), I am not dismissive of British School work and in fact see it as making a considerable contribution to psychoanalysis as a resource for social thought. However, my reasoning in reducing its role here has to do with the promise of relational theory and the way it encourages the kinds of encounters with social research that this book endorses. Particularly through the varied (and contrasting) uses of the notion of *recognition* by Benjamin and Butler, one can see the emergence of a productive engagement with philosophical work on otherness that can create an elaborated understanding of social subjectivity. Kleinianism has lent its own categories of intersubjectivity for use in this, projection, introjection and projective identification being chief amongst them. However, its unswerving postulation of a 'depth' model and its focus on a separable 'inner world' make it less congruent with the psychosocial model sought here, in which no distinction is made between 'inside' and 'out'. It is also, in many of its manifestations, an example of an expert system of psychoanalysis that 'knows' its subject too well, and is at odds with the approach advocated here. That said, there is a definite loss in omitting Klein from the central dynamic of this work. As noted in Chapter 2, the profound attention it gives to destructiveness has been an important source of the cultural currency that it has. Other approaches also deal with destructiveness, and it is here that the influence of Kleinianism can be seen in relational psychoanalysis, alongside that of Hegel. Lacanian thought is also attuned to it, as the material on the neighbour and the 'Thing' shows. But there can be little argument with the claim that Kleinian psychoanalysis has the most fully developed theory of, and the most unwavering focus on, the

forces of destruction, and one might consider that the contribution made by psychoanalysis to some of the more pressing contemporary social concerns could be lessened without it.

Other psychoanalytic approaches are also relatively absent, as are other fields of potential application/implication. The reasons behind the selections and omissions of this book are given in Chapter 1. However, looking back over this, and over other elements in my writing, what it seems to reveal is the types of 'seduction' that certain encounters outside the clinic hold for those of us who are enamoured of psychoanalysis, however ambivalently. The *intellectual* reasons for seeking to inform contemporary social science through an encounter with psychoanalysis, and vice versa, have been given continually throughout this book, and one hopes that the demonstration of their mutual fertility is convincing. It is not really that difficult to argue that psychoanalysis has one of the most elaborate vocabularies and conceptual systems addressing subjectivity, so it has to be brought into any debate that deals with this area of academic activity. Its power to query the surface of things is invaluable both as a tool and also as a continuing counterweight to tendencies towards claiming the truth of knowledge. So much has been asserted repeatedly here. But one is still left with a legitimate question about what the appeal might be, particularly if – as in this book – some of the more esoteric aspects of psychoanalysis are constantly drawn on, pushing readers away from its core, relatively simple ideas.

For Baudrillard (1979), in one of the founding texts of postmodernism, 'seduction' is opposed to psychoanalytic 'interpretation' in the same way that surface is opposed to depth. As it happens, he mistrusts depth. 'Getting beyond appearances is an impossible task', he writes (p.149), because every approach that tries to do this becomes seduced by its own terms, forms and appearances, until it becomes over-enamoured with its own presence, which it uses to persuade, flatter and deceive others. 'The havoc interpretation wreaks in the domain of appearances is incalculable', Baudrillard states (ibid.). The search for meaning is instructive because it reveals the attraction of that search, not because it actually discovers something meaningful lurking in the depths. Lacan (1991) addresses some similar issues when he outlines a number of the 'lures' of psychoanalysis, amongst which, as Parker (2008) points out, is belief in the progressive possibilities of psychoanalysis ('I am not a man of the left', asserts Lacan, 1991, p.114). This suggests that psychoanalysis itself is a kind of lure, a seduction that may have less to do with its intellectual weightiness and more with what its *associations* are, its flashy surface, one might say, or at least its appearance. This is rather a disconcerting thought for someone trying to write in a scholarly way about psychoanalysis, but it does seem apposite if

one is doing this whilst also distancing oneself from the everyday difficulty faced by psychoanalysts who are doing 'routine' clinical work. Without idealising the latter, for clinical work itself has plenty of seductions (how one thinks of oneself, how one presents oneself to others, the prospect of voyeurism, and so on), the grounding of clinical psychoanalysis in human suffering is real enough to act as a *memento mori*. Lacking it, perhaps we are only left with the *appearance* of something meaningful. This can drift into becoming a kind of intellectual game in which one can feel special because of the suggestion that speaking in a psychoanalytic voice puts one in touch with real human depths, when in fact it is just another way of talking about the same things, mostly in the same small rooms.

I hope, of course, that this is not the case, though my own predilection for Lacanian obscurity makes me wonder. There is clearly a need for care. Nevertheless, the presentation of examples or 'interventions' throughout this book has aimed to show that something real is added by and to psychoanalysis when it openly engages with the other disciplines of the academy. It is important to renounce claims of mastery, but it matters equally that we open something out here that will allow understanding of the social to develop further than it can with its current disciplinary constraints. The key argument, if one can put it like this, is that without psychoanalysis as an involved, critical body of theory and practice, social theory and research remain tied to rationalist models that find too little space for the irruptions of subjectivity. The domain of the psychosocial is called into being here as a possible arena in which this can be contested and in which the division between social and personal, which is a construct of disciplinary practices rather than something 'real', might be broken down. It is too early to tell whether this will work, but without psychoanalysis it has much less chance of doing so.

However, this has to be a certain kind of psychoanalysis. It needs to retain its awareness of its clinical grounding, whilst also being sensitive to how it loses its authority outside the clinic (and even within it when that authority is contested – though that is another discussion). It needs to adopt an attitude of curiosity to the results of its forays outside, and be willing to have even cherished theoretical premises challenged by what it finds there. It needs to engage with questions about its own seduction into mastery and try to find a way to maintain its analytic 'discourse' as something that throws itself, and everything else, off balance. It might need to withdraw at times, when it knows too little, and be critical of itself, when it seems to know too much. Most of all, if the implication of psychoanalysis outside the clinic is to produce rich encounters, it needs to step back from its own normativeness, its own conformist tendencies, and ask how it can be constantly renewed.

References

Abel, E. (1989) *Virginia Woolf and the Fictions of Psychoanalysis*. Chicago: University of Chicago Press.

Adorno, T. (1967) Sociology and Psychology, Part I and II. *New Left Review*, 46, 67–97.

Adorno, T., Frenkel-Brunswick, E., Levinson, D. and Sanford, R. (1950) *The Authoritarian Personality*. New York: Norton, 1982.

Agamben, G. (1995) *Homo Sacer: Sovereign Power and Bare Life*. Stanford, CA: Stanford University Press.

Agamben, G. (2002) *Remnants of Auschwitz*. New York: Zone Books.

Allen, J. and Fonagy, P. (eds) (2006) *Handbook of Mentalization-Based Treatment*. Chichester: John Wiley.

Althusser, L. (1971) Ideology and Ideological State Apparatuses. In L. Althusser, *Lenin and Philosophy and other Essays*. London: New Left Books.

Altman, N., Benjamin, J., Jacobs, T. & Wachtel, P. (2006) Is Politics the Last Taboo in Psychoanalysis? In L. Layton, N. Hollander and S. Gutwill (eds), *Psychoanalysis, Class and Politics*. London: Routledge.

Appignanesi, L. and Forrester, J. (1992) *Freud's Women*. London: Weidenfeld & Nicolson.

Badiou, A. (2004) *Theoretical Writings*. London: Continuum.

Banton, R., Clifford, P., Frosh, S., Lousada, J. & Rosenthall, J. (1985) *The Politics of Mental Health*. London: Macmillan.

Baraitser, L. (2006) Introduction to Seminar with Jessica Benjamin. Centre for Psychosocial Studies, Birkbeck College, London.

Baraitser, L. (2008) On Giving and Taking Offence. *Psychoanalysis, Culture & Society*, 13, 423–7.

Baraitser, L. (2009) *Maternal Encounters: The Ethics of Interruption*. London: Routledge.

Baudrillard, J. (1979) On Seduction. In J. Baudrillard, *Selected Writings*. Cambridge: Polity, 1988.

Beckett, S. (1984) *Worstward Ho*. London: Calder.

Benjamin, J. (1988) *The Bonds of Love*. London: Virago.

Benjamin, J. (1995) *Like Subjects, Love Objects: Essays on Recognition and Sexual Difference*. London: Yale University Press.

Benjamin, J. (1998) *Shadow of the Other: Intersubjectivity and Gender in Psychoanalysis*. New York: Routledge.

Benjamin, J. (2000) Response to Commentaries by Mitchell and by Butler. *Studies in Gender and Sexuality*, 1, 291–308.

Benjamin, J. (2004) Beyond Doer and Done To: An Intersubjective View of Thirdness. *Psychoanalytic Quarterly*, 73, 5–46.

Benjamin, J. (2009) A Relational Psychoanalysis Perspective on the Necessity of

Acknowledging Failure in Order to Restore the Facilitating and Containing Features of the Intersubjective Relationship (the Shared Third). *International Journal of Psychoanalysis*, *90*, 441–50.

Berman, M. (1983) *All That is Solid Melts into Air*. London: Verso.

Bernheimer, C. and Kahane, C. (eds) (1985) *In Dora's Case*. London: Virago.

Billig, M. (1997) The Dialogic Unconscious: Psychoanalysis, Discursive Psychology and the Nature of Repression. *British Journal of Social Psychology*, *36*, 139–59.

Billig, M. (2006) Lacan's Misuse of Psychology: Evidence, Rhetoric and the Mirror Stage. *Theory, Culture & Society*, *23*, 1–26.

Bion, W. (1959) *Experiences in Groups*. London: Tavistock.

Bion, W. (1962) *Learning from Experience*. London: Heinemann.

Bion, W, (1963) *Elements of Psychoanalysis*. London: Heinemann.

Bion, W. (1967) *Second Thoughts*. London: Heinemann.

Bloch, S. and Reddaway, P. (1984) *Soviet Psychiatric Abuse: The Shadow over World Psychiatry*. London: Victor Gollancz.

Bonaparte, M. (1933) *The Life and Works of Edgar Allan Poe*. Humanities Press, New York, 1971.

Bosteels, B. (2006) Alain Badiou's Theory of the Subject. In S. Žižek (ed.), *Lacan: The Silent Partners*. London: Verso.

Bourdieu, P. (1999) *The Logic of Practice*. Stanford, CA: Stanford University Press.

Brah, A. (1996) *Cartographies of Diaspora*. London: Routledge.

Braidotti, R. (2006) *Transpositions*. Cambridge: Polity.

Brennan, T. (ed.) (1989) *Between Feminism and Psychoanalysis*. London: Routledge.

Brooks, P. (1982) Freud's Masterplot. In S. Felman (ed.), *Literature and Psychoanalysis: The Question of Reading: Otherwise*. Baltimore: Johns Hopkins University Press.

Buber, M. (1959) *I and Thou*. Edinburgh: T&T Clark.

Burman, E. (2007) *Deconstructing Developmental Psychology*. London: Routledge.

Butler, J. (1990) *Gender Trouble: Feminism and the Subversion of Identity*. London: Routledge.

Butler, J. (1997) *The Psychic Life of Power*. Stanford, CA: Stanford University Press.

Butler, J. (2000) Longing for Recognition. *Studies in Gender and Sexuality*, *1*, 271–90.

Butler, J. (2005) *Giving an Account of Oneself*. New York: Fordham University Press.

Butler, J. (2008) *Frames of* War. London: Verso.

Butler, J., Laclau, E. and Žižek, S. (2000) *Contingency, Hegemony, Universality: Contemporary Dialogues on the Left*. London: Verso.

Casement, P. (2002) *Learning from our Mistakes: Beyond Dogma in Psychoanalysis and Psychotherapy*. Hove: Brunner-Routledge.

Castoriadis, C. (1995) Logic, Imagination, Reflection. In A. Elliott and S. Frosh (eds), *Psychoanalysis in Contexts*. London: Routledge.

Coward, R. and Ellis, J. (1977) *Language and Materialism*. London: Routledge & Kegan Paul.

Deleuze, G. and Guattari, F. (1977) *Anti-Oedipus*. New York: Viking.

Deleuze, G. and Guattari, F. (1988) *A Thousand Plateaus*. London: Athlone.

Derrida, J. (1975) The Purveyor of Truth. *Yale French Studies*, 52 (Graphesis: Perspectives in Literature and Philosophy), 31–113.

Ehrenzweig, A. (1967) *The Hidden Order of Art*. London: Weidenfeld & Nicolson.

Eickhoff, F. (2006) On Nachträglichkeit: The Modernity of an Old Concept. *International Journal of Psychoanalysis*, 87, 1453–69.

Eliot, T.S. (1922) The Waste Land. In *The Waste Land and Other Poems*. London: Faber, 1940.

Ellmann, M. (1990) Eliot's Abjection. In J. Fletcher and A. Benjamin (eds), *Abjection, Melancholia and Love: The Work of Julia Kristeva*. London; Routledge.

Ellmann, M. (1994) Introduction. In M. Ellmann (ed.), *Psychoanalytic Literary Criticism*. Harlow: Longman.

Empson, W. (1956) *Seven Types of Ambiguity*. London: Chatto & Windus.

Erikson, E. (1956) The Problem of Ego Identity. *Journal of the American Psychoanalytic Association*, 4, 56–121.

Ettinger, B. (2006) *The Matrixial Borderspace*. Minneapolis: University of Minnesota Press.

Evans, D. (1996) *An Introductory Dictionary of Lacanian Psychoanalysis*. London: Routledge.

Felman, S. (1982a) To Open the Question. In S. Felman (ed.), *Literature and Psychoanalysis: The Question of Reading: Otherwise*. Baltimore: Johns Hopkins University Press.

Felman, S. (1982b) Turning the Screw of Interpretation. In S. Felman (ed.), *Literature and Psychoanalysis: The Question of Reading: Otherwise*. Baltimore: Johns Hopkins University Press.

Flax, J. (1996) Taking Multiplicity Seriously: Some Implications for Psychoanalytic Theorizing and Practice. *Contemporary Psychoanalysis*, 32, 577–93.

Fletcher, J. (1999) Psychoanalysis and the Question of the Other. Introduction to J. Laplanche, *Essays on Otherness*. London: Routledge.

Fletcher, J. (2007) Seduction and the Vicissitudes of Translation: The Work of Jean Laplanche. *Psychoanalytic Quarterly*, 76, 1241–91.

Fonagy, P. and Target, M. (2007) The Rooting of the Mind in the Body: New Links between Attachment Theory and Psychoanalytic Thought. *Journal of the American Psychoanalytic Association*, 55, 411–56.

Foucault, M. (1976) *History of Sexuality: Vol. 1*. London: Allen Lane.

Fox, D., Prilleltensky, I. and Austin, S. (2009) *Critical Psychology: An Introduction*. London: Sage.

Fraser, N. and Honneth, A. (2003) *Redistribution or Recognition: A Political-Philosophical Exchange*. London: Verso.

Freud, S. (1905) Fragment of an Analysis of a Case of Hysteria. *The Standard Edition of the Complete Psychological Works of Sigmund Freud, Volume*

VII (1901–1905): A Case of Hysteria, Three Essays on Sexuality and Other Works, 1–122.

Freud, S. (1907) Delusions and Dreams in Jensen's *Gradiva. The Standard Edition of the Complete Psychological Works of Sigmund Freud, Volume IX (1906–1908): Jensen's 'Gradiva' and Other Works,* 1–96.

Freud, S. (1908a) Creative Writers and Day-Dreaming. *The Standard Edition of the Complete Psychological Works of Sigmund Freud, Volume IX (1906–1908): Jensen's 'Gradiva' and Other Works,* 141–54.

Freud, S. (1908b) 'Civilized' Sexual Morality and Modern Nervous Illness. *The Standard Edition of the Complete Psychological Works of Sigmund Freud, Volume IX (1906–1908): Jensen's 'Gradiva' and Other Works,* 177–204.

Freud, S. (1910a) Leonardo Da Vinci and a Memory of his Childhood. *The Standard Edition of the Complete Psychological Works of Sigmund Freud, Volume XI (1910): Five Lectures on Psycho-Analysis, Leonardo da Vinci and Other Works,* 57–138.

Freud, S. (1910b) 'Wild' Psycho-Analysis. *The Standard Edition of the Complete Psychological Works of Sigmund Freud, Volume XI (1910): Five Lectures on Psycho-Analysis, Leonardo da Vinci and Other Works,* 219–28.

Freud, S. (1913a) Totem and Taboo. *The Standard Edition of the Complete Psychological Works of Sigmund Freud, Volume XIII (1913–1914): Totem and Taboo and Other Works,* vii–162.

Freud, S. (1913b) The Theme of the Three Caskets. *The Standard Edition of the Complete Psychological Works of Sigmund Freud, Volume XII (1911–1913): The Case of Schreber, Papers on Technique and Other Works,* 289–302.

Freud, S. (1914) The Moses of Michelangelo. *The Standard Edition of the Complete Psychological Works of Sigmund Freud, Volume XIII (1913–1914): Totem and Taboo and Other Works,* 209–38.

Freud, S. (1915) The Unconscious. *The Standard Edition of the Complete Psychological Works of Sigmund Freud, Volume XIV (1914–1916): On the History of the Psycho-Analytic Movement, Papers on Metapsychology and Other Works,* 159–215.

Freud, S. (1917a) Introductory Lectures on Psycho-Analysis. *The Standard Edition of the Complete Psychological Works of Sigmund Freud, Volume XVI (1916–1917): Introductory Lectures on Psycho-Analysis (Part III),* 241–463.

Freud, S. (1917b) Mourning and Melancholia. *The Standard Edition of the Complete Psychological Works of Sigmund Freud, Volume XIV (1914–1916): On the History of the Psycho-Analytic Movement, Papers on Metapsychology and Other Works,* 237–58.

Freud, S. (1919) The 'Uncanny'. *The Standard Edition of the Complete Psychological Works of Sigmund Freud, Volume XVII (1917–1919): An Infantile Neurosis and Other Works,* 217–56.

Freud, S. (1920a) The Psychogenesis of a Case of Homosexuality in a Woman. *The Standard Edition of the Complete Psychological Works of Sigmund Freud, Volume XVIII (1920–1922): Beyond the Pleasure Principle, Group Psychology and Other Works,* 145–72.

Freud, S. (1920b) Beyond the Pleasure Principle. *The Standard Edition of the Complete Psychological Works of Sigmund Freud, Volume XVIII (1920–1922): Beyond the Pleasure Principle, Group Psychology and Other Works*, 1–64.

Freud, S. (1921) Group Psychology and the Analysis of the Ego. *The Standard Edition of the Complete Psychological Works of Sigmund Freud, Volume XVIII (1920–1922): Beyond the Pleasure Principle, Group Psychology and Other Works*, 65–144.

Freud, S. (1923) The Ego and the Id. *The Standard Edition of the Complete Psychological Works of Sigmund Freud, Volume XIX (1923–1925): The Ego and the Id and Other Works*, 1–66.

Freud, S. (1925) The Resistances to Psycho-Analysis. *The Standard Edition of the Complete Psychological Works of Sigmund Freud, Volume XIX (1923–1925): The Ego and the Id and Other Works*, 211–24.

Freud, S. (1926) Psycho-Analysis. *The Standard Edition of the Complete Psychological Works of Sigmund Freud, Volume XX (1925–1926): An Autobiographical Study, Inhibitions, Symptoms and Anxiety, The Question of Lay Analysis and Other Works*, 259–70.

Freud, S. (1927) The Future of an Illusion. *The Standard Edition of the Complete Psychological Works of Sigmund Freud, Volume XXI (1927–1931): The Future of an Illusion, Civilization and its Discontents, and Other Works*, 1–56.

Freud, S. (1930) Civilization and its Discontents. *The Standard Edition of the Complete Psychological Works of Sigmund Freud, Volume XXI (1927–1931): The Future of an Illusion, Civilization and its Discontents, and Other Works*, 57–146.

Freud, S. (1933) New Introductory Lectures On Psycho-Analysis. *The Standard Edition of the Complete Psychological Works of Sigmund Freud, Volume XXII (1932–1936): New Introductory Lectures on Psycho-Analysis and Other Works*, 1–182.

Freud, S. (1937) Analysis Terminable and Interminable. *The Standard Edition of the Complete Psychological Works of Sigmund Freud, Volume XXIII (1937–1939): Moses and Monotheism, An Outline of Psycho-Analysis and Other Works*, 209–54.

Freud, S. (1939) Moses and Monotheism. *The Standard Edition of the Complete Psychological Works of Sigmund Freud, Volume XXIII (1937–1939): Moses and Monotheism, An Outline of Psycho-Analysis and Other Works*, 1–138.

Freud, S. (1961) *Letters of Sigmund Freud 1873–1939* (ed. E. Freud). London: Hogarth Press.

Freud, S. and Einstein, A. (1933) Why War? *The Standard Edition of the Complete Psychological Works of Sigmund Freud, Volume XXII (1932–1936): New Introductory Lectures on Psycho-Analysis and Other Works*, 195–216.

Frosh, S. (1989) *Psychoanalysis and Psychology.* London: Macmillan.

Frosh, S. (1991) *Identity Crisis: Modernity, Psychoanalysis and the Self.* London: Macmillan.

Frosh, S. (1994) *Sexual Difference: Masculinity and Psychoanalysis*. London: Routledge.

Frosh, S. (1999) *The Politics of Psychoanalysis: An Introduction to Freudian and Post-Freudian Theory*. 2nd edn. Basingstoke: Palgrave.

Frosh, S. (2002) *After Words: The Personal in Gender, Culture and Psychotherapy*. Basingstoke: Palgrave Macmillan.

Frosh, S. (2003) Psychosocial Studies and Psychology: Is a Critical Approach Emerging? *Human Relations*, 56, 1547–67.

Frosh, S. (2005) *Hate and the Jewish Science: Anti-Semitism, Nazism and Psychoanalysis*. Basingstoke: Palgrave Macmillan.

Frosh, S. (2006) *For and Against Psychoanalysis*. 2nd edn. London: Routledge.

Frosh, S. (2007) Disintegrating Qualitative Research. *Theory and Psychology*, 17, 635–53.

Frosh, S., Phoenix, A. and Pattman, R. (2002) *Young Masculinities: Understanding Boys in Contemporary Society*. Basingstoke: Palgrave Macmillan.

Frosh, S., Phoenix, A. and Pattman, R. (2003) Taking a Stand: Using Psychoanalysis to Explore the Positioning of Subjects in Discourse. *British Journal of Social Psychology*, 42, 39–53.

Frosh, S. and Saville Young, L. (2008) Psychoanalytic Approaches to Qualitative Psychology. In C. Willig and W. Stainton-Rogers, *The Sage Handbook of Qualitative Research in Psychology*. London: Sage.

Gabbard, G. (2001) Introduction. In G. Gabbard (ed.), *Psychoanalysis and Film*. London: Karnac.

Gay, P. (1988) *Freud: A Life for Our Time*. London: Dent.

Gellner, E. (1985) *The Psychoanalytic Movement*. London: Paladin.

Giddens, A. (1991) *Modernity and Self-Identity*. Cambridge: Polity.

Goffman, E. (1969) *The Presentation of Self in Everyday Life*. London: Allen Lane.

Goldner, V. (2003) Ironic Gender/Authentic Sex. *Studies in Gender and Sexuality*, 4, 113–39.

Gould, S. (1996) *The Mismeasure of Man*. New York: Norton.

Greenacre, P. (1958) Early Physical Determinants in the Development of the Sense of Identity. *Journal of the American Psychoanalytic Association*, 6, 612–27.

Grinberg, L. and Grinberg, R. (1974) The Problem of Identity and the Psychoanalytical Process. *International Review of Psychoanalysis*, 1, 499–507.

Grünbaum, A. (1984) *The Foundations of Psychoanalysis: A Philosophical Critique*. Berkeley: University of California Press.

Guntrip, H. (1968) *Schizoid Phenomena, Object Relations and the Self*. London: Hogarth Press.

Habermas, J. (1968) *Knowledge and Human Interests*. Cambridge: Polity, 1987.

Hall, S. (1990) Cultural Identity and Diaspora. In J. Rutherford (ed.), *Identity: Community, Culture, Difference*. London: Lawrence & Wishart.

Hall, S. (1996) Who Needs 'Identity'? In S. Hall and P. du Gay (eds), *Questions of Cultural Identity*. London: Sage.

Haraway, D. (1991) *Simians, Cyborgs and Women: The Reinvention of Nature*. New York: Routledge.

Haraway, D. (2006) Encounters with Companion Species: Entangling Dogs, Baboons, Philosophers, and Biologists. *Configurations, 14*, 97–114.

Haraway, D. (2007) *When Species Meet*. Minneapolis: University of Minnesota Press.

Herzog, J. (2009) Triadic reality, same sex parents and child analysis: A response to Ann Smolen's 'Boys only! No mothers allowed'. *International Journal of Psychoanalysis, 90*, 19–26.

Hinshelwood, R. (1991) *A Dictionary of Kleinian Thought*. London: Free Association Books.

Hirst, P. (1979) *On Law and Ideology*. Basingstoke: Macmillan.

Hoggett, P. (2008) What's in a Hyphen? Reconstructing Psychosocial Studies. *Psychoanalysis, Culture & Society, 13*, 379–84.

Hollway, W. (2006) Paradox in the Pursuit of a Critical Theorization of the Development of Self in Family Relationships. *Theory and Psychology, 16*, 465–82.

Hollway, W. and Jefferson, T. (2000) *Doing Qualitative Research Differently*. London: Sage.

Hollway, W. and Jefferson, T. (2005) Panic and Perjury: A Psychosocial Exploration of Agency. *British Journal of Social Psychology, 44*, 147–63.

Hook, D. (2007) *Foucault, Psychology and the Analytics of Power*. Basingstoke: Palgrave.

Hook, D. (2008a) Fantasmatic Transactions: On the Persistence of Apartheid Ideology. *Subjectivity, 24*, 275–97.

Hook, D. (2008b) Articulating Psychoanalysis and Psychosocial Studies: Limitations and Possibilities. *Psychoanalysis, Culture & Society, 13*, 397–405.

Irigaray, L. (1985) *This Sex Which is Not One*. Ithaca, NY: Cornell University Press.

Isay, R. (1985) On the Analytic Therapy of Homosexual Men. *The Psychoanalytic Study of the Child, 40*, 235–54.

Jacobson, E. (1964) *The Self and the Object World*. London: Hogarth Press.

Jacoby, R. (1975) *Social Amnesia*. Sussex: Harvester.

Jacoby, R. (1983) *The Repression of Psychoanalysis*. New York: Basic Books.

Jameson, F. (1982) Imaginary and Symbolic in Lacan: Marxism, Psychoanalytic Criticism, and the Problem of the Subject. In S. Felman (ed.), *Literature and Psychoanalysis: The Question of Reading: Otherwise*. Baltimore: Johns Hopkins University Press.

Johnson, B. (1996) The Frame of Reference: Poe, Lacan, Derrida. In S. Vice (ed.), *Psychoanalytic Criticism*. Cambridge: Polity.

Jones, E. (1910) The Oedipus-Complex as An Explanation of Hamlet's Mystery: A Study in Motive. *American Journal of Psychology, 21*, 72–113.

Kelsen, H. (1924) The Conception of the State and Social Psychology – With Special Reference to Freud's Group Theory. *International Journal of Psycho-Analysis, 5*, 1–38.

Kerr, J. (1993) *A Most Dangerous Method*. New York: Knopf.

Kingsbury, P. (2007) Psychoanalytic Approaches. In J. Duncan, N. Johnson and R. Schein (eds), *A Companion to Cultural Geography*. Oxford: Blackwell.

Klein, M. (1927) Symposium on Child Analysis. *International Journal of Psycho-Analysis, 8*, 339–70.

Klein, M. (1932) *The Psycho-Analysis of Children*. London: Hogarth Press.

Klein, M. (1935) A Contribution to the Psychogenesis of Manic-Depressive States. *International Journal of Psycho-Analysis, 16*, 145–74.

Klein, M. (1955) The Psychoanalytic Play Technique. In M. Klein, *Envy and Gratitude and Other Works*. New York: Delta, 1975.

Klein, M. (1957) Envy and Gratitude. In M. Klein, *Envy and Gratitude and Other Works*. New York: Delta, 1975.

Kovel, J. (1995) On Racism and Psychoanalysis. In A. Elliott and S. Frosh (eds), *Psychoanalysis in Contexts*. London: Routledge.

Kristeva, J. (1983) Freud and Love. In T. Moi (ed.), *The Kristeva Reader*. Oxford: Blackwell, 1986.

Lacan, J. (1949) The Mirror Stage as Formative of the Function on the I as Revealed in the Psychoanalytic Experience. In J. Lacan, *Écrits: A Selection*. London: Tavistock, 1977.

Lacan, J. (1953) The Function and Field of Speech and Language in Psychoanalysis. In J. Lacan, *Écrits*. New York: Norton, 2005.

Lacan, J. (1954–55) *The Seminars of Jacques Lacan, Book II: The Ego in Freud's Theory and in the Technique of Psychoanalysis*. Cambridge: Cambridge University Press.

Lacan, J. (1956) The Quilting Point. In J. Lacan, *The Psychoses: The Seminar of Jacques Lacan Book III, 1955–6*. London: Routledge.

Lacan, J. (1959–60) *The Ethics of Psychoanalysis: The Seminar of Jacques Lacan Book VII*. London: Routledge, 1992.

Lacan, J. (1973) *The Four Fundamental Concepts of Psychoanalysis*. Harmondsworth: Penguin, 1979.

Lacan, J. (1991) *The Other Side of Psychoanalysis: The Seminar of Jacques Lacan Book XVII*. New York: Norton, 2007.

Laplanche, J. (1999) The Unfinished Copernican Revolution. In J. Laplanche, *Essays on Otherness*. London: Routledge.

Laplanche, J. (2003) Narrativity and Hermeneutics: Some Propositions. *New Formations, 48*, 26–9.

Laplanche, J. and Pontalis, J.-B. (1967) *The Language of Psychoanalysis*. London: Hogarth Press, 1973.

Latour, B. (2007) *Reassembling the Social: An Introduction to Actor-Network-Theory*. Oxford: Oxford University Press.

Layton, L. (2008) What Divides the Subject? Psychoanalytic Reflections on Subjectivity, Subjection and Resistance. *Subjectivity, 22*, 60–72.

Lear, J. (2005) *Freud*. London: Routledge.

Levi, P. (1960) *If This is a Man*. London: Abacus, 1987.

Levinas, E. (1985) *Ethics and Infinity*. Pittsburgh, PA: Duquesne University Press.

Levinas, E. (1991) *Entre Nous: On Thinking of the Other*. London: Athlone Press, 1998.

Lingis, A. (1994) *The Community of Those Who Have Nothing in Common.* Indianapolis: Indiana University Press.

Marcus, S. (1975) Freud and Dora: Story, History, Case History. In C. Bernheimer and C. Kahane (eds), *In Dora's Case.* London: Virago, 1985.

Marcuse, H. (1955) *Eros and Civilization.* Boston: Beacon Press, 1966.

Marcuse, H. (1965) *Negations.* Harmondsworth: Penguin.

Marks, E. and de Courtivron, I. (eds) (1981) *New French Feminisms.* Sussex: Harvester.

Marks, S. and Mönnich-Marks, H. (2003) The Analysis of Counter-Transference Reactions Is a Means to Discern Latent Interview-Contents. *Forum: Qualitative Social Research,* 4 (2), www.ph-freiburg.de/sozial/Marks/fqs.pdf (accessed 6 February 2008).

Mayes, L., Fonagy, P. and Target, M. (eds) (2007) *Developmental Science and Psychoanalysis: Integration and Innovation.* London: Karnac.

McNay, L. (2008) The Trouble with Recognition: Subjectivity, Suffering, and Agency. *Sociological Theory* 26, 271–96.

Metz, C. (1977) *Psychoanalysis and Cinema: The Imaginary Signifier.* London: Macmillan, 1982.

Mitchell, J. (1974) *Psychoanalysis and Feminism.* Harmondsworth: Penguin.

Mitchell, J. (2002) Reply to Lynne Segal's Commentary. *Studies in Gender and Sexuality,* 3, 217–28.

Moi, T. (1989) Patriarchal Thought and the Drive for Knowledge. In T. Brennan (ed.), *Between Feminism and Psychoanalysis.* London: Routledge.

Moore, B. and Fine, B. (1990) *Psychoanalytic Terms and Concepts.* New Haven, CT: Yale University Press.

Mulvey, L. (1975) Visual Pleasure and Narrative Cinema. In L. Mulvey, *Visual and Other Pleasures.* London: Macmillan, 1989.

Mulvey, L. (1989) *Visual and Other Pleasures.* London: Macmillan.

Nasio, J. (1992) *Five Lessons on the Psychoanalytic Theory of Jacques Lacan.* Albany: State University of New York Press, 1998.

Nobus, D. and Quinn, M. (2005) *Knowing Nothing, Staying Stupid.* London: Routledge.

Ogden, T. (1999) 'The Music of What Happens' in Poetry and Psychoanalysis. *International Journal of Psychoanalysis,* 80, 979–94.

Parker, I. (1997) *Psychoanalytic Culture: Psychoanalytic Discourse in Western Society.* London: Sage.

Parker, I. (2005a) Lacanian Discourse Analysis in Psychology: Seven Theoretical Elements. *Theory and Psychology,* 15, 163–82.

Parker, I. (2005b) *Qualitative Psychology: Introducing Radical Research.* Maidenhead: Open University Press.

Parker, I. (2007) *Revolution in Psychology: Alienation to Emancipation.* London: Pluto Press.

Parker, I. (2008) Temptations of Pedagogery: Seventeen Lures (review of Lacan's *Seminar XVII*). *Subjectivities,* 24, 376–9.

Perri 6, Radstone, S., Squire, C. and Treacher, A. (eds) (2006) *Public Emotions.* Basingstoke: Palgrave Macmillan.

Phillips, A. (1988) *Winnicott.* London: Fontana.

Phoenix, A. and Rattansi, A. (2005) Proliferating Theories: Self and Identity in Post-Eriksonian Context. *Identity, 5,* 205–25.

Pick, D. (1995) Freud's Group Psychology and the History of the Crowd. *History Workshop Journal, 40,* 39–61.

Potter, J. and Hepburn, A. (2005) Qualitative Interviews in Psychology: Problems and Possibilities. *Qualitative Research in Psychology, 2,* 281–307.

Quayson, A. (2007) Area Studies, Diaspora Studies, and Critical Pedagogies. *Comparative Studies of South Asia, Africa and the Middle East, 27,* 580–90.

Reinhard, K. (2005) Toward a Political Theology of the Neighbor. In S. ?i?ek, E. Santner and K. Reinhard, *The Neighbour: Three Inquiries in Political Theology.* Chicago: University of Chicago Press.

Rieff, P. (1966) *The Triumph of the Therapeutic.* Harmondsworth: Penguin.

Riley, D. (2005) *Impersonal Passion.* Durham, NC: Duke University Press.

Riviere, J. (1927) Symposium on Child Analysis. *International Journal of Psycho-Analysis, 8,* 370–7.

Riviere, J. (1936) On the Genesis of Psychical Conflict in Earliest Infancy. In J. Riviere, *Collected Papers 1920–1958.* London: Karnac, 1991.

Robinson, A. (2004) The Politics of Lack. *British Journal of Politics and International Relations, 6,* 259–69.

Rose, H. and Rose, S. (2000) *Alas, Poor Darwin: Arguments Against Evolutionary Psychology.* London: Vintage.

Rose, J. (1996) *States of Fantasy.* Oxford: Clarendon Press.

Rose, J. (2003) *On Not Being Able to Sleep.* London: Vintage.

Rose, J. (2005) *The Question of Zion.* Princeton: Princeton University Press.

Rose, J. (2007) *The Last Resistance.* London: Verso.

Rose, N. (1998) *Inventing our Selves: Psychology, Power and Personhood.* Cambridge: Cambridge University Press.

Roseneil, S. (2006) The Ambivalences of Angel's 'Arrangement': A Psychosocial Lens on the Contemporary Condition of Personal Life. *Sociological Review, 54,* 846–68.

Rustin, M. (1991) *The Good Society and the Inner World.* London: Verso.

Rustin, M. (1995) Lacan, Klein and Politics: The Positive and Negative in Psychoanalytic Thought. In A. Elliott and S. Frosh (eds), *Psychoanalysis in Contexts.* London: Routledge.

Rustin, M. (1999) Psychoanalysis: The Last Modernism? In D. Bell (ed.), *Psychoanalysis and Culture.* London: Duckworth.

Rustin, M. (2008) For Dialogue between Psychoanalysis and Constructionism. *Psychoanalysis, Culture & Society, 13,* 406–15.

Said, E. (2007) *On Late Style: Music and Literature against the Grain.* London: Bloomsbury.

Samuels, A. (1993) *The Political Psyche.* London: Routledge.

Sandler, J., Dare, C. and Holder, A. (1973) *The Patient and the Analyst.* London: Maresfield Reprints, 1979.

Saville Young, L. and Frosh, S. (2009) Discourse and Psychoanalysis: Translating Concepts into 'Fragmenting' Methodology. *Psychology in Society, 38,* 1–16.

Schwartz, J. (1999) *Cassandra's Daughter: A History of Psychoanalysis in Europe and America.* Harmondsworth: Allen Lane.

Index

Abel, E. 71, 78
abjection 79
Abraham, K. 42
acknowledgement 134–5, 156, 176
adaptation 10, 102, 105, 112, 162, 176
Adler, A. 8
administered society 171–3, 185, 192
Adorno, T. 6, 9, 166, 171–2, 182
aesthetics 44, 46–7, 51, 53, 60, 69, 70, 123
affect 38, 49, 58, 96, 99, 118, 119–20, 122–3, 139–41, 145, 175, 177, 187, 189, 196, 207
Agamben, G. 143–4
agency 7, 38, 59, 100, 103, 120, 135, 140, 144, 149, 152, 178, 196, 198, 200
aggression 61, 81, 132, 176
alienation 112–13, 115–16, 139–40, 174, 198
alienness 53, 127–8, 131, 141–5, 151–5, 177–8
Allen, J. 31
Althusser, L. 9, 34, 38, 170
Altman, N. 135
ambivalence 25, 78, 81, 161, 164, 167–8, 186, 205
analyst, discourse of 184, 186
analytic attitude 16, 68, 115, 199, 208
anthropology 40, 42, 43, 45, 65, 97
anxiety 7, 25, 81, 136, 149, 200, 202, 204, 209
Appignanesi, L. 71

Arendt, H. 162
art *see* psychoanalysis, and art
Austin, S. 192
authority 25–6, 61, 63, 90–1

Badiou, A. 145, 182
Banton, R. 192
Baraitser, L. 30, 131–2, 137–8, 216
Baudrillard, J. 223
Beckett, S. 93
Benjamin, J. 29, 30, 32–3, 111–12, 130–5, 137, 145, 153, 173, 175, 177, 222
Berman, M. 22
Bernheimer, C. 83
Billig, M. 115, 194, 201–2
biology 17, 31, 170
Bion, W. 32–3, 114, 222
Bloch, S. 191
body, and identity 104–5, 107–9, 112, 116–17, 120, 123, 196
Bonaparte, M. 71
Bosteels, B. 180
Bourdieu, P. 209–10
Brah, A. 101
Braidotti, R. 119
Brennan, T. 5
Brooks, P. 84–8, 91
Buber, M. 130, 136, 162–3
Burman, E. 191
Butler, J. 5, 29, 38, 119, 132–3, 145–153, 161–2, 177, 182, 222

capitalism 117, 121, 170, 173, 175, 193, 212
case history 82–4
Casement, P. 32

237

Wetherell, M. (2003) Paranoia, Ambivalence and Discursive Practices: Concepts of Position and Positioning in Psychoanalysis and Discursive Psychology. In R. Harré and F. Moghaddam (eds), *The Self and Others: Positioning Individuals and Groups in Personal, Political and Cultural Contexts*. New York: Praeger/Greenwood.

Wetherell, M. (2005) Unconscious Conflict or Everyday Accountability? *British Journal of Social Psychology, 44*, 169–73.

Wetherell, M. (2008) Subjectivity or Psycho-Discursive Practices? Investigating Complex Intersectional Identities. *Subjectivity, 22*, 73–81.

Wetherell, M. (2010) Introduction: The Field of Identity Studies. In M. Wetherell and C. Mohanty (eds), *The Sage Handbook of Identities*. London: Sage.

Wetherell, M. and Potter, J. (1992) *Mapping the Language of Racism*. London: Harvester Wheatsheaf.

Whitebook, J. (1995) *Perversion and Utopia*. Cambridge, MA: MIT Press.

Wilson, E. (1934) The Ambiguity of Henry James. In F. Dupee (ed.), *The Question of Henry James: A Collection of Critical Essays*. New York: Holt & Co., 1945.

Winnicott, D. (1960) Ego Distortion in Terms of True and False Self. In D.W. Winnicott, *The Maturational Process and the Facilitating Environment*. London: Hogarth Press, 1965.

Winnicott, D. (1967) The Mirror-role of Mother and Family in Child Development. In D. Winnicott, *Playing and Reality*. (1969).

Winnicott, D. (1969) The Use of an Object. *International Journal of Psychoanalysis, 50*, 711–16.

Wolfenstein, V. (1981) *The Victims of Democracy*. London: Free Association Books.

Zaretsky, E. (2004) *Secrets of the Soul*. New York: Knopf.

Žižek, S. (1991) *Looking Awry*. Cambridge, MA: MIT Press.

Žižek, S. (1994) *The Metastasis of Enjoyment*. London: Verso.

Žižek, S. (2005) *Neighbours and Other Monsters: A Plea for Ethical Violence*. In S. Zicek, E. Santner and K. Reinhard (eds), *The Neighbor: Three Inquiries in Political Theology*. Chicago: University of Chicago Press.

Žižek, S. (2006a) *How to Read Lacan*. London: Granta.

Žižek, S. (2006b) *The Parallax View*. Cambridge, MA: MIT Press.

Zweig, S. (1943) *The World of Yesterday*. London: Cassell.

Segal, H. (1979) *Klein*. Glasgow: Fontana.

Segal, H. (1991) *Dream, Phantasy and Art*. London: Karnac.

Segal, H. (1995) From Hiroshima to the Gulf War and After: A Psychoanalytic Perspective. In A. Elliott and S. Frosh (eds), *Psychoanalysis in Contexts*. London: Routledge.

Segal, L. (2001) Psychoanalysis and Politics: Juliet Mitchell, Then and Now. *Studies in Gender and Sexuality, 2*, 327–43.

Smolen, A. (2009) Boys Only! No Mothers Allowed. *International Journal of Psychoanalysis, 90*, 1–11.

Spivak, G. Chakravorty (1988) Can the Subaltern Speak? In C. Nelson and L. Grossberg (eds), *Marxism and the Interpretation of Culture*. Urbana: University of Illinois Press.

Spurling, L. (2009) *An Introduction to Psychodynamic Counselling*. 2nd edn. Basingstoke: Palgrave.

Stavrakakis, Y. (2007) *The Lacanian Left*. Albany: State University of New York Press.

Stepney, E. (2003) Bourdieu on Bourdieu: Reflexive Sociology and the Sociologist in Society. *Crossing Boundaries, 1*, 126–43.

Stokes, A. (1955) *Michelangelo*. London: Tavistock.

Stokes, A. (1963) *Painting and the Inner World*. London: Tavistock.

Stolorow, R. (2006) Intersubjectivity Theory and Intersubjective Systems Theory. In R. Skelton (ed.), *The Edinburgh International Encyclopaedia of Psychoanalysis*. Edinburgh: Edinburgh University Press.

Stonebridge, L. (1998) *The Destructive Element: British Psychoanalysis and Modernism*. London: Macmillan.

Summers, F. (2007) Psychoanalysis, the American Psychological Association, and the Involvement of Psychologists at Guantanamo Bay. *Psychoanalysis, Culture & Society, 12*, 83–92.

Tausk, V. (1933) On the Origin of the 'Influencing Machine' in Schizophrenia. *Psychoanalytic Quarterly 2*, 519–56.

Trilling, L. (1951) *The Liberal Imagination*. Harmondsworth: Penguin, 1970.

Ungar, V. (2009) A Contemporary Child Case Discussion. *International Journal of Psychoanalysis, 90*, 27–34.

Venn, C. (2006) *The Postcolonial Challenge: Towards Alternative Worlds*. London: Sage.

Venn, C. (2009) Identity, Diasporas and Subjective Change: The Role of Affect, the Relation to the Other, and the Aesthetic. *Subjectivity, 26*, 3–28.

von Dohnyani, K. (1986) Opening Ceremony, 34th IPA Congress. *International Journal of Psychoanalysis, 67*, 2–4.

Waddell, M. (1988) Infantile Development: Kleinian and Post-Kleinian Theory, Infant Observational Practice. *British Journal of Psychotherapy, 4*, 313–28.

Waddell, M. (1998) *Inside Lives: Psychoanalysis and the Development of the Personality*. London: Duckworth.

Walkerdine, V. (2008) Contextualizing Debates about Psychosocial Studies. *Psychoanalysis, Culture & Society, 13*, 341–5.

Wallerstein, R. (1998) Erikson's Concept of Ego Identity Reconsidered. *Journal of the American Psychoanalytic Association, 46*, 229–47.

DATE DUE

Demco, Inc. 38-293